MENTORING LITERACY PROFESSIONALS: CONTINUING THE SPIRIT OF CRA/ALER AFTER 50 YEARS

Association of Literacy Educators & Researchers

The Thirty-First Yearbook
A Doubled Peer Reviewed Publication of The College Reading Association

Co-Editors

Susan Szabo
Texas A&M University-Commerce

Mary Beth Sampson
Texas A&M University-Commerce

Martha M. Foote
Texas A&M University-Commerce

Francine Falk-Ross
Pace University in New York

Editorial Assistant

Karen Whalen
Texas A&M University-Commerce

Leslie Haas
Texas A&M University-Commerce

ISBN: 1-883604-15-X

Printed at Texas A&M-University-Commerce
Cover Design: Carlyn Ross Schlechter

Elections, Karen Bromley, Binghamton University SUNY
Awards, Ellen Jampole, State University of New York-Cortland
Research Kristy Dunlap, George Mason University
   Ruth A. Oswald, University of Akron
Publications, Janelle Mathis, University of North Texas

Organization Focus
Memberships, Doris Walker-Dalhouse, Minnesota State University Moorhead
   Mary DeKonty Applegate, St. Joseph's University
Public Information, Sylvia Read, (Webmaster), Utah State University
   Marie Holbein, State University of West Georgia
   Donna Harkins, State University of West Georgia
   Parker Fawson, Utah State University
Scholarship, Patsy Douville, University of North Carolina-Charlotte
Historian, Dixie D. Massey, University of Washington
Photographer, Robin Erwin, Niagara University
Resolutions & Rules, Jon Jones, Western Illinois University
Legislative & Social Issues, JoAnn Dugan, Ohio University-Athens
Professional Affairs, Jill Mizell Drake, State University of West Georgia

2008 Conference Planners
Program Chair, Mona W. Matthews, Georgia State University
Assistant to Program Chair, Camille Chapleau, Georgia State University
Conference Coordinator, Barbara J. Reinken, Grand Valley State University
Local Arrangements Chairs, Jennifer Bailey, University of West Florida
Reading Room, Tami Craft Al-Hazza, Old Dominion University
Exhibitors Coordinators, Pamela F. Summers, State University of New York-
   Cortland
New Member Luncheon Coordinators, Doris Walker-Dalhouse, Minnesota State
   University-Moorhead and Mary DeKonty Applegate, St. Joseph's University
50th Gala Event, Mary Beth Allen, East Stroudsburg University of Pennsylvania
Business Manager, Michael Pickle, St. Cloud St. University

Future Conference Sites
2009 November 5-8 Charlotte, NC Marriott City Center
2010 November 4-7 Omaha, NE Hilton Omaha
2011 November 3-6 Richmond, VA Omni Richmond Hotel
2012 November 1-4 Grand Rapids, MI Amway Grand Plaza

CRA Editorial Advisory Board

Linda Mahoney, Mississippi University for Women
Barbara Marinak, Penn State Harrisburg
Sally Martin, Eastern Kentucky University
Jane Matanzo, Florida Atlantic University
Brandi Mathers, Geneva College
Mona Matthews, Georgia State University
Rozanna May, Texas A&M University-Commerce
Barbara McClanahan, Southeastern Oklahoma State
Judith Mitchell, Weber State University
Virginia Modla, LaSalle University
Timothy Morrison, Brigham Young University
Andrew Pachtman, Mercy College
Larkin Page, Texas A&M University-Commerce
David Paige, Bellarmine University
Joel Palmer, Mesquite ISD
Debra Pane, Florida International University
Kelli Paquette, Indiana University of Pennsylvania
Seth Parsons, George Mason University
Miriam Pepper-Sanello, Adelphi University
Donna Phillips, Niagara University
J. Michael Pickle, St. Cloud State University
John Ponder, University of West Georgia
Debra Price, Sam Houston State University
LaVerne Raine, Texas A&M University-Commerce
Mary Robbins, Sam Houston State University
Valerie Robnolt, Virginia Commonwealth University
Mary F. Roe, Washington State University
Mary Rycik, Ashland University
Lou Ann Sears, University of Pittsburg
Alice Snyder, Kennesaw State University
Kathy Stephens, Le Tourneau University
Frances Steward, Western Illinois University
Melissa Stinnett, Western Illinois University
Agnes Stryker, Texas A&M University-Commerce
Denise Stuart, University of Akron
Rhonda Sutton, East Stroudsburg University
Jean Vintinner, University of North Carolina
Donna Wake, University of the Ozarks
Katherine Wiesendanger, Longwood University

TABLE OF CONTENTS

Mentoring Students **293**

ACKNOWLEDGEMENTS

This volume is a milestone year for the Yearbook, the conference, and the organization. At this conference, CRA celebrated its 50th year. Such longevity shows that the organization has vibrancy. However, many changes have occurred.

First, we must say good-bye to the old CRA Yearbook name and change the title of the publication to the Association of Literacy Educators and Researchers (ALER) Yearbook. In this transition year, we have used both the old logo and the new logo on the title page to show that we have changed the organization's name after 52 years. Second, this is the last volume for which the editorial team of Susan Szabo, Mary Beth Sampson, Martha Foote, and Francine Falk-Ross has assumed responsibility in the publication of the Yearbook. Third, we want to thank our graduate assistant Karen Whalen who received the articles, sent them out to be reviewed, and created the tracking process. Her last official task before she graduated was to train her replacement, Leslie Haas. Fourth, we said farewell to our publisher, Vivian Freemen, as she decided it was time to retire. Finally, we said goodbye to Timothy Morrison who was the Chairperson of the Publications Committee.

Even though many changes occurred during the work on this Yearbook, we have many people to THANK for the completion of this volume. Many colleagues have given their time and their expertise to make this Yearbook possible. First, we wish to thank all those authors who worked diligently through the editing process in order to share their research, thoughts, and stories of their good work to add to the body of literacy knowledge. In addition, we wish to thank the keynote speakers for their inspirational and motivational words of wisdom.

Likewise, we are indebted to our many reviewers who answered the call for help, as we needed more reviewers than had initially signed up. The response was overwhelming and this is the first year each reviewer only had two articles to review. The detailed feedback our reviewers provided helped both the new and the seasoned authors with ideas for revision, which helped to create many high quality articles and continued to add rigor to this Yearbooks publication. In addition, we are grateful to the members of the Board of Directors who have continually supported the editorial team and the publication of the Yearbook.

Our 'production crew' consisted of dedicated editorial whizzes Leslie Haas, Debbie Raney, Blake Shaw, and Carlyn Ross Schlechter. Leslie kept the publication process going through her organized manuscript tracking, her weekly schedule reminders, and her meticulous line editing. We are thankful to have had her expert eye on the flow of the papers in and out of our offices. Debbie turned the documents into PDF files and created our book while Blake corresponded with the printers. In addition, this is the fourth year Carlyn Ross Schlechter has designed the colorful front cover. Her unique portrayal of the Yearbook's theme beckons the readers to check out what's inside.

We are very fortunate and grateful for the ongoing support provided by our two universities. At Texas A & M University-Commerce, we send our heart-felt 'Thank You' to President Jones for his support of this scholarly endeavor, as well as Dr. Martha Foote who is the Curriculum and Instruction Department Head. In addition, we are very thankful for the many instances of assistance and help from the Department of Curriculum and Instruction's Administrative Assistants, Maureen Preston and Priscilla Nichols. At Pace University in New York, we wish to thank Dr. Harriet Feldman, Dean of the School of Education, Associate Deans Mary Rose McCarthy and Annjanet Woodburn who value the scholarship the Yearbook provides.

SS, MBS, MMF, & FFR

INTRODUCTION

When we meet in Saratoga, the organization celebrated two milestones. First, this was our Golden Anniversary Year in which we celebrated 52 years of sharing and mentoring literacy professional. Second, to celebrate this occasion, the membership decided it was time to change the organizational name from College Reading Association to Association of Literacy Educators and Researchers.

The title of the thirty-first yearbook mirrors the theme of the 2008 conference—"Mentoring Literacy Professionals for 50 Years." We chose the title *Mentoring Literacy Professionals: Continuing the Spirit of CRA/ALER after 50 Years* in an attempt to reflect the research and papers presented at the Golden Anniversary Conference held in Saratoga, Florida.

This organization has long been the home of some of our nation's most notable literacy experts. At the Florida conference, these literacy professionals once again engaged us in dialogue of the utmost importance through their presentations and informal conversations throughout the conference. The articles included in this volume are representative of these dialogues that can lead to transformation, possibilities, and risk.

The Yearbook begins with the article representing Ray Reutzel's presentation to the membership. In his presidential address, Ray delves into the power of words in our lives in his keynote presentation entitled, *So What's in a Word? The Power of Words*. He asked the audience to reflect on the power of words, as words are central to the work of becoming literate.

The second section reveals the specifics of a special group of presenters, the three invited keynote addresses. First, Linda Gambrell shared her work with motivation and the importance of helping students appreciate and value reading. Second, Barbara Walker spoke at the newcomers' luncheon. She presented to the group why she has found CRA/ALER to be a positive force in her career. Third, in his presentation entitled, *Speaking the Lower Frequencies 2.0: Digital Ghost Stories*, Jacobs explored not only the use of digital storytelling but also the power it had on his student's understanding of their actions and attitudes. In his college classroom, he encouraged his college students to produce a video about the strong but invisible forces that shaped their lives. He shared several of these videos with his audience. Finally, Maria Valeri-Gold gave us on update on *What Johnny is Reading*.

The next section of the Yearbook contains our award winner's research. This year there were two dissertation winners. First, Carla Wonder-McDowell from Utah State University did her research on *"The Hidden Peril of Differentiation: Fragmented Instruction."* The results of her research study suggest that at-risk second-grade students benefit from supplemental instruction that is aligned with the classroom core-reading program. Second, Cheryl L. Potenza-Radis from Kent State University did her research *"Study Examining How Struggling Third Grade Readers, as Members of a Guided Reading Group, Experience Peer-Led Literature Discussions."* The results of her research suggest that struggling readers take on unique roles in the discussion process; are capable of engaging in peer-led discussions that advances their understanding; gain independence and take on greater responsibility for their discussions; and build relationships with one another. Third, the Master Thesis Winner was Susan E. Perkins from the University of British Columbia, Vancouver. She did her research on *"PALS in Vietnamese: Implementing a bilingual family literacy program."* This study describes the development and implementation of a bilingual family literacy program for Vietnamese families with preschoolers at a suburban British Columbia elementary school.

The remaining sections of the volume contain articles that we sorted into four overarching categories: *Mentoring Literacy Leaders, Mentoring Classroom Teachers, Mentoring Preservice Teachers, and Mentoring Students.* The articles within each of these categories are a great read. It is our hope that the "scholarship of teaching" represented by our keynote speakers, our award winners, and our authors will provide new insights and possibilities that will support and extend literacy research.

SS, MMS, MF, FFR

PRESIDENTIAL ADDRESS

SO WHAT'S IN A WORD?
THE POWER OF WORDS

Presidential Address

D. Ray Reutzel
Utah State University

Ray Reutzel has been an active member of CRA/ ALER since 1985. He has served the organization in many ways, including as editor of Reading, Research and Instruction (now the Literacy Research and Instruction) and as Chair of the Research Awards Committee and former Board of Directors member. In 1999, CRA recognized Ray's numerous accomplishments selecting him as the recipient of the A.B. Herr Award for Outstanding Research and Published Contributions to Reading Education.

He has authored more than 175 refereed research reports, articles, books, book chapters, and monographs and has been published in Early Childhood Research Quarterly, Reading Research Quarterly, Journal of Literacy Research, Journal of Educational Research, Reading Psychology, Reading Research and Instruction, Language Arts, Journal of Adolescent and Adult Literacy, and The Reading Teacher, among others. Ray was the co-editor of The Reading Teacher from 2002-2007 and served as a member of the IRA Board of Directors from 2007-2010. In addition, he has received more than 5.5 million dollars in research/professional development funding from private, state, and federal funding agencies. Currently, Ray is the Emma Eccles Jones Distinguished Professor and Endowed Chair of Early Childhood Education at Utah State University.

Reprinted from *College Reading Association Legacy: A Celebration of 50 Years of Literacy Leadership Volume II*, pp. 665-672, by W. M. Linek, D. D. Massey, E. G. Sturtevant, L. Cochran, B. McClanahan, & M. B. Sampson, Eds., 2010, Commerce, TX: Association of Literacy Educators & Reseachers.

This presidential address asserts that words are central to the work of becoming literate. Words are not the only but surely among the most meaningful building blocks of language and literacy. Words are powerful. In this address, the focus is upon the power of six words in our lives—*paradox, teacher, change, label, laugh, and reading.*

As I have prepared for this speech over the past few months, I have reflected back upon the many erudite, insightful, moving, and entertaining CRA Presidential addresses given in the past. Last year, Ellen Jampole wowed us as she brought her southern wit along with her personal Sweet Potato Queen support group, and her CRA Boss Queen Wig and Tiara to the Crossroads of the West as we met in Salt Lake City. So, it seems only fair that I should bring the wit and wisdom of the west, my Jeff Foxworthy Redneck support group, and my Cowboy hat to the south as we meet here in Sarasota, Florida. So as the new self-declared CRA TRAIL BOSS, I declare this to be the final roundup of the College Reading Association after 50 wonderful years.

My talk today is entitled, "*So What's in a Word? The Power of Words.*" Words are central to the work of becoming literate. I am one of those people who when they get a new copy of *Reader's Digest* immediately turns to the long running and ever popular "Word Power" feature each month. Words are not the only but surely the most meaningful building blocks of language and literacy. Words are powerful. Today I want to just focus upon a few words, just eight words, seven if we don't count "the," as demonstrations of the power of words in our lives. So for a moment today, let us get carried away by the words. Years ago, Emily Dickinson (1924) wrote poignantly about the power of words in this poem:

> He ate and drank the precious words,
> His spirit grew robust;
> He knew no more that he was poor,
> Nor that his frame was dust.
> He danced along the dingy days,
> And this bequest of wings
> Was but a book. What liberty
> A loosened spirit brings!

The image of that young man in the picture, pouring over the words in a book is powerful. You and I, as literacy professionals, weave artfully the tapestry of literacy word by word.

So, let us begin our journey of words with a short story from one of my favorite books, *The Weighty Word Book,* by Levitt, Berger and Guralnick (1985), Professors of English at the University of Colorado, yup that's right, a western university! This wonderful book contains 26 stories that explain the meanings of 26 weighty words, one each for each letter of the English alphabet. The story I am about to share with you is the "P" word story. It is your job now, to see if you can figure out the "P" word before I reach the end of the story.

Paradox

Have you truly considered the power of the word—*paradox*? In a world, even a universe, composed of seemingly divinely or cosmically appointed opposites, how does considering the meaning of paradox help us live more wholly, peacefully, and joyfully? Parker Palmer, a Quaker Spiritualist, writer of such books as *To Know as We are Known: Education as a Spiritual Journey* (1993) and *The Courage to Teach: Exploring the Inner Landscape of a Teacher's Life* (1998) writes penetratingly about the concept of a paradox.

He reminds us of the dangers brought on by embracing and nurturing a polarizing culture. He reminds us that our Western commitment to thinking in polarities elevates disconnection "into an intellectual virtue." Palmer suggests, "Truth is not approximated best by splitting the world into endless *either-ors* but by embracing the world as a place of *both-and*." Palmer argues that, "We need to argue for the paradoxical—the joining of apparent opposites. We must very often learn to embrace opposites as one. Paradoxes need not be esoteric or exotic. They are found in our everyday living" (Palmer, 1998 p. 63).

Take, for example, breathing. Indeed, breathing itself is a form of paradox, requiring inhaling and exhaling to be whole. Imagine a vitriolic debate about the relative importance of exhaling and inhaling among respiratory therapists? Yet as a literacy profession, we often find colleagues forcefully representing either phonics or whole language as the cure for what ails kids in learning to read. As I have contemplated the notion of the joining of opposites such as we find in paradox, I find myself recently more of a mind to find the "win-win"; more willing to seek that place of wholeness in the joining of opposites as represented by the single word—paradox.

Teacher

Now onto the second word—*teacher*. I don't remember exactly when the moment came that I felt called to teach. Was it when I played school in the basement of our home where my mother had created a little school room complete with desks, bookshelves, and chalkboard? I am not sure? But I do remember a profound feeling that this was to be my life's vocation and avocation.

Frederick Buechner (1993) offers a generous and humane image of one's vocation as "the place where your deep gladness and the world's deep hunger meet" (Buechner, 1993, p. 119). Those of us in this room have chosen to make our contribution to alleviate the world's hunger through teaching the world to read and write, listen and hear, see and express. I also know that I did not find literacy as the focus of my teaching life, rather literacy found me. Parker Palmer (1998) in the *Courage to Teach* illustrates the power of the subject upon the teacher when he wrote:

> Knowing begins with our intrigue about some subject, but that intrigue is the result of the subject's action upon us: geologists are people who hear

rocks speak, historians are those who hear the voices of the long dead, writers are people who hear the music of the words. (p.105)

Thus, the teacher of literacy gladly feeds the world's deep hunger by helping others feel, hear, and sing the music of the words. A poem authored by Brod Bagert (1999. p. 8-9) in a book entitled, *Rainbows, Headlice, and Pea Green Tile: Poems in the Voice of the Classroom Teacher*, brings home this point far better than I. In his poem, *The Answer Machine*, Brod relates how a veteran teacher, one who was wondering about her life and calling as a teacher noticed the light flashing on her answering machine, and remembered why she had spent a lifetime teaching children to read.

Change

The next word on our journey of words is *change*. I was, truthfully, a bit hesitant to select this word since it has been so thoroughly used and abused in the recent presidential campaign by both sides. But if there is one constant in our lives as educators and researchers, it is embodied in the word—change. Last summer I was introduced to the contents of a book while attending the 3rd Annual Institute of Education Sciences Research Conference in Washington, D.C. The luncheon speaker was talking about the concept of "best practice" and how this idea had influenced the medical profession and was now creeping gradually into the education profession. The book, *Better* (2007) was authored by Atul Guwande who has also authored the book, *Complication: A Surgeon's Notes on an Imperfect Science.* In the opening section of this book, entitled, "Diligence," Guwande details the difficulties of promoting change in the medical establishment. He writes about Dr. Ignac Semmelwies, who in 1847, deduced that by not washing their hands consistently or well enough, doctors and nurses were causing childbed fever in hospitals. Remember this was well before we knew about things called germs. Semmelwies had noted that 600 of 3000 women, 20%, who came to the hospital died after childbirth whereas women who remained at home to give birth died much less often, 30 women out of 3000, or 1%. He was determined to implement the "best practice" of hand washing in his hospital. He did so using somewhat dictatorial techniques which eventually cost him his job. But after a year of "diligence" in using the best practice of hand washing, Semmelwies had successfully lowered maternal death rates in the hospital to 30 women in 3000 or just 1%. Coupled with the later discovery of bacteria and viruses, one would expect that the medical profession would submit to the evidence-based practice of diligently washing its collective hands. But this is not the case. We read in Guwande's (2008) book that, "Our hospital's statistics show what studies everywhere else have shown—that we doctors and nurses wash our hands one-third to one-half as often as we are supposed to" (p.15). Change does not come easily in a profession. Like medicine, education is changing to make diligent use of effective, evidence-based practices in teaching literacy that will eventually become common place in classrooms.

And sometimes, change isn't all that transformative! In the writings of the western cowboy poet, Wallace McRae (1992), in his book entitled, *Cowboy Curmudgeon*, McRae writes of the changes associated with reincarnation.

Label

Our next word on the journey of words is *label*. Consider with me for a moment the power of labels—simple little words printed on a variety of goods and services we select or refuse every day. What is the difference between the labels—Cadillac and Yugo? Substantial, right. But how do labels work their magic upon our thinking? Take for example this box and label, Milkbone™ Crunchy Original Dog Treats. The label says—dog treats—which of course would never allow us, as people, to reach into this box and have treat. After all, it says dog food. I have here a new, unopened box of Milkbone™ Crunchy Original Dog Treats. Would you please open this new box for the others to see that it is indeed new and the contents are in fact dog treats? Thank you.

Would anyone like to join me in eating a dog treat? Why won't you eat one? Do you see how the label is limiting your thinking? Ah, the power of a label, just one little word, "dog" when attached to treats and we won't eat. Labels often obfuscate important details that are often over looked or outright dismissed. Labels tend to stop our thinking, obstruct investigation, and close down dialog. Once we label something or someone, it's as if the discussion has ended, the debate terminated, and the investigation ended. So, let's have a deeper look beyond the label. Let's examine the ingredients. Let's read and talk about them as I offer them again to you as the audience....

I often wonder how the power of labels act to constrain our thought rather than to liberate it. If it can be labeled, it can often be dismissed. How do the labels of disability or gifted or failing constrain our thought, limit our investigation, and cause us to refuse to see what lies beneath the surface of the label. We must be cautious so that we are not taken in by the mischief of words when masquerading as labels. Mahatma Gandhi reminds us that:

> Your beliefs become your thoughts. Your thoughts become your words. Your words become your actions. Your actions become your habits. Your habits become your values. Your values become your destiny.

Remember this demonstration of the power of labels. Think beyond the labels we put on things, ideas, people, beliefs, etc. For, if we are not vigilant about our use of labels, they may close our minds to beckoning possibilities and burgeoning human potential.

Laugh

Our next word along the road of our journey of words is, *laugh*. Laughter has often been referred to as the most powerful medicine known to humanity. In the spirit of this final CRA Western Reading Roundup where I am the CRA Trail Boss, we turn our attention to my fractured attempts at humor. As a westerner, we are often thought of as "rednecks" by those who live outside our region. Foxworthy offers many examples of Rednecks to define this particular human species more colorfully. For example, you might be a Redneck if....You burn your yard rather than mow it.

So in the spirit of Jeff Foxworthy, today I unveil a new form of Literacy humor in the genre of a true western Redneck. This new literacy form of humor should become known far and wide as "READNECK" jokes. Please note on the Redneck book cover the black editor's carrot indicating a change to the word Redneck to a new word—READNECK. To help you come to a more complete appreciation of the definition of the word, READNECK, let me offer a few examples for your sophisticated literary consumption....

You might be a READNECK if...
Your idea of a good read is the menu at the local diner.
You might be a READNECK if...
You read 20 minutes a day to your huntin' dog.
You might be a READNECK if...
When you're pregnant you get a tattoo on your belly that says—
READ TO YOUR BABY!
You might be a READNECK if...
You put a book in front of your TV and try to read it with the TV remote.
You might be a READNECK if...
You are caught reading a steamy romance novel in your driver's license photo.
You might be a READNECK if...
You expect to receive a Pan Pizza certificate from Pizza Hut when you return your books to the public library.
You might be a READNECK if...
You put your copy of *Field and Stream* inside your Bible for readin' at church.
You might be a READNECK if...
You carry a canvas tote full of books for protection when rushing into the exhibit hall opening at an IRA conference.

Reading

Now we move onto the one word we all came here to celebrate at this 50th Anniversary of CRA, read. To this end—*reading* and the teaching of *reading*, we here in this room have devoted a considerable portion of our lives. When I was in Canada this past winter speaking for a couple of days on an IRA Board assignment, I was told the following amusing anecdote about a young reader named Jake and his early reading experiences.

Learning to Read

Jake is 5 and learning to read.
He points at a picture in a zoo book and says,
"Look Mama! It's a frickin' Elephant!"
Deep breath.... "What did you call it?"
"It's a frickin' Elephant, Mama! It says so on the picture!"
And so it does.....

AFRICAN ELEPHANT

The word *read*, Ah, the mere thought of it conjures up such transformative and liberating power. Oprah Winfrey writes and talks frequently about her love of reading. She says, *"Reading opened the door to all kinds of possibilities for me. I loved books so much as a child, as they were my outlet to the world"* (Winfrey, para 5).

I love the music of the word—read as captured in the exceptionally well crafted story of Booker T. Washington by Marie Bradby (1995) in the children's book entitled, *More than Anything Else*. Frederick Douglass once observed as did Booker T. Washington, "Once you learn to read you will be forever free" (Douglass, 2008). Reading is truly the *hinge upon which the gate of social justice swings*!

And now, the two words for which you have more than likely patiently waited...the end. Indeed it is the end, the end of an era. At this meeting we say good-bye to an old friend—the name of the College Reading Association—a name that has come to represent, for many of us, an association of welcoming, nurturing, and friendly literacy colleagues. But alas, with every passing, there is a new birth. So in the spirit of our Western Reading Roundup, let's whoop and holler a bit for our new beginning as the Association of Literacy Educators and Researchers.

My time as President of this organization has drawn to a close and fortunately for you, my speech as well. So I close in the words of Wallace McRae (1992) in his western cowboy poem entitled, *Requiem*.

Thank you so much for the honor of serving you and this exceptional organization for the past several years—an organization which by any other name still smells as sweet!

References

Bagert, B. (1999). *Rainbows, head lice, and pea-green tile: Poems in the voice of the classroom teacher.* Gainesville, FL: Maupin House Publishing, Inc.

Beuchner, F. (1993). *Wishful thinking: A seeker's ABC.* San Francisco, CA: Jossey-Bass.

Bradby, M. (1995). *More than anything else.* New York: Orchard Books.

Dickinson, E. (1924). *Part One: Life, XXI. Complete Poems.* Retrieved January 19, 2010 from   http://www.bartleby.com/113/1099.html

Douglass, Frederick (2008). Quote taken from Abilene Christian University Archives. Retrieved January 20, 2010, from http://www.acu.edu/academics/library/reference/quotes.html

Foxworthy, J. (2008). *You might be a redneck if 2008 calendar.* Kansas City, MO: Andrews McMeel Publishing, LLC.

Gandhi, M. K. (1927). *An autobiography, or the story of my experiments with truth.* Ahmedabad, India: Navajivan Press.

Guwande, A. (2007). *Better: A surgeon's notes on performance.* New York: Picador.

Guwande, A. (2002). *Complications: A surgeon's notes on an imperfect science.* NY: Henry Holt & Co, LLC.

Levitt, P. M., Burger, D. A., Guralnick, E. S. (1985). *The weighty word book.* Longmont, CO: Bookmakers Guild, Inc.

McFeely, W. S. (2006). *Fredrick Douglass.* New York: W. W. Norton & Co., Inc.

McRae, W. (1992). *Cowboy curmudgeon and other poems.* Layton, UT: Gibbs Smith Publisher.

Palmer, P. J. (1993). *To know as we are known: Education as a spiritual journey.* San Francisco, CA: Jossey-Bass.

Palmer, P. J. (1998). *The courage to teach: Exploring the inner landscape of a teacher's life.* San Francisco, CA: Jossey-Bass.

Winfrey, O. (1991, February 21). Quote taken from her interview for the American Academy of Achievement. Retrieved from http://www.achievement.org/autodoc/page/win0int-

KEYNOTE ADDRESSES

HELPING STUDENTS APPRECIATE THE VALUE OF READING

Keynote Speaker

Linda B. Gambrell
Clemson University

Linda B. Gambrell is Distinguished Professor of Education in the Eugene T. Moore School of Education at Clemson University where she teaches graduate and undergraduate literacy courses. Prior to coming to Clemson University in 1999, she was Associate Dean for Research in the College of Education at University of Maryland. She began her career as an elementary classroom teacher and reading specialist in Prince George's County, Maryland. From 1992-97, she was principal investigator at the National Reading Research Center at the University of Maryland where she directed the Literacy Motivation Project. She has served as an elected member and President of the Board of Directors of the International Reading Association, National Reading Conference, and College Reading Association.

Her major research areas are literacy motivation, the role of discussion in teaching and learning, and comprehension strategy instruction. Her research has been published in major scholarly journals including Reading Research Quarterly, Educational Psychologist, and Journal of Educational Research. She has served on the editorial review boards for the most prestigious peer reviewed journals in the field of literacy.

Linda has received professional honors and awards including the College Reading Association A.B. Herr Award for Outstanding Contributions to the Field of Reading,

---

Reprinted from *College Reading Association Legacy: A Celebration of 50 Years of Literacy Leadership Volume II*, pp. 997-1006, by W. M. Linek, D. D. Massey, E. G. Sturtevant, L. Cochran, B. McClanahan, & M. B. Sampson, Eds., 2010, Commerce, TX: Association of Literacy Educators & Reseachers.

1994; International Reading Association Outstanding Teacher Educator in Reading Award, 1998; National Reading Conference Albert J. Kingston Award, 2001; College Reading Association Laureate Award, 2002; and in 2004 she was inducted into the Reading Hall of Fame.

In the area of reading, recent theory and research have focused on understanding the construct of reading motivation and the components of that construct. Motivation to read is defined, for the purposes of this discussion, as the likelihood of engaging in reading or choosing to read. This definition has been used for decades in research conducted by behavioral, humanistic, cognitive and social-cognitive psychologists.

Motivation is central to all stages of reading development. Students who are highly motivated to read will pursue reading, make time for reading, and develop the reading habit. One of the primary reasons motivation is so central to reading proficiency is that the more one reads the better reader one becomes (Cunningham & Stanovich, 1998; Gambrell, 2009). While all students deserve high quality instruction in phonemic awareness, phonics, vocabulary, fluency and comprehension, it is clear that if students are not motivated to read, they will never reach their full literacy potential. Because motivation exerts a tremendous influence on literacy development, it is important for us to consider theory and research on motivation and its influence on our developing understanding of reading motivation.

According to Turner and Paris (1995), motivation does not reside solely in the child; rather it is in the interaction between students and the reading context of the classroom. The role of the teacher in creating a classroom culture that supports and nurtures reading motivation cannot be over-estimated. Alvermann (2008), building on the work of Barton and Hamilton (1998) and Street (1995), defines classroom practice as the "cultural ways in which teachers make sense of what they do, including their interactions with students. These ways involve attitudes, feelings, values, and social relationships, which, while not readily observable, nonetheless serve to regulate who gets to produce or access what textual content, at what point, and for what purposes" (p. 9). The big question, then, is "How can teachers help students' develop an appreciation for the value of reading?"

Three Central Issues in Reading Motivation

Brophy (2008) has urged educators and researchers to focus more specifically on developing students' appreciation for what is taught in school. While he focused more on content knowledge, there are many insights that can be drawn from his work with respect to reading motivation. According to Brophy, issues in motivation in general fall into three major categories: social context, expectancy, and value. The social context or social milieu is the classroom climate or the context in which the learning takes place. Issues relating to expectancy reflect what is commonly referred to as self-concept of the reader (How do I feel about my chances of being successful at reading?). Issues relating to value reflect the students' appreciation of engaging in reading and the benefits of doing so (Why should I care about this?). Brophy further contests that we know a great deal more about establishing a social context and addressing expectancy problems than we do about helping students appreciate the value of learning tasks such as reading. Brophy (2008) states:

> Work on the social milieu points to the importance of making students feel a sense of belonging and well-being: meeting their needs of autonomy, competence, and relationships (self-determination theory); and maintaining master-goal rather than performance-goal structures (goal theory). Work on the expectancy aspects indicates that the content and learning activities should be at an optimal level of difficulty (neither too easy nor too hard), and the teacher should orient students toward attributing their learning progress to internal and controllable factors (attribution theory), developing positive self-efficacy perceptions (self-efficacy theory), and viewing their abilities as incrementally improvable rather than fixed and limited…Except for difficulty level, these principles do not identify aspects of curricular content domains or learning activities that might affect students' appreciation of their value…Addressing value requires attention to the learners' beliefs and feelings about the content, as well as the processes involved in learning and applying it…Until recently, only a few lines of theory and research did this. (p. 132)

With respect to the motivational aspects of school learning, Brophy (2008) advocates shifting our conversations about motivation away from "intrinsic motivation" to "motivation to learn." Taking a cue from Brophy, I think it may well serve the field of reading to change the way we talk about motivation – moving away from the term "intrinsic motivation" to using the more descriptive and richer term, "motivation to read". At present, reading theory and research do not have much to say about how to help students develop an appreciation of reading and its benefits. Clearly, what is taught must be worth learning, but students may not appreciate the value of reading unless we scaffold instruction in ways that help them to do so.

Motivation to Read: Situational Affordances

In order to fully understand Brophy's emphasis on developing appreciation for what is taught in school, an understanding of situational affordances is needed. We often say that we want students' to be intrinsically motivated to read "for its own sake." This is not truly the case. Highly motivated readers do not engage in reading "for its own sake"—instead they read because it provides some valued benefit—for example, pleasure, satisfaction, or information. These situational affordances carry motivational implications for engagement in reading. The highly motivated reader recognizes the value of reading and the affordances it offers.

In order for reading to hold value for our students it is necessary for students to understand the authentic applications to life outside of school. In most classrooms there are frequent opportunities for students to read both narrative and informational text; however, there is little emphasis on when, where, or why they might use this information in meaningful ways. For reading educators and researchers the challenge is to learn more about the affordances for reading and how we can help students learn to appreciate the value of reading, particularly with respect to authentic applications to life outside of school.

Fostering Appreciation of the Value of Reading with Authentic Literacy Tasks

Embedding instruction in authentic and relevant experiences holds great promise for increasing motivation to read. Situating literacy learning in such tasks allows students to access and apply relevant knowledge (Brophy, 2004; 2008; Cunningham & Allington, 1999; Guthrie, 2008). This notion is perhaps summed up best by Brophy's challenge to researchers and educators to "…learn more about situational affordances for acquiring and using K-12 content in ways that serve valued human purposes, then develop ways to enable students to exploit these affordances with appreciation of opportunities to engage in worthwhile activities" (2008, p. 136).

Some scholars regard the concept of moving everyday life into schools to reflect more authentic literacy experiences as essential to literacy learning (Brophy, 2004, 2008; Brown, Collins, & Duguid, 1989; Neuman & Roskos, 1997; Scribner & Cole, 1973). Authentic literacy experiences are analogous to those that are encountered in the everyday lives of people, as opposed to school-like activities such as completing worksheets or answering teacher-posed questions. Authentic literacy tasks acknowledge and play into students' needs and desires to do things that are "real life." According to Purcell-Gates (2002), authentic literacy tasks involve meaningful, purposeful, and functional experiences that motivate and engage students.

Authentic literacy has three dimensions: meaning making, purpose, and ownership (Edelsky, 1991). Literacy tasks that encourage purposeful student cognition and result in the construction of new meanings would be considered more authentic than tasks that simply require extraction and recall of information. Authentic tasks, in Edelsky's view, would also provide some personal relevance and require some ownership or control on the part of the learner; a consideration that requires knowledge of what students and society value in terms of literacy events.

Other scholars contend that authentic academic achievement is determined by the extent to which the learner constructs new knowledge, develops and utilizes a cognitive frame for constructing that knowledge, and the value of the newly created knowledge outside of school (Newmann, Marks, & Gamoran, 1996). In their study, Newmann, Marks, & Gamoran (1996) report findings of the School Restructuring Study, a review of the organizational and pedagogical features of 23 recently restructured schools. Although this operational definition appears to involve cognitive elements alone, the researchers acknowledge that the learning they observed was the result of a negotiation of meaning rather than a transmission of information and relied heavily on the student's prior knowledge and the social exchange of ideas.

Street (1995) makes a distinction between autonomous and ideological models of literacy. Autonomous models position literacy as a collection of skills rather than a cultural practice. While skills are necessary for the cognitive process of reading, the practice of reading that prepares students for real world literacy experiences is situated in an ideological model that provides activities and interactions that require meaningful exchanges and responses. Accordingly, Au and Raphael (2000) posit that reciprocity exists between ownership and proficiency, where ownership of literacy learning leads to greater proficiency and proficiency engenders empowerment when faced with authentic, real-life literacy practices.

Authentic Learning and Cognitive Processes

In their commentary on authentic learning activities, Clayden, Desforges, Mills, and Rawson (1994) bring to light the distinction between teaching that is viewed as a transmission of knowledge and teaching that utilizes the social context of learning. Literacy as a socially situated practice involves more than the passing on of knowledge from teacher to student; rather, bodies of knowledge are created through negotiation and interaction of members of a learning community. Knowledge is acquired as the result of social exchanges rather than transmitted in one-way release from teacher to student.

Fisher and Hiebert (1990) found in their investigation of skills-based and literature-based elementary classrooms that lessons planned around literary works rather than skills development involved a greater level of cognitive complexity and allowed for more input and engagement on the part of the students. Cognitive complexity was operationalized in their research as moving along a continuum that progressed from recall of information (low cognitive complexity) to tasks that required the student to synthesize and integrate (moderate cognitive complexity) to learning that resulted in the development of novel constructions of knowledge (high cognitive complexity).

Neuman and Roskos (1997) position their discussion of literacy development with those of Brown, Collins, and Duguid (1989) who describe literacy learning as a process of enculturation into literacy practices. With young children, this involves creating literacy tasks that will prepare them to engage with texts by simulating real life literacies in play settings such as post offices, restaurants and medical offices. In these learning centers, young children have opportunities to engage in literacy activities in authentic contexts of communication and literacy.

Recent Research on Fostering Students' Appreciation for the Value of Reading

In a recent study, reading, writing, and discussion were explored within the context of authentic tasks (Gambrell, Hughes, & Calvert, 2009). Specifically, students read books, discussed their interpretations of the books with others, and engaged in letter writing about the books with adult pen pals. Findings revealed that students' literacy motivation increased for both boys and girls from pre assessment at the beginning of a school year to post assessments at the end of the same school year, and that the increase was particularly salient for boys. In addition, the study found that students engaged in important higher order thinking skills as they talked and wrote about their books.

Several important conclusions can be drawn from the results of this study. First, it appears that authentic literacy tasks support and sustain students' literacy motivation. Evidence of the influence of the nature of the task on student engagement was found in both quantitative and qualitative data sources. The results of the Literacy Motivation Survey (LMS; Gambrell, Palmer, Codling, & Mazzoni, 1996) revealed that the means of total scores for both boys and girls increased significantly from fall to spring, in contrast to the robust findings in the research that reading motivation declines across the school year and as students progress through the grades (McKenna, Kear, & Ellsworth, 1995).

Of particular interest in this study was the finding that on the pre-intervention administration of the LMS girls had significantly higher scores on value of reading than did boys. This was not an unexpected finding, given that one of the most consistent findings in the motivation literature is that girls have more positive attitudes toward reading than boys (Marinak & Gambrell, in press; McKenna, Kear, & Ellsworth, 1995). However, on the post-intervention administration of the LMS there were no significant gender differences. One possible explanation of this finding is that the authentic and purposeful nature of the pen pal exchange with an adult carried sufficient social value for boys so that they perceived a utility value for engaging in the reading, discussion, and writing activities that would support them in the pen pal exchange. Exchanging ideas with an adult who is personally interested in their ideas may provide a context for scaffolding the school-related tasks of creating, revising, and communicating personal interpretations of a commonly read book. The results of this study suggest that authentic literacy tasks such as book discussions and literacy pen pal exchanges support and sustain literacy motivation.

In another study exploring the reward proximity hypothesis, students reported high motivation while engaged in an authentic reading task (Marinak & Gambrell, 2008). The reward proximity hypothesis (Gambrell, 1996) posits that when there is a close relationship between the reward and the desired behavior (reading), intrinsic motivation is enhanced. In classrooms, both teacher praise and feedback are ideally linked to the desired student behavior. Conversely, extrinsic rewards are usually unrelated to the desired behavior. The reward proximity hypothesis suggests that a student's motivation to read is enhanced when the incentive not only rewards the behavior of reading but also reflects the value of and encourages future engagement in that behavior. In the Marinak and Gambrell (2008) study, students completed an authentic reading task and then received a reward according to treatment condition: book reward, token reward (erasers, rings, charms, etc.), or no reward. The children were asked to browse a selection of newly published books, choose one, read an excerpt, and offer their opinion regarding whether the book should be purchased for their library. After receiving their "reward" (book, token, or no reward) for helping to select books for the library, the students were allowed to choose from three activities to spend the remaining free time: continue reading, do a puzzle, or do a math game. At the end of the period the children were asked, "If your best friend asked you, 'What was the best or most fun thing to do in this room?' What would you tell them?" Every one of the seventy-five children in the study responded that reading or reading the library books was the most fun thing they did in the room that day. Interestingly, this response was given even by children who chose to play the game or complete the math puzzle during their free time. Clearly, the authentic task of reading books to render an opinion about purchase for their school library proved motivating regardless of the reward offered for reading.

Concluding Thoughts

Most educators would agree with the contention that if students are not motivated to read, they will never reach their full literacy potential. Motivation is clearly linked to the notion that the more students read the better readers they become. Students who are motivated to read will make time for reading, will read more, and as a result are likely to increase in both reading ability and intelligence. Just as we must give attention to making sure that students have sufficient amounts of time to read, we must also promote and support classroom cultures that encourage and nurture motivation to read.

In order to increase motivation to read, we must help students develop an appreciation of the value of reading. To do so, we must broaden our definition of reading tasks from one that is school bound to one that is based on real life experiences. Reading instruction needs to be more closely tied to authentic tasks that are connected to real life experiences and context-based problems. According to Neuman and Celano (2001), a better balance between decontextualized learning and authentic learning may take advantage of what students bring to the academic setting. Neuman and Celano contend that we need to create literacy tasks that engage students in problem-solving activities that reflect the types of real purposes and routines we use in everyday life.

The New London Group (1996), has asserted "…if one of our pedagogical goals is a degree of mastery in practice, then immersion in a community of learning engaged in authentic versions of such practice is necessary" (p. 84). While recognizing that it is not possible for every reading curriculum standard to be easily transposed into a relevant and authentic purpose, if we take the time to know more about our students and their lives, their communities and their interests, connections can be made between learning and living. And if the learning target is not easily tied to some authentic aspect of living in society, perhaps we should question why we must teach it (Malloy & Gambrell, 2008).

References

Alvermann, D. (2008). Why bother theorizing adolescents' online literacies for classroom practice and research? *Journal of Adolescent & Adult Literacy, 52*, 8 – 19.

Au, K. H., & Raphael, T. E. (2000). Equity and literacy in the next millennium. *Reading Research Quarterly, 35*, 170-188.

Barton, D., & Hamilton, M. (1998). *Local literacies: Reading and writing in one community.* London: Rutledge.

Brophy, J. (2008). Developing students' appreciation for what is taught in school. *Educational Psychologist, 43*(3), 132-141.

Brophy, J. (2004). *Motivating students to learn* (2nd ed.). Mahwah, NJ: Lawrence Erlbaum Associates.

Brown, J. S., Collins, A., & Durguid, P. (1989). Situated cognition and the culture of learning. *Educational Researcher, 18*, 32-42.

Cunningham, P. M., & Allington, R. L. (1999). Classrooms that work: They all can read and write (2nd ed.). Reading, MA: Addison Wesley Longman.

Cunningham, A. E., & Stanovich, K. E. (1998). What reading does for the mind. *American Educator*, Spring/Summer, 8-15.

Edelsky, C. (1991). *With literacy and justice for all: Rethinking the social in language and education. Critical perspectives on literacy and education.* London: Falmer.

Fisher, C. W., & Hiebert, E. H. (1990). Characteristics of tasks in two approaches to literacy instruction. *The Elementary School Journal 91* (1), 3-18.

Gambrell, L. B. (2009). Creating opportunities to read more so that our students read better. In E.H. Hiebert (Ed.), *Reading more, reading better* (pp. 251-266). NY: Guilford.

Gambrell, L.B., Palmer, B. M., Codling, R. M., & Mazzoni, S. A. (1996). Assessing motivation to read. *The Reading Teacher, 49*, 2-19.

Gambrell, L. B., Hughs, E., & Calvert, W. (2009, May) *Authentic literacy tasks: Reading, writing, and discussion*, Paper presented at the meeting of the International Reading Association, Minneapolis, MN.

Guthrie, J. (2008). Growing motivation: How students develop. In J. Guthrie (Ed.) *Engaging adolescents in reading* (pp. 99-114). Thousand Oaks, CA: Corwin Press.

Malloy, J. A., & Gambrell, L. B. (2008). New insights on motivation in the literacy classroom. In C.C. Block & S.R. Parris, *Comprehension instruction: research-based best practices*, 2nd ed. (pp. 226-238). New York: Guilford.

Marinak, B., & Gambrell, L. B. (in press). Reading motivation: Exploring the elementary gender gap. *Literacy Research and Instruction.*

Marinak, B. & Gambrell, L.B. (2008). Intrinsic motivation and rewards: What sustains young children's engagement with text? *Literacy Research and Instruction, 47.* 9-26

McKenna, M. C., Kear, D. J., & Ellsworth, R. A. (1995). Children's attitudes toward reading: A national survey. *Reading Research Quarterly, 30*, 934-956.

Neuman, S. B., & Celano, D. (2001). Access to print in low-income and middle-income communities: an ecological study of four neighborhoods. *Reading Research Quarterly, 36*(10), 8-26.

Neuman, S. B.,& Roskos, K. (1997). Literacy knowledge in practice: Contexts of participation for young writers and readers. *Reading Research Quarterly, 32*, 10-32.

New London Group. (1996). A pedagogy of multiliteracies: Designing social futures.*Harvard Educational Review, 66*, 60-92.

Newmann, F. M., Marks, H. M., & Gamoran, A. (1996). Authentic pedagogy and student performance. *American Journal of Education, 104*(4), 280-312.

Purcell-Gates, V. (2002). Authentic literacy in class yields increase in literacy practices. *Literacy Update, 11*, 7.

Scribner, S., & Cole, M. (1973). *The psychology of literacy*. Cambridge, MA: Harvard University Press.

Street, B. (1995) Social Literacies. London: Longman.

Turner, J.,& Paris, S. G. (1995). How literacy tasks influence children's motivation for literacy. *The Reading Teacher, 48*(8), 662-673.

College Reading Association: Academic, Conversational, and Collaborative

Keynote Speaker
Given at the Newcomers Luncheon

Barbara J. Walker
Oklahoma State University

Barbara J. Walker is president of the International Reading Association and a past board member of the college reading association. She received the College Reading Association's 1997 A. B. Herr Award for outstanding contributions to reading. Currently she is professor of reading at Oklahoma State University where she teaches courses in reading difficulties and literacy coaching. Dr. Walker graduated from Oklahoma State University in Curriculum and Instruction, specializing in reading difficulty. Dr. Walker's passion is teaching struggling readers and supporting teachers as they teach these readers. Her books Diagnostic Teaching of Reading (6th ed., 2008), Supporting Struggling Readers and Literacy Coaching: A Collaborative Approach demonstrate her understanding of students who struggling with reading as well as how teachers can support their learning. Dr. Walker has been director of the reading at both Montana State University-Billings and Oklahoma State University. Most important to her, however, is preparing teachers to work with struggling readers. In this capacity, she has helped more than 3,000 struggling readers improve their literacy.

Abstract

As this is the last year for the conference being called College Reading Association (next year we will be known as ALER, Association of Literacy Educators and Researchers), I am happy to talk with you about what CRA embodies for me. First, CRA is where I learn new information and construct knowledge about teaching reading and teaching teachers. Second, College Reading Association is where I can share my ideas about literacy with other colleagues. Finally, at CRA, I have developed collaborative relationships and lifelong friends.

New Learning

College Reading Association has always had insightful keynote speakers as well as collegial sessions with easy access to speakers. So many members take advantage of the many excellent academic presentations. It is at this conference where I always learn something new. In my early years, for example, I learned about qualitative research in a presentation by Kathy Roskos and Joanne Vacca as well as others. This inspired me to conduct a small qualitative study with preservice teachers in the reading clinic course that I taught. I did a study on teacher reflection in a reading clinic setting and my path of research began. Thus, my academic learning led to many more presentations where I learned as I prepared the sessions and listened to other extraordinary presentations on work done in reading clinics, as well as teacher education.

Conversational Interactions

When I first began attending CRA, I did so because there was both a clinical division and a teacher education division. My academic knowledge was growing, but it was through conversations with other members that I began to rethink my understandings. As Vygotsky (1978) has purported, learning does not occur until you weave your understanding with everyday experiences, first using informal language but then connecting our knowledge to academic language. This occurs as we have conversations about what we are learning.

Second, the College Reading Association has always meant conversing and talking through ideas. As I attended various CRA conferences, I met others who shared my ideas. Thus, we learned and deepened our understanding during our social interactions. Not so long ago, I remember a heated discussion about phonics instruction with Dee Nichols as well as a conversation with Tim Rasinski about constructivist approaches to teaching phonics. This conversation inspired me to put together a CRA session on alternate ways to teach phonics with Tim Rasinski, Mindy Smith, Callie Fortenberry, and Ray Reutzal. During conversations, we used our everyday language creating a "sea of the known." Then, we intertwined our personal language and ideas with the academic language from our peers and our academic reading. For me, these conversations produced ideas that I could not think of alone. Involving colleagues in jointly constructing and reconstructing meaning through conversations happens most frequently at the College Reading (soon to be ALER) conference.

Collaborative Endeavors

College Reading Association has always meant collaboration as well as conversations. At the heart of collaboration are individuals who believe that collaboration adds value to learning. They believe their differing viewpoints and experiences add strength and power to joint projects. From the conversations and presentations, new academic collaborations could occur. Through conversations, Kathy Roskos and I collaborated on research projects within our reading clinic courses. As we began, we used concrete examples to explain our perspectives. Finally, we found common ground and developed a series of research studies. This collaboration began from a small academic research presentation and grew to publications of research articles and a book. As I had conversations with Linda Gambrell and Pat Koskinen, I often discussed imagery and comprehension another interest of mine. These conversations challenge me to state my perspectives concisely. Later, we collaborated on some imagery studies and published several articles. In addition, I have collaborated and presented with graduate students as they are beginning their career. Thus, within CRA (ALER) we develop collaborative relationships that help us make our interesting ideas become academic projects.

Conclusion

As I look back on my comments last year, I realize that College Reading Association is a great big learning community. According to DuFour (2004), a learning community involves a focus on learning and interactions valuing everyone's perspective. This organization has always valued the perspectives of its members. Thus, individuals within the community discuss ideas freely and reflect personally on their learning. The members, as a whole, value all perspectives creating a supportive learning community. At the conference and through e-mail we share our ideas because of this support. It is at CRA that I feel safe enough to share some of my emerging perspectives with my friends and colleagues. I hope that as you begin your CRA/ALER journey, you will develop collaborative relationships and lifelong friends as well.

References

DuFour, Richard (2004). Leading edge: Culture shift doesn't occur overnight—or without conflict. *Journal of Staff Development, 25*, 29-34.

Vygotsky, L. S. (1978). *Mind in society*. Cambridge, MA: Harvard University Press.

Speaking the Lower Frequencies 2.0: Digital Ghost Stories

Keynote Speaker

Walter R. Jacobs

University of Minnesota

University of MinnesotaWalter R. Jacobs is an Associate Professor and Chair of the Department of African American & African Studies at the University of Minnesota. A sociologist (PhD, Indiana University, 1999), Jacobs is the author of Ghostbox: A Memoir and Speaking the Lower Frequencies: Students and Media Literacy, and co-editor of If Classrooms Matter: Progressive Visions of Educational Environments. His current research explores personal and social possibilities of students' generation of creative nonfiction.

Abstract

In *Speaking the Lower Frequencies: Students and Media Literacy* Walter R. Jacobs explores how college students can become critical consumers of media while retaining the pleasure they derive from it. *Speaking the Lower Frequencies 2.0: Race, Learning, and Literacy in the Digital Age* builds on its predecessor by examining pedagogy and literacy through theories and practices of digital media making, specifically digital storytelling methods used in a fall 2008 undergraduate class, "Digital Storytelling in and with

Reprinted from *College Reading Association Legacy: A Celebration of 50 Years of Literacy Leadership Volume II*, pp. 1007-1014, by W. M. Linek, D. D. Massey, E. G. Sturtevant, L. Cochran, B. McClanahan, & M. B. Sampson, Eds., 2010, Commerce, TX: Association of Literacy Educators & Reseachers.

Communities of Color." Jacobs begins his keynote with the course description and then examines one component of the class project: students' engagement with "social ghosts," the strong but usually hidden and unexamined forces that structure their educational experiences.

"Digital Storytelling in and with Communities of Color," fall 2008. Storytelling is a tool for preserving memory, writing history, learning, entertaining, organizing, and healing in communities of color. It is in the telling of stories that communities build identities, construct meaning, and make connections with others and the world. In this course we will investigate modes and power dimensions of digital storytelling, analyze the role of digitized media as a method of individual healing, and examine media as tools for community organizing and development. We will explore media making, creative writing, and memoir in both literary and digital writing, and examine the gendered, racialized, and classed dimensions of digital storytelling. We will create projects to tell our stories, examine our social ghosts, and work with community members as part of the 40th Anniversary of the African American and African Studies Department to develop digital stories about Twin Cities communities of color. Students will learn to produce creative work (writing, video, photography, sound, and artwork) and gain technical proficiency in Mac-based editing. Students will produce photographic and video work that will be shared on the course blog. No technical expertise is necessary!
—course description for "Digital Storytelling in and with Communities of Color" undergraduate class, University of Minnesota, fall 2008.

In my 2005 book, *Speaking the Lower Frequencies: Students and Media Literacy*, I investigated strategies for encouraging undergraduate students to become critical consumers of the media without losing the pleasure they derive from it (Jacobs, 2005). Sonia Livingstone, however, notes that in the digital age literacy should provide students with "the ability to access, analyse, evaluate and create messages across a variety of contexts" (Livingstone, 2004, p. 3). In other words, students need to become producers of media content in addition to being critical consumers of media worlds. In my new project, I explore this expanded understanding of literacy. *Speaking the Lower Frequencies 2.0: Race, Learning,* and *Literacy in the Digital Age* examines pedagogy and literacy through theories and practices of digital media making, specifically digital storytelling (Jacobs, Raimist, & Doerr-Stevens, 2009). This project is centered on a fall 2008 undergraduate course I co-taught at the University of Minnesota; the epigraph above provides an overview of the main elements of the class. In this chapter, I examine one component of the project: students' engagement with "social ghosts," the strong but usually hidden and unexamined forces that structure their educational experiences (Jacobs, Reynolds, & Choy, 2004).

Kristina Woolsey notes,

We are extending infrastructures to support the newest digital technologies that are introduced by industry. However, at the core, we are not focused on learning with technologies. We are supporting students with computers so that they can better take advantage of an educational system that is at its heart still an idiosyncratic face-to-face, text-based enterprise. (Woolsey, 2008, p. 218)

My co-instructor (Rachel Raimist) and I attempted to challenge this unfortunate reality for many students. In our "Digital Storytelling in and with Communities of Color" class, students learned to use technology to transform their learning experiences, to see themselves as active agents who can use technology in ways not always envisioned by the designers. While the class did employ text-based readings, these were delivered in non-traditional electronic formats. More importantly, the readings provided a foundational structure on which we built the computer-mediated tools and processes that formed the core of the class. Students developed a new paradigm for confronting the many social ghosts fostered by the educational systems they inhabit. I believe that instructors in a diverse array of education locations can deploy technology in ways to facilitate constructive engagement with these ghosts. I present one method here.

Using the Center for Digital Storytelling method

The Center for Digital Storytelling is a California-based non-profit 501(c)3 arts organization rooted in the art of personal storytelling. We assist people of all ages in using the tools of digital media to craft, record, share, and value the stories of individuals and communities, in ways that improve all our lives.

Many individuals and communities have used the term "digital storytelling" to describe a wide variety of new media production practices. What best describes our approach is its emphasis on personal voice and facilitative teaching methods. Many of the stories made in our workshops are directly connected to the images collected in life's journey. But our primary concern is encouraging thoughtful and emotionally direct writing.
—Center for Digital Storytelling website (http://www.storycenter.org/index1. html)

According to Leslie Rule's oft-quoted definition, "Digital storytelling is the modern expression of the ancient art of storytelling. Digital stories derive their power by weaving images, music, narrative and voice together, thereby giving deep dimension and vivid color to characters, situations, experiences, and insights" (Rule, 2009). Such digital stories are both created and shared via the use of computer tools. One of the leading proponents of using Apple Macintosh computer-based products in digital storytelling is the Center for Digital Storytelling (CDS) in Berkeley, CA. As one can readily discern from reading the first page of their website (reprinted in this section's epigraph above), CDS has created a powerful approach to digital storytelling, one that has influenced thousands of individuals and groups.

At the center of the CDS approach to digital storytelling is the 3-day "Basic Workshop." In a setting of 8-12 participants, each student designs and produces an individual digital story. Students are taught to scan and edit images using Adobe Photoshop, craft and record first-person narratives, and use Apple Final Cut Express to combine the elements into a rough draft of a 3-5 minute digital story. After the workshop CDS staff polish the digital story and mail a compact disc (CD) to the participants. The CD contains the final version of the digital story, along with all of the source materials in order to allow students to complete additional edits on their own.

Upon completion of the Basic Workshop students can attend an "Educator Workshop" or a "Facilitator Intensive Training Workshop." The 3-day Educator Workshop is designed to guide K-12 teachers in the practical application of digital storytelling as a classroom program for K-12 age students. The week-long Facilitator Intensive Training Workshop explores curricular and technological issues educators should consider when adapting the CDS digital storytelling process to their own pedagogical environments.

I enrolled in a Basic Workshop in May 2008, and produced a digital story called "Letter to my Mother." (This digital story may be viewed at http://tinyurl. com/JacobsDS/). "Letter to my Mother" is a memorial to my mother, who I believed helped me survive adolescence with an abusive stepmother. It is the digital story manifestation of my memoir *Ghostbox*, in which I explored a life where family problems were blamed on "disrespectful" children who refused to accept "Mom's" authority (Jacobs, 2007). My stepmother is one of my social ghosts, a force that limited my thoughts and decisions until I filled a special shoebox with objects that evoke significant memories: good, bad, and ugly. My "ghostbox" has rendered my stepmother's seething presence benign.

In our fall 2008 "Digital Storytelling in and with Communities of Color" course the students read *Ghostbox* and discussed it with Rachel and me in class. Students also watched and discussed the "Letter to my Mother" digital story. In these discussions, students interrogated the social processes of digital storytelling. For example, students learned that it takes courage to share their stories publicly; they risk judgment from others. But once they develop confidence and commitment to the storytelling process, students can generate many new insights. After a thorough analysis of CDS's seven social elements of digital storytelling (Lambert, 2006), we conducted several classes where we taught students the technical skills necessary for creating their own digital stories. These digital stories can be viewed online: http://tinyurl.com/UMstories/.

A digital story on literacy and learning

This is a story examining my time teaching in Brooklyn, New York. Through layering of images, voice, and music, I try to explore my memories as I've stored them in my

mind. In many ways my memories are limited, focusing only on certain aspects. This story is an attempt to open up that past and perhaps re-remember these moments in new ways in order to reshape how I view myself now.
—*Candance Doerr-Steven's description of her digital story,* "White Teacher"

We did not explicitly require students to include social ghosts in the digital stories, but some students did. One student not only produced a story that engaged a social ghost, this social ghost was one explicitly about learning and literacy. Candance Doerr-Stevens' "White Teacher" provides us with a powerful example for rethinking how K-12 educators can view classrooms with diverse student populations. ("White Teacher" may be accessed at http://tinyurl.com/WhiteTeacherDS/).

The fall 2008 "Digital Storytelling in and with Communities of Color" course was a 3000-level class, meaning that it was primarily designed for juniors and seniors. We did, however, enroll several sophomores. Graduate student Candance Doerr-Stevens also enrolled in the class using a graduate directed studies mechanism, given that it fit perfectly with her interests in new media literacies. Rachel and I were so impressed with her early contributions to that class that we invited her to be the third author on our in-progress *Speaking the Lower Frequencies 2.0* manuscript (Jacobs, Ramist, & Doerr-Stevens, 2009).

Candance analyzes "White Teacher" in chapter 6 of the manuscript. She writes,

> *I chose to focus on my experience as a fifth grade teacher in Brooklyn, New York, looking specifically at my identity as a White teacher. My choice to revisit this particular memory was inspired by reading Walt's memoir Ghostbox. In his book, Walt describes social ghosts as memories from our past that haunt us. Walt proceeds to present the process of creating a "ghostbox," as a space and process through which to re-visit traumatic memories for purposes of "productive haunting." To avoid and forget these memories, Walt argues, is "to let them be born anew in another shape, a form that rots my identity and crumbles my self-worth" (Jacobs, 2007, p. 16).*

> *Wanting to channel some of my own productive haunting, I hoped the process of digital storytelling would help me work through some of the shame and regret I had attached to my memories of teaching in New York City. I decided to revisit this memory through examining the trope of teacher as White savior, looking specifically at how this trope may have influenced my thinking and teaching at the time.*

Candance goes on to interrogate dominant discourses that position urban students of color as "downtrodden," "poor and disadvantaged students," or "second class citizens." She was able to present her students less as victims and more as the happy 5th graders that they were; she captured the energetic children who had loving families and enjoyed school. At the same time, she avoided representing herself as a villain who did not understand students from a social world that was very different than her own. She posed complex questions about intersections of race, literacy, and learning in public school systems. She shunned easy answers; instead she presented the story as more complicated than "nice White lady goes to Brooklyn." In an age where we are increasingly seeing mainstream commentary such as "The End of White America?" (Hsu, 2009), we need digital stories like Candance's to remind us that race will not go gently into that good night...if ever.

Conclusion

One way forward for higher education is to nudge more digital content into the open web, combining our honed wariness about privacy and security with our awareness of the full-blown social web. (Alexander, 2008, p. 199)

Bryan Alexander explores ways in which we can integrate social networking tools like blogging and wikis and/or sites such as Facebook and MySpace into collegiate learning environments (Alexander, 2008). An integral component of the "Digital Storytelling in and With Communities of Color" website was for students to post their digital stories to the course blog, http://blog.lib.umn.edu/afroam/storytelling/. In light of issues of privacy and confidentiality (alluded to above by Alexander), Rachel and I allowed students to choose pseudonyms under which they could post their work. Most students used their real names, however, in order to fully create a space where everyone could freely share aspects of their lives, and receive support and encouragement in confronting their social ghosts digitally.

One of the comments posted in response to the "White Teacher" digital story states:

I enjoyed the mix of images and the music, which was present but not overpowering. Even more, I appreciated the self-critique and the critique of identity in relation to the classroom—both yours and that of your students. Positioning is a powerful factor that often goes unnoticed, unacknowledged.

Indeed, "Digital Storytelling in and with Communities of Color" students explored how "colonized and subjugated people who, by way of resistance, create an oppositional subculture within the framework of domination, recognize that the field of representation (how we see ourselves, how others see us) is a site of ongoing struggle" (Hooks, 2006, p. 389). Students learned to not fear this site of struggle; they discovered how each and every one of us can explore our combination of privileged and disadvantaged identities in a quest to create a more democratic society. "If we want our students to engage the world as critical, informed people, then we need to reshape our plans as that world changes" (Alexander, 2008, p. 200). Digital stories help our students (and ourselves!) confront a world in constant motion by opening windows into spaces we don't know, as well as by guiding us in complicating understandings of contexts we believe that we thoroughly comprehend.

By the end of the semester, the students in the fall 2008 "Digital Storytelling in and with Communities of Color" class at the University of Minnesota viewed digital stories as gifts: "Those of us fortunate enough to be able to talk out loud should love our voices, because they tell everyone so much about who we are, both how strong we can be and how fragile" (Lambert, 2006, p. 54). I invite readers from places throughout the educational spectrum to explore how they may similarly help their students develop strong voices and create digital stories as gifts for themselves and others.

References

Alexander, B. (2008). Social networking in higher education. In R. Katz (Ed.), *The tower and the cloud: Higher education in the age of cloud computing* (pp. 197-201). Boulder, CO: Educause.

Hsu, H. (2009). The end of white America? *The Atlantic, 303*(1), 46-55.

Hooks, B. (2006). In our glory: Photography and black life. In L. Wells (Ed.), *The photography reader* (pp. 387-394). New York: Routledge.

Jacobs, W. (2007). *Ghostbox: A memoir*. New York: iUniverse.

Jacobs, W. (2005). *Speaking the lower frequencies: Students and media literacy*. Albany, NY: State University of New York Press.

Jacobs, W., Raimist, R., & Doerr-Stevens, C. (2009). *Speaking the lower frequencies 2.0: Race, learning, and literacy in the digital age*. Unpublished manuscript.

Jacobs, W., Reynolds, T., & Choy, G. (2004). The educational storytelling project: Three approaches to cross-curricular learning. *Journal of College Reading and Learning, 35*(1), 50-66.

Lambert, J. (2006). *Digital storytelling: Capturing lives, creating community* (2nd ed). Berkeley, CA: Digital Diner.

Livingston, S. (2004). Media literacy and the challenge of new information and communication technologies. *The Communication Review, 7*(3), 3-14.

Rule, L. (2009). Digital Storytelling. Accessed January 18, 2009 at http://electronicportfolios.org/digistory/.

Woolsey, K. (2008). Where is the new learning? In R. Katz (Ed.), *The tower and the cloud: Higher education in the age of cloud computing* (pp. 212-218). Boulder, CO: Educause.

What is Johnny Reading?
A Research Update

Keynote Speaker

Maria Valeri-Gold
George State University

I will begin my talk this morning with a quote taken from the writer, Janet Ruth Falon (2001), in her article titled "Life Among the Debris."

A book, as a physical object, develops a life of its own, one other than a story written on its pages. We read books as we experience the story of our lives....

We teach many readers who approach books as Falon has described in this quote. What draws readers to these physical objects? Why do readers choose books that appear to develop a life of their own? What books are they selecting? How do these books affect them? As a lifelong reader and as a college educator who teaches at-risk learners, I understand the importance of reading interest and its effect on reading attitude, reading behavior, intrinsic and extrinsic motivation, and reading comprehension. I have incorporated literature as a positive catalyst to motivate my reluctant college readers to read and to create that literary spark to help them develop an interest in reading.

I will present to you this morning a brief research update on the reading interests of elementary, middle, junior-high, high school, college at-risk students, and mature adults.

Reprinted from *College Reading Association Legacy: A Celebration of 50 Years of Literacy Leadership Volume II*, pp. 603-610, by W. M. Linek, D. D. Massey, E. G. Sturtevant, L. Cochran, B. McClanahan, & M. B. Sampson, Eds., 2010, Commerce, TX: Association of Literacy Educators & Reseachers.

The assessment of readers' reading interests has been well documented since 1889 (Weintraub, 1987), and researchers have continued to investigate the reading preferences of readers using a variety of data-gathering materials, such as open-ended questions and responses, Likert scaled survey instruments, reading logs, and journals (Monson & Sebesta, 1991).

During the past decade, numerous research studies have been conducted that examine the reading interests of elementary, middle, junior-high, and high school students (Beck, Bargiel, Koblitz, O'Connor, Pierce, & Wolf, 1998; Belden & Beckman, 1991; Cope, 1997; Diaz-Rubin, 1996; Fisher & Ayres, 1990; Fox, 1996; Fronius, 1993; Isaacs, 1992; Johns & Davis, 1990; Jordan, 1997; Laumbach, 1995; Lewis & Mayes, 1998; Richards, Thatcher, Shreeves, & Timmons, 1999; Rinehart, Gerlach, Wisell, & Welker, 1998; Simpson, 1996; Snellman, 1993; Sullivan & Donoho, 1994; Weiss, 1998; Worthy, 1996; Wray & Lewis, 1993). Yet, a limited number of research studies have been conducted to investigate the reading interests of college at-risk students (Blackwood, Flowers, Rogers, & Staik, 1991; Gallik, 1999; Jeffres & Atkin, 1996; Martinez & Nash, 1997; McCreath, 1975; Schraw, Flowerday, & Reisetter, 1998; Sheorey & Mokhtari, 1994) and mature adults (Black, 1998; Gourlie, 1996) in the last ten years.

Other research studies have examined how physical characteristics (visual appeal, size), age, grade level, reading ability, intrinsic and extrinsic motivation, reading attitude, reading habits, book choice, assigned reading, income, and gender play a significant role in determining the reading interests of students in varying grade levels (Cherland, 1994; Cope, 1997; Kincade & Kleine, 1993; Ley, 1994; Reutzel & Gali, 1998; Wigfield & Guthrie, 1997; Worthy, 1996; Worthy, Moorman, & Turner, 1999).

Additional studies have investigated the role of realistic fiction books focusing on societal issues, such as prejudice, racism, cults, child abuse, peer pressure, self-esteem, family struggles, violence, crime, rape, death, alcohol, and drugs, and their impact on reading interests (Weiss, 1998). These books discuss controversial problems that are realistic portrayals of readers' issues and their lives, and they can help students cope and solve their personal, social, and academic concerns in the real world.

Other investigations examine how self-selection, intrinsic and extrinsic motivation, peer relationships, and teacher interest influence reading interests rather than the school's media center, school collections, and libraries (Worthy et al., 1999).

After reviewing the literature, I noted that the majority of students from elementary through college grade levels enjoy listening to stories and reading books (Richards et al., 1999), and they also find pleasure in reading "light materials" such as comics and magazines (Worthy et al., 1999). Regardless of grade level, however, both females and males preferred fiction over nonfiction; females preferred fiction more strongly than males; males preferred male main characters more strongly than females; and females preferred female main characters more than the males (Segel, 1986). Simpson (1996) found that females read more, while males read less. Fox (1996) noted that students read more than they are generally believed to read, but their reading interests are not often tapped in school. Overall, the majority of students want books that they can read, relate to, think about, discuss, and write about (Harkrader & Moore, 1997).

I will present the reading interests of students by grade levels, ages, and categories. It should be noted, however, that the changes found in students' reading interests as they grow older are well documented (Wigfield & Asher, 1984). Methods of assessing readers' reading interests and the use of different populations, terminology, and data collecting methods can also affect the various reading categories. In addition, categories may represent a mixture of genre, theme, and topic and may be too broad to pinpoint students' reading interests (Monson et al., 1991).

Elementary school readers (ages-5-8) were interested in reading the following types of books: 1) picture books, 2) animals, 3) scary books /mystery/suspense/horror, 4) humor/riddles/jokes, 5) media (television/movies), and 6) adventure.

Preadolescent readers (middle and junior high school students, ages 9-13) reported that they were interested in reading these types of books: 1) horror, 2) humor, 3) mystery, 4) historical fiction, 5) adventure, 6) science fiction/fantasy, 7) animals, 8) media (television/movies, 9) realistic fiction, and 10) magazines (video games, teen magazines).

Higginbotham's study (1999) conducted with middle school readers (ages 9-11) noted that females reported an interest in romance, friendship, animal stories, adventure, and historical fiction; while the males reported preferences for sports and science. The results also indicated that males had a stronger preference for non-fiction than did the females.

An earlier study conducted by Fisher and Ayres (1990) compared the reading interests of children between the ages of 8 and 11 years old in England and in the United States is noteworthy. The rank order of mean scores by country is as follows:

England	United States
1. Jokes	1. Jokes
2. Mystery	2. Mystery
3. Adventure	3. Crafts
4. Crafts	4. Adventure
5. Animals	5. Animals
6. Sports	6. Science
7. Fairytales	7. Sports
8. Science	8. Fairytales
9. Poetry	9. Poetry
10. History	10. History
11. Biographies	11. Biographies

The top 10 areas of interest for high school students (ages 14-17) are the following (Diaz-Rubin, 1996): 1) adventure, 2) horror, 3) mystery, 4) humor, 5) murder, 6) love, 7) fantasy, 8) crime, 9) sports, and 10) media (television/ movies).

The reading interests of college at-risk students (Blackwood et al., 1991; Gallik, 1999; Jeffres & Atkin, 1996; Nelson, 1989) are: 1) newspapers, 2) magazines, 3) comic books, 4) poetry, 5) letters/e-mail/chat rooms, 6) Internet, 7) novels, 8) fiction, 9) non-fiction, and 10) media (television/movies).

Black's (1998) study conducted with mature adults indicated the following interests according to genre and preferences:

Fiction Preferences for Women
1. Romance
2. Mystery
3. Historical fiction

Non-fiction Preferences for Women
1. Biography
2. History
3. Travel

Fiction Preferences for Men
1. Western fiction
2. Mystery
3. Historical fiction and Romance

Non-fiction Preferences for Men
1. Travel
2. Fine Arts
3. Biography

I would like to recommend three books written by Kathleen Odean for future reference. One book is titled *Great Books about Things Kids Love* (Odean, 2001), and two earlier guides titled *Great Books for Girls* (1997) and *Great Books for Boys* (1998). *Great Books about Things Kids Love* (Odean, 2001) describes over 750 books recommended for ages three to fourteen that are arranged by high interest subjects such as ghosts, computers, robots, insects, and disasters. *Great Books for Girls* (Odean, 1997) contains more than 600 books recommended for girls three to fourteen, and *Great Books for Boys* (1998) has more than 600 books for boys aged two to fourteen.

I will end my presentation with a quote written by the writer Charlotte Gray. This quote was found in Glaspey's (1998) book titled *A Passion for Books*:

> Books become as familiar and necessary as old friends. Each change in them, brought about by much handling and by accident only endears them more. They are an extension of oneself.

Educational Resources for Selecting Books

Recommended websites for selecting books:
Award Winning Children's Books
 http://awardbooks.hypemart.net/
Bibliotherapy
 http://www.indiana.edu/~eric_rec/ieo/digests/d82.html
The Bulletin of the Center for Children's Books
 http://www.lis.uiuc.edu/puboff/bccb/
Horn Book Magazine
 www.hbook.com

Book Links
www.ala.org/BookLinks/
Book: *The Magazine for the Reading Life*
bookmagazine.com
Children's Literature Web Guide from the University of Calgary
www.acs.calgary.ca/~dkbrown/
Fairrossa Cyber Library of Children's Literature
www.dalton.org/libraries/fairrosa/
American Library Association
www.ala.org
International Reading Association
http://www.reading.org./choices/tc2000.html
http://www.reading.org./choices/cc2000.html
HtmlResAnchor
http://www.reading.org./choices/yac2000.html
Takoma Park Maryland Library—Middle School and High School Students
Selected Resources-Books, Magazines, Websites
HtmlResAnchor http://cityoftakomapark.org/library/ya/midbook.html

Recommended websites for renting audio books:
Recorded Books
www.recordedbooks.com
Books on Tape
www.booksontape.com
Blackstone Books
HtmlResAnchor www.blackstoneaudio.com

Recommended reference books for selecting children's books that are arranged and indexed by subject.
Cavanaugh, M., Freeman, J., Jones, B., & Rivlin, H. (Eds.). (2000). *The Barnes and Noble guide to children's books*. New York: Barnes & Noble.
Gillespie, J. T., & Naden, C. J. (Eds.). (1998). *Best books for children: Preschool through grade 6* (6th ed.). New York: Bowker.
Homa, L. L. (Ed.). (2000). *Elementary school library collection* (22nd ed.). New York: Brodart.
Lima, C. W., & Lima, J. A. (1998). *A to Zoo: Subject access to children's picture books* (5th ed.). New York: Bowker.
Lipson, F. R. (Ed.). (2000). *The New York Times parent's guide to the best books for children* (3rd ed.). New York: Three Rivers Press.
Rand, D., Parker, T. T., & Foster, S. (1998). *Black books galore: Guide to great African American children's books*. New York: John Wiley.

References

Beck, C., Bargiel, S., Koblitz, D., O'Connor, A., Pierce, K. M., & Wolf, S. (1998). Books for summer reading (Talking about books). *Language Arts, 75,* 320-328.

Belden, E. A., & Beckman, J. M. (1991). Finding new harmony, then and now: Young women's rites of passage (Books for the teenage reader). *English Journal, 80,* 84-86.

Black, B. A. (1998). *Outreach services for older adults at the Wadsworth Public Library.* Unpublished master's research paper, Kent State University, Ohio.

Blackwood, C., Flowers, S. S., Rogers, J. S., & Staik, I. M. (1991, November). *Pleasure reading by college students: Fact or fiction.* Paper presented at the annual meeting of the Mid-Southern Educational Research Association Conference, Lexington, KY.

Cherland, M. (1994). Untangling gender: Children, fiction, and useful theory. *New Advocate 7,* 253-264.

Cope, J. (1997). Beyond "voices of readers": Students on school's effects on reading. *English Journal, 86,* 18-23.

Diaz-Rubin, R. C. (1996). Reading interests of high school students. *Reading Improvement, 33,* 169-175.

Falon, J. R. (2001, May/June). Life among the debris: *Book: The Magazine for the Reading Life* (p. 92). New York: West Egg Communications.

Fisher, P. J. L., & Ayres, G. (1990). A comparison of the reading interests of children in England and the United States. *Reading Improvement, 2,* 111-115.

Fox, D. L. (1996). Learning to teach through inquiry (New teachers). *English Journal, 85,* 114-117.

Fronius, S. K. (1993). *Reading interests of young adults in Medina County, Ohio.* Unpublished master's research paper, Kent State University, Ohio.

Gallik, J. D. (1999). Do you read for pleasure? Recreational reading habits of college students. *Journal of Adolescent & Adult Literacy, 42,* 480-489.

Glaspey, T. W. (1998). *A passion for books.* Eugene, OR: Harvest House.

Gourlie, S. K. (1996). Reading interests in older adult public library users. Unpublished master's thesis, Kent State University, Ohio.

Harkrader, M. A., & Moore, R. (1997). Literature preferences of fourth graders. *Reading Research and Instruction, 36,* 325-339.

Higginbotham, S. (1999). *Reading interests of middle school students and reading preferences by gender of middle school students in a southeastern state.* Unpublished master's thesis, Mercer University, Macon, Georgia.

Isaacs, K. T. (1992). "Go ask Alice": What middle schoolers choose to read. *New Advocate, 5,* 129-143.

Jeffres, L. W., & Atkin, D. J. (1996). Dimensions of student interest in reading newspapers. *Journalism and Mass Communication Educator, 51,* 15-23.

Johns, J., & Davis, S. J. (1990). Reading interests of middle school students. *Ohio Reading Teacher, 24,* 47-50.

Jordan, A. D. (1997). Space, the final frontier: Books on space and space exploration. *Teaching and Learning Literature with Children and Young Adults, 7,* 15-16.

Kincade, K. M., & Kleine, P. E. (1993). Methodological issues in the assessment of children's reading interests. *Journal of Instructional Psychology, 20,* 224-237.

Laumbach, B. (1995). Reading interests of rural bilingual children. *Rural Educator, 16,* 12-14.

Lewis, V. V., & Mayes, W. M. (1998). *Vaki & Walter's best books for children: Lively, opinionated guide.* New York: Avon.

Ley, T. C. (1994). Longitudinal study of the reading attitudes and behaviors of middle school students. *Reading Psychology, 15,* 11-38.

Martinez, M., & Nash. M. F. (1997) Heroes and heroines. *Language Arts, 74*, 50-56.

McCreath, E. E. (1975). An investigation of reading habits, reading interests, and their relationship to reading improvement of students in an urban open door junior college. In G. McNinch & W. Miller (Eds.), *Reading: Convention and Inquiry* (pp. 100-106). Clemson, SC: National Reading Conference.

Monson, D. L, & Sebesta, S. (1991). Reading preferences. In J. Flood, J. Jensen, D. Lapp, & J. Squire (Eds.), *Handbook of Research in Teaching the Language Arts* (pp. 664-673). New York: Macmillan.

Nelson, R. L. (1989, October). *College students' views of reading*. Paper presented at the annual meeting of the Great Lakes Regional Reading Association, Cincinnati, OH.

Odean, K. (1997). *Great books for girls*. New York: Ballantine.

Odean, K. (1998). *Great books for boys*. New York: Ballantine.

Odean, K. (2001). *Great books about things kids love*. New York: Ballantine.

Reading Today. (June/July, 2001). *Reading remains popular among youths, according to polls*, p. 13.

Reutzel, D. R., & Gali, K. (1998). The art of children's book selection: A labyrinth unexplored. *Reading Psychology, 19*, 3-50.

Richards, P. O., Thatcher, D. H., Shreeves, M., & Timmons, P. (1999). Don't let a good scare frighten you: Choosing and using quality chillers to promote reading. *Reading Teacher, 52*, 830-840.

Rinehart, S. D., Gerlach, J. M., Wisell, D. L., & Welker, W. A. (1998). Would I like to read this book?: Eighth graders' use of book cover choices to help choose recreational reading. *Reading Research and Instruction, 37*, 263-279.

Schraw, G., Flowerday, T., & Reisetter, M. F. (1998). The role of choice in reader engagement. *Journal of Educational Psychology, 90*, 705-714.

Segel, E. (1986). As the twig is bent . . .: Gender and childhood reading. In E. Flynn & P. Schweickart (Eds.), *Gender and Reading: Essays on Readers, Texts, and Contexts* (pp. 165-186). Baltimore, MD: John Hopkins University Press.

Sheorey, R., & Mokhtari, K. (1994). The reading habits of college students at different levels of reading proficiency. *Reading Improvement, 31*, 351-362.

Simpson, A. (1996). Fictions and facts: An investigation of the reading practices of girls and boys. *English Education, 28*, 268-279.

Snellman, L. M. (1993). *Sixth grade reading interests: A survey*. (ERIC Document Reproduction Service No: ED 358 415).

Sullivan, E. P., & Donoho, G. E. (1994, November). *Reading interests of gifted secondary school writers*. Paper presented at the annual meeting of the Mid-South Educational Research Association, Nashville, TN.

Weintraub, S. (1987). Two significant trends in reading research. In H. A. Robinson (Ed.), *Reading and Writing Instruction in the United States: Historical Trends* (pp. 59-68). Newark, DE: International Reading Association.

Weiss, M. J. (1998). Potpourri (The Publisher's Connection). *ALAN Review, 26*, 40-41.

Wigfield, A., & Asher, S. R. (1984). Social and motivational influences on reading. In P. D.Pearson (Ed.), *Handbook of Reading Research* (pp. 423-452). New York: Longman.

Wigfield, A., & Guthrie, J. T. (1997). Relations of children's motivation for reading to the amount and breath of their reading. *Journal of Educational Psychology, 89*, 420-432.

Worthy, J. (1996). A matter of interest: Literature that hooks reluctant readers and keeps them reading. *Reading Teacher, 50*, 204-212.

Worthy, J., Moorman, M., & Turner, M. (1999). What Johnny likes to read is hard to find in school. *Reading Research Quarterly, 34*, 12-27.

Wray, D., & Lewis, M. (1993). The reading experiences and interests of junior school children. *Children's Literature in Education, 24*, 252-263.

RESEARCH AWARDS

THE HIDDEN PERIL OF DIFFERENTIATION: FRAGMENTED INSTRUCTION

Doctoral Dissertation Award

Carla Wonder-McDowell

Utah State University

Abstract

This paper describes the process of aligning intervention and commercial materials with the classroom scope and sequence of instruction in phonemic awareness, phonics, fluency, vocabulary, and comprehension to support struggling readers. The results of a two group, pre-post experimental study suggest that at-risk second-grade students benefit from supplemental instruction that is aligned with the classroom core-reading program.

Teaching young students to read has been described as one of the most important responsibilities of primary grade teachers, and yet, a significant number of students struggle to develop proficient skills (Snow, Burns, & Griffin, 1998). To address the varied needs of students who are at-risk of failure, teachers often provide small group, differentiated instruction. Providing more intense instruction with smaller groups of students has the intended outcome of establishing an accelerated learning trajectory, ultimately resulting in grade level performance of at-risk students. Unfortunately, recent data would suggest that efforts to differentiate instruction through small-group instruction alone are insufficient for making a substantial difference with at-risk readers (Torgesen, 2004).

In many schools, supplemental instruction, in addition to that provided by the classroom teacher, is delivered in a variety of formats in an attempt to address the greater instructional needs of students who are at risk of failure. Student achievement data is used to identify students who are lagging behind peers in the development of proficient reading skills through classroom instruction alone. After receiving comprehensive literacy instruction in the classroom, students are identified as at-risk readers and are labeled as non-responders to instruction (Vaughn, 2003). Once identified, the non-responders are often placed with reading specialists, special education teachers and/or paraprofessionals to receive additional reading instruction time where progress data is carefully monitored through a response-to-intervention (RTI) model. During supplemental instruction periods, specialists and paraprofessionals use a variety of commercial materials and programs to address the needs of at-risk students who struggle to learn to read (Adams & Englemann, 1996; Clay 1985; Sprick, Howard & Fidanque, 1998). Although Mathes, Denton, Fletcher, Anthony, Francis & Schatschneider (2005) provided evidence that delivering supplemental instruction through a variety of programs and methods positively impacts student achievement, the rate of growth is often not accelerated to a high enough degree to allow at-risk students to catch up with grade-level peers.

In a meta-analysis of studies over a 20-year period, Borman & D'Augostino (1996) reported that students served in Title I programs failed to achieve or maintain levels of success when compared to mainstream peers. Allington (1994) and Torgeson (2004) have asserted that special education has failed in its promise to lift at-risk students out of school failure. While the 2007 National Assessment of Educational Progress has suggested increases in the overall reading achievement of U.S. fourth-grade students (http://www.nationsreportcard.gov), the proportion of students reading below basic levels (approximately 40%) did not change noticeably from 1993 to 2005 and gains noted in overall achievement were not always accompanied by significant closing of racial/ethnic and gender gaps.

Differentiated Instruction

Over the past fifteen years, many structural changes have been implemented in our large, urban school district to enable teachers to deliver differentiated instruction that was sensitive to individual student need. At-risk students were grouped together in separate, smaller classrooms within grade levels and across grade levels to provide increased adult assistance and instruction. Paraprofessionals in Title I schools delivered supplemental instruction for at-risk students during the literacy block and in small, homogenous groups. Special education services were provided through a resource, pull-out model and through a push-in, inclusive model. In spite of providing supplemental reading instruction through the use of different grouping arrangements and differentiated instruction for each group, data from our at-risk student population indicated they were not accelerating enough to catch up to their grade-level peers. Thus, our data, which is supported by data from other studies, showed that making structural changes to support instructional differentiation is not any more effective than using other traditional accelerated learning approaches (Boorman, & D'Augostino, 1996; Pogrow, 2002; Powell, 1964).

It was felt that the district teachers were putting forth great effort implementing a variety of methods to differentiate instruction in order to meet the needs of our at-risk readers. However, our at-risk students were not gaining the needed reading skills. As a school district serving a majority of at-risk students, it was determined that the next step in our efforts to help our students was to examine the various reading curricula used by the district for reading instruction. It was hoped that this analysis would provide a solution to helping increase our at-risk students' reading achievement.

Literature Review

Reading Instruction

In our school district's attempt to reach our struggling readers, our at-risk readers received reading instruction from a variety of sources. The regular education classroom teachers provided reading instruction using the basic core or basal reader. However, this instruction alone did not provide the needed support to enable the at-risk student to become successful readers. Therefore, the at-risk readers were also grouped and required to attend a supplementary reading class, where more intense differentiated instruction was provided. This increased both their instructional reading time and their time to practice reading in a small group setting. Even though our teachers were doing everything they could, our at-risk readers were not improving. Thus, it was determined that the reading curriculum needed to be analyzed.

Our curriculum analysis showed that all the reading instructional materials bought by the district were supported by scientific research. However, our analysis also revealed some unsettling facts. First, the core-reading program and the supplemental reading program taught the various reading skills listed on the scope and sequence chart at different times. Second, each reading program had sight words for the students to learn but they were basically different and had very little overlap. Third, the various reading programs used different reading terminology to teach similar reading skills, strategies, and concepts. Finally, the instructional approach to teaching varied from a highly scripted, behaviorally approach to a responsive, social approach (Adams & Englemann, 1996; Clay, 1985; Morris, Tyner & Perney, 2001; Torgeson, 2000).

In essence, we were acting on the hope that if one program did not work for our at-risk students, a different program might be more effective. Moreover, in our attempt to give them more reading time and differentiated instruction to meet their needs, we were putting our at-risk students in peril, as they were being taught by two very different reading programs that were asking them to do and learn different things. Thus, our at-risk students were being asked to learn more with less instructional time to master either program (Allington & Johnston, 1986).

It was determined that we needed to adjust our various reading curricula so that we could make them more compatible or aligned. Curricular alignment occurs when the core-reading curriculum found in the regular classroom is aligned with the reading curriculum found in supplemental reading classes. This alignment allows at-risk students to receive instruction that is more effective. Learning the same thing in both classroom environments gives at-risk students more time to learn the necessary skills found on the scope and sequence chart, as they are receiving the instruction twice and have more time to develop the necessary skills to become successful readers. Thus, the first purpose of this study was to align our supplementary reading programs with our core-reading program that was found in all our classrooms.

Aligning Our Reading Curricula

Nine years ago, the U.S. Congress commissioned a synthesis of reading research, resulting in a meta-analysis of current reading research. The results of this analysis were presented in a report by the National Reading Panel (NICHD, 2000). The report identified five essential reading elements that should be included in instruction in order for students to attain competency and become a successful reader. These five reading elements are phonemic awareness, phonics, fluency, vocabulary, and comprehension and are the foundation upon which most comprehensive classroom core-reading programs and supplemental reading programs are based. However, different reading programs provide different instructional methods and different scope and sequence skill charts in which the five reading elements are taught.

Our process of designing our aligned reading instruction began with the second-grade core basal reader. First, we looked at the core-reading program's scope and sequence chart and developed a second-grade curriculum map using the five essential elements of reading instruction identified by the National Reading Panel (NICHD, 2000). Second, this curriculum map was then used to help us work on the alignment with the scope and sequence for supplemental instruction. Third, instructional materials were listed on the curriculum map so that teachers could easily access resources when working with at-risk students. Finally, assessment of mastery was essential to placing students in appropriate instruction and monitoring individual understanding. Although the general process was clear, we ran into many challenges along the way.

Phonemic Awareness

The second grade classroom core-reading program included no explicit phonemic awareness (PA) training since students at this age level are expected to have mastered oral blending and segmentation skills. However, the classroom core reading intervention materials provided thirty PA review lessons for students. These lessons were designed to support the development of oral blending and segmentation skills, moving from blending and segmenting syllables to initial phonemes, ending phonemes and finally, medial phonemes.

During supplemental instruction, reading specialists used portions of the lessons to determine where students struggled within this progression of skills. Supplemental instruction began where the students were unable to blend or segment phonemes and continued through from that point to the end of the series of thirty lessons. The instruction using the classroom core intervention materials was referred to on the curriculum map; however, we did not align this instruction to the phonics strand because it was intended to be provided for only those students who were unable to blend and segment phonemes and was to be terminated as soon as blending and segmenting three phonemes was established.

Phonics

The National Reading Panel provided evidence supporting systematic phonics instruction (NICHD, 2000). Phonics skills are presented in increasing difficulty during the first grade year and, in most comprehensive classroom core programs, are reviewed in the second grade. It is assumed that students have a foundational knowledge of the sound/spelling relationships of the English language and instruction is designed to build upon this knowledge, gradually increasing difficulty as words with multiple syllables are presented. Classroom core intervention programs often provide a review of phonics elements; however, because it is considered review, content is presented very rapidly.

Many at-risk second-grade students have mastered basic consonant sounds; however, long vowel spellings, diphthongs, and even short vowels can present a challenge for at-risk students. Since our goal was mastery of each skill, it was clear that we needed to identify the scope and sequence of instruction within the classroom core on a curriculum map. The phonics strand was developed in a four-step process that took about two months to complete. First, the order in which each phonics element was presented in the classroom core intervention program was listed on a curriculum map. The skills taught in each lesson were noted on the curriculum map and became the foundation for the aligned treatment (see Figure 1, Step 1 below). Second, each decodable text from the second grade classroom core-program was analyzed to determine vowel spellings being practiced and added to the map where the target spellings were to be taught. As we analyzed the second grade decodable text that was intended for practice, we found that the core program often directed teachers to provide text for students as a review when sounds and spellings in the books had not yet been taught. In order to address these issues, we listed each book on the curriculum map, matching the scope and sequence even if it meant placing books in a different order than the publisher recommended. Although we attempted to align both the consonants and vowel spellings, this became very challenging and in the end, we prioritized the vowel spelling scope and sequence of instruction knowing that many of our students had mastered single consonant spellings.

After listing all of the second grade text provided with the classroom core program on the curriculum map, we could clearly see what classroom teachers had been telling us. For some lessons, there were no practice materials. For others, there was only one piece of connected text provided (see Figure 1, Step 2). Although this was not as concerning for single consonant spellings, we knew that our at-risk second grade students had not mastered vowel spellings and needed ample materials to practice them. Our goal was to provide a wealth of materials for reading specialists to use with students to bring them to mastery. To increase the supply of practice materials, we added all of the first grade core decodable books and practice decodable books to the second grade curriculum map, noting when each book should be read within the second grade scope and sequence. To prevent dependence upon picture clues and to provide a more challenging format, the text from all first grade decodable books was printed in paragraph format on a single page.

We spent extensive hours aligning the first grade decodable text with the second grade scope and sequence and yet, our goal of having multiple practice opportunities to bring students to mastery was not in place. Since there were no more materials to align within the classroom core program, we gathered additional pieces of connected text from *The Six Minute Solution*, which is a supplemental program designed to increase student reading fluency (Adams & Brown, 2003). In this program, sound/spelling relationships are taught and practiced through repeated readings of word lists and paragraphs of decodable text that focus on a specific spelling. As we added text from *The Six Minute Solution* to the curriculum map, we altered the author's intended order of presentation so that all fluency practice was aligned to the phonic element listed on our second grade curriculum map (see Figure 1, Step 4).

Figure 1: Curriculum Mapping of Phonics Instruction

Week	Step 1 Phonics	Step 2 2nd Grade Decodable	Step 3 1st Grade Core Decodable	Step 3 1st Grade Practice Decodable	Step 4 Six Minute Solution Fluency	Step 4 Six Minute Solution Passage
Unit 1: Lesson 2	/k/ spelled c	#8	#9	#4	p. 168	
	/k/ spelled ¨ck		#10	#5	p. 127-128	p. 262
	/k/ spelled k		#11	#6	p. 130	p. 263
	/ĭ/		#12	#7	p. 131	
	Review /ă/		#13		p. 132-133	
	Review /ĕ/		#14	#8		
			#19			
			#20			

The classroom core-reading program introduced large number of sight words, mixing together high frequency words, content words, and words with irregular spellings. As we analyzed the core-reading program sight words, we discovered that there were many words presented quickly with limited practice opportunities. Originally we were planning to align the sight words within the text that students were reading; however, the core reading program lacked consistency of emphasis across lessons with very little practice opportunities for student reading in connected text. In each lesson, however, the classroom core intervention materials provided connected text in blackline master form (BLM) that included the sight words, sounds, and spellings cumulatively taught through the lesson. We analyzed each BLM to identify when common sight words were assessed in the core intervention program and the first 200 words were added to the curriculum map (*www.usu.edu/teachall/text/reading/Frylist. pdf*). We included words from the first 200 words because in the Utah state core curriculum it is expected that all second graders will master these two hundred sight words (See Figure 2, step 6).

Figure 2: Curriculm Mapping of Reading Assessment and Sight Words

Week	Step 5	Step 6	
	Core Program Assessment Text	High Frequency Words	
		First 100	2nd 100
Unit 1: Lesson 2	p. 3	at	hand
		did	
		her	
		is	
		it	
		like	
		look	
		she	
		to	

Fluency

Fluency was primarily taught through a repeated reading format. The curriculum map identified multiple pieces of decodable text that reading specialists could use during supplemental instruction. As reading specialists provided instruction, they were given direction to have students read as much text as needed to attain mastery, but to move quickly on to the next skill in the scope and sequence once mastered. In other words, students did not have to read each piece of text on the curriculum map; they simply had to read the text fluently. The reading specialist's goal was to move students through the scope and sequence of instruction as quickly as possible.

Figure 3: Sample Reading Assessment Proficiency Scores

Lesson	No Pass Errors: 3=>	Weak Pass Errors: 2=<	Pass Errors: 2=<	Strong Pass Errors: 2=<
2.5	47 or less	48 - 55	56 - 64	65 or greater
2.6	48 or less	49 - 57	58 - 67	68 or greater
2.7	49 or less	50 - 59	60 - 70	71 or greater
3.1	50 or less	51 - 61	62 - 73	74 or greater
3.2	51 or less	52 - 63	64 - 76	77 or greater
3.3	52 or less	53 - 65	66 - 79	80 or greater
3.4	66 or less	54 - 67	68 - 82	82 or greater
3.5	54 or less	55 - 69	70 - 85	86 or greater
3.6	55 or less	56 - 71	72 - 88	89 or greater

Although the classroom core intervention reading selections (BLM) were intended to be used as the only connected text for fluency practice in each lesson, we used this piece of text to assess mastery of all skills taught thus far. Reading fluency norms were used to establish acceptable rate and accuracy levels to determine mastery of the phonics elements taught (brt.uoregon.edu/tech_reports.htm). To move on to a new element, three of the four students in each small group must pass with a strong pass or weak pass. If this level of mastery was not attained, supplemental instruction was provided using additional phonics lessons with connected text to bring students to mastery.

Although establishing mastery levels would ensure that students were not taught more complex sounds and spellings before mastering simple ones, once instruction began we found that students had difficulty attaining these fluency levels and therefore, instruction was not progressing. To remedy this, materials were organized to highly scaffold students. The decodable text was broken down into component parts, practiced, and then presented as connected text. Initially, students were taught the sounds for target spellings, next they read words with those spellings. As fluency developed with words, practice was given with phrases using the target words from the book. When the students became successful with phrases, they read the decodable text. This process was repeated for the next decodable book that focused on the same sounds and spellings; however, different words and phrases were taught. Students spent ten to fifteen minutes a day working on fluency, orally reading for the majority of time. We discovered that student fluency development was best supported when we provided instruction of phonics elements in isolation, provided immediate practice in reading words and phrases with the target sound/spellings, and then provided numerous pieces of decodable text that contained the practiced words and phrases. It is important to note, however, that reading specialists varied the number of decodable books read for each group, progressing through the scope and sequence of phonics instruction as quickly as possible.

Vocabulary

The classroom core program identified vocabulary words that supported units in science and social studies. As with most comprehensive reading programs, the classroom core intervention program provided a lower level comprehension text that followed the unit theme in the basal reader - it was shorter and less dense. We began by adding the intervention text provided for comprehension instruction on the curriculum map (See Figure 4, Step 7 below). Next, we selected key vocabulary words from the comprehension text in the intervention program and added them to the curriculum map (See Figure 4, Step 8 below).

To support instruction of each vocabulary word, we created a vocabulary compact disc for each reading specialist that contained the printed word, pictures of each word and a child-friendly definition for every word on the curriculum map. During the development of the vocabulary compact disc, care was taken to ensure that the words identified for vocabulary instruction would support understanding of the shorter comprehension text while being directly related to the content and themes being taught in the classroom basal reading program. As a result of this design, at-risk students were receiving additional vocabulary instruction. However, words presented during the supplemental reading instruction were related to themes being read in the classroom core reading program.

Figure 4: Curriculum Mapping of Reading Comprehension and Vocabulary Instruction

Step	7	8	9	10
Week	Comprehension Text	Vocabulary	Comprehension Strategy	Comprehension Skill
Unit 1: Lesson 2	Core Intervention Program Shorter Reading Selection	wreck		
		tacks	Making Connections	Compare and Contrast
		destroyed	Predicting	

Comprehension

There is evidence that students benefit from multiple strategy comprehension instruction and explicit instruction in text features (NICHD, 2000; Vacca & Vacca, 2008). In comprehensive reading programs, comprehension strategies are modeled as students read the anthology. Graphic organizers are used to help students understand features of text and text structure (Houghton Mifflin, 2005; Open Court, 2000).

The curriculum map was again very useful for aligning classroom core and supplemental instruction. First, we analyzed the classroom core content to identify what reading strategies and features of text (skills) were being taught. This information was added to the curriculum map and we prepared a packet of graphic organizers taught in the classroom core-reading program for each reading specialist. As we aligned the comprehension instruction between the classroom core-reading program and the supplemental instruction, our goal was to provide at-risk readers with text that was less dense but that engaged students in reading text that was conceptually at grade level. Initial comprehension instruction was provided for all students as an anthology selection was read the classroom. For example, as the class read an expository piece of text on animals, classroom teachers modeled predicting and making connections. During a second reading, the classroom teachers would model the use of a Venn diagram to compare and contrast the characteristics of two different animals. When receiving supplemental instruction, at-risk students would read an additional, shorter selection on animals from the classroom core intervention program. As they read the expository text, the smaller group size of four enabled each student to practice predicting and making connections. On a second reading of the supplemental text, students filled in a Venn diagram, comparing and contrasting two animals that were described in the shorter text. Again, the key feature of this instruction was the direct link between the classroom core and supplemental instruction scope and sequence.

Comprehension instruction was given several days a week (a portion of the second fifteen minutes allocated to fluency in connected text and comprehension) in the supplemental groups. Two primary issues came up within this area. First, the students had such limited decoding ability that we had to bridge the gap between what could be decoded and having enough content for students to be able to use strategies and practice analyzing text structures. Initially the leveled text was not at an instructional level (95% + accuracy, 70%+ comprehension) due to limited student skills. Reading specialists were instructed to support the decoding so that they could work with vocabulary and comprehension instruction (choral reading, modeled reading, etc.). As student decoding improved, reading specialists gradually moved students from developing listening comprehension to reading comprehension. Reading specialists struggled at first; however, when they understood the instructional intent of fluency with decodable text and comprehension with the reading selection, they were able to adapt the support level to reach the objective.

The second problem that we identified was that, once again, the classroom core-reading program did not provide enough intervention text for students to read. To address this gap, we provided additional leveled text, carefully aligning the text with the scope and sequence of classroom core instruction. The text was carefully monitored to ensure that it was at an instructional reading level and that it was appropriate for providing instruction in the comprehension strategies and text structures that were identified on the curriculum map.

Methods

Participants/Setting

The participants were 133 second-grade students who attended eleven elementary schools throughout the district. Overall, the schools served students who were 48% White, 38% Hispanic, and 14% African American. Almost half of these 133 at-risk students were identified as being English language learners (46%) and primarily from low-income households, with 81% receiving free and reduce breakfast and lunch.

The setting was in eleven elementary schools where twelve reading specialists provided supplementary reading instruction. One group of at-risk students received reading instruction using the new aligned materials, while the other group of at-risk students received reading instruction using *Read Well*, a commercially available program designed to support struggling readers (Sprick, Howard & Fidanque, 1998).

Treatment Intervention

In both the aligned treatment group and the unaligned treatment (control) group, instruction occurred for 20 weeks. In the aligned treatment group, there was little flexibility provided in *what to teach* because content followed the classroom scope and sequence. However, in the *how to teach*, reading specialists used their knowledge and expertise to provide varied practice activities. For example, using the target sounds and spellings in phonics, reading specialists explicitly taught blending by writing words on a white board as students read. "Toughie Charts" had words, phrases, and sentences with the target content written for fluency practice. Words with new or difficult spellings were written on flash cards and practiced to develop fluency. Sorting activities were used to support student understanding of common spelling patterns, which culminated in the oral reading of each set of words. To increase the amount of individual practice, the same spellings, words, and phrases were written on sentence strips and read simultaneously while being passed from student to student. Sight words were randomly written on a sheet of paper, practiced as timed readings and correct words per minute were graphed by students. It is important to note that all spellings, words, and phrases that were practiced during word study lead directly to fluency practice of identical words embedded in connected, decodable text.

To ensure that there was equal time spent on word level work and reading of connected text, lesson formats for reading specialists were developed (See Figure 5). Each day, students were to receive 15 minutes of decoding practice and 15 minutes of fluency practice. Vocabulary and comprehension were consistently taught within the thirty-minute block of time.

Figure 5: Reading Intervention Lesson Format

Supplemental Instructional delivery	Treatment 1: Aligned instruction	Treatment 2: Nonaligned instruction
Decoding practice: Word study (15 minutes per lesson)		
Phonological processing	Classroom core program; oral blending and segmenting activities.	Read Well®; segmenting activities.
Word study: Fluency practice	Classroom core program sequence of skills; sound review, blending, repeated reading of words, sight word review.	Read Well® sequence of skills; sound review, blending, repeated reading of words, sight word review.
Vocabulary	Introduce three words from classroom core program that are related to the core anthology stories.	Introduce three words from Read Well® text (on a different topic than the classroom core content).
Fluency in connected text and comprehension (15 minutes per lesson)		
Fluency in connected text	Repeated reading in text practicing target spellings from word study in decodable text from core program. Additional fluency practice following classroom core scope and sequence from supplemental resources (Six Minute Solution®).	Read Well® solo text, practice target spellings from word study, fluency practice following Read Well® scope and sequence
Comprehension	Classroom core intervention two page reading selection (narrative and expository), applying comprehension strategies and text structure skill that was modeled in whole group classroom instruction (use of strategies and graphic organizers).	Read Well® comprehension strategy and text structure instruction, based on scope and sequence of nonaligned supplemental program

Initially, reading specialists struggled with the challenge of selecting activities for instruction and monitoring the 15-minute instructional blocks. At the beginning of the study, reading specialists reported that they preferred the more scripted, non-aligned treatment. As reading specialists proficiency increased during the study, however, the preference of treatment changed to the aligned curriculum. Reading Specialists reported that they were better able to differentiate instructional activities to meet the needs of students and they felt that students were progressing faster in the aligned treatment.

Assessment Instrument

All students who received the supplemental reading instruction were assessed using two different instruments. First, the oral reading fluency (ORF) in the Dynamic Indicators of Basic Early Literacy Skills (DIBELS) was taken. Students who scored in the lowest quartile were placed in supplemental reading classes (Good & Kaminski, 2002). Second, the Woodcock Reading Mastery Test-Revised (WRMT-R) subtests of Word Identification, Word Attack, Word Comprehension, and Passage Comprehension were administered to all students at pretest and posttest as outcome measures (Woodcock, 1998). These instruments were used as a pre/post to determine the effects of the aligned reading instruction on students reading scores.

Data Analysis and Results

A *t*-test for independent samples analysis was used to examine differences in mean scores between groups at posttest. Next, an ANCOVA analysis was used. After controlling for pretest scores and accounting for the variance between reading specialists by using the ANCOVA, posttest scores for each treatment condition were compared. Using the WRMT-R, student responses to supplemental instruction were examined for the dependent variables of oral reading fluency, word identification, word attack, word comprehension, and passage comprehension. The composite standardized scores received on reading comprehension and total reading were examined for each treatment condition.

On the pretest, the *t*-test for independent samples showed no statistically significant differences between the aligned, supplemental and nonaligned, supplemental reading instruction interventions on oral reading fluency, word identification, word attack, word comprehension, or passage comprehension. A table of random numbers was used to establish equivalent groups and pretest data confirmed the efficacy of the random assignment procedures.

After controlling for pretest scores and accounting for the variance among reading specialists, there were statistically significant differences found between the aligned condition and nonaligned condition in favor of the aligned treatment for posttest scores on the DIBELS oral reading fluency assessment $F(1,108) = 10.640$, $p = .000$, Word Identification subtest (sight words), $F(1, 108) = 4.729$, $p = .01$, the

Word Attack subtest (ability to decode phonetically regular words), F (1, 108) = 8.141, p =.001), the word comprehension subtest (vocabulary), F (1, 108) = 15.489, p = .000, the passage comprehension subtest, F (1, 133) = 32.670, p = .000, reading comprehension, F (1,108) = 11.569, p = .000 and total reading composite scores, F (1, 108) = 5.183, p = .007. The results of these analyses indicated that providing aligned supplemental reading instruction had a statistically significant positive effect on students' oral reading fluency development, ability to read sight words, ability to decode phonetically regular words, vocabulary development, and comprehension. Although most effect sizes were small, moderate effect sizes were identified for vocabulary and comprehension development in favor of the aligned treatment.

Implications

It is imperative that effective reading instruction is found in order to accelerate the reading growth of at-risk students. Students at the highest risk of failure are often supported through special education or reading specialist services where they receive a "different" reading curriculum than the one used in the classroom core reading program. Historically, it has been shown that students who receive supplemental reading instruction in pull-out settings rarely make strong enough gains to catch up with peers and maintain grade-level performance (Al Otaiba, & Fuchs, 2002; Bean, 1991; Borman & D'Augostino, 1996; Elbaum, Vaughn, Hughes, & Moody, 2000; Kenk & Kibby, 2000; Vaughn, 2003). Thus, there has been a renewed interest in push-in supplemental services where supplemental instruction occurs within the classroom for at-risk students. This study suggests that the answers to accelerating reading growth might not be found in location of services, the amount of adult assistance or through the use of a different supplementary reading instructional program, but in the alignment of the scopes and sequences of instruction between the classroom core reading program and supplementary reading interventions.

These findings suggest that at-risk students benefit from increased "FIT" of instruction: (a) with content mirroring the scope and sequence of the core classroom instruction that is highly *"focused"* on individual need, (b) in small groups of four or less to increase *"intensity"* and (c) that provides a double dose of instruction, increasing instructional *"time."* To collaborate in this manner means that classroom teachers and reading specialists must not only use similar methods and materials when instructing students, they must also have a common, pre-determined scope and sequence of instruction that at-risk students practice. This practice allows various professionals supporting at-risk readers to work collaboratively to ensure accelerated student learning and success. While effective differentiation may not be found in providing different materials or instructional methods, it may be found in the provision of comprehensive literacy instruction where the amount of individual practice is varied to support student development of proficiency within a common scope and sequence of instruction.

References

Adams, G., & Englemann, S. (1996). *Research on direct instruction: 25 years beyond DISTAR.* Seattle, WA: Educational Achievement Systems.

Adams, B., & Brown, S. (2003). *The six-minute solution: Primary level.* Natick, MA: Cambium Learning.

Allington, R. (1994). What's special about special programs for children who find learning to read difficult? *Journal of Reading Behavior, 1*(26), 95-115.

Allington, R., &. Johnston, P. (1986). The coordination among regular classroom reading programs and targeted support programs. In B. I. Williams, P. A. Richmond, & B. J. Mason (Eds.), *Designs for compensatory education: Conference proceedings and papers* (pp. 440-478). Chapel Hill, NC: Research Evaluation Associates.

Al Otaiba, S., & Fuchs, D. (2002). Characteristics of children who are unresponsive to early literacy intervention: A review of the literature. *Remedial and Special Education, 23,* 300-316.

Bean, R. C. (1991). In class or pull out: Effects of setting on the remedial reading program. *Journal of Reading Behavior, 4,* 445-464.

Borman, G., & D'Augostino, J. V. (1996). Title I and student achievement: A meta-analysis of federal evaluation results. *Educational Evaluation & Policy Analysis, 18,* 309-326.

Clay, M. (1985). *The early detection of reading difficulties.* Portsmouth, NH: Hineman.

Elbaum, B., Vaughn, S., Hughes, M., & Moody, S. (2000). How effective are one-to-one tutoring programs in reading for elementary students at risk for reading failure? A meta-analysis of the intervention research. *Journal of Educational Psychology, 92,* 605-619.

Englemann, S. (1997). *Preventing failure in the primary grades.* Eugene, OR: Association for Direct Instruction.

Good, R., & Kaminski, R. (2002). *DIBELS oral reading fluency passages for first through third grades* (Technical Report No. 10). Eugene: University of Oregon.

Houghton Mifflin Reading (2005). Boston, MA: Houghton Mifflin Publishing.

Kenk, L., & Kibby, M. (2000). Re-mediating reading difficulties: Appraising the past, reconciling the present, constructing the future. In M. M. Kamil (Ed.), *Handbook of reading research* (Vol. 3, pp. 667-690). Mahwah, NJ: Erlbaum.

Mathes, P.G., Denton, C. A., Fletcher, J. M., Anthony, J.L., Francis, D. J., & Schatschneider, C. (2005). The effects of theoretically different instruction and student characteristics on the skills of struggling readers. *Reading Research Quarterly, 40, 148-182.*

Morris, D., Tyner, B., & Perney, J. (2001). Early steps: Replicating the effects of an early first grade reading intervention program. *Journal of Educational Psychology, 92*(4), 681-693.

National Institute of Child Health and Human Development (NICHD) (2000). *Report of the National Reading Panel. Teaching children to read: An evidence-based assessment of the scientific reearch literature on reading and its implications for reading instruction: Reports of the subgroups (NIH Publication No. 00-4754).* Washington, DC: US Government Printing Office.

Open Court Reading (2000). *Intervention guide, second grade.* Columbus, OH: SRA/ McGraw-Hill.

Pogrow, S. (2002). Success for all is a failure. *Phi Delta Kappan , 83,* 463-468.

Powell, W. R. (1964). The joplin plan: An evaluation. *The Elementary School Journal, 64,* 387-392.

Snow, C.E., Burns, M.S., & Griffin, P. (Eds.). 1998. *Preventing reading difficulties in young children.* Washington DC: National Academy Press.

Sprick, M. M., Howard, L. M., & Fidanque, A. (1998). *Read well: Critical foundations in primary reading.* Longmont, CO: Sopris West.

Taylor, B., Pearson, P., Cark, K., & Walpole, S. (1999). *Beating the odds in teaching all children to read.* Washington, DC: U.S. Department of Education.

Torgesen, J. (2004). Lessons learned from research on interventions for students who have difficulty learning to read. In P. C. McCardle (Ed.), *The voice of evidence* (pp. 355-382). Baltimore, MD: Brookes Publishing.

Torgesen, J. (2000). Individual differences in response to early intervention in reading: The lingering problem of treatment resisters. *Learning Disabilities Research and Practice , 15,* 55-64.

Vacca, R., & Vacca, J. (2008). *Content Area Reading.* New York: Pearson Publishing.

Vaughn, S. (2003). *How many tiers are needed for response to intervention to achieve acceptable prevention outcomes.* Paper presented at the National Research Center on Learning Disabilities RTI Symposium, Kansas City, MO.

Woodcock, R. (1998). *The Woodcock Reading Mastery Tests-Revised: Normative update.* Circle Pines, MN: American Guidance Service.

A Study Examining How Struggling Third Grade Readers, as Members of a Guided Reading Group, Experience Peer-Led Literature Discussions

Doctoral Dissertation Award

Cheryl L. Potenza-Radis

Kent State University

Abstract

The purpose of this study was to describe how struggling readers experienced peer-led literature discussions within the context of Guided Reading. Using a multiple case study design to discover patterns in the experiences of five participants, qualitative data and descriptive statistics were analyzed to describe what students did and said as they progressed through three discussion contexts. Over a 7-month period, students participated in teacher-led, guided-practice, and peer-led literature discussions. Primary data included discussion transcripts, videotapes, and student interviews. Secondary sources included teacher interviews, questionnaires, and field notes. Results found this group of struggling readers (a) took on unique roles in the discussion process; (b) were capable of engaging in peer-led discussions which advanced understanding; (c) gained independence and took on greater responsibility for their discussions; (d) built relationships with one another; and (e) understood the purpose of peer-led discussions as being social and supportive in nature.

In classrooms across the country, there exists a population of struggling readers who have not been identified as having a learning disability but who nonetheless have trouble in reading. Because the reasons for which they struggle are as varied as the readers themselves, literacy professionals must take into account the individual nature of becoming literate as they embrace "integrated, comprehensive approaches to literacy and literature that are theoretically and research based" (Short, 1999, p.

131). One such approach, small group literature discussions, has gained renewed interest over the past decade (Almasi 1996). Whether called literature circles (Daniels, 1994), book clubs (McMahon & Raphael, 1997), literature discussion groups (Peterson & Eeds, 1990), or peer-led literature discussion groups (Almasi & Gambrell, 1994), each with their own subtle distinctions, the basis is the same. That is, small groups of children read, respond, and discuss texts together in an effort to construct meaning and enhance understanding. As discussions occur among the children, ideas are transformed, adapted, and eventually internalized by the participants. Thus, reading becomes a social endeavor in which all students, including those who struggle, read with the purpose of responding to and discussing texts with others in an effort to collaboratively construct meaning about the text.

Another approach that has regained popularity is Guided Reading. Guided Reading consists of small, flexible groups where students using similar reading processes come together to read similar levels of text with instructional support provided by their teacher (Antonacci, 2000; Fountas & Pinnell, 1996, 2001; Routman, 2000). Opitz and Ford (2001) summarized, "While those who write about guided reading interpret its subtle complexities somewhat differently, all agree that guided reading is planned, intended, focused instruction" (p.2). Recently, however, questions have been risen regarding a narrower interpretation of Guided Reading; one that has resulted in authentic activities such as literature discussions being replaced with a focus on strategy instruction alone (Opitz & Ford; Short, 1999). When strategic reading is valued over thoughtful reading, all readers, especially struggling readers suffer, as their perspective of the reading process is needlessly limited. Acknowledging the value of Guided Reading and its role in providing necessary strategy instruction along with the positive benefits associated with literature discussions, some have proposed "the current vision of Guided Reading should be expanded so that it is broad enough to include literature circles and other grouping formats" (Opitz & Ford, 2001, p. 7). In this way, Guided Reading groups could serve as a platform for introducing students to thoughtful literature discussions. Having the opportunity to discuss texts in a supportive context benefits all students, but seems of paramount importance for those who struggle with reading; as they, typically, have received isolated, decontextualized skills instruction rather than experiencing reading as a meaningful whole (Allington, 1977, 1983, 2001; Allington & Cunningham, 2002; Allington & Walmsley, 1995; Primeaux, 2000; Routman, 2003; Sawyer, 1991; Strickland & Walker, 2004).

But how does this look? What are the experiences of struggling readers as they learn about and participate in these discussions? Having identified this gap in the research, the purpose of this study was to describe the experience of five struggling third grade readers as they participated in peer-led literature discussions within their established Guided Reading groups.

Theoretical Framework

Both Guided Reading and literature discussion groups find theoretical grounding in Rosenblatt's transactional theory of reading and Vygotsky's social constructivist view of learning. The cornerstone of Rosenblatt's theory is the understanding that:

> Every reading act is an event, a transaction involving a particular reader and a particular configuration of marks on a page, and occurring at a particular time in a particular context....The "meaning" does not reside ready-made in the text or in the reader, but happens during the transaction between the reader and text. (Rosenblatt, 1986, p. 4)

Furthermore, "Rosenblatt argued that personal response must be elaborated through a social exchange of ideas" (McMahon & Raphael, 1997, p. 14). Through these interchanges, readers discover how others have engaged in different transactions with the text and this awareness contributes to the construction of meaning (Rosenblatt, 1978).

The idea that reading is situated in a social context is grounded in the work of Vygotsky (1962, 1978) who believed in the importance of a community of learners and the social context of learning. Vygotsky did not assume children learned naturally on their own, but rather, in concert with more knowledgeable others. Of central importance is Vygotsky's Zone of Proximal Development (ZPD) which is defined as "the distance between the child's actual developmental level as determined by independent problem solving and the level of potential development as determined through problem solving under adult guidance or in collaboration with more capable peers" (Vygotsky, 1978, p. 86). Clearly, Guided Reading and literature discussion groups embrace the need to identify a student's current level and provide scaffolded opportunities for growth within a social context.

Method

As the purpose of this study was to describe the experience of struggling readers within a specific instructional context, this work emanates from the qualitative paradigm. A multiple case study design was utilized in an effort to understand the experiences of five struggling third grade readers as they participated in peer-led literature discussions within their Guided Reading group. Each participant's experience was treated independently, and only after each individual case was fully developed, group patterns were discerned.

Setting

A third grade classroom was used for this study. Located in the Midwest, this public school classroom was part of a district that served approximately 3000 students in a middle class suburb of nearly 14,000 residents. Third through fifth grade students attended this school and its demographic composition closely mirrored that of the larger community. Of the 697 students, 95.5% (665) were Caucasian, 2.6% (18) were African-American, and 1.9% (14) were Asian/Pacific Islander, Hispanic, American Indian, or those or multiracial descent (Demographic Profiles, 2000).

Third grade was specifically chosen for a number of reasons. First, there already exist numerous studies investigating peer-led literature discussions focusing on grades four and higher (Allen, 1997; Almasi, 1995; Almasi & Gambrell, 1997; Alvermann & Hayes, 1989; Alvermann, Hynd, & Qian, 1995; Boyd, 1997; Boyd & Galda, 1997; Close, 1992; Commeyras, Pearson, Ennis, Garcia & Anderson, 1992; Diehl, 2005; Dugan & Bean, 1996; Evans, 1997; Evans, Alvermann, & Anders, 1998; Goatley, Brock & Raphael, 1995; Peterson & Belizaire, 2006). Second, although studies including primary-aged participants in kindergarten through grade three exist, they were not only less abundant but tended to focus on procedures involved in implementing literature circles rather than the experience of the readers (Commeyras, 1994; Commeyras & Heubach, 1994; Farinacci, 1998; Grattan, 1997; Maloch, 1999; McCormack, 1997; Roller & Beed, 1994; Scherer, 1997). Finally, research examining the experience of young struggling readers was even more scarce (Triplett & Buchanan, 2005).

Classroom Teacher

Ms. P was a veteran teacher with 25 years of elementary teaching experience including time as a reading interventionist. She believed in the effectiveness of Guided Reading for her entire class, but particularly for those who struggle. In previous years, she had experienced success implementing literature circles; however, since the district's adoption of Guided Reading and the ever-increasing pressure to prepare students for spring testing, she felt her schedule no longer allowed for the additional block of time this activity required. She was intrigued with the notion of using Guided Reading groups as a platform for introducing readers to thoughtful literature discussions, eventually leading to their own peer-led literature discussions. From the onset, the classroom teacher was an active partner in the study and was *"excited by the idea"* of giving voice to these struggling readers (personal communication, August 19, 2004).

Participants

The five participants (3 girls and 2 boys) were third-grade students who were defined as struggling readers. In this study, a struggling reader was defined as a reader who had no identified learning disability but who had trouble in the reading process based on his or her performance on the Developmental Reading Assessment (DRA; Beaver, 2000) and teacher observations.

While detailed reader profiles are presented later, in brief, these students brought unique histories and personalities to the study. Though none had been retained, each had had trouble in reading and received supplemental instruction in the district's pullout reading program in the past. Attitudes toward reading varied with some more positive than others, although most commented they would choose another activity before reading. Each could list various characteristics of a good reader but had more difficulty discussing their own reading ability; each acknowledged reading was not always an easy task.

Tests

In an effort to better understand the participants' experiences and because reading is a complex process involving a variety of abilities, various assessments were administered. These assessments helped in the triangulation of data and eliminated any question that these five students had a learning disability. Table 1 summarizes these tests and the components they measured. Results of these, along with Fall DRA scores, cumulative school records data, and teacher interview data were used to confirm participation and aid in the construction of individual reader profiles.

Table 1: Assessment Measures

Instrument in references	Date Administered	Word identification	Phonological awareness	Comprehension	Fluency	Vocabulary
Developmental Reading Assessment (DRA) (Beaver, 2000)	September 2004	X		X	X	
Peabody Picture Vocabulary Test – 3rd Edition (PPVT-III); (Dunn & Dunn, 1997)	November 2004					X
Qualitative Reading Inventory-3 (QRI-3) (Leslie & Caldwell, 2000)	January 2005	X		X	X	
Woodcock Johnson III, Tests of Achievement. Woodcock, Mather, McGrew, 2001)	February 2005		X			

Guided Reading Procedures

Ms. P spent the first four to six weeks of the school year establishing classroom procedures and assessing students' abilities in reading. She organized students into three Guided Reading groups based on her observations, the results of the Developmental Reading Assessment (Beaver, 2000), and established grade level benchmarks. Throughout the year, three or four Guided Reading groups ran concurrently, with group membership changing as students demonstrated varying abilities and/or needs.

The teacher met with each group multiple times a week, usually daily, and served as teacher and guide to students as they read appropriately leveled, teacher-chosen texts. Mini-lessons occurred at the beginning of most Guided Reading sessions. Topics included a variety of word recognition, comprehension, and fluency strategies along with lessons focused on the discussion process and specific discussion techniques.

Data Collection

Data collection occurred during the 2004-2005 school year from October to May. In an effort to remain objective and allow interaction between the participants and the process of discussion to unfold naturally, the researcher did not participate in the literature discussions but instead, sat off to the side recording observations in a field log. These detailed notes were used along with the actual discussions, which were audio- videotaped, and transcribed for later analysis. Pseudonyms were assigned to each student at the time of transcription.

Although data collection began in October, February served as an important transition, as the group moved from teacher-led discussions (TLD) to a teacher-supported format, referred to as guided-practice. During guided-practice discussions (GPD), students still met in the presence of the teacher but began taking charge of discussions, as Ms. P sat on the periphery of the circle, offering support to students only when needed. This differed from teacher-led discussions where Ms. P controlled the conversation and was central to the process. In April, the first peer-led literature discussion (PLD), a discussion completely led by students *without* the presence of a teacher, began.

Focusing on what students *did* and *said* in discussion sessions and interviews provided a basis for accurately reconstructing and describing the experience of these readers. In doing so, multiple methods of data collection were utilized in each phase of the study, including numerous hours of observation, student interviews, and post-discussion interviews with their teacher.

Individual student interviews were conducted to capture participants' thoughts on their experiences. Immediately after literature discussions, students were interviewed on a random, yet rotating basis to insure each was provided an equitable opportunity to share their thoughts. Interviews averaged approximately 13 minutes and followed a semi-structured approach, starting with a grand tour probe, *"Tell me about the discussion today."* From here, the researcher allowed the data to emerge naturally, encouraging students to elaborate on their thoughts until a natural end to a line of discussion occurred. Interviews were not driven by a standard set of questions, although when the situation presented itself, similar questions were asked in an effort to form comparisons among this group of readers.

Efforts to verify data occurred over time as questions were purposefully revisited in order to confirm students' thoughts or flesh out changes or contradictions. When analysis of discussions and interviews showed a repetition in the data, the researcher concluded that adequate data verification and saturation had occurred. Final interviews and exit from the field took place in mid-May.

Data Management

Data collection, management, reduction, and analysis were recursive in nature, each helping "to guide the next move in the field" (Miles & Huberman, 1994, p. 8). Large categorical themes such as "gradual release of responsibility," "participation," and "thoughts on discussion" emerged and were used to show patterns regarding individual participation and experiences. This type of data reduction was critical to analysis as it "…sharpens, sorts, focuses, discards, and organizes data in such a way that 'final' conclusions can be drawn and verified" (Miles & Huberman, 1994, p. 11).

Discussion transcripts were coded showing specific lines of discussion (LODs). LODs referred to the various topics of conversation occurring in discussion sessions. Two main categories of talk emerged: meaning making and process talk. Meaning-making talk included those portions of the discussion that aided in the construction of meaning. These contributions were further coded as talk that was (a) tied to the reader (MR), (b) the text (MT) or (c) the social context of discussion (MS). Process talk referred to talk that kept the discussion moving but was directive in nature, not necessarily tied to meaning making. Appendix A provides a descriptive guide to these codes, along with examples of student comments.

Not surprisingly, during teacher-led discussions, talk was most often teacher controlled with Ms. P asking a specific question, a student responding and Ms. P commenting on the response. This common initiate-respond-evaluate sequence has been referred to as an I-R-E participatory structure (Cazden, 1986; Mehan, 1979); therefore, instances of teacher-controlled talk were coded "I-R-E." As Ms. P gradually released responsibility to students, this pattern of talk was replaced with more authentic discussions among participants. Finally, there were instances when talk was unintelligible or inaudible, as students responded with laughter but no words. Occassionally, their talk was not related to the discussion in any way; for example, talk that was centered on a fire drill that occurred during taping. These instances were categorized as "non-coded" passages (NC).

As the study unfolded, discussion transcripts also yielded interesting quantitative data, reported in the form of descriptive statistics. Data included: (a) number of contributions, (b) word count, and (c) number of initiated lines of discussion. Analysis of these served to add another layer in describing the participants' experiences. Descriptions of each of these are found in Appendix B.

Finally, videotapes were analyzed for student interactions; that is, each occurrence of talk was coded according to who said it and to whom it was directed. Because of occasional limits in videotaping (e.g., obstructed view), student interaction codes did not provide exact quantitative data, but rather, patterns of interaction for each participant.

Credibility was established through prolonged engagement and persistent observation; the triangulation of multiple data sources and methods; member checking, and peer debriefing (Guba & Lincoln, 1983). The result was a study rich in description, filled with student voice detailing how this group of five struggling readers experienced peer-led discussions within their Guided Reading group individually and collectively.

Results

Although the primary focus was to describe the experience of struggling readers in the context of *peer-led* discussions, it soon became apparent that describing their individual and collective experiences required developing an interpretive understanding of the *evolution* of their experience, as it was undoubtedly shaped over time as they transitioned from teacher-led to peer-led discussions. The following profiles pull together data documenting those experiences in an effort to answer the primary research question, "How do struggling third grade readers, as members of a Guided Reading group, experience peer-led literature discussions?"

Reader Profile #1: Holly—Primary Leader, Active Contributor

Bubbly and light-hearted, Holly had a dynamic personality that shined especially in small group and individual settings. She was a dominant, vocal presence throughout the study consistently ranking in the top two for word count and contributions regardless of the discussion context (Table 2).

Holly maintained a pattern of talk in which most of her contributions were social in nature (MS), followed by text-based responses (MT) and reader-related responses (MR). Holly's process talk steadily increased over time (Table 3).

Holly exhibited a subtle confidence in her abilities and viewed herself as both a contributor and listener. She did not wait for others to invite her to participate; rather, she initiated lines of discussion, responded to others, and could often be seen applying her growing knowledge of the process by keeping the discussion going and encouraging others to participate. She appreciated the social nature of discussion stating, *"I like when we all do it [discuss] together 'cause I like hearing other people's ideas"* (personal communication, 01/11/05). Holly felt a sense of responsibility in keeping the discussion going. However, she showed an understanding of the reciprocal nature of discussion, explaining, *"I can't keep on thinking of stuff to say and no one else is jumping in, so I'm sort of stuck . . . I like it when everybody started talking, and I wasn't just the one talking all the time"* (personal communication, 12/07/04). Moreover, Holly articulated her role as leader as did her peers, citing her ability to initiate new lines of discussion and keep the group on task. The group's recognition of Holly's role was revealed not only overtly in interviews, but also more subtly during discussions as contributions were directed toward Holly more than any other group participant.

Table 2: *Percentages of Student Word Count, Contributions, Initiated Lines of Discussion over Three Contexts

	Word Count			Contributions			Initiated Lines of Discussion		
	TLD	GPD	PLD	TLD	GPD	PLD	TLD	GPD	PLD
Holly	15	21	29	14	22	25	7	20	39
Allie	14	22	23	9	16	19	10	16	14
Lisa	14	21	24	17	24	26	8	21	28
Jim	10	20	15	10	19	16	10	20	9
Andy	6	5	9	11	8	13	3	6	10
Multiple Voices	0	0	0	3	2	1	0	0	0
Teacher	38	11	0	36	9	0	63	17	0

*Because the number of discussion sessions in each of the three phases (TLD, GPD, and PLD) varied, these data are presented as percentages for the basis of making comparisons.

Reader Profile #2: Allie—Primary Listener, Developing Leader

Quiet and unbothered, to the casual observer, Allie could have easily been labeled unenthusiastic or unmotivated in terms of overall contributions during discussions. Despite outward appearances, Allie was very much present in the literacy happenings occurring in her small group. Individual interviews were vital to uncovering and understanding her experience. Allie's responses, although short and succinct, were meaningful and mature.

Looking at participation, Allie showed increases in word count and contributions over time (see Table 2). By May, she ranked third for word count, contributions and initiated lines of discussion. Like Holly, Allie showed a pattern of talk in which most contributions were social in nature (MS), followed by text-based responses (MT) and reader-related responses (MR; see Table 3).

Allie's story unfolded to show a cautious reader who longed for independence. Here, she candidly expressed,

> *I like reading by myself because sometimes it bugs me when people are looking right over your shoulder to make sure you read it right and stuff . . . because sometimes I want to read by myself for once 'cause everybody else gets to.* (personal communication, 05/11/05)

Interestingly, although Allie craved independence, she also showed an appreciation for teacher guidance during discussions. During the guided-practice phase, Allie explained,

> *I think I like it when we bring up the topics and start because sometimes it helps us remember things more. . . . like, if something happened in the chapter that we liked, and we forgot it, and somebody else remembered it, it's like, they refresh our memory so we remember it.* (personal communication, 02/03/05)

Later though, she added,

> *Whenever we got off the topic, [Ms. P] would tell us to go back to the topic. But since she's not there anymore, she can't do that with us and like, she would*

give us good tips for the next time, but she can't do that 'cause we're in the hall and with each other. (personal communication, 04/14/05)

Allie articulated her role, accurately describing herself as more of a "follower" than "leader" explaining, *"sometimes if you're a follower, there's just more to say . . . because whenever somebody thinks of something, if you didn't think of that, then you can always add on to it"* (personal communication, 05/02/05). Although Allie appreciated her more subdued role, her participation gradually increased over time including instances during peer-led discussions when she questioned others, facilitated discussion, and attempted to bring the discussion to a close.

Reader Profile #3: Lisa—Vocal Participant

The youngest participant, Lisa was eager and talkative from the onset. She made successive gains regarding word count, contributions, and initiated lines of discussion (see Table 2). Regardless of the discussion context, Lisa consistently ranked first and second in terms of contributions and word count, respectively. Socially based meaning responses (MS) dominated her contributions (see Table 3). Although she often supplied a large percentage of recorded words, observation and interview data revealed a reader who grasped concepts on a superficial level. Typically, Lisa's contributions were loosely connected to the topic, thus adding length to the discussion rather than depth. This was often a source of tension as her peers voiced resentment toward Lisa's tendency to lead the discussion astray. Therefore, although she was as vocal as Holly, she did not communicate the same level of competence and thus, did not garner the same level of leadership or respect.

Table 3: Meaning Code (Types of Student Contributions) Percentages Across Discussion Contexts

	Socially Based Meaning Codes (MS)			Text Based Meaning Codes (MT)			Reader Based Meaning Codes (MR)			Process Talk (P)			Teacher-Controlled Talk (IRE)			Non-Coded Talk (NC)		
	TLD	GPD	PLD	TLD	GPD	PLD	TLD	GPD	PLD	TLD	GPD	PLD	TLD	GPD	PLD	TLD	GPD	PLD
Holly	14	48	50	10	18	20	2	2	3	1	17	25	71	11	0	3	5	2
Allie	16	50	57	12	31	16	2	2	2	2	6	23	66	9	0	2	1	1
Lisa	12	48	54	7	23	11	1	2	3	1	12	27	73	9	0	5	5	5
Jim	12	47	48	10	25	12	7	1	4	1	14	31	66	8	0	4	4	5
Andy	18	44	55	3	29	16	0	0	5	1	3	17	69	13	0	9	11	8

* This data is presented as percentages for the basis of making comparisons.

Reader Profile #4: Jim—Quiet Contributor

Jim experienced peer-led discussions as a quiet contributor. He was one of the least vocal participants, consistently ranking third or fourth in word count and/or contributions in each of the discussion contexts. Unique to Jim's experience, his participation peaked during guided practice but decreased during peer-led discussions (see Table 2). He was the only student to show a decrease in word count, contributions, and initiated lines of discussion during peer-led discussions. Examining Jim's limited contributions, responses were mostly social in nature (MS; see Table 3) and he could be characterized as joining in the conversation rather than initiating it.

Despite Jim's less dominant vocal presence, he nonetheless demonstrated a positive affect toward being part of the group, stating, "it's…always fun to discuss.…*You get to say your own opinions and…your thoughts*" (personal communication, 05/11/05). Interestingly, although Jim considered himself a "good reader," he often expressed needing confidence in order to contribute. In explaining his role, Jim said,

> "*A leader is somebody that starts off a book thought and…a follower is like when somebody piggybacks off of somebody…I'm more of a follower.… 'Cause usually, it takes courage to like start…and I just don't want to like, to do that.*" (personal communication, 03/10/05)

Reader Profile #5: Andy—Quiet Contributor

Polite and respectful, Andy was a tentative boy whose voice had a slight tremor when he spoke. Like Jim, he was a quiet contributor. Despite making year-end participation gains (see Table 2), he ranked last across almost every participation category regardless of the discussion context. Andy's contributions followed the same pattern as his peers; that is, socially based meaning responses (MS) were predominant (see Table 3). His contributions tended to be short affirmations, interjections, or questions rather than extended responses. Early on, interview data shed light on Andy's pattern of participation as he shared, "*I just wait for someone to be finished or if they're talking, then if someone talks before me, I'll just wait after them and then I'll talk*" (personal communication, 12/02/04). Despite his quiet demeanor, Andy was an attentive listener and demonstrated comprehension of the stories as he politely corrected others when they misspoke. Andy was content with his role as quiet contributor and listener explaining, "*I like thinking about more things than, than like, telling other people*" (personal communication, 05/06/05).

Cross-Case Analysis

Data analysis revealed cross-case patterns for this group of struggling readers. One of the most apparent patterns was the girls' vocal dominance regardless of discussion context. Descriptive statistics revealed an increase in word count and contributions for each of the girls during each successive discussion context (see Table 2).

Another pattern included students' recognition of the social nature of discussion, expressed in terms of appreciating the support the group provided its members; the sharing of ideas; and the cultivation of relationships that grew over time. Additionally, students' understanding of the purpose of discussion was closely tied to the social nature of the group. Other themes included an awareness of and appreciation for the roles each took on, a focus on the procedural elements of discussion, and an appreciation of the independence peer-led literature discussions provided. All participants expressed a preference for being part of a literature discussion group over traditional reading groups.

Although the design of this study never intended to show that literature discussion had an "effect" on student performance, spring testing data revealed patterns among the group. Four out of five participants showed improvement in their overall informal reading inventory scores from fall to spring, with one participant showing similar scores. If nothing else, this data showed participation was not detrimental to this group of struggling readers.

Limitations and Significance

As with any research, limitations existed in this study including the small number of cases. While the purpose was to describe the experiences of a subset of students rather than generalize to larger populations, a larger participant pool would have potentially yielded additional information. Another limitation in studies with young children involves a naturally occurring "authority dimension . . . that separates research with adults from research with children" (Fine & Sandstrom, 1988, p. 14). To offset this, rather than assuming the role of supervisor or leader, the researcher assumed the role of "friend" as "adopting the friend role suggests that the participant observer treats his or her informants with respect and that he or she desires to acquire competency in their social worlds" (Fine & Sandstrom, p. 17).

Some may consider the life-experience of the researcher (e.g., being a classroom teacher for 11 years) to be a potential limitation as "educators, linguists and others . . . [have been] trained to interpret behaviors and experiences from a particular vantage" (Holmes, 1998, p. 111). Although life experience is also often considered to add depth and richness to one's understandings, in terms of objectivity in research, the researcher must (and did) acknowledge any potential for bias. Being a classroom teacher carries with it perceptions and attitudes toward classroom practices and underlying philosophies. Therefore, in an effort to remain objective to the data, peer debriefing was incorporated as part of the methodology to establish the veracity of the themes and patterns. Finally, the researcher also acknowledged that despite her belief in the value of literature discussions, there existed no underlying motive in conducting this research to compromise the results.

The significance of this study lies in understanding and giving voice to the experiences of struggling readers as they participated in authentic literature discussions. The findings have the potential to influence the implementation of Guided Reading groups and peer-led literature discussions in the primary grades, helping to refine practice so that students who have trouble reading experience more than strategy instruction.

Discussion

This study resulted in several key findings. First, each reader took on a unique role within the group. Whether as leaders, contributors, and/or listeners, these roles developed over time and helped describe how these children experienced discussions. Similarly, Goatley, Brock and Raphael (1995) summarized, "peer-led literature discussion groups provided students with the opportunity to develop and maintain 'a unique discourse community' in which each member contributed to the group's construction of meaning as students participated in a variety of ways, taking on different roles such as leader, facilitator, and observer" (p. 376). In this study, student voice provided evidence of the existence of these roles as students were asked to comment on their own and others' performance. This suggests that regardless of reading ability and/or level of participation, students had an awareness of the part they played in the discussion process, lending support to struggling readers' inclusion in thoughtful literacy activities such as literature discussions.

The data showed several other key findings about these 5 struggling readers. The findings included:

- *These readers were capable of engaging in discussions that advanced understanding in a supportive community.* The high occurrence of socially-based responses (MS) coupled with a low occurrence of unrelated, non- coded talk supports these readers were capable of maintaining discussions (see Table 3).

- *These readers became more independent and took on greater responsibility for their discussions.* As Jim said, *"I think the change is good because it helps us with discussions because [Ms. P] would tell us to get back on track, but without her, we have to remember that on our own"* (personal communication, 05/06/05). Successive increases in process talk also provided evidence supporting students increased responsibility (see Table 3). Naturally, the least amount of process talk occurred during teacher-led sessions, where Ms. P held the most control. As responsibility was gradually released, increases in process talk occurred.

- *These readers built relationships with one another, and developed a supportive community of learners within their Guided Reading group.* Students positively referenced having the opportunity to: (a) hear others' ideas; (b) share with their peers; (c) help others and be helped; (d) meet people and become friends; and (e) not be embarrassed when they made a mistake. Similarly, Raphael, Brock and Wallace (1997) explained, "it is within smaller groups that diverse learners seem more safe" (p. 195). Other research asserting the social-emotional benefits of literature discussions lends support to this key finding (Almasi, 1996; Almasi & Gambrell, 1997; Triplett & Buchanan, 2005).

- *These readers developed an understanding of the purpose of peer-led discussions that was social and supportive in nature.* Each participant described the purpose of literature discussions in terms of helping each other and the sharing of ideas. Ketch (2005) summarized, "Hearing ideas discussed orally from another's point of view increases understanding, memory, and monitoring of one's own thinking. Ideas transition on the basis of the conversation. The oral process helps students clarify and solidify their thoughts" (p. 10). Andy commented, *"I like reading with the group because I can help other people and people can help me"* (05/11/05).

Implications and Conclusion

Numerous implications for literacy leaders including classroom (and pre-service) teachers, reading specialists, principals, teacher-educators, and researchers were revealed including the importance of learning about students in terms of their reading histories, current reading ability and thoughts regarding literacy processes. For educators, this means abandoning the oversimplification that often comes with labeling students "proficient" or "not proficient" (Buly & Valencia, 2002). When a more holistic approach is taken to learning about students, it embraces a social constructivist perspective on learning, one that values the community of learners, focuses on strengths, and views differences among learners as "variability, not disability" (Roller, 1996).

Equally compelling is the importance of providing learners with multiple and varied opportunities in which to have their voices heard. Great instructional potential exists in providing opportunities for students to talk about the discussion process. In doing so, student voice is honored and valued. "Learning from students' own perspectives regarding the conditions conducive to discussions can provide teachers with important information to use in instructional planning and in shared decision making with students" (Evans, 2002, p. 65).

Another implication includes recognizing the promising role Guided Reading played in providing readers with a platform to successfully negotiate (and eventually lead) literature discussions. In this study, within the context of Guided Reading, struggling readers were afforded both time and opportunity to engage with texts on their instructional level, just as their more capable peers. This was important because "students, even those labeled 'at risk' or 'struggling,' learn to read by reading—having time, opportunity, and support for active construction of meaning from text" (Strickland & Walker, 2004, p. 401).

In conclusion, this study sought to describe the experience of young, struggling readers as they participated in peer-led literature discussions within their Guided Reading group. The convergence of these topics in a cohesive study was not only unique to the field, but timely and important in terms of its contributions as the results suggested that for this group of five readers, participation in peer-led literature discussions had both cognitive and social-emotional benefits. Furthermore, the results lend support to educators' efforts to provide environments for learning that are engaging, motivating, challenging, and meaningful. This kind of thoughtful literacy instruction is vital for all students, but especially critical to those who find reading difficult. Diehl (2005) stated, "Raising all students to higher levels of thoughtful literacy is the lens through which to view opportunity" (p. 56). Clearly, there are opportunities for struggling readers to succeed in classrooms where their voices are encouraged and valued. Peer-led literature discussions provide but one way for these readers to express their thoughts, build relationships and provide the adults charged with teaching them, a window into their world; a world that is indeed "special and noteworthy" (Fine & Sandstrom, 1988, p. 12).

References

Allen, S. H. (1997). Talking about literature "in depth:" Teacher-supported group discussions in a fifth-grade classroom. In N. J. Karolides (Ed.), *Reader response in elementary classrooms: Quest and discovery* (pp. 53-68). Mahwah, NJ: Lawrence Erlbaum.

Allington, R. L. (1977). If they don't read much, how they ever gonna get good? *Journal of Reading*, 57-61.

Allington, R. L. (1983). The reading instruction provided readers of differing reading abilities. *Elementary School Journal*, 83, 548-559.

Allington, R. L. (2001). *What really matters for struggling readers: Designing research-based programs.* New York: Addison-Wesley Educational Publishers.

Allington, R. L., & Cunningham, P. M. (2002). *Schools that work: Where all children read and write* (2nd ed.). Boston: Allyn and Bacon.

Allington, R. L., & Walmsley, S. A. (Eds.). (1995). *No quick fix: Rethinking literacy programs in America's elementary schools.* New York: Teachers College Press.

Almasi, J. F. (1995). The nature of fourth graders' sociocognitive conflicts in peer-led and teacher-led discussions of literature. *Reading Research Quarterly*, 30, 314-351.

Almasi, J. F. (1996). A new view of discussion. In L. B. Gambrell & J. F. Almasi (Eds.), *Lively discussions!* (pp. 2-24). Newark, DE: International Reading Association.

Almasi, J. F., & Gambrell, L. B. (1994). *Sociocognitive conflict in peer-led and teacher-led discussions of literature. Reading research report No. 12.* (No. CS011687). Athens, GA: National Reading Research Center.

Almasi, J. F., & Gambrell, L. B. (1997). Conflict during classroom discussions can be a good thing. In J. R. Paratore & R. L. McCormack (Eds.), *Peer talk in the classroom: Learning from research* (pp. 130-155). Newark, DE: International Reading Association.

Alvermann, D., & Hayes, D. A. (1989). Classroom discussion of content area reading assignments: An intervention study. *Reading Research Quarterly*, 24, 305-335.

Alvermann, D., Hynd, C., & Qian, G. (1995). Effects of interactive discussion and text type on learning counterintuitive science concepts. *Journal of Educational Research*, 88, 146-154.

Antonacci, P. (2000). Reading in the Zone of Proximal Development: Mediating literacy development in beginner readers through guided reading. *Reading Horizons*, 41(1), 19-33.

Beaver, J. (2000). *Developmental Reading Assessment.* Parsippany, NJ: Celebration Press.

Boyd, F. (1997). The cross-aged literacy program: Preparing struggling adolescents for book club discussions. In S. I. McMahon & T. E. Raphael (Eds.), *The book club connection: Literacy learning and classroom talk* (pp. 162-181). New York: Teachers College Press.

Boyd, F., & Galda, L. (1997). Lessons taught and lessons learned: How cross-aged talk about books helped struggling adolescents develop their own literacy. In J. R. Paratore & R. L. McCormack (Eds.), *Peer talk in the classroom: Learning from research* (pp. 66-87). Newark, DE: International Reading Association.

Buly, M., & Valencia, S. (2002). Below the bar: Profiles of students who fail state reading assessments. *Educational Evaluation and Policy Analysis*, 24, 219-239.

Cazden, C. B. (1986). Classroom discourse. In M. C. Wittrock (Ed.), *Handbook of research on teaching* (3rd ed., pp. 432-463). New York: Macmillan.

Close, E. E. (1992). Literature discussion: A classroom environment for thinking and sharing. *English Journal*, 81, 65-71.

Commeyras, M. (1994). Were Janell and Nessie in the same classroom? Children's questions as the first order of reality in story book discussions. *Language Arts*, 71, 517-523.

Commeyras, M., & Heubach, K. M. (1994). *Second grade children's storybook questions and discussion: A qualitative analysis* (Speech). San Diego: National Reading Conference.

Commeyras, M., Pearson, P. D., Ennis, R. H., Garcia, G., & Anderson, R. C. (1992). *Dialogical-thinking reading lessons: Promoting critical thinking among "learning-disabled" students.* Urbana-Champaign: University of Illinois Center for the Study of Reading.

Daniels, H. (1994). *Literature circles: Voice and choice in the student-centered classroom*. York, ME: Stenhouse.

—*Demographic Profiles for Places in Ohio*. (2000).Retrieved April 21, 2007, from http://censtats.census.gov/data/OH

Diehl, H. L. (2005). Snapshots of our journey to thoughtful literacy. *The Reading Teacher*, 59(1), 56-69.

Dugan, J. R., & Bean, R. M. (1996, April 8-12). *Can I say what I think? A case study of at-risk readers making meaning during transactional literature discussions*. Paper presented at the American Educational Research Association, New York.

Dunn, L. M., & Dunn, L. M. (1997). PPVT-III: *Peabody Picture Vocabulary Test-Third Edition* (3rd ed.). Circle Pines: AGS.

Evans, K. S. (1997). Exploring the complexities of peer-led literature discussions: The influence of gender. In J. R. Paratore & R. L. McCormack (Eds.), *Peer talk in the classroom: Learning from research* (pp. 156-173). Newark, DE: International Reading Association.

Evans, K. (2002). Fifth-grade students' perceptions of how they experience literature discussion groups. *Reading Research Quarterly*, 37(1), 46-69.

Evans, K., Alvermann, D., & Anders, P. L. (1998). Literature discussion groups: An examination of gender roles. *Reading Research and Instruction*, 37(2), 107-122.

Farinacci, M. (1998). "We have so much to talk about": Implementing literature circles as an action-research project. *Ohio Reading Teacher*, 32, 4-11.

Fine, G. A., & Sandstrom, K. L. (1988). *Knowing children: Participant observation with minors* (Vol. 15). Newbury Park: Sage.

Fountas, I. C., & Pinnell, G. S. (1996). *Guided reading: Good first teaching for all children*. Portsmouth, NH: Heinemann.

Fountas, I. C., & Pinnell, G. S. (2001). *Guiding readers and writers grades 3-6: Teaching comprehension, genre, and content literacy*. Portsmouth, NH: Heinemann.

Goatley, V. J., Brock, C. H., & Raphael, T. E. (1995). Diverse learners participating in regular education "Book Clubs". *Reading Research Quarterly*, 30, 352-380.

Grattan, K. W. (1997). They can do it too! Book club with first and second graders. In S. I. McMahon & T. E. Raphael (Eds.), *The book club connection: Literacy learning and classroom talk* (pp. 267-283). New York: Teachers College Press.

Guba, E. G., & Lincoln, Y. S. (1983). Epistemology and methodological bases of naturalistic inquiry. In G. F. Madauss, M. Scriven & D. L. Stufflebeam (Eds.), *Evaluation models: Viewpoints on educational and human services evaluation* (pp. 325-329). Boston: Kluwer-Nijhoff.

Holmes, R. M. (1998). *Fieldwork with children*. Thousand Oaks: Sage.

Ketch, A. (2005). Conversation: The comprehension connection. *The Reading Teacher*, 59(1), 8-13.

Leslie, L., & Caldwell, J. (2000). *Qualitative Reading Inventory-3* (3rd ed.). New York: Allyn & Bacon.

Maloch, B. (1999, April 19-23). *Shifting to student-centered, collaborative classrooms: Implementing student-led discussion groups*. Paper presented at the Annual meeting of the American Educational Research Association, Montreal, Quebec, Canada.

McCormack, R. L. (1997). Eavesdropping on second graders' peer talk about African trickster tales. In J. R. Paratore & R. L. McCormack (Eds.), *Peer talk in the classroom: Learning from research* (pp. 26-44). Newark, DE: International Reading Association.

McMahon, S. I., & Raphael, T. E. (1997). The book club program: Theoretical and research foundations. In S. I. McMahon & T. E. Raphael (Eds.), *The book club connection: Literacy learning and classroom talk* (pp. 3-25). New York: Teachers College Press.

Mehan, H. (1979). *Learning lessons*. Cambridge, MA: Harvard University Press.

Miles, M. B., & Huberman, A. M. (1994). *Qualitative data analysis* (2nd ed.). Thousand Oaks, CA: Sage.

Opitz, M. F., & Ford, M. P. (2001). *Reaching readers: Flexible and innovative strategies for guided reading*. Portsmouth, NH: Heinemann.

Peterson, R., & Eeds, M. (1990). *Grand conversations: Literature groups in action*. New York: Scholastic.

Peterson, S., & Belizaire, M. (2006). Another look at roles in literature circles. *Middle School Journal*, 37, 37-43.

Primeaux, J. (2000). Focus on research: Shifting perspectives on struggling readers. *Language Arts*, 77, 537-542.

Raphael, T. E., Brock, C. H., & Wallace, S. M. (1997). Encouraging quality peer talk with diverse students in mainstream classrooms: Learning from and with teachers. In J. R. Paratore & R. L. McCormack (Eds.), *Peer talk in the classroom: Learning from research* (pp. 176-206). Newark, DE: International Reading Association.

Roller, C. M. (1996). *Variability not disability: Struggling readers in a workshop classroom*. Newark, DE: International Reading Association.

Roller, C. M., & Beed, P. L. (1994). Sometimes the conversations were grand, and sometimes...*Language Arts*, 71, 509-515.

Rosenblatt, L. M. (1978). *The reader, the text and the poem*. Carbondale: Southern Illinois University Press.

Rosenblatt, L. M. (1986, October). *Writing and reading: The transactional theory*. Paper presented at the Conference on Reading and Writing Connections, Urbana-Champaign, IL.

Routman, R. (2000). *Conversations: Strategies for teaching, learning and evaluating*. Portsmouth, NH: Heinemann.

Routman, R. (2003). *Reading essentials: The specifics you need to teach reading well*. Portsmouth, NH: Heinemann.

Sawyer, D. (1991). Whole language in context: Insights into the current great debate. *Topics in Language Disorders*, 11, 1-13.

Scherer, P. (1997). Book club through a fishbowl: Extensions to early elementary classrooms. In S. I. McMahon & T. E. Raphael (Eds.), *The book club connection: Literacy learning and classroom talk* (pp. 250-263). New York: Teachers College Press.

Short, K. G. (1999). The search for "balance" in a literature-rich curriculum. *Theory Into Practice*, 38, 130-137.

Strickland, K., & Walker, A. (2004). "Re-valuing" reading: Assessing attitude and providing appropriate reading support. *Reading and Writing Quarterly*, 20, 401-418.

Triplett, C. F., & Buchanan, A. (2005). Book talk: Continuing to rouse minds and hearts to life. *Reading Horizons*, 46, 63-75.

Vygotsky, L. S. (1962). *Thought and language* (E. Hanfmann & G. Vakar, Trans.). Cambridge, MA: M.I.T. Press.

Vygotsky, L. S. (1978). *Mind in society: The development of higher psychological processes* (M. Cole, V. Alfred-Steiner, S. Scribener & E. Souberman, Eds., & Trans.). Cambridge, MA: Harvard University Press.

Woodcock, R., Mather, N., & McGrew, K. (2001). *Woodcock Johnson III - Tests of Achievement*: Riverside.

Appendix A: Meaning-Making and Process Code Examples

Meaning tied to the reader (MR):	Examples
• Personal connection	"I remember when that happened to me…" or "One time, me and my friend got into a fight like Pam and Julie did."
• Putting self in character's shoes	"If I were (character), I would…"
Meaning tied to text (MT):	
• Retelling events, recounting details of text events	"Max tried to bake cookies but he left out the eggs."
• Opinions of text events	"I thought it was sad when Julie and Pam got into a fight."
• Prediction of future text events	"I think Max *will* make a million dollars in the next chapter!"
• Asking a question that is text-based in nature	"I wonder why Max was always copying Austin."
• Providing a text-based correction or clarification of a peer's contribution	Participant #1: "I wonder if Tom tamed the cat?" (MT) Participant #2: "It said he did in chapter 8."
Meaning tied to the social nature of discussion (MS):	
• Overtly agreeing/disagreeing with a peer	"I agree with (participant), it was sad when Julie and Pam got into a fight." "Well, I don't agree, I thought it was stupid that friends were fighting."
• Acknowledging a peer's contribution	Participant #1: I wonder if Max will tell Austin to stop copycatting? (MT) Participant #2: Yeah, me too. Every time Max comes up with an idea, Austin copycats. (MS; agreement with Participant #1, keeping the conversation going)
• Expanding on a thought (either one's own or another's)	Participant #1: "Max tried to bake cookies but he left out the eggs." (MT) Participant #2: "Yeah, you can't leave out eggs and think the cookies will work." (MS)
• Questioning a peer	Participant #1: "I remember when my friend and I got in a fight like Pam

	and Julie." (MR) Participant #2: "What happened?" (MS)
• Helping peers	Participant #1: I liked it when Max forgot to add . . . oh wait, (MT) Participant #2: the chocolate chips? (MS)
Process talk (P):	
• Reminding others to stay on task	"Let's get back to the book"
Encouraging participation	"Lisa, do you have anything?" "Jim?"
• Deferring to another	"I thought . . . no you go . . ." "Holly, you can go first . . ."
• Encouraging the use book or book thoughts	"Let's look in the book." "You got any more book thoughts?"
• Changing lines of discussion or offering a contribution	"I got something." "Can I change the subject?"
• Comments that started the discussion off but were not related to text or reader	"Anyone want to start?"
• Comments that brought the discussion to close	"I think we're done" "I'm out." (Meaning out of ideas, out of thoughts)

Appendix B: Explanation of Descriptive Statistics

Number of Contributions

In this study, a contribution was defined as an "occurrence of talk" in a discussion session. It had no limit as to the amount of words it could contain; it could even be as short as a one-word response. A contribution was simply a participant's addition to the conversation, in other words, his or her occurrences of talk during a discussion session. By coding and tallying contributions, a pattern of each student's participation emerged. The following excerpt provides an example of how contributions were tallied.

Andy: *Like, um, he said "No, that's my new . . . secret."*
Allie: *Yeah, he's like// (interrupted by teacher)*
Teacher: *//Oh (affirming Andy's comment)*
Allie: *He said, "No, how about that's my new secret?" And then he was, that's the end of the book.*
Teacher: *And that was the end of it?*
Allie: *That was the last page.*

In this example, Andy was credited with 1 contribution, Allie with 3, and the teacher with 2. Allie's first contribution was (probably unintentionally) cut short by the teacher, but rather than staying out of the conversation, Allie regained the floor and continued on with her comment. Therefore, Allie was credited with 3 contributions or "occurrences of talk" in this short excerpt. Her first two contributions were more spontaneous and the third directly answered a teacher question.

Word Count

Word count data were also derived from each transcript, as counting contributions alone did not provide an entirely accurate picture of the extent of a student's participation. For example, a student may have contributed numerous times with frequent one-word contributions as opposed to another who contributed less often but supplied longer, more thoughtful comments that helped in the social construction of meaning.

Initiated Lines of Discussion

Transcripts were also analyzed to determine who initiated lines of discussions. Initiating lines of discussion demonstrated a different degree of participation as students took control of the discussion by introducing a change in the direction of the conversation. At times, this initiation was "shared" by more than one student. This type of "sharing" most commonly occurred when a participant suggested that the group "get back on topic" without any further elaboration or contribution of thought. This simple redirection proved to be constructive as it provided another student with the opportunity to contribute his or her thought. In a coding sense, both students, the one who redirected talk and the other who introduced a new topic, were credited with initiating a line of discussion. Regardless of whether they were shared or not, initiating lines of discussion showed a type of risk-taking behavior necessary for discussion to continue (and possibly deepen) rather than reach a premature end. As with contributions and word count data, this information helped in the construction of experiences and roles in the group.

PALS in Vietnamese: Implementing a Bilingual Family Literacy Program

Master's Thesis Award Winner

Susan E. Perkins

University of British Columbia, Vancouver

Abstract

This study describes the development and implementation of a bilingual family literacy program for Vietnamese families with preschoolers at a suburban British Columbia elementary school. The benefits and challenges of family literacy programs, especially in cross-cultural contexts, and of the PALS program in particular, are reviewed. In examining the program from it conception to the end of its second year implementation, several themes emerged: the need to be flexible, the need to be creative and responsive to the needs and wishes of the community, the importance of a strong team, the need for a community liaison person, the need for adequate and consistent funding, the advantages to families and the advantages to schools.

Parents as Literacy Supports (PALS) program was created to get parents and children (four-and five-years-of age) involved in literacy learning and the schooling process. Teachers and other school officials noticed that even when a translator was made available, the Vietnamese population of their school district did not participate in school activities. Therefore, in the spring of 2005, school staff and other interested persons initiated the Vietnamese PALS program to find ways to help get Vietnamese families actively involved in school life. The purpose of this paper is to talk about that two-year journey.

Literature Review
Building Family/School Connections

It is generally accepted that parents have an important role in their children's success in school, and that increased parent-school cooperation is a worthy goal (Cairney, 2002b; Griffith, 1996; Snow, Dickinson & Tabors, 2000). In addition, Cairney (1995) and Handel (1999) suggested that to develop this parent-school cooperation, the first overtures should come from the school.

However, connecting with families when students' ethnic background differs from that of the teachers is a challenge. This was highlighted in Li's (2006) study, which found that upper-middle class Chinese parents did not understand school practices, while Euro-Canadian teachers had little information about students' home life, parental beliefs, and desire to support children at school. Weinberg (1997) reported that in three Michigan schools Vietnamese students were asked what they wished their teachers understood about them, and the major theme was, "I wish my teachers understood more about my homeland and culture and the experience I've been through" (p. 147). These ideas are supported by Cairney (2002b), who pointed out that a truly effective family literacy program should be based on a school staff's commitment to dialogue between school and home that values students' languages and cultures.

There are a number of reasons for schools to support home literacy in students' first language. If children become literate in their first language, many of the skills will transfer to the second language (Atwill, Blanchard, Gorin & Burstein, 2007; Sparks, Patton, Ganschow & Humbach, 2009). Students who are proficient in neither language are at risk of school failure (Novick, 1996). Family relationships may be endangered if the adults are not fluent in English and the children lose their heritage language (Puchner, 1997). Shanahan, Mulhern and Rodriguez-Brown (1995) found in their study that the school can communicate that it values the home language by encouraging parents to use their most proficient language with their children and by offering books to read written in their first language.

Cross-Cultural Family Literacy Programs

Schools' efforts to involve parents in their children's schooling often consist of one-way, English-only transmissions from home to school (Auerbach, 1997a; Edwards, 2004; Epstein, Sanders, Simon, Salinas, Jansorn, & Van Voorhis, 2002; Tett, 2001). When using this model, opportunities are missed by school personnel to learn about the literacy practices of the community, for parents to learn from each other, or for families to find out about community services (Auerbach). Handel (1999) pointed out that the model of unidirectional transmission of literacy, from adult to child, does not account for the fact that in immigrant families, a child may be called upon to interpret the English-speaking world for his/her parents. The one-way model also undervalues the role that siblings can play in the development of literacy skills (Puchner, 1997).

Initial recruitment for a family literacy program can be difficult when there is a cultural divide (Paratore, 2001). Location, scheduling, transportation, and childcare can all affect families' ability to participate (Nurss, 1992; Thomas & Skage, 1998). One advantage to holding programs in the school is that parents become more comfortable there (Paratore). The participation of a paid bilingual community liaison to assist with recruitment of participants and to facilitate communication in both directions can be very helpful (Auerbach, 1997b; Colombo, 2004; Linguistic diversity, 2001).

Planning a family literacy program should be a process of negotiation. Program development should be a compromise between school staff and parents in order to collaboratively make plans and set goals (Cairney, 1995). When families are involved in making decisions about "… a program that is intended 'to help them,' the program becomes more effective and the effect more durable" (Gadsden, 1995, p. 293).

Considerations for Implementation of Family Programs

In work with Vietnamese families in Philadelphia, Puchner (1997) found that the goals of the community were different from those of the school. The school wished to facilitate parent-teacher communication, but the parents wished to learn English. Hendrix (2000) expressed concern that a family literacy program that adds adult literacy or ESL instruction into a pre-school program runs the risk of doing neither program well; many family literacy programs skimped on the time for parents and children to explore materials together in favor of separate instructional time for parents.

Securing adequate, long-term funding for staffing and other program costs has been a barrier for family literacy programs. Thomas and Skage (1998) found that family literacy funding follows an uneven pattern across Canada, with program providers often having to rely on volunteers and short-term grants. Auerbach (1997a) put obtaining funding at the top of her list of suggestions for establishing and maintaining partnerships, because many other strategies depend on having adequate funds. She noted that "when school personnel are expected to reach out to parents and communities on their own time, it very often doesn't get done" (p. 211).

Public awareness and fundraising are more accessible if good data is available, but "program evaluation in family literacy often amounts to little more than testimonials" (Thomas & Skage, 1998, p. 20). Measuring impacts of an intergenerational, cross-cultural program that is intended to be flexible and responsive to participants' needs is difficult, and gathering data is time-consuming. However, documentation of cross-cultural programs is important because the experience is different from traditional practices (Puchner, 1997). Such information also needs to be shared widely.

Parents as Literacy Supports (PALS) Program

One family literacy program which has been successful is the Parents as Literacy Supporters program (PALS), developed in 1999 by Dr. Jim Anderson, of the Language and Literacy Department at the University of British Columbia, and Fiona Morrison, currently director of family literacy and early learning for British Columbia's 2010 Legacies Now. PALS began in four schools and is currently being implemented in 21 school districts.

PALS was designed to help parents and caregivers of four- and five-year-olds. Parents are given ideas on how to work with their children at home to improve their children's literacy and numeracy skills. There are usually ten to twelve sessions throughout the year. A resource binder is given to schools with suggested formats and resources for popular topics, but the developers recommend that each site have open sessions where topic suggestions from their particular group can be included (see http://www.2010legaciesnow.com/pals/ for more information, including a list of topic suggestions and a typical session plan).

In a typical PALS program, a session begins with a shared meal or snack. The adults then spend about one-half hour discussing the session topic while the children go to the kindergarten classroom. Next, adults and children explore together theme-related activity centers in the classroom. At the end of each session, parents reflect on what they had observed and thought about during the session. Often families are given a book and other materials to take home. In the words of one early participant, "Some of the strengths I see in a family literacy program such as PALS are food, child care, respect, and freebies" (Cody, 2005, p. 88).

As with many other family literacy initiatives, obtaining funding for PALS has required some creativity and extra work. Most PALS facilitators are kindergarten teachers who coordinate PALS in addition to their teaching assignment. Childcare for younger siblings is also the responsibility of the schools. In some sites, funding affects the availability of suitable materials and services. With English-speaking participants, children's picture books were well received (Anderson, Morrison & Manji, 2005). In schools where a variety of languages were spoken and translation services were not always available, parents expressed a wish for bilingual materials or materials in their first language, which are more costly (Anderson, Smythe & Shapiro, 2005; Anderson, Smith, Shapiro & Morrison, 2003).

The most consistent results shown in several PALS studies is increased parent confidence and the formation of social networks (Anderson & Morrison, 2007). Parents have said that they feel more confident in their ability to contribute to their children's literacy development (Cody, 2005), and that they have an increased understanding of the value of play and daily literacy events (Anderson, Smythe & Shapiro, 2005). Parents report an increased sense of connection to the school staff and to each other (Anderson, Morrison & Manji, 2005).

Implementing the Vietnamese PALS Program

After reviewing the strengths and challenges of various programs to support family literacy, it is clear that while there are many promising ways to form partnerships between parents and schools, the most effective approaches are responsive to and respectful of the local community. The following section looks back at the first two years of the school's Vietnamese PALS program.

The First Year: 2005-2006

In the fall of 2005-06, local Vietnamese parents met with the District's cultural liaison to discuss forming a PALS group. They indicated that they wanted to meet twice a month and asked that an additional part of the program be to add adult-alone time for conversational English lessons. One mother told her story of not being able to understand her child's teacher when she was trying to communicate something about the child and of signing something that she did not understand.

As the sessions got underway, the author/researcher found or bought and organized center materials, set up tables and chairs in an empty classroom, put out and labeled the centers, and put up the schedule for each session. Parents signed up to bring refreshments, and the local McDonalds provided free juice and muffins. Older Vietnamese-speaking students and their friends did childcare for small siblings.

PALS sessions included a take-home package, with books and materials related to the theme. The school district buys paperback picture books in quantity for the English PALS programs. For the Vietnamese program we purchased picture books written in both Vietnamese and English, which were considerably more expensive, in order to reinforce the message that literacy should be encouraged in both languages. The books that were bought had limited amounts of large print, with the pictures containing much of the meaning.

One of the kindergarten parents at the school had taught English in Japan, and she agreed to teach the conversational English portion. She approached the project with warmth, enthusiasm, and gentle encouragement for reluctant speakers. The district's ESL coordinator also came to all sessions and helped with feedback, ideas, and materials. She sometimes assisted with instruction. The author/researcher also attended every meeting.

Twelve families attended the first PALS session in January 2006. Parents and children responded to the warm and encouraging tone set by the facilitator, to the hands-on centers, to the chance to share snacks brought by some of the families, and to the take-home packages in special bags. The second session had a number of new faces, and they all knew to expect goody bags.

Once the session had started, the parents continued to chat while the facilitator was speaking, until our translator reminded them to listen. In the early sessions, she translated everything the facilitators said into Vietnamese, and she translated most responses into English. However, as the sessions progressed, she did less verbatim translation and focused on clarifying when parents seemed confused. She said that she found that when she translated everything, the parents did not pay attention during the English part, and that since one of the parents' goals was to learn English they needed to practice listening and responding.

During the parent discussions, we learned how very different some of their lives had been. Even in this small group, there was considerable variation in family background, with some parents coming from rural backgrounds, others from urban, some from poor families, and others from middle class. All the parents seemed to agree, however, that in Vietnam, school was for studying and play was mostly unstructured free time. Some told us that they had contact with books mostly at school, that there were few books in their homes. They told how hard their parents had worked, getting up early and going to bed late. It was rare for the parents to have time to play with their children.

Throughout the sessions some parents needed prompting to participate with their children, and some seemed more inclined to socialize with other parents than to join their children in the learning centers activities. In general, activities in which parents were most willing to participate were the ones that resulted in a product. Parents tended to skip centers where the activity was to have a conversation with their child, although we emphasized that conversations could be in Vietnamese. Many of the parents joined enthusiastically in making things with play dough, but few joined their children at the imaginative play centers.

The first time we used wordless picture books a number of parents seemed confused about their purpose. One mother said, "There is nothing here." In the next session, the facilitator modeled how to tell a story from that session's take-home book, Raymond Briggs' wordless story, The Snowman. After this, many of the parents engaged in telling the story to their children, some in Vietnamese, and some in English.

At the end of the first year, the cultural liaison said that she had noticed several benefits of the program. First, at the beginning of the program parents were hesitant to attend, but that once they understood the purpose and benefits of the program they started coming regularly, although their work still sometimes interfered. One of the most regular participants said that in order to be able to attend the "graduation" session, she started work on the mushroom farm where she was employed at 3 a.m. Second, the sessions provided a way for the Vietnamese parents to get together, which had not happened before. Third, the liaison felt the Vietnamese parents had more understanding that as parents, they had an important role in their young children's literacy development.

The Second Year: 2006-2007

In the second year, the ESL teacher could not continue due to work commitments so the school district's ESL coordinator took on the ESL instruction component of the program. As the parents had requested help with computers, in the first session she introduced some computer terminology and spoke about Internet safety. However, it quickly became apparent that we had overestimated the computer experience of our parents, as most of them were not able to use a mouse or scroll down a page.

For the next session, computer basics were the focus, and it was arranged that the Vietnamese students from the intermediate grades would act as mentors to the parents. The Vietnamese students enjoyed showing-off their technological abilities to the adults and liked being able to invite other students to assist them. We noted that some Vietnamese students who had seemed somewhat embarrassed by their ethnic background were proud to be part of the helping group. Because these students could work one-on-one and could explain the process in Vietnamese, many of the parents quickly caught on, and by the fourth session, many were proudly showing us e-mailed photographs they had sent to or received from relatives in Vietnam.

The computer time became the focal point of our ESL instruction in the second year, and we progressed from sending e-mails to using on-line ESL resources, such as sites that helped participants practice English pronunciation or grammar. The student mentors also showed the adults sites that would be good resources for their children. One unintended but welcome consequence was that members of the Vietnamese community who did not have young children attended some of our sessions. One father whose nine-year-old son attended a school some distance from ours came to several sessions, and a pair of young women with no children also came to a few sessions, drawn by the opportunity to practice on the computer and learn more computer skills

A session about parenting with the school counselor prompted requests for an additional session with her. At these sessions, topics common to all parents, such as effective discipline, expectations for chores, and allowances were discussed. Parents talked about the way their work hours affected their ability to be at home for dinnertime and bedtime, how hard it was to find time to spend on the kinds of activities that were talked about in PALS, and how sometimes their children took advantage of their parents' limited English.

We had some new faces among the parents, but many of the second year's participants had been part of the first year's program. In the first year of Vietnamese PALS, we spoke with some parents about the need to come with their children to the sessions, as some would send their children with another parent. The second year, however, some parents were reluctant to take their children out of pre-school or primary programs, and they came without their children. Some parents said that they felt that they had "done" PALS the previous year, and that their purpose in coming the second year was their own learning in a comfortable environment. In all circumstances, in both years, our focus was on being welcoming to all who came and flexible in meeting their needs.

Results

In their brief written answers at the end of the second year evaluation form, parents again expressed positive reactions to the activities. A number of participants specifically mentioned liking the computer times while others wrote that they had appreciated the parenting sessions.

No longitudinal test studies have yet been done on these Vietnamese children to determine how participating in a PALS program affected their reading test scores. However, many compelling arguments to continue with the program came from the qualitative data from the parents. There was a core group of parents who rarely missed a session and actively participated in the planned activities. In addition, other parents and community members felt comfortable enough that they attended sessions intermittently. Attendance ranged from a high of fifteen parents to a low of six parents; usually there were ten to twelve parents at a session. Harder to quantify is the joy with which the Vietnamese parents took part in the program and they began to feel more comfortable with the school altogether.

It is equally hard to assign a numerical value to the sense of pride the older Vietnamese students felt because of assisting with the program. Some of these students had not shown pride in their heritage that they now exhibit. It was important to the Vietnamese students that the their school personnel showed they valued the

Vietnamese language and culture, that books in Vietnamese were available in the school library, and that the school reached out to Vietnamese families whose children attended the school, as well as to the Vietnamese community. At our PALS "graduation" ceremony, which combined the English and Vietnamese groups, language created barriers to mingling of the groups of adults, but the children were much less shy about playing together, and all participants enjoyed the eclectic mix of treats brought by various parents.

While it became apparent that there is no single way to make a program like this work, many lessons were learned as the district's PALS program was started. They include:

- A visionary is needed, someone who can translate the many possibilities into a course of action (in our case this was provided by Fiona Morrison and Jim Anderson).
- A liaison to work with the parents in the community is invaluable. In our case, the community liaison and translator was known and well respected in the community.
- Having a liaison/interpreter at the school on a predictable basis was important to these Vietnamese families. In the past, students had to act as interpreters for their families, and not all the students had taken information home from their teachers. Now teachers know that they can put a note in the interpreter's mailbox, and that she will facilitate a conference.
- A welcoming school climate where staff participate and administration support the program.
- An understanding that such a program needs to be dynamic, creative, flexible, and responsive to the needs of the families it serves.
- For program stability, adequate funding for personnel and materials is important.

Author's Final Reflection of the PALS Program

Our primary goal, which was to involve a group of parents who had not previously joined in the school's family literacy programs, was achieved. These parents demonstrated a strong commitment to learning, both for their children and for themselves. If we had not been willing to go beyond traditional methods of involving parents, we might not have understood the depth of this commitment. In addition, if we had tried to accommodate Vietnamese speakers within the "English" PALS group, they would not have come, as they needed their own group and their own identity.

In any family literacy program run by a school, many questions need to be asked. These questions include but are not limited to the following: Have we gotten beyond the one-way transmission model that Auerbach (1997b), Handel (1999) and Puchner (1997) cautioned against? Have we tapped into the parents' "funds of knowledge" (Moll, 1997)? Have we entered into the kind of dialogue suggested by Li (2006) and Weinberg (1997), in which our pedagogical practices are informed by what we learn from the parents? Do our program objectives include change or learning on the part of the school staff, as well as on the part of the parents, as proposed by Nakagawa, McKinnon, and Hackett (2001)?

PALS developed because parents wanted to know how their children could be successful in school, and it is mostly geared to providing this information. This framework worked well in helping the Vietnamese PALS members to get to know each other. However, I think we have to answer Cairney's question (2002b) about whether we are propagating the literacy practices of European English families in the affirmative. From what I understood from the Vietnamese parents, reading to children, engaging in purposeful dialogue and learning through play have not been part of their tradition. I hope we have been respectful, possibly adding to their repertoire of ways to encourage their children's learning without devaluing their cultural practices.

There has been a trend over time toward reciprocity between this group and the program organizers. However, we have not fully tapped into the funds of knowledge of these parents. We still have much to learn about their stories, their daily lives, and their dreams, and there is more work to do before we approach Cairney's (2002a) ideal of a school culture in which staff is committed to a dialogue between school and home that values all students' languages and cultures. I believe, though, that this Vietnamese PALS program was a step along this road.

Epilogue

Since this paper was originally written, the bilingual PALS program has expanded to become Immigrant PALS, with funding for a three-year pilot project funded by Citizenship and Immigration Canada and the provincial Ministry of Education. Seven schools in five Lower Mainland communities participate in programs in Farsi, Karen, Mandarin, Punjabi and Vietnamese. Preliminary results are promising. While no longitudinal studies have yet been done, Anderson and Morrison (2009) documented growth in children's literacy development in four year olds who participated with their parents in the Immigrant PALS program at four sites. Pre- and post-test comparisons of children's Normal Curve Equivalent scores (N=42) on the Test of Early Reading Ability (TERA) II [Form A in October 2008 and Form B in May 2009] using paired t-tests, revealed significant increases [t (42) = -4.617, p =.05] and a moderate/large effect size (d=.71).

References

Anderson, J., & Morrison, F. (2007). "A Great Program...for Me as a Gramma": Caregivers Evaluate a Family Literacy Initiative. *Canadian Journal of Education*, 30, 68-89.
Anderson, J., & Morrison, F. (2009, June). Some preliminary findings from the PALS in Immigrant Communities Project. Presentation to the PALS in Immigrant Communities Conference, Vancouver, BC.
Anderson, J., Morrison, F., & Manji, T. (2005). *Valuing family literacy: What parents have to say*. Paper presented at the American Educational Research Association, Montreal.

Anderson, J., Smith, S., Shapiro, J., & Morrison, F. (2003). *Issues in family literacy programmes in inner city communities.* Paper presented at the Twelfth European Conference on Reading, Dublin.

Anderson, J., Smythe, S., & Shapiro, J. (2005). Working and learning with families, communities, and schools: A critical case study. In J. Anderson, M. Kendrick, T. Rogers & S. Smythe (Eds.), *Portraits of literacy across families, communities, and schools* (pp. 63-85). Mahwah, NJ: Lawrence Erlbaum Associates.

Atwill, K., Blanchard, J., Gorin, J., & Burstein, K. (2007). Receptive vocabulary and cross-language transfer of phonemic awareness in kindergarten children. *Journal of Educational Research*, 100, 336-346.

Auerbach, E. (1997a). Partnerships with linguistic minority communities. In D. Taylor (Ed.), *Many families, many literacies: An international declaration of principles* (pp. 211-215). Portsmouth, NH: Heinemann.

Auerbach, E. (1997b). Reading between the lines. In D. Taylor (Ed.), *Many families, many literacies: An international declaration of principles* (pp. 71-81). Portsmouth, NH: Heinemann.

Cairney, T. H. (2002a). New directions in family literacy: Building effective partnerships between home and school. In O. N. Saracho & B. Spodek (Eds.), *Contemporary perspectives in literacy in Early Childhood Education* (Vol. 2, pp. 99-125). Greenwich, Conn.: Information Age Publishing.

Cairney, T. H. (2002b). Bridging home and school literacy: In search of transformative approaches to curriculum. *Early Child Development and Care*, 172, 153-172.

Cairney, T. H. (1995). Developing Partnerships: The home, school and community interface (Vol. 1). Sydney: UWS Nepean.

Cody, S. (2005). A single mother's journey of rediscovery. In J. Anderson, M. Kendrick, T. Rogers & S. Smythe (Eds.), *Portraits of literacy across families, communities, and schools* (pp. 87-89). Mahwah, NJ: Lawrence Erlbaum Associates.

Colombo, M. W. (2004). Family literacy nights...and other home-school connections. *Educational Leadership*, 48-51.

Edwards, P. A. (2004). *Children's literacy development: Making it happen through school, family, and community involvement.* Boston: Pearson.

Epstein, J. L., Sanders, M. G., Simon, B. S., Salinas, K. C., Jansorn, N. R., & Van Voorhis, F. L. (2002). *School, family, and community partnerships: Your handbook in action* (2nd Ed.). Thousand Oaks, CA: Corwin Press.

Gadsden, V.L.(1995). Representations of Literacy: Parents' images in two cultural communities. In Morrow, L.M. (Ed.). *Family literacy connections in schools and communities.* Newark, DEL: International Reading Association.

Griffith, William. (1996). Relation of parental involvement, empowerment, and school traits to student academic performance. *Journal of Educational Research*, 90, 33-42.

Handel, R. D. (1999). *Building family literacy in an urban community.* New York: Teachers College Press.

Hendrix, S. (2000). Family literacy education: Panacea or false promise? *Journal of Adolescent and Adult Literacy*, 43, 338-346.

Li, G. (2006). *Culturally contested pedagogy: Battles of literacy and schooling between mainstream teachers and Asian immigrant parents.* Albany: State University of New York Press.

Linguistic diversity and early literacy: Serving culturally diverse families in Early Head Start. (2001). Washington, D.C.: Head Start Bureau Early Head Start National Resource Center @ Zero to Three.

Moll, L. C. (1997). The creation of mediating settings. *Mind, Culture and Activity*, 4, 191-199.

Nakagawa, K., McKinnon, A., & Hackett, M. R. (2001). *Examining the discourse of strengths vs. deficits in a family literacy program.* Paper presented at the 2001 Annual Meeting of the American Educational Research Association, Seattle, WA.

Novick, R. (1996). *Developmentally appropriate and culturally responsive education: Theory in practice.* Portland, OR: Child and Family Program, Northwest Regional Educational Laboratory.

Nurss, J. R. (1992). *Clayton Family Literacy and School Support Services. Project Class: Final report.* Atlanta: Georgia State University Center for the Study of Adult Literacy.

Paratore, J. R. (2001). *Opening doors, opening opportunities: Family literacy in an urban community.* Boston: Allyn and Bacon.

Puchner, L. D. (1997). *Family literacy in cultural context: Lessons from two case studies* (Publication No. NCAL TR 97-01). Philadelphia: National Center on Adult Literacy, University of Pennsylvania.

Reid, D., Hresko, W., & Hammill, D. (1989). *Test of Early Reading Ability II.* Austin, Texas: Pro-Ed Inc.

Shanahan, T., Mulhern, M., & Rodriguez-Brown, F. (1995). Project FLAME: Lessons learned from a family literacy program for linguistic minority families. *The Reading Teacher*, 48, 586-593.

Snow, C., Dickinson, D., & Tabors, P. (2000). The Home-School Study of Language and Literacy Development. Retrieved July 13, 2003 from Harvard University web site: http://gseweb.harvard.edu/~pild/homeschoolstudy.htm

Sparks, R., Patton, J., Ganschow, L., Humbach, N. (2009). Long-Term Crosslinguistic Transfer of Skills from L1 to L2. *Language Learning* 59, 203-243.

Te, H. D. (1995). Understanding Southeast Asian students. In L. L. Cheng (Ed.), *Integrating language and learning for inclusion* (pp. 107-122). San Diego: Singular Publishing Group.

Tett, L. (2001). Parents as problems or parents as people? Parental involvement programmes, schools and adult educators. *International Journal of Lifelong Education*, 20, 188-198.

Thomas, A., & Skage, S. (1998). Overview of family literacy research and practice in Canada. In A. Thomas (Ed.), F*amily Literacy in Canada: Profiles of Effective Practice*. Welland, ON: Soleil.

Weinberg, M. (1997). *Asian-American education: Historical background and current realities.* Mahwah, NJ: Lawrence Erlbaum Associates.

MENTORING
LITERACY LEADERS

A Different Kind of Coaching:
The Professional Preparation of Graduate Level Reading Specialists Combining Videocoaching with Concurrent Feedback

Elaine Marker

Delaware State University

Antonia D'Onfrio

Widener University

Abstract

The purpose of this study was to determine if videocoaching with concurrent feedback offered any advantages for preparing reading specialists. This investigation chronicles the experiences of 18 reading specialist candidates who participated in videocoaching conferences using videotapes of lesson taught during their clinical experience. Thematic analysis was based on four sources of information: conversations occurring during videocoaching sessions; entries in dialogic-reflective journals; the culminating reflection for the course; and students' comments on course evaluations. Three major themes synthesized the perspectives of 18 students who were participants in the videocoaching framework: conversation and reflection transforms teaching practices, learning to see theory in action, and discovering that reflection really can inform practice.

Struggling readers use a variety of strategies when they develop the skills needed for reading comprehension (Hitchcock, Prater & Dowrick, 2004). Improving the reading comprehension of struggling readers may, therefore, require intervention strategies that are more differentiated than the use of generic questions, or techniques that assume that any and all students can learn to comprehend text because a teacher engages them in tactical questioning (Guthrie, Anderson, Alao & Rinehart, 1999; Young, Bolla, Schumm, Moreyra, Exley, Morrow & Woo, 2001). Reading specialists may even misunderstand how to match teaching strategies to students' comprehension strategies. Professional training that makes concurrent use of videotapes, coaching and feedback from peers and clinical supervisors can help candidates for reading specialist certification build a more differentiated repertoire of clinical skills.

Key to understanding the approach to clinical supervision reported in this investigation are several key elements: the ability to give immediate feedback to reading specialists candidates; teaching candidates to be more opportunistic and to change their interventions in response to the challenges sequencing lessons in real time; and tailoring the coaching aspects of clinical supervision to the candidates' clinical experiences and personal instructional challenges. The way that videotapes are used in athletic coaching provides some instructive parallels. Videotapes capture a complete sequence of actions that are frozen in time, and can be later discussed. The athlete in training can devise an improvement plan from detailed, visual analysis of strategies that are helpful, as well as those that are not so helpful. An athlete in training can also examine the strategies of athletes who have attained champion status and learn from them. The videocoaching model used by athletes and their trainers mirrors all the essential elements needed to move the skills of reading specialists to higher levels of expertise.

The purpose of this study was to share how candidates for reading specialist certification described the impact of video coaching on their ability to make connections between their understanding of comprehension problems encountered by students and the actions they took to correct readers. The questions to be answered in this investigation were as follows: Why should the use of videotapes demonstrate particular advantages for training of reading specialists? Did candidates for reading specialist certification judge themselves to be more effective reading teachers when they were coached using videotapes accompanied by concurrent feedback from their clinical supervisor? Did they change their personal understanding of how to be more effective reading teachers, and is this an overlooked advantage of videocoaching?

Theoretical Framework

This investigation offers some insight into how 18 reading specialist candidates changed their perceptions and beliefs about the effectiveness of their teaching, and ultimately chronicles reading specialist candidates descriptions of how they believed their teaching strategies had become more effective and had a positive impact on individual students. They weighed and evaluated the choices they made by viewing their teaching on videotape, and receiving concurrent feedback from their clinical instructor.

The goal of clinical training is to develop more proficient clinicians, who in turn will meet the training needs of classroom teachers, and improve the learning experiences of struggling readers. Key to the attainment of this goal are training contexts in which reading specialists are able to assess their classroom performance with the aim of making keener clinical judgments and better decisions about instruction and intervention. Decision-making in the clinic takes assessment to the next level because reading specialists are expected to choose among a variety of possible intervention strategies based on the information they have gained from diagnostic tests. In this research, the relevant program components could be identified as Coaching, Collaboration, and the use of Videotapes. Thus, the theoretical framework will discuss relevant literature for each of these components.

Coaching

How does coaching foster improved judgment and decision-making? Coaching processes reinforce many of the cognitive proficiencies that are needed to understand why and how some readers struggle with comprehension. The cognitive proficiencies that are gained through coaching include observing, modeling, hypothesizing, reasoning, and analysis.

Kibby (1995) recommended that coaching be a process of "intensive instructional intervention" that capitalized upon having comprehensive knowledge of a learner's reading performance, strategies, skills, and instructional needs. Kibby's model fostered thorough and accurate observation for the purpose of modifying instruction. Moreover, Kibby affirmed the importance of collecting observational data about student performance in order to maintain a diagnostic and reflective stance in teaching. His approach infused instruction with diagnostic decision-making. Similarly, Horwitz (2002) urged that teachers assume an instructive stance, a perspective that balance content and process. Horwitz argued that maintaining this balance helps students to move forward continually from earlier moments of focus and to more comprehensive levels of understanding as they process the complexities of text.

Collaboration

Collaborative aspects of coaching also foster greater awareness of students' difficulties in comprehending written materials (Rochelle, 1992). The professional collaboration between a clinical supervisor and a teacher yields an exchange of perspectives and experiences (Fauske, 2002; Sawyer, 2007). There are opportunities for both to observe and evaluate a certification candidate's performance; there are also opportunities to evaluate strengths and limitations over an entire range of teaching strategies (Cobb, 2000; Cobb, Bufi, McClain & Whiteneck, 1997). Collaboration also provides opportunities for debriefing because the experiences of more experienced clinicians, who have worked effectively with struggling readers, encountered many different reading problems, and weighed the effectiveness of varied interventions, can be shared (Bereiter & Bird, 1985; Pressley, El-Dinary, Gaskins, Schuder, Bergman, Almasi, & Brown, 1992).

Stigler's (1975) earliest investigations in the Third International Mathematics and Science Study (TIMSS) suggested that the use of videotapes fostered collaboration among teachers because they coached one another and learned by sharing successful classroom strategies. More recently the use of videotapes has been viewed as an effective way to capture mistakes, and to make the record of less than optimal teaching available for observation, analysis and reflection (Stigler & Hiebert, 1999; Stigler, Gallimore & Hiebert, 2000). These authors believe that videotaping takes teacher-collaboration beyond brainstorming about best practices, and leads them toward informed practice. By using videotapes, teachers working together can test the use of research-based strategies and critique their performance on video (Guthrie, Anderson, Alao & Rinehart, 1999; Stigler, Gallimore, & Hiebert, 2000).

Bussye, Sparkman and Wesley (2003) have noted that teachers rarely think of teaching as a shared enterprise in which they should collaborate with other teachers. Bransford and Brown (2002), Palincsar and Brown (1984) and Hayes and Alvermann (1986) claimed that professional judgment and informed decision-making are gained in part from active involvement with colleagues. There have been studies that argued that collegial interactions among teachers can be fostered by the use of videotapes (Murphy, 1999). Both Lewis and Tsuchida (1998) and Stigler and Hebert (1999) found that Japanese teachers regularly videotaped learners who experienced difficulties with lessons; they would later gather and debrief a lesson as colleagues.

Use of Videotaping

Watching an experienced teacher on video is not a new professional development strategy. The New Teachers' Network, sponsored by the University of Chicago, provides individualized coaching to both novice and experienced teachers, using video technology extensively to create a framework for the analysis of classroom practice (New Teachers' Network). Video also provides opportunities for the observation of expert performance. By watching videotapes of experienced teachers in action, less experienced teachers receive continuous support and feedback. Video also makes it possible to demonstrate research-based teaching strategies. This professional development initiatives pairs teachers with teaching coaches. Together teachers and coaches can view videotapes of expert teachers. The tapes are presumed to become part of an interactive and ongoing exploration of teaching.

Watching oneself teach on videotape combines the value of observation with that of collaboration. Stigler's earliest investigations were able to demonstrate what average teaching looked like. However, unsuccessful lessons, according to Stigler, also have instructional value. Stigler concluded that even tapes of unsuccessful lessons are valuable because when a teacher observes a problem on tape he/she is able to ask what may have caused that problem. His (1999) revised version of TIMSS is based on a number of LessonLabs in which teachers plan lessons together, view their own teaching on videotape, and critique and analyze various samples of classroom teaching.

By comparing the use of video to self-modeling, Hitchcock, Prater, and Dowrick (2004) suggested that teachers should use videotapes as part of their instructional planning. They commented that an array of reading interventions can be planned, designed and evaluated prior to being implemented as part of a teacher's repertoire of strategies. Similarly, Taylor and Pearson (2000) found that videotapes facilitated information sharing among teachers; their conversations focused on what they had observed. Alvermann and Hayes (1989) discovered that teachers, who observed lessons on tape and later analyzed their observations, were subsequently more attentive to students' remarks (Alvermann & Hayes; Hayes & Alvermann, 1986). Teachers whose perceptions about their learners have been primed by watching videotapes also tended to respond in more elaborate ways, as their students engaged in more text-connected speech and language that involved analysis and inference.

Normally the training of reading specialists makes heavy use of case-based instruction in diagnostic decision-making. However, the literature tends to be silent on how clinical supervision can support teachers throughout their own learning of diagnostic skills. The approach to videocoaching described in this study was consequently influenced by the need to support teachers, and the intensive interventions recommended by Kibby and Scott (2002) and the instructivist stance of Horowitz (2002) were starting points for the design of the coaching model.

In conclusion, both novice and experienced teachers gain from professional development experiences where learning from colleagues is valued. The use of videotapes increases opportunities to learn from observation, analysis and reflection. By linking collegial discussion to the use of video, the acquisition of new instructional strategies can seem far less hypothetical because it is grounded in collaborative sharing of experience and expertise.

Methods and Procedures

Participants

Eighteen candidates, pursuing certification as reading specialists, at a small, comprehensive university in New Jersey, were the participants in this study. They comprised a cohort in its culminating clinical core course in the Master of Arts in Reading. Their range of experience as teachers was kindergarten through high school; they had been teaching from 2 to 15 years. All were teachers in both regular classrooms and in special education settings.

All of the participants tutored one or two children, who had been identified as needing reading remediation, in a university reading clinic. The teachers worked with the students 4 days a week, for one hour and 15 minutes each session. Each teacher was observed at least one time, for periods lasting at least 30 minutes. Each teacher was also asked to videotape a reading comprehension lesson.

The principal investigator (PI) in this study served as both course instructor and sole clinical supervisor, thereby taking the role of participant-observer. The PI, who was also the Director of the Reading Clinic, was a full-time tenure track professor at the university, possessing a terminal degree in reading. Additionally, she had over 20 years experience in the role of clinical supervisor to students completing the clinical experience in pursuit of a reading specialist certificate.

Videocoaching Procedures

Videocoaching in this investigation adapted both intensive intervention (Kibby, 1995) and instructivism (Horowitz, 2002). Once teachers had completed their videotapes, each previewed their videos and listed talking points based on what they believed was significant about a lesson. (A guide to the videocoaching process is included as an appendix.) When listing talking points, they were asked to consider four aspects of their teaching:

1. The comprehension strategies that they would teach students;
2. The stage of the teaching process: i.e., scaffolding, coaching or reflecting;
3. Which of 5 comprehension processes was being accessed in the lesson (Irwin, 1986); and
4. Key functions of schemata that students needed to use (Anderson, 1994).

The teachers were not required to elaborate on the talking points. They scheduled individual conferences with the clinical supervisor in order to review the videotaped lessons. At these conferences, the teachers provided an oral synopsis of their lessons and which talking points or aspects of their teaching they believed the clinical supervisor would see on the videotapes.

Teachers and the clinical supervisor took notes while viewing the tapes. These were informal sessions, and the teachers could stop the tape at any time if they wished interject comments about their teaching. The clinical supervisor posed questions designed to provide points of comparison between what teachers had listed as talking points and what she, the clinical supervisor, actually observed. The goal of the discussion was to arrive at a balanced view of the teachers' strategies. Thus, questions were intended to focus teacher attention either on teaching sequences that contradicted the taking points, on the practices teachers believed they had used, or on missed opportunities to comment on aspects of their teaching that may have been particularly effective.

The coaching sessions were also intended to open up a collegial dialog about the crafting of a particular lesson, as opposed to question and answer sessions in which the teacher would seek expert advice. Note-taking continued during the dialog. For the clinical supervisor, these notes served as information that would be used later to interpret the impact of the videotapes and conferencing on the teachers. These interpretations would be important later during clinical teaching, because they provided the frameworks for monitoring the teachers in subsequent lessons to see if they modified their tutoring practices after conferencing with their clinical supervisor. The teachers used their notes to write reflections about their lesson.

Data Collection and Analysis

Documentation included the following sources of information: the field notes of the clinical supervisor, observations of teachers, teacher reflections, and culminating reflections (a final course assignment). Documentation through an assignment known as the Sequence of Instruction gathered by the clinical supervisor in a prerequisite course (*Correction of Remedial Reading Difficulties*) was predominantly used to establish baselines for teacher performance. In that assignment, teachers were instructed to focus on one specific strand of instruction as they tutored one child. They kept a record of their observations as they worked with children, and recorded their reflections on their responsiveness to student needs. Finally they recorded their personal evaluations of their progress in being more responsive to their students.

The analysis of information collected by the clinical supervisor from the teachers was aimed at understanding whether teachers had used reflection to inform their teaching practice. Axial coding, the process of relating codes (categories and concepts) to each other, via a combination of inductive and deductive thinking, was used to interpret and analyze the collected documents (Strauss & Corbin, 1997). Axial coding was selected because it lends itself to uncovering relationships within data sets. Not only was interpretation needed to see if teachers' were becoming more self-analytic; interpretations of this information also needed to be individualized and tailored to track the progressive improvement of teachers to see if they were conscious of their impact on students' reading ability. This was a way to discover whether teachers' became more aware of the quality of their instructive stance. Had their stance become more diagnostic and more reflective?

Each data set was read for initial coding. Comments within reflections, supervisor field notes of student from videocoaching sessions, and each student's culminating course reflection were coded using the following designations: tutee information (ti), lesson description (ld), questions for instructor (qfi), self-analytic statements (sas), diagnostic-reflective statements (d/r), teaching practices (tp), changes in perspective (cip), theory application (ta), and comments unrelated to teaching (unrc). A limitation in student evaluations as a data set must be noted. The course evaluation data consisted of a summary of comments compiled by a senior staff member. Thus, comment tallies for a set of evaluations was not possible.

Next, the entire record for an individual teacher (excluding student evaluations) was read to identify evidence that pointed to self-analysis (SAS), diagnostic and reflective thinking about the act of teaching (D/R), personal awareness that one had changed as a teacher, changes in perspective about teaching practices (APC), and recognition that theories were being applied (TA). At this point axial coding was applied. (See Table 1 for frequencies for each data source). Information about the teachers could then be categorized, and restated as the thematic structure of the videocoaching experience.

Table 1: Frequencies of types of comments found in each data source

	Comment type			
Data Source	SAS%	D/R%	APC%	TA%
Baseline (Sequence)	55.6	55.6	0	11.1
Journal Reflections	66.7	50.0	0	22.2
Videocoaching				
Conference	72.0	83.3	50.0	33.3
Culminating Reflection	100	83.3	71.1	50.0

n = 18

Coding of the data, categories identified and themes constructed through linkages were reviewed by a researcher in the role of disinterested observer who questioned any inconsistencies observed in coding decisions and in the identification of relationships.

Results

Thematic analysis was based on four sources of information: conversations occurring during videocoaching sessions; entries in dialogic-reflective journals; the culminating reflection for the course; students' comments on course evaluations. Three major themes synthesized the perspectives of 18 students who were participants in the videocoaching framework. The themes were:

1. Conversation and reflection transforms teaching practices;
2. Learning to see theory in action; and
3. Discovering that reflection really can inform practice.

Conversation and reflection transforms teaching practices

This theme was evidenced many times as teachers reported or commented that they became their own observers. One teacher voiced an extreme reaction stating, "Observing your professional skills on video can be a humiliating experience." Others made more positive comments but initially a level of discomfort with video taping oneself was certainly present. A certain detachment was possible because teachers were able to view their own instruction from the vantage point of a disinterested observer through the use of video. The New Teachers Network (2007), sponsored by the University of Chicago, also provided individualized coaching to both novice and experienced teachers, using video technology extensively to create a framework for the analysis of classroom practice. Because the video coaching allowed them to move out of the active context of working with children and gave them a needed perspective on their own classroom behavior. This was the intention of the video coaching conference. By watching themselves on video, reading specialist candidates could back up and review their instruction. By conferencing with the clinical supervisor they could talk through instructional decisions. They could evaluate whether their instructional strategies had positive consequences for the children in the clinic, and they could determine whether their mistakes could be analyzed in ways that led to new learning. From the teacher who thought observing oneself was humiliating came this comment, "Video lessons provide opportunities for collegial collaboration and assessment. It is a wonderful opportunity to learn from one another and provide important feedback to confirm your teaching skills and strategies." Most teachers viewed the videoconference as collegial and collaborative, and not as an evaluative moment. A number of teachers echoed the sentiments of the comment above; they embraced the opportunity to learn from each other. The teachers came to realize that their past experiences and personal skills could be connected to new knowledge about theories of literacy. They became increasingly aware of how to connect theory to practice.

What is remarkable about the emergence of this theme is the extent to which it represents a dramatic shift from teachers' initial responses to being videotaped and to conferencing with the clinical supervisor. Initially their emotions ranged from skeptical to resistant. At the end of the clinical experience, the most common assessment included on course evaluations was, "The video observations were helpful and maybe more should be incorporated."

In the following sections, comments from the teachers via journals, conversation, and culminating reflections are shared. Names have been changed and any identifying information has been deleted to protect identities.

Learning to see theory in action

Theories of literacy are grounded in evidence that describes and explains how readers interact with text to construct meaning. Therefore, once a teacher assumes an analytical stance, connections between teaching strategies and evidence that children really are constructing meaning makes a theory of literacy real. The teachers in this study began to acquire a deeper understanding of theories of literacy that supported their practice because they were able to look analytically at their interactions with children. They were able to relate their interactions directly back to literacy theories.

In the previous semester, teachers videotaped themselves and turned in their videotapes and journals later in the clinical experience. For that reason, feedback from the clinical supervisor may have occurred too late in the semester to apply it to that teaching experience. Teachers may have been able to store and tap into feedback. But if a teacher had taken a wrong turn in the middle of the semester, there was no easy way to intervene. In the previous semester, written feedback to reflective journals included questions asking the teachers to draw upon theories of literacy; but responses were perceived as evaluative and probably left the teachers more concerned about grades, and less focused on how feedback would help them refine their teaching practices.

Table 2: Distribution for the types of each comments occurring in each data source

Subj. code	COMMENT TYPE	Baseline (Sequence)				Journal Reflections				VC Conference Field Notes				Culminating Reflection			
		SAS	D/R	APC	TA	SAS	D/R	APC	TA	SAS	D/R	APC	TA	SAS	D/R	APC	TA
T1		X				X	X			X	X	X		X	X	X	X
T2			X			X			X	X	X	X		X	X	X	
T3		X			X		X			X	X	X	X	X	X		X
T4			X			X	X			X	X		X	X	X		X
T5		X				X				X	X			X	X		X
T6			X							X	X			X	X	X	
T7														X			
T8		X	X			X	X		X	X	X	X	X	X	X	X	X
T9		X				X				X				X			
T10			X				X			X	X	X		X	X	X	
T11		X	X			X				X	X			X	X		
T12		X		X		X	X		X	X	X	X	X	X	X	X	X
T13						X								X		X	
T14		X	X			X				X	X	X		X	X	X	
T15			X				X			X	X	X		X	X	X	X
T16		X				X			X	X	X			X	X		
T17			X			X	X			X	X	X	X	X	X	X	X
T18		X	X				X			X	X		X	X	X	X	X

An "X" signifies that the subject made the type of statement indicated by column heading somewhere within that artifact.

Most problematic was that written responses to their written reflections left little opportunity for a professional exchange of ideas. Dale's comment illustrates how important dialog between professionals is, "I thought I was teaching thematically…I was spending an inordinate amount of time on word study, and not enough time on the actual reading of text." Dale remarked that a single question posed by the clinical supervisor in her journal was startling and motivated her to take stock of the actual teaching that took place. Our interpretation is that by perceiving the clinical supervisor as a colleague giving feedback, rather than as a professor giving admonishment, Dale was independently moved to be analytical about her own performance.

Finding out that reflection really can inform practice

Standing outside of the active context of teaching affords a teacher the advantages that come with being an outsider. Context can be so complex that a teacher cannot really process what may be beneficial for a student. As an outsider, one must reflect in order to understand. Trudy related such a moment, "A videotaped observation provided me with a chance to see my lesson, and David's reactions, as an outsider." Trudy understood that the outsider's perspective is one more point of view, which contributes to greater personal awareness of her impact and the impact of her teaching.

Stella, who had been using questioning and prompting strategies with Jake, a struggling reader, learned that struggling readers develop greater confidence when they experience success. When presented with new challenges, struggling readers will persist. Continued reflection made it possible for Stella to understand how readers like Jake internalize comprehension strategies. Susan connected the process of daily reflection to thoughtful analysis teacher-student interactions. "The daily reflections were very helpful to me. I found myself analyzing each of the lessons and the students' reactions to them. Self-analysis is underrated."

According to Susan, "The videotaped lesson was an immeasurable learning experience." During a taped lesson, Susan was working with two children, Dianna and Charles. Dianna was a stronger reader; she had more strategic reading skills. Dianna observed Susan giving praise and attention to Charles, the weaker reader. During the taped lesson, Dianna withdrew. It was only after watching the videotape that Susan realized she had been praising only Charles, and that Dianna had made a conscious choice to withdraw. Until then Susan blamed herself for the event; but Susan now realized that she had been vulnerable to being manipulated. Susan also concluded that in the future she would take a more collaborative approach, praising both children, as Dianna needed positive reinforcement as much as Charles, even if she was the stronger reader.

Professional awakening: Three teachers who changed

Three teachers—Stella, Valerie, and Barbara—changed their perspective of their own diagnostic practices in dramatic ways. Each of them evolved individually, and each became aware of how to be more reflective in ways that illustrated the desired outcomes of this diagnostic and reflective model. Their comments and reflections follow.

Stella

Stella's earlier reflections, recorded in a previous clinical course on corrective reading, showed that she was somewhat inflexible because she used diagnostic and teaching interventions that had been prescribed by her school district. These were prescriptive plans that did not address individual students' instructional needs. For example, she required a student who had difficulties internalizing story structure to retell a passage using a story rubric devised by the district, and without looking back at the story's text. When confronted, she explained the district "expected the boy would be able" to accomplish this task. If she were to adapt the task "it would be enabling to the boy", and would cause him "to be overly dependent on resources he would not have during district assessment. After she shared this reflection along with a video clip during a coaching session, her clinical supervisor asked her to reflect on what she was actually teaching. Was her intent to help the boy structure information in the story? Or, was she preparing him for district reading assessment? Stella at that moment felt the clinical supervisor had made an important point, but she also remarked that the episode was over and done with.

The clinical supervisor felt that Stella had not really internalized the implications of feedback for clinical practice.

In the following semester, videocoaching had been combined with the normal clinical routine. Stella and her clinical supervisor watched a videotape together in which she tutored another boy named Jake. She had planned to teach word identification and comprehension as two separate strands of instruction. She explained, "As I began working with Jake, I found myself carrying on this internal dialog that contained the frequent refrain, 'Why can't Jake do this?'...Now my internal conversation has changed. I say, 'He is using meaning, re-reading and is self correcting his miscues.' " She added, "This experience has provided me with the opportunity to see the power of literacy coaching."

Stella now spoke explicitly about the value of being a diagnostic and reflective. Stella witnessed how theory could be translated into practice, for example implement scaffolding with instruction. Stella said that she "realized only 20 percent of word work should occur in isolation and the remaining 80 percent should be taught in context. Working in context proved to be well worth the effort. Attaching meanings to phonograms, sight vocabulary and sound letter relationships helped Jake transfer learning to long-term memory." Stella's realization taught her much about expectations for classroom teachers. "It can be an exercise in jumping through the documentation hoop." Through her experiences within the diagnostic-reflective clinical framework, she realized that being a reflective diagnostician and teacher should be a top priority, and not something one had to learn about at a later point in one's professional development.

Valerie

Valerie's change in perspective became clear during a discussion immediately following our conversation about one of her videotapes. As she watched the clip with me, she said that it "was becoming evident to her that Danny's reading processes were breaking down at the macro-processing level." Danny was unable to connect meanings in text to his experiences, prior knowledge and to the rest of the text. He seemed to process and remember in bits and pieces and did not seem to be able to combine information or synthesize parts of the text. Valerie later wrote in her journal, "I was using a lot of questioning, scaffolding and guided discussion during lessons, but in initially did not understand why I needed to provide him with [this] explicit framework." She added, "The turning point in my understanding came after meeting with Dr. M— to review a video taped lesson. Through much questioning and discussion, she led me to understand the way (sic) that Danny was lacking in integrative comprehension processes."

Much like Stella's reflection, Valerie wrote that she had the opportunity to delve deeply into comprehension practices, in ways that her previous experiences had not allowed. She saw theory become a practical reality. Valerie felt she could now create meaningful lessons that had a positive impact on learners.

Valerie essentially began to understand that although she had been scaffolding consistently, she did not understand why she was using scaffolding. She knew she needed to; she didn't know why. Up to that point she had been presenting Danny with many strategies, hoping that one of them would become meaningful for him. A few days after our coaching session, Valerie reported that Danny was exhausted during clinic. He had stayed up all night to finish a book. Danny had responded on the pre-clinic survey that he would rather clean his room than read a book. Valerie attributed the change in Danny to the video coaching, "After our discussion, I was able to focus on his specific learning needs." Once she made this realization, Valerie remarked that Danny's confidence began to soar, and he began to show dramatic growth.

Barbara

Sometimes gaining expertise is not the most important outcome for a teacher. Barbara was a reading specialist who lacked confidence. She was never "quite certain that she was on the right track." Because she is a high school teacher, the teaching in the clinic was Barbara's first experience working with intermediate level students. "I had conjured up horrific scenarios of how tough it was going to be and how miserably I was going to fail in tutoring younger children." Barbara's challenge was to teach two middle school boys who had admitted their aversion to reading. She had to help them realize that reading wasn't going to go away and that it was part of school Barbara needed to help them understand the importance of reading, and perhaps even gain enjoyment from it.

In her reflection, Barbara wrote that through videocoaching she learned that perfect teaching was not the goal. For Barbara, changing perspective meant discovering that making mistakes and fixing them was a continuous process. It was more helpful to be comfortable analyzing one's mistakes and learning from them. Barbara described the specific value of the videocoaching framework in the following way, "I realized what a nice boost of confidence it is to have someone critique your teaching and give positive feedback. Just when I felt as though I was not sure I was on the right track, this observation was helpful in reminding me that I am doing my best and was organizing the lessons around Will's and Jared's needs." Barbara learned that doing one's best often is good enough.

Discussion

In the course of this investigation, several patterns surfaced. Initially, most students had an adverse reaction to videotaping themselves. This sentiment did not change when taping continued and they wrote personal reflections. They discovered the value of videotaping only when they began discussing their strategies and interventions with their clinical supervisor and each other. Another discovery pertained to the structure of the clinical supervision conference itself. The teachers tended to think of the process as collaborative and collegial; and this sentiment was true whether the conversation was with the clinical supervisor or with colleagues.

Suddenly, it was acceptable to be wrong and to talk about mistakes. It was no longer important that they were being evaluated in a summative way, or were brainstorming about better decisions and more effective strategies. The conferencing seemed to make reading theory come alive: to become palpable and understandable in the moment. Scaffolding, for example, was no longer a chosen objective; rather it became an integrated part of a personal repertoire. From the time these teachers began their reading specialist curriculum, they had heard that students' needs drive instruction. Many participants in this study began to see there was a difference between planning that was based on assessed needs, and responding based on needs observed in real time. Theory became an intuitive part of teaching.

Participants understood why they were effective teachers of reading when they began to see that observation and reflection is an opportunity for collaboration. They learned from action and reflection. They also affirmed in many cases that they were doing things well, and understood why they were effective. Valerie tied substantial improvements in reading comprehension for a specific student to specific aspects of conversations about her videotapes, making her own teaching demonstrably more effective. Observation and reflection was also an opportunity to change practices. From her comment, "Reflection is like an internal dialog on paper," Stella disclosed that coaching was powerful because it changed her internal dialog for the better. The teachers began to see how theory presents opportunities for changes in practice and becomes practice. They changed their teaching repertoire in a relatively short time; and they were ultimately less defensive about feedback, which was seen as helpful rather than as admonishment.

As their personal understanding about how to be effective teachers of reading changed, many began to identify previously unsuspected advantages to videocoaching. Dale began to describe her own teaching as diagnostic. She saw herself looking through another lens, analyzing her own performance. This was the way that that videocoaching helped her to change. Susan was able to view a lesson that went awry from a different perspective. The problem with the lesson had little to do with flawed teaching and very much to do with her interpersonal responses to a manipulative student. Because Susan had prepared a list of questions to help Dale observe her own performance on videotape, she eventually assumed the perspective an observer might have and came to understand why the lesson went awry.

Limitations of the Study

A limitation of the study was having only one supervisor participate. Having the perspective of several supervisors or even one other supervisor, particularly in the interpretation of student responses during videocoaching conferences would have been invaluable to provide better triangulation of the data. Any future replication of this study would provide for multiple supervisors and employ interrater reliability scales. Best case scenario would be to replicate this research in multiple sites concurrently. Another limitation came from having no additional reading personnel to review and analyze transcripts, written artifacts, and field notes or to independently code data. An independent researcher reviewed all of the data and monitored each phase of the data analysis thereby adding additional safeguards against supervisor bias. However, while this researcher is considered an expert in qualitative research design, she is not well-versed in the field of literacy. An additional reviewer with expertise in literacy would have provided needed balance.

Implications for Practice

It is important for videocoaching to be first and foremost an individualized experience before it becomes a collaborative and interpersonal experience. A clinical supervisor needs to grasp that the reading specialist, not unlike the student who is learning to overcome reading difficulties, has specific needs that should be the basis of training. Observation and reflection will be most effective when they focus on individual needs for change. The value of videocoaching when accompanied by concurrent feedback and reflection comes from the change in perspective about the nature of teaching itself. As learners, graduate students, therefore, need to have experiences that are optimal if they are to make personal cognitive gains. Another overlooked advantage of videocoaching, when accompanied by concurrent feedback and reflection, comes from the context it creates for teachers to be free to make mistakes, take risks, and benefit from the perceptions and expertise of others, including peers and clinical supervisors. In understanding the classroom dynamics of teaching and learning. Through videocoaching, a teacher can also be a learner, and teachers enjoy opportunities to learn from students. Videocoaching helps teachers understand the limitations of recurring posturing as knowers, and it sets the stage for teachers to become more comfortable to learn from participation and discovery. The structure of the conference also prevents clinical supervisors from being only purveyors of knowledge about teaching; new parameters are established in which even clinical supervisors must model collaborative and interactive teaching strategies.

Additionally, the videocoaching conference expands the opportunities for distance learning by making "distance supervision" a viable method of monitoring instruction. Using software such as Skype, a free internet video calling service, and web formats, like RSS (Really Simple Syndication) and podcast, the supervision of online clinical experiences could become common practice. According to Hartsell and Yeun (2006), video streaming applications "can help increase online interactivity and communication between instructors and students." Video streaming and RSS/podcast formats allow the student to post teaching videos for the supervisor or a cohort of peers to view. Software, such as that offered by Skype, offers the possibility for conducting the videocoaching conference or a group videocoaching conference online in real time. Perhaps these developments in technology would bring the collegiality and interactivity valued in face-to-face conferences to the virtual learning experience.

References

Alvermann, D. E., & Hayes, D. A. (1989). Classroom discussion of content area reading assignments: An intervention study. *Reading Research Quarterly*, 24, 305-335.

Anderson, R. C. (1994). Role of the reader's schema in comprehension, learning, and memory. In R. B. Ruddell, M. R. Ruddell, & H. Singer (Eds.) *Theoretical models and processes of reading* (4th edition). International Reading Association Publications. Newark, DE: International Reading Association. Pp. 469-482,

Artiles, A. J. (1994). Assessing the link between teacher cognitions, teacher behaviors, and pupil responses to lessons. *Teaching and Teacher Education*, 10, 65-81.

Bereiter, C., & Bird, M. (1985). Use of thinking aloud in identification and teaching of reading comprehension strategies. *Cognition and Instruction*, 2, 131-158.

Bransford, J. D., & Brown, A. L. (2002). How people learn: Brain, mind, experience, and school. Washington, DC: National Academies Press.

Buysse, V., Sparkman, K.L., & Wesley, P.W. (2003). Communities of practice: Connecting what we know with what we do. Exceptional Children, 69, 263-277.

Cobb, P. (2000). *Conducting teaching experiments in collaboration with teachers*. Amahwah, NJ: Lawrence Erlbaum Inc.

Cobb, P., Bufi, A., McClain, K., & Whiteneck, J. (1997). Reflective discourse and collective reflection. *Journal for Research in Mathematics Education*, 28, 258-277.

Fauske, J. (2002). Preparing school leaders: Understanding, experiencing, and implementing collaboration. *International Electronic Journal for Leadership in Learning*, 6. Retrieved February 25, 2007. http://www. ucalgary.ca/~iejll/

Guthrie, J. T., Anderson, E., Alao, S., & Rinehart, J. (1999). Influences of concept-oriented reading instruction on strategy use and conceptual learning from text. *The Elementary School Journal*, 99, 343-367.

Hartsell, T., & Yuen, S. (2006). Video streaming in online learning. *AACE Journal*, 14(1), 31-43.

Hayes, D. A., & Alvermann, D. E. (1986). Video-assisted coaching of textbook discussion skills. Its impact on critical reading behavior. Paper presented at the annual meeting of the American Educational Research Association, San Francisco, April 1988. 11 pp. ED 271 734.

Hitchcock, C. H., Prater, M. A., & Dowrick, P. W. (2004). Reading comprehension and fluency: Examining the effects of tutoring and video self-modeling on first-grade students with reading difficulties. *Learning Disability Quarterly*. Retrieved February 25, 2007, http://www.cldinternational.org/LDQ/ldq.asp.

Horwitz, P. (2002), Instructivism: Between CAI and microworlds. A paper presented to the National Science Foundation, REC Principal Investigators' Meeting. Washington, DC: National Science Foundation.

Irwin, J. (1986). Cohesion and Comprehension: A Research Review. In J. Irwin, (Ed.) *Understanding and Teaching Cohesion Comprehension*. International Reading Association Publication. Newark, DE: International Reading Association. Pp 31-43.

Kibby, M. W. (1995). Practical steps for informing literacy instruction: A diagnostic decision-making model. International Reading Association Publication. Newark, DE: International Reading Association.

Kibby, M. W., & Scott, L. (2002). Using computer simulations to teach decision-making in reading diagnostic assessment for remediation. *Reading Online*, 6, Retrieved February 25, 2007. http://www.readingonline.org/articles/art_index.asp?HREF=kibby/index.html.

Lewis, C. C., & Tsuchida, I. (1998). A lesson is like a swiftly flowing river. *American Educator*, Winter, 12-17/50-52.

Murphy, C. U. (1999). Use of time for faculty study. *Journal of Staff Development*, 20. http://www.nsdc.org/library/publicatons/jsd/murpy202.cfm

New Teachers Network. University of Chicago. Retrieved February 25, 2007. http://usi.uchicago.edu/schooldev.html/

Pressley, M., El-Dinary, P.V., Gaskins, I., Schuder, T., Bergman, J. L., Almasi, J., & Brown, R. (1992). Beyond direct explanation: Transactional instruction of reading comprehension strategies. *The Elementary School Journal*, 92, 513-555.

Palincsar. A. S., & Brown, A. L. (1984) Reciprocal teaching of comprehension-fostering and comprehension-monitoring activities. *Cognitive Instruction*, 1, 117-175.

Rochelle, J. (1992). Learning by collaborating: Convergent conceptual change. *Journal of the Learning Sciences*, 2, 235-276.

Sawyer, R. D. (2001). Teachers who grew as collaborative leaders: The rocky road of support. *Education Policy Analysis Archives*, 9. Retrieved February 25, 2007. http://epaa.asu.edu/epaa/v9n39.html.

Stigler, J. W., & Hiebert, J. (1999), *The Teaching Gap: Best ideas from the world's teachers for improving education in the classroom*. New York, NY: Free Press.

Stigler, J., Gallimore, R., & Hiebert, J. (2000). Using video surveys to compare classrooms and teaching across cultures. Educational Psychologist, 35, 87-100.

Strauss, A., & Corbin, J. (1990) *Basics of qualitative research; Grounded theory procedures and techniques*. Newbury Park, NJ: Sage.

Taylor, B, & Pearson, P. D. (2000). School-reading improvement. What does the research say? How can we make it happen? Retrieved February 25, 2007. http://www.ciera.org/library/presos/2000/2000-IRA/taylor/taylor-ira-2000.pdf

Young, J., Bolla, J., Schumm, J., Moreyra, A., Exley, R., Morrow L.M., & Woo, D.G., (2001). Tutoring programs for struggling readers. *The South Florida America Reads Coalition: A Synergistic Effort*. Retrieved February 25, 2007. http://www.americareadsmiami.org.

Appendix A

Videocoaching Conference: What to expect

- Typically, the initial conference lasts anywhere from 30-60 minutes. Subsequent conferences are usually 20-30 minutes in length.
- Conferences are not intended to be evaluative in nature. It creates an opportunity for the tutor and supervisor to both view the instruction as interested observers and discuss it.
- Conference must be scheduled ASAP after the lesson is taught, (Within a week is preferable but with such a large clinic group, this may not happen.)

Before Videocoaching Conference

- You will videotape a lesson—one must be a comprehension lesson—during clinic tutoring session.
- You will review the tape and complete the following 3 tasks:
  - Complete a Rubric for Classroom Observation form for your lesson.
  - Construct a Talking Point Guide

- What comprehension/word identification strategy were you teaching?
- At what stage of the teaching process were you working? (Scaffolding/ Gradual Release of Responsibility)
- How engaged was your learner?
- Which of the student's strengths did you build upon during this lesson?
- How did make sure that this lesson worked toward Success, Independence, and Improved Self-Esteem?
- How was this lesson an example of authentic reading and/or writing?
- Choose a ten minute portion of the tape to view during the conference.

Bring both of these to your video coaching conference.

During the Videocoaching Conference

- Presents talking points to the supervisor. (That means hand her the paper)
- Both tutor and supervisor take notes as we chat.
- The conference is informal. You are urged to interject comments into the conversation.
- As the lesson is viewed questions are posed about the instruction based on the your talking points in comparison to what is occurring in the lesson.
  - The questions are designed to open a dialogue about the crafting of the lesson.
  - The questions are intended to focus the your attention on instances where the video lesson contradicts a talking point or where you have missed the opportunity to comment on a particularly effective strand of instruction.

After the Videocoaching Conference

- You will submit a critical reflection structured using the video lesson talking points, based on our dialogue about the instruction and the question guide for critical reflection. You will also complete a Lesson Observation Rubric.
- In subsequent lessons we look for evidence that issues raised during the video coaching conference are addressed during teaching.
  - If necessary, a follow-up conference is scheduled.

From Questions to Answers: Education Faculty Members Learn about English Language Learners

Laura Chris Green

Martha Foote

Carole Walker

Texas A&M University-Commerce

Cindy Shuman

Kansas State University

Abstract

Due to increases in the population of English language learners (ELLs) throughout the nation, many PK-12 teachers are responsible for linguistically diverse students, but few receive adequate preparation for this task. With support from the US Department of Education's Office of English Language Acquisition, project ¡Listo! was launched as curriculum and instruction faculty members collaboratively developed a new paradigm of professional development building on the Reggio-inspired pedagogical philosophy in order to infuse ELL instruction into their university courses. Faculty members joined one of five professional learning communities (PLCs) to revise the syllabi of key undergraduate courses, including five literacy courses. The overarching research question was: "What happens when C&I faculty members participate in the ¡Listo! Professional Learning Community for the purpose of improving teacher education instruction for preservice teachers to learn best practices for teaching ELLs?" Changes in faculty members' knowledge and attitudes were measured through an online survey and through content analysis of a reflection protocol. Analysis revealed four themes of growth in faculty members' knowledge and change in their attitudes toward ELL instruction during the first year of the five-year project.

O ur inservice and preservice teacher education programs can no longer ignore the needs of the large and ever-growing population of English language learners (ELLs) as we prepare teachers for our nation's schools. English language learners are the fastest growing segment of the school-age population with over five million enrolled in our nation's public schools. For the 2005-2006 school year, the National Clearinghouse for English Language Acquisition (NCELA, 2007) reported that 5,074,572 of the 49,324,829 students enrolled in PK-12 were officially identified as LEP (Limited English proficient) students. This was 10.3% of the total student population and represented a 57.7% growth rate over the previous ten years. By 2001 the proportion of all teachers who had taught at least one ELL student had grown to 43% (Zehler, Fleischman, Hopstock, Stephenson, Pendick, & Sapru, 2003). At the current annual growth rate, projections are that by 2050, virtually all classrooms in the United States, especially at the elementary level, will have ELLs enrolled (Green, 2006).

Historically speaking, ELLs have primarily resided in the states where immigrants first enter the US (Southwest, Northeast, and Florida). Texas, where the authors of this study are located, for example, has the second largest ELL population in the nation with the Texas Education Agency (2009) reporting over 800,000 officially identified students. The states experiencing the most explosive growth (400% to 500%), however, are not in these traditionally high ELL regions as immigrants move into "the heartland." Four of the five states with the highest increases are in the Southeast and the fifth is in the Midwest. English language learners are in every state of the Union, and increasingly they are in areas they have not been in before.

Multiple sources reveal a profound shortage nationally of bilingual and ESL teachers. Most needed are elementary bilingual teachers and teachers in urban areas. Over ten years ago, the General Accounting Office (1994) reported a shortage of 175,000 bilingual teachers at the national level. Recent data collected from Texas school districts found that districts were unable to fill 26% of open secondary bilingual/ESL positions and lacked 2,906 elementary bilingual and ESL teachers (Lara-Alecio, Galloway, Palmer, Arizpe, Irby, Rodríguez, & Mahadevan, 2003). The severe shortage of bilingual and ESL specialists coupled with the dramatic increases in the number of ELLs means many of these students are placed in mainstream classrooms for all, or at least part, of the day.

Unfortunately, few mainstream teachers have been trained to meet the linguistic and cultural needs of ELL students. According to Ballantyne, Sanderman & Levy (2008), only 30% of teachers who have ELLs in their classrooms have had the training to do so effectively and only 26% of teachers have had training regarding ELLs in their staff development programs. According to Alexander, Heaviside, & Farris (1999), 57% of the teachers believe they need additional training in order to provide effective instruction to ELL students. In addition, only 20 states require training on working with ELLs in their preservice preparation programs and less than one-sixth of all colleges provide such training (Ballantyne, Sanderman, & Levy, 2008; Menken & Atunez, 2001). Perhaps even more damaging is the fact that many mainstream educators, including school administrators, who work with linguistically diverse students, believe many deficit-based myths and misconceptions about them (Minaya-Rowe, 2008; Harper & de Jong, 2004). Reeves (2006), for example, found that 71% of teachers surveyed thought that ELLs should be able to learn English within two years, and Karbenick and Noda (2004) found that 52% of teachers believed that speaking one's first language at home inhibits English language development.

A Growing Call among Teacher Educators

In view of this great need, many professional organizations are calling for better preparation of all teachers for the realities of today's classrooms. For example, the National Association for the Education of Young Children in its latest edition of its Developmentally Appropriate Practices (Copple & Brederkamp, 2009), integrates references to the teaching of ELLs throughout its standards for early childhood program as does the National Council of Teachers of Mathematics (2000)in its Equity Principle from *Principles and Standards for School Mathematics.*

Reading/language arts associations have been particularly active in sounding the call. In synthesizing research on teacher preparation for reading instruction, the *International Reading Association* (2007), concluded that excellent teacher education programs " . . . are saturated with an awareness of diversity, their faculties and students reflect diversity and they produce teachers who know how to teach diverse students in diverse settings" (p. 1). Such awareness leads to moving away from deficit models towards respect for all kinds of diversity, including cultural and linguistic diversity, as well for struggling readers of all kinds, which many ELLs often are.

At the annual 2007 College Reading Association conference, the Teacher Education division led discussions on issues that drive reading education policies and initiatives (Ferree, Falk-Ross, Gambrell, Long, Sampson, Mohr, & Flippo, 2008). Both the elementary and secondary discussion groups called for increased attention to the teaching of ELLs in our teacher education programs as well as helping to make districts, legislators, and the public aware of the need.

We heard this call. The Department of Curriculum and Instruction at our university made a decision to infuse content about the teaching of ELLs into elementary and secondary education courses. In order to help our undergraduate and graduate students learn about best practice for ELLs, a grant from the US Department of Education was obtained to provide five years of funding for the effort.

The authors will describe the process used and the progress made by the 31 faculty members, only one of whom had formal bilingual/ESL credentials, during the first year of the project, 2007-2008, in their implementation of Project ¡Listo!: Strategies for ELL Student Success. We offer this description and analysis of our first year in hopes that others can see how we launched this ambitious project and what lessons we have learned on our journey thus far.

The ¡Listo! Professional Development Framework

Methods for teaching that are non-intimidating to teachers and their students, build on their existing knowledge and skills, and result in *engaging work* were needed to accomplish *¡Listo!* instructional goals. It was necessary to change what and how we taught in our university courses so that our preservice teachers and graduate students would be equipped to teach ELLs in their public school classrooms. The *¡Listo!* project design, therefore, included an embedded professional development component modeled after three frameworks: Universal Design of Instruction (Burgstahler, 2007), the *Reggio Approach* (Edwards, Gandini, & Forman, 1998) and *Phillip Schlechty's "Working on the Work" framework* (2002). The result is a newer paradigm, one of professional development through action research and collaboration.

Table 1: Comparison of Universal Design Qualities and Schlechty's Critical Design Qualities of Student Work and the Values of the Reggio-Inspired Approach

8 Universal Design Principles	10 Schlechty Design Qualities	8 Reggio-Inspired Values
Class climate valuing diversity and inclusiveness	Choice	The integral role of relationships with parents in the life of the school
Interaction among students and instructor	Affiliation	The critical importance of relationships: teacher-learner, learner-learner, & teacher-parent
Accessible and useable physical environments and products		The importance of a rich, engaging environment for promoting learning
Accessible delivery methods	Organization of knowledge	Learners represent their knowledge through many media
Engaging, flexible, accessible information resources and technology	Content and substance, Novelty, Authenticity	Learner's experiences and questions as the basis on which curriculum is built
Regular, specific, formative feedback	Product focus Affirmation of performance	Negotiated Learning, teachers responsiveness to learner's current level of learning
Multiple, accessible methods and tools for assessing student progress	Clear and compelling standards	Documentation and the study of student's learning as the core of practice
Accommodations for students whose needs are not being met	Protection from adverse consequences of initial failure	Learners with Special Rights

In higher education, as within Pre-K through grade 12, most teachers plan and teach in isolation. This practice may stem from long-held beliefs about the need for individual accountability, as well as the lack of fiscal resources to provide more teachers at all levels of education with joint planning times. However, working in isolation actually impoverishes a teacher's potential and makes building capacity as a designer and leader of learning for students less likely. In contrast, the ¡Listo! approach is to collaborate following the Reggio-inspired *Pedagogy of Listening* (Rinaldi, 2000), as we redesigned our courses.

> In order to educate ourselves, we must try to understand differences rather than wanting to cancel them. This means approaching each individual in terms of his or her background and personal story, and with great sensitivity. It means 'listening' to the differences (what we refer to as "the pedagogy of listening"), but also listening to and accepting the changes that take place within us, which are generated by our relationships, or better, by our interactions with others. It means letting go of any truths that we consider to be absolute, being open to doubt and giving value to negotiation as a strategy of the possible. All of this means—or more precisely, can mean—greater possibilities for us to change, but without making us feel displaced or that we have lost something (Rinaldi, 2006, p.140).

Such is the kind of interaction that we wish for our collaborative endeavors toward preparing our teachers to teach English language learners.

Co-construction is the basic premise of the *Pedagogy of Listening*. Teachers work collaboratively to make instructional decisions based on their close observation of their students. They listen to each other and to their students and study the evidence available from students' work and learning progress. Working collegially to reflect on the documentation gathered (e.g., transcriptions of student comments in class discussions, papers, reflection journals, other artifacts, performance on tests, etc.), the collaborative teams study the data in a systematic fashion, functioning as action researchers, reaching conclusions from their joint analyses of their students' work and making thoughtful, data-driven decisions. In this study, faculty members used this new paradigm of collaboration. Through this collaborative process, the faculty members uncovered not only how English language learners learn and experience success in our schools systems, but also how to prepare teachers to better support ELL learning in their individual content areas.

In our department, 28 faculty members agreed to participate in book study groups and interact with visiting scholars within the ¡Listo! project. Provocations for their participation included a $1,000 stipend, the opportunity to interact with highly regarded researchers and protected time to work with colleagues in professional learning communities (Dufour, 2004) on engaging instructional design tasks. ¡Listo! used five existing departmental work teams: Early Childhood Education, Elementary Education, Middle Level Education, Secondary Education, and Reading. The C&I teams included both those primarily teaching undergraduate courses and those teaching mostly at the graduate level. They became instructional redesign teams for one or more of the 12 upper-level, preservice courses within their program area. Our new paradigm is graphically represented in Figure 1.

Figure 1: *¡Listo!* Reggio-Inspired Professional Development Model

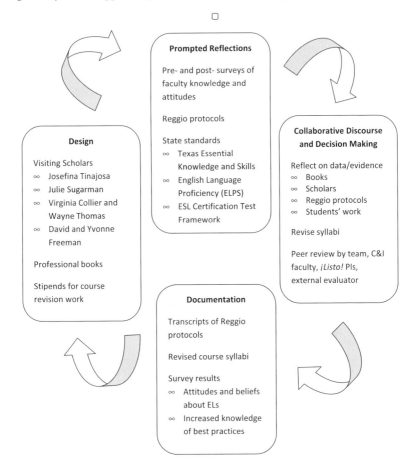

Prompted Reflections

Pre- and post- surveys of faculty knowledge and attitudes

Reggio protocols

State standards
- ∞ Texas Essential Knowledge and Skills
- ∞ English Language Proficiency (ELPS)
- ∞ ESL Certification Test Framework

Design

Visiting Scholars
- ∞ Josefina Tinajosa
- ∞ Julie Sugarman
- ∞ Virginia Collier and Wayne Thomas
- ∞ David and Yvonne Freeman

Professional books

Stipends for course revision work

Collaborative Discourse and Decision Making

Reflect on data/evidence
- ∞ Books
- ∞ Scholars
- ∞ Reggio protocols
- ∞ Students' work

Revise syllabi

Peer review by team, C&I faculty, *¡Listo!* PIs, external evaluator

Documentation

Transcripts of Reggio protocols

Revised course syllabi

Survey results
- ∞ Attitudes and beliefs about ELs
- ∞ Increased knowledge of best practices

Research Design

Our research on the faculty development process in the first year of Project ¡Listo! has been guided by one key question and two sub-questions. The key question is what happens when C&I faculty members participate in the ¡Listo! Professional Learning Community (PLC)? The two subquestions are:

1. What changes occurred in faculty members' knowledge of best practices for teaching English language learners?
2. What changes occurred in faculty members' attitudes toward preparing teachers to teach English language learners?

We measured changes in faculty members' knowledge and attitudes through the collection of two kinds of data: a pre- and post-online survey and through content analysis of a Reggio-inspired reflection protocol administered throughout the year at all of the Visiting Scholar roundtables.

The survey consisted of seven Likert-scale questions and six open-ended questions and was designed to provide some basic, baseline data on how the faculty members felt about the project's goals and objectives before the beginning and at the end of the first project year. The survey was designed by one of the project principal investigators (PI) in collaboration with the project's outside evaluator and the other two PIs. The survey asked the faculty members to rate three statements: 1) the importance of the project's faculty development goal ("to better prepare our students to teach ELLs"); 2) the effectiveness of our efforts in meeting this goal; and 3) how "knowledgeable" they themselves as individuals were about the characteristics of ELLs, effective teaching strategies for ELLs, and the assessment of ELLs. This self-reported data is dependent on each respondent's individual interpretation of terms like "better prepared," "effectively … preparing" and "knowledgeable." This is a limitation of the survey data, both pre- and post-, but the surveys provided an additional source of data to measure the growth in faculty members' knowledge and change in their attitudes that was also observed in the Reggio-inspired protocol responses.

This article reports on the responses to the seven Likert-scale items, not on the responses to the six open-ended questions. The survey was sent to the 28 participating faculty members in September, 2007, in an email message providing a link to the online form and was followed by another invitation to participate in May, 2008. Twenty-seven of the 28 faculty members responded to the fall survey for an exceptionally high response rate of 96% and up to 18 of the 28 responded in the spring, a still respectable response rate of 64%. It is possible that the attrition from the pre- to post-survey is due to more of those who least supported the project not participating in the spring, but it is also believed the timing of the spring survey, right during the end of the semester, had its effects. Like public school classroom teachers, university faculty members, and instructors have many testing, grading, and other responsibilities at this time of the year. We also noted that the attendance of our faculty members at our four all-day Visiting Scholar events was quite high (95% overall), indicating that faculty members who did not support the project did not feel they should not participate, as they sometimes let us know quite clearly as they articulately stated their positions in our whole group meetings. The rather large attrition rate, however, should be viewed as a limitation of the survey data.

In order to prompt thoughtful reflection, discussion, and sharing of new ideas, a modified version of Project Zero's Collaborative Reflection Protocol (2001) was utilized to provide a series of prompts for individual and group responses after each Visiting Scholar Day, at the conclusion of book study group sessions, as well as, at other strategic points. The questions served to scaffold the Professional Learning

Communities (PLCs) in their collaborative discourse so that shifts in thinking could be identified and shared, perspectives thoughtfully considered, hypotheses/predictions about teaching practices formulated, and possibilities for future instruction articulated. The prompts helped to examine the implications for infusing ELL instruction into our undergraduate courses in a systematic, yet detailed, way. Our analysis looked at the protocol responses of over 30 faculty members and occasional visitors at all four of our first Visiting Scholar Days. This rich source of faculty members' reflections and discussions provided us with formative, qualitative data we used to track changes in faculty members' knowledge and attitudes about ELLs and teacher preparation for ELLs throughout the first project year.

Survey Results

The first three questions on the online surveys dealt with faculty members' attitudes toward preparing teachers to teach ELLs. Twenty-seven full-time faculty members responded to the fall survey and 18 faculty members responded to the spring survey. As discussed above, this represents some significant attrition from fall to spring. Percentages of respondents are reported so that comparable judgments can be made. Results for the first question are as follows:

Question 1. How important do you feel it is to better prepare our students (preservice and inservice teachers) to teach ELLs?		
Rating	Fall N=27	Spring N=18
Not at all important	0.0	0.0
Of little importance	3.7	0.0
Neutral	0.0	11.1
Important	22.2	27.8
Extremely important	74.1	61.1

Comparisons of the pre-and post surveys show clearly that the faculty members felt the issue of better preparing teachers to address the needs of ELLs was important both before the project began and at the end of the first year of implementation. No one felt the issue was of little importance on the post-survey, a minor change from the pre-survey. However, the percentage of those who felt neutrally about the topic increased, perhaps because those with more negative attitudes moved from a "Of little importance" to a "Neutral" position.

The second and third questions asked how the faculty members felt about the department's effectiveness in preparing preservice and inservice teachers to teach ELLs. The results for those two questions are as follows:

Question 2.1. How effectively do you feel our C&I department has done preparing preservice teachers to teach ELLs thus far?		
Rating	Fall N=27	Spring N=18
Very ineffectively	0.0	5.6
Ineffectively	25.9	27.8
Neutral	55.6	11.1
Effectively	3.7	50.0
Very effectively	0.0	5.6
Don't know	14.8	0.0
Questions 2.2. How effectively do you feel our C&I department has done preparing inservice teachers to teach ELLs thus far?		
Rating	Fall N=27	Spring N=15
Very ineffectively	3.7	0.0
Ineffectively	37.0	26.7
Neutral	22.2	26.7
Effectively	14.8	46.7
Very effectively	0.0	0.0
Don't know	22.2	0.0

The pre-survey, done in the fall, showed that only a few faculty members felt that the department had done an effective job preparing teachers to teach ELLs (3.7% for preservice teachers and 14.8% for inservice teachers). No one thought it had done so very effectively (0% for both preservice and inservice teachers). The rest chose "Ineffectively," "Neutral" or "Don't know" responses with only one person responding "Very ineffectively" for preservice teachers. Comparisons on these two questions to the post-survey, spring results show that faculty members increasingly felt that the department has improved its effectiveness and somewhat lowered its ineffectiveness for both kinds of teachers. Significant, too, is that "Don't Know" responses dropped to zero, showing that faculty appear to have more knowledge about each other's teaching in this area now.

The next three questions revealed changes in how much faculty members felt they individually had learned about English language learners over the course of the year.

Question 3.1. My knowledge of the characteristics (demographic data, strengths, needs) of ELLs.		
Rating	Fall N=27	Spring N=18
No knowledge of these issues	0.0	0.0
Minimal knowledge	18.5	0.0
Somewhat knowledgeable	51.9	16.7
Knowledgeable	22.2	66.7
Very knowledgeable	7.4	16.7

Question 3.2. My knowledge of effective teaching strategies that maximize academic success for ELLs.		
Rating	Fall N=27	Spring N=18
No knowledge of these issues	3.7	0.0
Minimal knowledge	22.2	0.0
Somewhat knowledgeable	48.1	11.1
Knowledgeable	18.5	72.2
Very knowledgeable	7.4	16.7
Question 3.3. My knowledge of how to assess ELLs in culturally and linguistically fair ways.		
Rating	Fall N=27	Spring N=18
No knowledge of these issues	7.4	0.0
Minimal knowledge	22.2	0.0
Somewhat knowledgeable	44.4	44.4
Knowledgeable	14.8	50.0
Very knowledgeable	11.1	5.6

Substantial increases in faculty members' knowledge of ELLs were seen in their responses to these questions. Adding together the two lowest categories on the Likert scale, the pre-surveys had from 18.5 to 29.6% who responded that they had no or minimal knowledge of ELL issues; zero percent responded to either no knowledge or minimal knowledge on the post-survey. In addition, many respondents on the post-survey moved up from "Somewhat knowledgeable" to "Knowledgeable" and from there to "Very knowledgeable." It is also worth noting that the faculty members felt most knowledgeable about teaching strategies and least knowledgeable about ELL assessment.

The last question asked faculty members about the application of their new knowledge on ELLs and how effectively they felt they had infused this knowledge into their courses.

Question 4.1. Please think about a course you currently teach. Overall, how effectively have you infused content about effective practices for ELL instruction in your course?		
Rating	Fall N=27	Spring N=16
Very ineffectively	11.1	6.3
Ineffectively	14.8	12.5
Neutral	18.5	6.3
Effectively	40.7	56.3
Very effectively	0.0	18.8
I have not infused this content in my course	14.8	0.0

Comparing the pre-survey results to the post-survey results for the last question, we see decreases in the percentage of faculty members who responded that they had done so "Very ineffectively," "Ineffectively," or not at all and increases in those who felt they now could do so "Effectively" or "Very effectively." During the pre-survey, 14.8% of the faculty members reported they did not infuse ELL content at all while on the post-survey, 0% of the faculty members reported not doing so. In addition, 18.8% of the faculty members chose "Very effectively" in the spring, showing that the faculty members believe they have become more knowledgeable but still have much to learn and assimilate.

In summary, by comparing the faculty members' responses to the pre- and post- surveys, four findings were discovered: 1) faculty member continue to see the issue of better teacher preparation for ELLs as important; 2) faculty members feel the department has improved in its effectiveness in this area; 3) faculty members reported that they themselves had increased their knowledge of ELL issues; and 4) faculty members had effectively infused content about ELLs into their courses, many moving from little or no infusion at all.

Protocol Results

As has been described previously, faculty members participating in sessions with four visiting scholars during the first year of the project reflected on their experiences by responding to five prompts based the Reggio Emilia approach. These five prompts were:

1. What did you learn (new information or "ah-has!") or notice?
2, What do you wonder/question?
3. What do you speculate (hunches about instructional practices that might be effective or factors about learning context or learners that could be important as instruction is designed)?
4. What are the implications?
5. How might we proceed?

Individual and group responses for each of these prompts for each visiting scholar were transcribed by the external evaluator. From her analyses of these data, she presented key ideas within each of the five sets of responses for each of the four visiting scholar sessions during year one of the project. In addition, the authors independently analyzed the transcripts. One identified four overarching themes found across the four data sets. Another looked for quotations from the data sets to support those themes. In the process, the initial themes were expanded; however, no new themes were identified. For example, an initial theme *from awareness to advocacy* was expanded to *from antagonism to awareness toward advocacy*.

Table 2: *Themes within PLC Data with Sample Statements*

Themes	Sample Statements
Theme 1: • From Antagonism (6 responses; one on Sept 07 –1, & five on Oct 07;) • To Awareness (3 responses; one on Jan 08 & two on Apr 08); Toward Advocacy (5 responses; one on • Oct 07 –1, one on Jan 08 –1, & three on Apr 08.	• Antagonism: *If we disagree, what—or are there—outlets to express differing beliefs?* (October 2007) • Awareness: *Need to "value" other viewpoints, languages, home life, etc.* (January 2008) • Advocacy: *We need to storm Austin.* (April 2008)
Theme 2: • From Complacency (3 responses on Sept 07) • To Questions (4 responses; one on Sept 07, & three on Oct 07) • Toward Answers (6 responses; four on Jan 08, & two on Apr 08)	• Complacency: *Diversity is not appreciated in schools (though it is claimed to be).* (September 2007) • Questions: *How long does it take to learn a second language? (September 2007)* • Answers: *Continue advocating best practice with addition of conscious effect on language development.* (January 2008)
Theme 3: • From Denial (5 responses; three on Sept 07, & two on Oct 07) • To Appreciation of Issues (6 responses; two on Sept 07, & four on Oct 07) • Toward Course Applications (12 responses; one on Sept 07, one on Oct 07, five on Jan 08, & five on Apr 08)	• Denial: Need for more studies or more background on studies presented. (September 2007) • Appreciation: For instructional strategies to be sustained over time, teachers must be helped to address the "myths about bilingualism." (October 2007) • Applications: SIOP protocol may be framework to use to teach instructional strategies in teacher ed. (April 2008)
Theme 4: • From Me (5 responses; four on Sept 07, & one on Apr 08) • To Us (5 responses; one on Sept 07, one on Oct 07, & three on Apr 08) • Toward Them - Expanding the Network (9 responses; two on Oct 07, five on Jan 08, & two on Apr 08)	• Me: Why don't we have speakers that specifically extend my knowledge base? (April 2008) • Us: How can faculty become more bilingual? (April 2008) • Them: Why do we not include doctoral students? Evening program? (April 2008)

While each theme suggests a growth continuum, our professional development during the first year of the project has not been linear. Nevertheless, the themes corroborate changes in attitudes and dispositions. These findings support the changes suggested by the analyses of the survey data reported earlier. While there are exceptions, comments aligned with the first anchor word in each theme at the beginning of the project year (September 2007) and comments aligned more with the last anchor word in each theme at the end of the project year (April 2008). Taken as a whole, these snippets provide evidence that over the course of the year changes occurred within the knowledge bases and attitudes of faculty participants.

Concluding Remarks

The survey results and the protocol responses are supported by additional anecdotal evidence of strong faculty commitment to the goals of the project:

- their high attendance rate of 95% at the all-day Visiting Scholar Days,
- their avid engagement in the presentations and group discussions,
- their consistent participation in monthly book study groups,
- their revision of 12 undergraduate course syllabi by the end of May, and
- their agreement to participate in group action research studies focusing on their revision of the undergraduate courses.

Bilingual/ESL education is a controversial, complex field. There are no simple answers because ELLs are themselves very diverse, in their native languages and cultures, their socio-economic statuses, the amount of schooling they have had (or not had), the degree of their parental support, their levels of educational skills and abilities, as well as a host of other factors. Add to this a plethora of different state and district policies and procedures as well as the complexity of first and second language teaching methods and one could easily throw up one's hands, and say "It's all too much!" We should recognize the difficulty and complexity of the issues, giving everyone – university faculty, school administrators, and classroom teachers – plenty of resources and lots of time to absorb and process new ideas. We must model the valuing perspectives and high expectations we advocate that educators use with ELL students if we wish to achieve genuine change.

References

Alexander, D., Heaviside, S., & Farris, E. (1999). *Status of education reform in public elementary and secondary schools: Teachers' perspectives.* Washington DC: U.S. Department of Education, National Center for Education Statistics. Retrieved on January 11, 2010 from http://nces.ed.gov/pubs99/1999045.pdf

Copple, C., & Bredekamp, S. (2009). *Developmentally appropriate practice in early childhood programs: Serving young children from birth to age 8* (3rd ed.). Washington, DC: National Association for the Education of Young Children.

Ballantyne, K. G., Sanderman, A.R., & Levy, J. (2008). *Educating English language learners: Building teacher capacity.* Washington, DC: National Clearinghouse for English Language Acquisition. Retrieved on January 13, 2010 from http://www.ncela.gwu.edu/practice/mainstream_teachers.htm.

Burgstahler, S. (2007). *Universal design of instruction (UDI): Definition, principles, and examples.* Seattle: DO-IT, University of Washington. Retrieved on January 11, 2009 from http://www.washington.edu/doit/Brochures/Academics/instruction.html.

Dufour, R. (2004). Schools as learning communities. *Educational Leadership, 61*(8), 6-11.

Ferree, A.M., Falk-Ross, F., Gambrell, L., Long, R., Sampson, M.B., Mohr, K., & Flippo, R.F. (2008). Confronting teacher education issues head-on: Increasing our knowledge and choosing our options for strengthening teacher education programs. In M. Foote, F. Falk-Ross, S. Szabo, & M.B. Sampson (Eds.) *Navigating the literacy waters: research, praxis, & advocacy, The twenty-ninth yearbook by the College Reading Association* (pp. 168-178). Commerce, TX: College Reading Association.

General Accounting Office, (1994). *Limited English proficiency: A growing and costly educational challenge facing many school districts.* Washington, DC: General Accounting Office.

Green, L.C. (2006). Major demographics and schooling trends for English language learners and their teachers. In P. Dam & M. Cowart (Eds.), *Cultural and linguistic Issues for English language learners* (pp. 26-55). Denton, TX: Texas Women's University.

Harper, C., & de Jong, E. (2004). Misconceptions about teaching English-language learners. *Journal of Adolescent & Adult Literacy, 48*(2), 152-162.

International Reading Association (2007). *Teaching reading well: A synthesis of the International Reading Association's research on teacher preparation for reading instruction.* Newark: DE, International Reading Association. Retrieved on January 13, 2010 from http://www.reading.org/Libraries/SRII/teaching_reading_well.sflb.ashx.

Karabenick, S.A., & Noda, P.Q. (2004, Spring). Professional development implications of teachers' beliefs and attitudes toward English language learners. *Bilingual Research Journal, 28*(1), 55-76.

Lara-Alecio, R., Galloway, M., Palmer, D., Arizpe, V., Irby, B.J., Rodríguez, L., & Mahadevan, L. (2003). *Study of bilingual/ESL teacher recruitment and retention in Texas school districts.* College Station, TX: Texas A & M University. Retrieved on January 3, 2009 from http://ldn.tamu.edu/Archives/recruitmentretention.pdf

Menken, K., & Atunez, B. (2001). *An overview of the preparation and certification of teachers working with limited English proficient students.* Washington, D.C.: National Clearinghouse of Bilingual Education. Retrieved January 2, 2009 from http://www.ericsp.org/pages/digests/ncbe.pdf.

Minaya-Rowe, L. (2008, November). Myths and misconceptions. *School Administrator, 65*(10), 22-22.

National Clearinghouse for English Language Acquisition. (2007). *The Growing Numbers of Limited English Proficient Students.* Washington, DC: Author. Retrieved on December 14, 2009 from http://www.ncela.gwu.edu/policy/states/ reports/statedata/2005LEP/ GrowingLEP_0506.pdf.

National Council of Teachers of Mathematics (2000). *Principles and Standards for School Mathematics.* Reston, VA: National Council of Teachers of Mathematics. Retrieved November 15, 2009 from http://standards.nctm.org/.

Project Zero, & Reggio Children. (2001). *Making learning visible: Children as individual and group learners.* Reggio Emilia, Italy: Reggio Children.

Reeves, J. R., (2006). Secondary teacher attitudes toward including English-language learners in mainstream classrooms. *Journal of Educational Research, 99*(3), 131-142.

Rinaldi, C. (2000). *The pedagogy of listening.* Paper presented at the 2000 Reggio Study Tour, sponsored by Reggio Children, Reggio, Emilia, Italy.

Rinaldi, C. (2006). I*n dialogue with Reggio Emilia: Listening, researching, and learning.* New York, NY: Routledge.

Schlechty, P.C. (2002).*Working on the work: An action plan for teachers, principals, and superintendents.* San Francisco, CA: Jossey Bass.

Texas Education Agency. (2009) Academic Excellence Indicator System, 2008-09 State Performance Report. Retrieved November 29, 2009 from http://www.tea.state.tx.us/ perfreport/aeis/2008/state.html.

Zehler, A.M., Fleischman, H.L., Hopstock, P.J., Stephenson, T.G., Pendick, M.L., & Sapru, S. (2003). *Policy Report: Summary of Findings Related to LEP and Sp-Ed LEP Students.* Washington DC: U.S. Department of Education, Office of English Language Acquisition, Language Enhancement, and Academic Achievement of Limited English Proficient Students (OELA). Retrieved on January 5, 2010 from http://www.ncela.gwu.edu/resabout/research/descriptivestudyfiles.

Time to Focus on the Impact of Graduate Reading Programs on the Expertise and Practice of Literacy Professionals

Lois K. Haid

Cynthia Fisher

Nancy Masztal

Joyce V. W. Warner

Joanna Marasco

Barry University

Abstract

Are we teaching our graduate students what they need to know in order to address the diverse populations they serve in southeastern Florida and the expectations of their academic environments? This guiding question is the core of an ongoing study of a graduate reading program (GRP) at a diversely populated, southeastern urban university. This study is unique in that research in the area of reading teacher education primarily investigates undergraduate programs. This mixed method, multiphase study uses various data types to investigate, from different perspectives, the impact of the GRP on the self-efficacy and instructional practices of the program's graduates. The study question provides a broad lens through which to view the impact of a graduate reading program that prepares graduates to become reading professionals. The results help clarify the praxis between the theoretical framework of the GRP and the graduates' teaching practice and suggest the need for other universities to research the impact of their graduate literacy programs.

Historically, research on the impact of reading education programs at the graduate level is absent from investigative research (Anders, Hoffman, & Duffy, 2000; Roller, 2001). Yet, recently, a surge of professional development for teachers, scrutiny of teacher preparation programs, and examinations of the role of the reading specialist have caused there to be more research and information available about teacher education programs, although generally at the undergraduate (initial certification) level, which often includes the preparation of educators who teach reading (Haid, 2006; Hoffman & Roller, 2001; IRA, 2007; Johnson, 2006; Lalik & Potts, 2001; Lyon, 1998; Walsh, Glaser, & Wilcox, 2006). A search of current, peer reviewed journals reveals an increase in studies pertaining to undergraduate programs and professional development for working teachers (Hoffman & Roller; Johnson; Lalik & Potts). Still, there remains a lack of research investigating the impact of graduate reading programs on the graduate students and the reading professionals that universities graduate.

In the late 1990s, an International Reading Association's (IRA) Commission on the Role of the Reading Specialist was charged with several tasks. One responsibility was to develop a literature review and to summarize the, then, current view of the various personae reading professionals/specialists may assume in the school setting. The Commission report confirmed there are many, varied roles and responsibilities, each of which depends on the context of the instructional setting and situation. Additionally, they found that these many roles and responsibilities were viewed differently by education professionals, i.e. the principal (Quatroche, Bean, & Hamilton, 2001).

In a later study on the changing role of the specialists, five primary roles were identified: resource to teachers; school and community liaison; coordinator of reading programs; contributor to assessment, and literacy instructor (Bean, Swan, & Knaub, 2003). The authors concluded that these roles represented leadership responsibilities and described the components of each role from that point of view, concluding with the finding that "reading specialists in exemplary schools displayed…characteristics that promote shared leadership in schools" (Bean, et. al, p. 453). As a result, these researchers (Bean, et al; Quatroche, et al., 2001) suggested that teacher educators must provide programs that are broad and acknowledge the multiple tasks of the reading professionals, and charged that teacher educators and researchers must research this area more thoroughly.

Purpose

The focus of our study was to both formatively evaluate our university's graduate program as well as to add to the limited body of knowledge addressing the impact of university graduate reading programs. For the purposes of this study, the reading professional/specialist was defined as an educator who held a Master's degree in reading or Education Specialist's degree in reading.

Cognizant of the scarcity of research, and acknowledging the wide range of roles, the university's graduate reading faculty members asked, "Are we teaching our graduate students what they need to know in order to address their diverse populations and the expectations of their academic environments?" This study investigated the impact of one graduate reading program from the point of view of the graduate students themselves.

In an earlier study done to answer the above question, we asked our graduate students about the impact of the program's final course, the reading practicum. This practicum requires the implementation of content learned throughout the program's coursework. During this first phase, data collected from graduate students showed that they valued this course as a safe arena to practice the new roles expected of them (Warner, Masztal, & Murphy, 2005). The data also suggested that although the graduate students felt prepared, they were tentative about their new responsibilities. The researchers concluded a more in-depth investigation was needed. This current investigation took the form of a longitudinal, multiphase look at the graduate reading program itself, to determine if the education that students received supported the reality of their roles after graduation. Further, it was clear that the ongoing investigation needed to rely on the multiple lenses of quantitative and qualitative data to serve as a formative evaluation and to achieve the purposes of the study.

The foci of this phase were to research and evaluate the: (a) usefulness of the curricula to the current instructional practices of the graduate students; (b) pressing daily needs of the graduate students as they meet the ever-changing milieu of the urban educator; (c) formative data to assess and improve the graduate program's practices; and (d) graduate students' responses to the faculty's initial question: "Are we teaching our graduate students what they need to know to address their diverse populations and the expectations of their academic environments?" Finally, this study addressed the need for further research to inform the field, which includes researchers, policy makers, administrators and educators (Pearson, 1996, 2001; Purcell-Gates, 2000; Roller, 2001).

Theoretical Framework

Paulo Freire's (Hasbrock, 2002) theories of praxis formed a foundation for the theoretical framework of this graduate program for educating teachers. As such, it is also the theoretical foundation for this study. This theoretical framework encompasses the philosophy that learning is not one person acting on another but rather a community of learners working, dialoging, and reflecting with each other. The underlying praxis is based on the belief that the best investment a country can make is in the professional development and ongoing preparation of its teachers (Darling-Hammond, 1997; 2000). However, understanding that teacher education is a wise investment is not enough, as this complex undertaking needs formative research with actionable results (Patterson, Michelli, & Pacheco, 1999).

Literature Review

In 2007, *Teaching Reading Well: A Synthesis of the International Reading Asso-*

ciation's Research on Teacher Preparation for Reading Instruction was published. The report was based on the work of the IRA's Teacher Education Task Force (TETF) and its National Commission on Excellence in Elementary Teacher Preparation for Reading Instruction. The report states, "Putting a quality teacher in every classroom is key to addressing the challenges of reading achievement in schools" (TETF, 2007, p. 1). Therefore, colleges and universities "must examine seriously the content and structure of their teacher preparation programs…" (TETF, p. 2). The research of the TETF and the Commission identified six essential criteria for programs that teach teachers how to teach reading. These include components in the areas of content; faculty and teaching; apprenticeships, field experiences, and practica; diversity; candidate and program assessment; and governance and vision (p. 1). A complete explanation of each component is offered in the report. Though this report refers to undergraduate programs, our ongoing study embodies the theoretical beliefs undergirding the six components.

Our study is also based on the belief that teacher education is not just knowledge of a subject area, but also the development of a theoretical base and the ability to critically think and plan for instruction (Anders, Hoffman & Duffy, 2000). Moreover, the graduate student is impacted by theoretical knowledge and field experience (Burk, 1989; Flint et al., 2001; Hoffman & Roller, 2001; Maloch, Flint, Eldridge, & Harmon, 2003; O'Callaghan, 1997; Pearson, 2001; D. S. Strickland, 2001; K. Strickland, 1990; Wilson, Floden, & Ferrini-Mundy, 2001). It is this praxis between theory and experience that influences instructional planning and ultimately impacts the development of literacy skills and strategies in learners, be they children/students or colleagues (Hoffman & Pearson, 2000; Hoffman & Roller, 2001).

Methods

Participants

Sixty-three graduate students from a midsized, private, southeastern Florida, urban university participated in the second phase of this study. The graduate reading program (GRP) has been offered at this multiethnic, international university since the mid-1960s. Our graduates serve the highly diverse school populations found in southeastern Florida. The GRP was designed to meet and incorporate state and federal requirements and mandates, professional association guidelines, and evidence-based research requirements. The graduate participants (n=63), who received either their MS or Ed S. degree in reading, were representative of the university's ethnically rich population. Seventy-six percent (n=48) of the responding graduates were classroom teachers; 13% (n=eight) were reading resource leaders, 8% (five) were involved in non P-12 academic roles, such as community college education and 3% (two) who did not answer the career question.

Data Collection and Analysis

This multiphase study used various data types to investigate, from different perspectives, the impact of the graduate reading program on the instructional practices of the program's graduates (Worthen & Sanders, 1987). In the initial phase of the study, the findings that emerged from discussion with recent graduate students about the impact of their graduate studies on their instructional planning and classroom practice drove the implementation of the study's second phase that incorporated qualitative and quantitative survey data. The survey (see Appendix) contained three types of questions: 1) demographic data; 2) questions that participants answered using a Likert scale; and 3) opened-ended question responses. Graduate students were asked to rank courses in relation to how effective they were to their daily instructional practice. Courses were ranked on a scale of 5 (most useful) to 1 (least useful). Responses to three open-ended questions provided the content for qualitative analysis. The questions asked graduates to: (a) identify three successes with students/colleagues which can be attributed to the graduate program (GP); (b) identify three pressing issues that impact the teaching of literacy, and (c) list strategies learned in the GP which are used in daily practice.

Descriptive statistics of the Likert data were used to determine the participants' attitudes about the importance of individual courses in the GP. Data were analyzed using an analysis of variance (ANOVA) to determine differences among groups based on years of experience, and teaching responsibility. Content analysis and constant comparison of verbatim responses on the open-ended questions provided rich descriptions of participants' evaluations and perceptions, and cross-validated qualitative data. Constant comparison is the process of collecting and analyzing initial data; developing tentative conclusions, hypotheses, and themes; collecting and analyzing additional data; testing against initial conclusions, hypotheses, and themes; and seeking new perspectives and data sources (Worthen & Sanders, 1987). Content analysis serves a similar purpose.

Results

The results provided information through descriptive, inferential, and qualitative data. Table 1 displays descriptive statistics of the scores for the top seven courses. Their mean scores are above four on a five-point scale. The two courses ranked highest for "usefulness" were diagnostic reading and corrective reading. Of the ten courses required for the MS and state certification in reading, six were ranked "most useful." All these courses required field experience, hands-on implementation of strategies, and scientifically based theory and research in literacy practices.

Analysis of Variance (ANOVAs) were used to determine if there was any variability among groups based on years of education experience and job title. As stated previously, there were three categories of participants based on their job titles: classroom teachers, reading resource leaders, and those in non P-12 academic roles, such as community college education. There were also participants who did not answer the question. When investigating differences from the view of career type, Language Arts had a significant difference among the groups. It was significant at 0.05 (p=0.045). Post Hoc analysis could not be performed because at least one group had fewer than two cases.

Table 1: Courses Rated by Usefulness in Career

Course	Mean	Range
* 590 Corrective	4.74	3-5
*584 Diagnosis	4.50	3-5
*567 Foundations	4.39	2-5
*568 Content Reading	4.39	3-5
*535 Language Arts	4.37	1-5
604 Vocab/Comp	4.33	2-5
*717 Practicum	4.32	1-5

*Required for MS, Ed.S., and State certification

In addition to job title, participants were divided into four categories based on years of experience. Fifty-one percent (n=32) were *novice,* with less than 5 years teaching experience; fourteen percent (n=22) were *experienced,* with 5-10 years teaching experience; twelve percent (n=8) were *veteran,* with 11-20 years experience; and fourteen percent (n= 9) were *senior educations* with 20 + years of experience. In investigating groups by experience, there was a statistically significant difference (p=0.020) among groups for the Language Arts course. A post hoc Bonferroni indicated that there was a significant difference between *novice* and *veteran* teacher groups; *novice teachers* found the Language Arts course more useful than *veterans teachers did.* Similarly, though no statistical significance was found at the .05 level for the reading practicum, practical significance could be implied at 0.051. The *novice* (m=4.75) teacher found this course more useful than the *veteran* teacher did (m=3.60).

The researchers used constant comparison to analyze the three open-ended questions. Several patterns emerged from the data: growth in professional relationships, literacy strategies transferred to daily practice; value of diagnostic and corrective strategies, and high stakes testing as a pressing issue. Content analysis was used to analyze these data to corroborate both quantitative and qualitative results. See Table 2 for verbatim comments from graduate students.

Content analysis showed similar patterns to both constant comparison and quantitative data analysis. Sixty-five percent of the comments to the open-ended questions described "learned" reading strategies as supportive in their work as reading professionals and 38% describe the knowledge from the diagnosis and corrective reading courses as valuable in their current position. This analysis of these data served to cross validate the descriptive data. Sixty-six percent of the comments attributed increased collegiality and professional growth in knowledge gained from the program. Twenty-five percent of the comments highlighted two of the pressing issues as high stakes testing and working with struggling readers. Twenty-nine percent of the comments refer to specific assessment procedures learned in the diagnosis and corrective reading courses (EDU584 & EDU590), thus adding deep descriptive data and cross validating the quantitative ranking of these two required courses.

Table 2: Verbatim Comments that Support the Patterns

Emerging Patterns	Typical Verbatim Responses
Growth in Professional Relationships	• "I am able to speak to my colleagues in a professional manner about reading issues in the reading profession." • "The final and most important success that I have had through my experiences has been collegiality and the understanding of its importance in my professional development."
Literacy Strategies Transferred into Daily Practice	• "Modeled reading strategies for science, social studies, and music." • "[Course work] helped me create a foundation on which to help {struggling} readers…I was given innovative strategies supported by research."
Value of Diagnostic and Corrective Strategies	• "As a result of attending Corrective Reading I now understand the value of assessing before instructing…from Reading Diagnosis I know to get an idea of what the child knows and teach to [those] strengths."
High Stakes Testing as a Pressing Issue	• "Course work gave me a calmer perspective on dealing with high-stakes testing. I now know strategies I can use daily to help my students learn."

Discussion

This study served two purposes. It was a formative evaluation of our graduate reading program's impact on our graduates' instructional practice. The study questions and subsequent methodology serve to provide a broad lens through which to view the impact of a graduate program, which prepares reading professionals in the highly diverse urban environments in which they live and work. Furthermore, the study results helped clarify the praxis between the theoretical framework of a graduate reading program, the graduates' teaching practices, and their subsequent impact as literacy resource experts.

These data suggest that our program positively affects the instructional decisions and practices of our graduates in their literacy communities. We also use these data to understand what activities impact learning in our courses, and to facilitate differentiated assignments so that coursework is appropriate to graduate students who are in varying stages of their careers. Simply put, these data serve to motivate improvement within our courses and our program as a whole. Additionally, the results suggest that other faculty researchers need to be proactive in providing evidence that documents the important role of their graduate programs in preparing highly qualified reading specialists.

This study also provides insight into the needs of our graduate students and the value they place on specific graduate reading coursework as it influences their daily instructional work. Analysis of the responses to the question asking which courses they valued most suggests that they valued the classes that exposed them to assessment, diagnosis, and strategic strategies. This aligns with the research of Bean, et al. (2003), Quatroche et al. (2001), and the IRA Commission on Reading Specialists (2000) which indicated that the primary roles of the reading specialist include assessor, instructor and resource provider. The quantitative data, cross-validated by qualitative data, suggested that of the 10 required courses in the state-approved graduate reading program, seven had been ranked as most helpful when graduates consider the impact of these courses on their work in the field. All of these courses not only presented evidence-based reading research and exemplify proven strategies, but included field experiences where graduate students had the opportunity to design and implement appropriate strategies with students.

Finally, the graduate students reported that their courses, along with their field experiences, have increased their confidence as collegial professionals acting as reading specialists. Their comments suggested that their pedagogical expertise has allowed them to move into positions outside the classroom where they act with confidence as reading resource personnel, reading coaches, and reading leaders in diverse urban environments. Their confidence as reading professionals seems to be an important issue as we look at their varying roles as emerging leaders. The importance of this confidence has been supported by researchers and theorists (Bean et al., 2003; IRA, 2000).

High stakes testing and working with struggling readers were most often cited as pressing issues. Of these, high stakes testing emerged as the most vital. While this may be perceived as an issue over which the graduate reading program has the least control, the data from the rankings for diagnosis and corrective imply that a key remedy to this issue is to provide pertinent and practical content in assessment courses. As the IRA position statement (IRA, 1999, 2000) notes, the reading specialist must know how to serve as a resource to help schools and students to meet this critical challenge. When referring specifically to high stakes testing, the IRA (2000) position statement recommends that the role of teachers is to create assessment rich environments in classrooms and schools and to recognize that accountability is a necessary part of education. The position statement (IRA, 2000) further recommends that teachers be prepared to explain the validity and the role of classroom assessment, which also implies that colleges of education that have graduate reading programs must also meet this challenge through research and proactive coursework in assessment and diagnosis.

This investigation provides one piece of evidence to begin to rebut reports that suggest that teacher preparation programs do not adequately prepare educators for the use of "scientifically based research" methodology in their instructional planning for the teaching of reading (Lyons. 1998; Teacher liberation, 2003). While these data are interesting, further research needs to be enacted to highlight components of not only graduate reading programs that enhance the graduates' ability to be effective in their roles as reading professionals, but of graduate reading programs in general. Next steps in this long-term study will be to include a continuation of the survey instrument with new graduates, and the addition of focus groups, observations, and interviews in an attempt to gather rich, in-depth information about the impact of our graduate students on their literacy communities.

Given the scarcity of evidence-based literature on graduate reading programs and their impact on teacher/educator practices, this study hones in on a niche yet to be explored. This research is important to teacher educators and researchers because it addresses imperative issues in literacy education. This study's results point to areas of future research in graduate literacy education while beginning to fill the need for empirical (both robust qualitative and quantitative) evidence regarding how to invest our resources to improve teacher graduate education in the field of literacy (Hoffman & Pearson, 2000; Hoffman & Roller, 2001; Langenberg et al., 2000; Pearson, 2001; Roller,2001; Strickland, 2001; Wilson et al., 2001). This is only the beginning of research that produces data on the effective practices of graduate reading programs. It is time to focus on graduate reading programs' positive impact on the expertise and practice of reading specialists and their students' learning by designing, evaluating and valuing programs "to encourage the continuing improvement of college and university curricula and encourage preparation programs for teachers and reading specialists" (Association of Literacy Educators and Researchers, 2009).

References
Anders, P., Hoffman, J. V., & Duffy, G. G. (2000). Teaching teachers to teach: Paradigm shifts, persistent problems, and challenges. In M. L. Kamil, P. B. Mosenthal, P. D. Pearson & R. Barr (Eds.), *Handbook of Reading Research* (Vol. III, pp. 719-742).

Mahwah, NJ: Lawrence Erlbaum.

Association of Literacy Educators and Researchers (2009) Goals of the Association of Literacy Educators and Researchers. Retrieved January 12, 2009 from, the Association of Literacy Educators and Researchers Web Site: http://aleronline.org/index.html.

Bean, R. M., Swan, A. L., & Knaub, R. (2003). Reading Specialist in schools with exemplary programs: Functional, versatile, and prepared. *The Reading Teacher, 56*, 446-454.

Burk, J. A. G. (1989). *Six case studies of preservice teachers and the development of language and learning theories.* Unpublished Dissertation, Texas A & M University, College Station, TX.

Darling-Hammond, L. (1997). *Doing what matters most: Investing in quality teaching.* New York: National Commission on Teaching and America's Future

Darling-Hammond, L. (2000). Solving the problems of teacher supply, demand, and standards: How can we ensure a competent, caring, and qualified teacher for every child. New York: Teachers College Press.

Flint, A. S., Leland, C. H., Patterson, B., Hoffman, J. V., Sailors, M. W., Mast, M. A., & Assaf, L. C.. (2001). I'm still figuring out how to do this teaching thing: A cross-site analysis of reading preparation programs on beginning teachers' instructional practices and decisions. In C. M. Roller (Ed.), *Learning to teach reading: Setting the research agenda* (pp. 100-118). Newark, DE: International Reading Association.

Haid, L. K. (2005) A preliminary look at the effect of a change in pre-service literacy curricula on the pedagogical content knowledge of literacy and theoretical orientation to reading of teacher candidates. In P. Linder, M. B. Sampson, J.A. Dugan, & B. Brancato (Eds.), *Building Bridges to Literacy*, (pp 115-135). Commerce, TX: College Reading Association.

Hasbrook, M. (2002). *Blah or Praxis? Reflection in Freirean Pedagogy.* Paper presented at the Annual Meeting of the National Council of Teachers of English. from http://search.ebscohost.com/login.aspx?direct=true&db=eric&AN=ED474969&site=ehost-live.

Hoffman, J. V., & Pearson, P. D. (2000). Reading teacher education in the next millennium: What your grandmother's teacher didn't know that your granddaughter's teacher should. *Reading Research Quarterly, 35*, 28-44.

Hoffman, J. V., & Roller, C. M. (2001). The IRA excellence in Reading Teacher Preparation Commission's report: Current practices in reading teacher education at the undergraduate level in the United States. In C. M. Roller (Ed.), *Learning to teach reading: Setting the research agenda* (pp. 32-79). Newark, Delaware: International Reading Association.

International Reading Association. (1999). High-stakes assessments in reading: A position statement of the International Reading Association. J*ournal of Adolescent & Adult Literacy, 43*, 305.

International Reading Association. (2000). *Teaching all children to read: The roles of the reading specialist. A position statement of the International Reading Association.* (No. 1081-3004): Journal of Adolescent & Adult Literacy.

International Reading Association. (2007). *Teaching reading well: A synthesis of the International Reading Association's research on teacher preparation for reading instruction.* Newark, DE.

Johnson, M. (2006). Preparing reading specialists to become competent travelers in urban settings. *Urban Education, 41*, 402-426.

Lalik, R., & Potts, A. (2001). Social reconstruction as a framework for literacy teacher education. In C. M. Roller (Ed.), *Learning to teach reading: Setting the research agenda* (pp.119-135). Newark, DE: International Reading Association.

Langenberg, D. N., Correro, G., Ehri, L., Ferguson, G., Garza, N., Kamil, M. L., et al. (2000). T*eaching children to read: An evidence-based assessment of the scientific research* *literature on reading and its implications for reading instruction.* Washington, DC: National Institute of Child Health and Human Development.

Lyon, R. G. (1998). *Overview of reading and literacy initiatives* (No. CS 014 072 075). Washington, DC: National Institute of Child Health and Human Development.

Maloch, B., Flint, A. S., Eldridge, D., & Harmon, J. (2003). Understandings, beliefs, and reported decisions made by first-year teachers from different reading teacher preparation programs. *The Elementary School Journal, 103*(5), 431-457, 536.

O'Callaghan, C. M. (1997, March 1997). *Social construction of preservice teachers' instructional strategies for reading.* Paper presented at the Annual meeting of the American Education Research Association, Chicago, IL.

Patterson, R. S., Michelli, N. M., & Pacheco, A. (1999). *Centers of Pedagogy: New structures for renewal* (Vol. 2). San Francisco: Jossey-Bass.

Pearson, P. D. (1996). Six ideas in search of a champion: What policy makers should know about the teaching and learning of literacy in our schools? *Journal of Literacy Research, 28*, 301-309.

Pearson, P. D. (2001). Learning to teach reading: The status of the knowledge base. In C. M. Roller (Ed.), *Learning to teach reading: Setting the research agenda* (pp. 4-19). Newark, DE: International Reading Association.

Purcell-Gates, V. (2000). Family Literacy. In M. L. Kamil, P. B. Mosenthal, P. D. Pearson & R. Barr (Eds.), *Handbook of Reading Research* (Vol. 3, pp. 853-870). Mahwah, NJ: Lawrence Erlbaum Associates.

Quatroche, D. J., Bean, R. M., & Hamilton, R. L. (2001). The role of the reading specialist: A review of the research. *The Reading Teacher, 55*, 282-294.

Roller, C. M. (2001). A proposed research agenda for teacher preparation in reading. In C. M. Roller (Ed.), *Learning to teach reading: Setting the research agenda.* (pp. 198-205) Newark, DE: International Reading Association.

Strickland, D. S. (2001). The interface of teacher preparation, and research: Improving the quality of teachers. In C. M. Roller (Ed.), *Learning to teach reading: Setting the research agenda* (pp. 20-29). Newark, DE: International Reading Association.

Strickland, K. (1990). *Changes in perspective student teachers' development of a reading philosophy* (Research No. ERIC Document Retrieval Service No. ED331037). Las Vegas, NV: Annual Meeting of the Association of Teacher Educators.

Walsh, K., & Thomas B. Fordham Foundation, W., DC. (2006). *Teacher Education: Coming Up Empty. Fwd: Arresting Insights in Education. Volume 3, Number 1:* Thomas B. Fordham Foundation & Institute.

Warner, J.V.W., Masztal, N.B., & Murphy, A., (2005) Literacy practicum experiences in an urban setting: Building bridges with the school, home, and community. In P. Linder, M. B. Sampson, J.A. Dugan, & B. Brancato (Eds.), *Building Bridges to Literacy*, (pp 258-274). Commerce, TX: College Reading Association.

Wilson, S. M., Floden, R. E., & Ferrini-Mundy, J. (2001). *Teacher preparation research: Current knowledge, gaps, and recommendations* (Research Report No. R-01-3). Seattle, WA: Center for the Study of Teaching and Policy.

Worthen, B. R., & Sanders, J. R. (1987). *Educational evaluation: Alternative approaches and practical guidelines.* White Plains, NY: Longman.

Appendix: Survey

Name_____

(1) I am currently a (circle one): classroom teacher, reading coach, reading specialist, reading leader or other (specify) _____

(2) School & grade level where I presently work_____

(3) School district where I am employed _____

(4) Number of years employed in education_____

(5) Grade levels taught _____

(6) Phone number _____

(7) E-mail address _____

(8) Degrees held and majors: respond as applicable

B.A. /B.S. in_____ from _____ (university)

        major _____

M.S. /M.A. /M.Ed. in _____ from _____ (university)

        major _____

Ed.S. in _____ from _____ (university)

        major _____

Location of [name of school] graduate studies:

Main campus _____ or Cohort location_____

National Board Certification in _____

Ed.S. in _____ from _____

1. Rate the [name of school] Graduate Reading courses that are most useful in helping you solve your professional challenges by ranking each course from 1 to 5, with **5 being the most useful** OR Did Not Take (DNT). Circle your response.

REQUIRED COURSES:

		Least Useful - Most Useful
EDU 601	Methodology of Research	1 – 2 – 3 – 4 – 5 DNT
EDU 535	Teaching of Language Arts	1 – 2 – 3 – 4 – 5 DNT
EDU 567	Foundations of Reading Instruction	1 – 2 – 3 – 4 – 5 DNT
EDU 568	Reading in the Content Area	1 – 2 – 3 – 4 – 5 DNT
EDU 584	Reading Diagnosis	1 – 2 – 3 – 4 – 5 DNT
EDU 590	Corrective Reading	1 – 2 – 3 – 4 – 5 DNT
EDU 607	Beginning Reading for the Primary Years	1 – 2 – 3 – 4 – 5 DNT
EDU 718	Developmental Reading	1 – 2 – 3 – 4 – 5 DNT
EDU 716	Advanced Diagnosis & Remediation in Reading	1 – 2 – 3 – 4 – 5 DNT
EDU 717	Practicum in Reading	1 – 2 – 3 – 4 – 5 DNT

ELECTIVE COURSES:

EDU 604	Teaching Vocabulary & Reading Comprehension	1 – 2 – 3 – 4 – 5 DNT
EDU 611	Reading and Thinking Skills	1 – 2 – 3 – 4 – 5 DNT
EDU 612	Teaching Reading to Secondary, College & Adult Students	1 – 2 – 3 – 4 – 5 DNT
EDU 613	Methods of the Reading Resource Teacher	1 – 2 – 3 – 4 – 5 DNT
EDU 631	Administration and Supervision of Reading Programs of Reading Programs	1 – 2 – 3 – 4 – 5 DNT
ECT 676	Computer/Tech Applications in the Teaching of Reading	1 – 2 – 3 – 4 – 5 DNT

2. Identify a minimum of three (3) successes or positive experiences you have had with your students and/or your colleagues that you can attribute to your graduate coursework in Reading at [name of school]. Describe each event in a brief paragraph.

3. Identify, at least three (3) pressing issues that impact the teaching of reading and writing which you face in your current job as a reading professional. Briefly explain each issue. In addition, describe how your graduate coursework in Reading at [name of school] has helped you meet these challenges.

4. List the successful strategies, learned in your graduate Reading coursework, that you use in your daily work as a reading professional..

   Please return this survey in the enclosed postage prepaid envelope.
   Thank you for your participation.

If you would be interested in participating in a focus group relating to this important research please check the box below. The focus group would take about 1.5 hours of your time. It would help us immensely in evaluating and improving our program.

   ☐ Yes, I would like to participate in a focus group.

ACTION RESEARCH: ARE WE EFFECTIVELY PREPARING OUR FUTURE READING SPECIALISTS?

Roberta Linder, Ed.D.

Wittenberg University

Abstract

This article describes a study which was conducted in order to determine how action research could help master's candidates transform from classroom teachers into future reading specialists ready to utilize the research process in their school settings. The action research concept was taken directly from existing master's programs at the university and integrated into a recent master's degree for reading specialists. Utilizing surveys to collect data at the beginning, mid-point, and end of the research project, the researcher has been able to identify ways to support and guide the candidates as they undertake their action research projects.

Although action research projects are frequently a requirement of numerous master's degree programs, candidates often initially respond to this assignment with anxiety, indifference, or annoyance. For many, the term *research* conjures up images of control groups, independent and dependent variables, and statistical analyses. The candidates become overwhelmed with the notion of designing a study, and the action research introductory course and instructor must first dispel many misconceptions about research. However, once the candidates understand how action research differs from traditional forms of research and how they can investigate issues involving their own pedagogy and students, they may develop and continue to embrace an inquiry stance toward their profession (Snow-Gerono, 2005).

Action research is a process that can be utilized by reading specialist candidates both during their degree programs and hopefully continuing after their degree completion. Whether remaining in the classroom or entering new positions as literacy coaches or reading specialists, action research provides a framework for studying questions related to educational practices or for engaging teachers in a problem-centered approach to professional development (Puig & Froelich, 2006). For example, one component of the Literacy Educators Assessing and Developing Early Reading Success (LEADERS) professional development project (Bean,

2004) involved an action research project designed by the teachers to address an area of need identified as the result of their Literacy Assessment Battery (LAB). The careful collection and analysis of data enabled one group of teachers to document improvement in their students' writing. In addition, the International Reading Association (IRA) has acknowledged the value of action research, including it as part of Standard 6, Professional Learning and Leadership, in its proposed *Standards for Reading Professionals 2010* (IRA, 2008).

The purpose of this article is to describe how the researcher studied the action research requirement in a master's program in order to improve this project so candidates will view it as a natural part of effective instruction, a form of professional development, and a process which empowers them as educators. This study was guided by the research question, "How can an action research project be designed in order to help master's candidates engage in a meaningful experience which enables them to develop the knowledge, skills, and vision of future reading specialists?" The researcher intentionally used the term *vision* in the research question based on her observations that candidates who were nearing the completion of their programs were not yet "seeing" themselves or envisioning themselves as future reading specialists. She felt that if action research were to be such a significant component of the master's program, an outcome would be that candidates viewed themselves as reading specialists. The next section provides definitions for action research and places it within the context of adult learning theory.

Action Research

Definitions

Action research is a type of educational investigation that is conducted by educational practitioners within the context of the school. Mills (as cited in Mertler, 2009) provided this definition.

> Action research is defined as any systematic inquiry conducted by teachers, administrators, counselors, or others with a vested interest in the teaching and learning process or environment for the purpose of gathering information about how their particular schools operate, how they teach, and how their students learn. (p. 4)

Action research can be undertaken by members of an educational community in order to address problems and present solutions (Calhoun, 2004), build a professional culture and make progress on school priorities (Sagor, 2000), or promote social justice (Brydon-Miller, Greenwood, & Maguire, 2003).

Similar terms, such as *teacher research* or *teacher inquiry* are often used interchangeably with action research although these terms indicate that the study is being conducted by the classroom teacher (Lassonde, Ritchie, & Fox, 2008). References to teacher inquiry may be more applicable in situations when an emphasis is being placed on the role of questions and inquiry in classroom investigations or when the objective is to make the research process less intimidating.

All of these forms of research represent investigations conducted in an educational setting for the purpose of making improvements within that specific context, and they follow a similar series of steps within the research process: identifying a need; writing research question(s); designing a study; collecting, analyzing, and interpreting the data; explaining the findings; and determining conclusions and implications (Falk-Ross & Cuevas, 2008).

Adult Learning Theory

Action research incorporates many of the elements that promote adult learning, making it a valuable component of a master's program serving practitioners. For example, Rosemary, Roskos, and Landreth (2007) stated that adults learn best when their learning is active, based on their background knowledge, and places an emphasis on learning to understand. Because it engages the teacher as an active learner, action research can provide teachers with a sense of empowerment (Godt, 2007; Levin & Merritt, 2006). According to Burnaford, Beane, and Brodhagen (1994), teacher action research "enables a teacher to explore her/his own classroom as a decision-maker, a peer, a leader, and a learner—not just as an implementer, curriculum consumer, and recipient of external change mandates" (p. 5). Trotter (2006) acknowledged the importance of teachers' past experience, but she also noted the significance of learner input and choice and the need for reflection and inquiry. Teachers can choose to implement and study ideas presented at workshops (Burnaford et al., 1994), or they can use action research as a means for gaining new knowledge, strengthening existing skills, refining their diagnostic skills in analyzing their own practice, and learn to see their classroom and instruction from the students' view (Stark, 2006). Because action research requires teachers to be active learners as they investigate and reflect on self-selected topics that are relevant to their professional experiences, adult learners can engage in an activity that acknowledges their unique learning needs.

Description of the Study

Research Design

This study utilized survey research in order to collect data from candidates attending classes in many different locations. Data collection began in April, 2008 and concluded twelve months later. A cross-sectional design (Mertens, 1998) allowed the researcher to sample responses from groups of candidates at three different points in their master's programs: beginning research class, mid-point of the program, and the final research class.

The survey instruments contained both closed and open formats. The closed format section contained items which were rated on a scale of 1 to 4 by the candidates. In the surveys for the research courses, the candidates rated the usefulness of various materials and activities used within the courses. In the mid-point survey, candidates rated the amount of progress they had been able to make on their investigation and their writing. The open format portion of the surveys contained questions designed to elicit responses from the candidates related to the impact the action research process had made upon them, their students, and other stakeholders such as colleagues, parents, and administrators. For a number of reasons, the questions focused on the candidates' classroom activities rather than the types of reading specialist activities included in the IRA standards (2004). First, the action research project was originally implemented in the same manner as the other master's programs, focusing on the classroom settings of the candidates. Second, because the initial research course occurs so early in the program sequence, candidates have had limited experience with assignments related to coaching and collaboration. These activities are embedded in other courses which they encounter throughout the program. Third, action research projects have more recently been conducted by candidates who are employed as reading specialists and literacy coaches, and these projects are investigating topics related to working with colleagues and the students of classroom teachers. Appendices A, B, and C contain examples of the three surveys used in the study.

Structure of the Action Research Project in the Study

This action research project is a component of a 36-semester hour master's program preparing candidates for reading specialist certification. The introductory course generally occurs as the third or fourth course within the sequence, and the course for the culmination of the project takes place near the end of the program. This format allows the candidates to have some flexibility in the initiation and conclusion of their projects and to engage in their research project for an extended period of time within a school year. The instructor for the introductory course maintains contact with the candidates throughout the research process via e-mail and/or individual or group meetings and teaches the final course devoted to the completion of the projects. The candidates are required to adhere to the requirements of the informed consent process before initiating their research. Their final product is a written document containing five well-developed chapters: (1) introduction, (2) review of the literature, (3) methodology, (4) findings, and (5) implications and conclusions. They must also prepare a PowerPoint presentation based on their research and present to their building or district personnel, if possible. In cases where candidates do not have the opportunity to present in their own districts or buildings, other arrangements are made to provide an audience other than the members of their cohort. For example, some candidates have made their presentations to other cohorts in the reading specialist program, offering those candidates a glimpse at the outcomes of action research projects and giving them an authentic audience for their presentations.

Context and Participants

This study was conducted in a small, private, mid-western institution offering degrees at the undergraduate, graduate, and doctoral levels. The campus is situated in a diverse, suburban community located about 40 miles west of a major metropolitan area. The graduate programs are held primarily off-campus in facilities offered by hosting school districts and Regional Offices of Education. The master's program for the preparation of reading specialists is one of the most recent additions to the College of Education, offering courses for the first time in 2005. The concept of the action research project was cloned from existing master's programs which required the project for program completion, and many of the same materials were initially used in the course instruction (e.g., text, action research manual). However, as the action research courses were implemented and evaluated, the text was changed and the action research manual was revised to be more specific to the needs of reading specialist candidates, incorporating examples from the field of literacy rather than educational leadership or general classroom pedagogy. The introductory and concluding research courses are each three semester hours of credit and are offered as 8-week courses during the school year and as 2-week courses in the summer.

In addition to the researcher, five other instructors have worked with the candidates on the action research projects. In terms of rank, two were full-time faculty (one assistant professor and one professor), two were pro-rata, and two were part-time instructors. Five of the instructors had doctorates and one was ABD, in the process of completing her degree in literacy education. All of the action research instructors had a master's or doctorate in reading. The full-time faculty members supervised the research of candidates in 3 to 4 cohorts, and the pro-rata and part-time instructors each worked with one cohort.

Data were collected from 14 cohorts at different points in their master's programs and action research projects. Each of the cohorts was located in an area with distinctive demographic characteristics. Four of the cohorts were comprised of candidates from the communities adjacent to the university and met on the campus. Located east of the campus and closer in proximity to the major metropolitan area were two cohorts: one containing predominantly white middle class students, and the other predominantly Hispanic lower income families. Three cohorts met in two geographic areas north of the campus with differing demographics. One of the cohorts met in a large, urban area containing a large percentage of non-white, lower income families, and the other cohorts were situated in communities populated by mostly white, middle class families. The remaining five cohorts lay west of the campus in rather dissimilar communities. Two cohorts met in a predominantly white, middle class, small town communities; one met in a working class community which was experiencing a growing population of Black and Hispanic students (35%); and two cohorts were located in rural communities which contained very little racial/ethnic diversity. The average size of the cohorts ranged between 11 and 16 candidates. Responses were collected from the candidates involved in the action research courses, therefore excluding candidates enrolled for the reading endorsement rather than the reading specialist certification and degree.

Data Collection and Analysis

At the appropriate times in the cohorts' programs (i.e., introductory research course, mid-way point, final research course), packets of survey materials were disseminated to the instructors who were directed to conduct the surveys in their final class meeting. Each packet contained a sheet of directions to be read to the candidates, surveys for the candidates, a survey for the instructor, and an envelope in which the completed surveys were placed and sealed. Although the researcher, the chair of the master's program and one of the research instructors, had prepared the materials for the surveys, her identity was not associated with the study. The materials were distributed and collected through the secretary of the master's programs, and this enabled the researcher to survey her own classes without their knowledge of her involvement with the study.

Because the surveys contained both numerical ratings and written responses to open-ended questions, different types of data analysis were employed. Descriptive statistics were computed for the candidates' ratings using SPSS 16.0 for Windows. Candidates' written responses were coded and analyzed for patterns and themes.

Findings

The purpose of this study was to address the question, "How can an action research project be designed in order to help master's candidates engage in a meaningful experience which enables them to develop the knowledge, skills, and vision of future reading specialists?" The data gathered from the candidate surveys and action research report reflections yielded findings at each of the three evaluation points within the study.

First Evaluation Point: After the Introductory Course

The candidates completed the survey instrument in the last session of their introductory course. Table 1 summarizes the elements that the candidates considered to be most useful in the course as well as the materials and activities that the candidates rated as least useful.

Table 1: Ratings from Introductory Course—4 Highest and 3 Lowest Rated Materials and Activities

Material	Number of responses	Mean[a]	Standard Deviation
Instructor's professional resources	77	3.83	0.44
Access to computers during class	77	3.78	0.58
Feedback from instructor on rough drafts	77	3.75	0.59
Action research manual	77	3.71	0.53
Peer editing of chapters	77	3.13	0.83
Guest speaker— electronic resources[b]	16	2.81	1.17
Text: *The Art of Classroom Inquiry*	77	2.60	1.02

[a] 1 indicates the item was not useful, 4 indicates it was very useful
[b] This activity was discontinued and later handled by course instructors

As shown in Table 1, the candidates valued materials which provided them with concrete examples of completed projects and specific guidelines for the completion of the project (i.e., the action research manual). They also found the assistance of the instructor to be helpful, particularly when professional materials were brought to the candidates for their use. This was especially important in cohorts located 75 to 100 miles from the campus that did not have access to the types of texts which would generally be available in the university library.

Candidates' responses to the open-ended questions also yielded valuable feedback. In addition to the materials rated as most useful in the course (see Table 1), the candidates also felt that PowerPoint presentations which provided them with information critical to their action research projects (e.g., introduction to action research, APA style, academic writing) were helpful. In particular, candidates were often intimidated and frustrated when attempting to use the APA manual and felt they benefitted by seeing the most common forms of APA style that would be needed for their written reports. The most effective use of class time for the beginning researchers included being given time to share their ideas and struggles and opportunities to use computers for research and writing with the guidance of the instructor. Several candidates also appreciated instructors who provided prompt feedback via electronic editing of texts.

Candidates reported gaining numerous new skills and insights as a result of their introductory research class. First, they acquired skills related to the research process such as locating sources of information, using APA style, conducting research with greater confidence, and understanding how action research can be used to inform their instructional practices. One candidate wrote, "*I've really learned how to research! And have been made aware of all the sources available to me for when I become a read-*

ing specialist." Second, they responded that the project impacted their pedagogy by demonstrating how research and theory can be connected to classroom instruction and how they can improve aspects of their teaching. One candidate reflected back to her undergraduate coursework, *"Theories were very good. I had not thought about theories or theorists since my undergrad classes, and at that point I had no teaching experience to fall back on."* Another candidate wrote about her current classroom instruction.

> *This class made me choose an area in my teaching that I was not comfortable with and do something about it. I would have never researched it to the depth I did if it was something I was doing on my own. As a result I feel I am in part a better educator and will do a better job meeting the needs of my students.*

Third, a number of candidates noted that the action research project had led them to improve their own literacy skills, particularly their writing mechanics and their ability to synthesize current research.

Second Evaluation Point: At the Mid-point of the Project

The candidates completed the survey instrument when their instructor/advisor met with them near the mid-point of their program (i.e., 18 semester hours). Table 2 summarizes how candidates rated their progress on their research projects half-way through the master's program.

Table 2: Ratings from Progress Survey (after approximately 18 semester hours)

Status of project	Number of responses	Mean[a]	Standard Deviation
Obtained parent permissions	50	3.38	0.83
Implemented intervention	50	3.07	0.78
Began collecting data	51	2.98	0.72
Worked on revisions to chap. 1 & 2	54	3,07	0.86
Began writing methodology chapter 3	52	2.32	0.99

[a]1 indicates the study is progressing very poorly, 4 indicates it is progressing very smoothly

As seen in Table 2, the items related to the implementation of their research were rated as progressing smoothly (i.e., rated > 3), but the items related to the writing of their reports were rated as progressing somewhat poorly (i.e., rated > 2 > 3).

Candidates also responded to questions regarding the impact the action research has had upon them and those around them. As shown in Table 3, the vast majority of the candidates felt they had implemented a research project that addressed an area of need in their classroom or program, produced changes in their students' reading habits/skills/attitudes, led to a deeper understanding of one aspect of literacy instruction, and attracted the interest of their colleagues, administrators, and/or parents. For example, one researcher stated that *"We share ideas in our team meetings. Several colleagues have used several strategies,"* and another wrote *"My first grade team mates are looking forward to implementing Text Talk in their day next school year."* Additional responses revealed that the most rewarding aspects of the projects were the changes noted in students' reading performance and attitudes toward reading, changes in pedagogy or philosophy, improved relationships with parents, and expanded knowledge about reading. As stated by one candidate, *"I feel much more knowledgeable about teaching reading fluency to my first grade students as well as being able to share my knowledge with my fellow teachers."* Another noted a change that had taken place in her classroom, writing *"I feel that reading is a very positive thing in my classroom where it hadn't always been that way."* Candidates' responses also indicated that 23 of them had made some minor changes in their research plans which were usually related to their intervention, assessment and data collection, or duration of their study.

Table 3: Responses from Progress Survey

Project Outcome	Yes	No	Comments
Able to implement intervention that addressed an area of need	48	5	N/A--6
Observe changes in students	39	12	N/A--7 Too soon Reading for enjoyment (nonfiction texts)
Deeper understanding of one aspect of literacy instruction	52	2	N/A--4 Learned from reading the research Would not have found the time had it not been for the action research project
Interest in project from others	42	13	N/A--4 19 mentioned colleagues 8 mentioned administrators 5 mentioned parents

Although candidates were able to articulate many positive outcomes as they were conducting their studies, three areas of challenge were noted. First, time presented the greatest obstacle, interfering with the implementation of the studies and with the continued writing of the action research reports. Second, aspects of the research process were noted by the candidates, specifically issues with getting the necessary materials and participants to get started and organizing and collecting data. Third, elements of the classroom context often impeded the research process, such as dealing with students and colleagues, trying to stay on track and not slip back into old habits, and having to conduct the research in a setting other than a classroom.

Third Evaluation Point: After the Final Course

The survey results were obtained by instructors who completed action research projects with their cohorts. In addition to the surveys, the researcher was able to review the reflections written in the conclusions in the finished reports of the completers, and these reflections provided additional information for the study.

Similar to the responses provided by candidates in the introductory research course, these candidates indicated that the activities that were most useful to them were computer access and time to work on the computers during class. Candidates benefitted from the immediate feedback from the instructors, guidance on using the software, and access to the most current versions of the software. Surprising in their low ratings from the candidates were the presentations made to colleagues and/or candidates and the peer review process. Sharing results with other professionals should be an expected outcome of an action research project, however, a number of candidates did not view this as a beneficial activity. The peer review process received low ratings from some candidates because they felt they had not been given the opportunity to do this in their class or had not been given ample time for the editing. Mentioned again as one of the least useful aspects of the class was the text, *The Art of Classroom Inquiry* (Hubbard & Power, 2003) along with supplemental readings distributed by the instructors.

Table 4: Ratings from Final Course—3 Highest and 4 Lowest Rated Materials and Activities

Material	Number of responses	Mean[a]	Standard Deviation
Access to computers during class	40	3.98	0.16
Time to work on report during class	40	3.85	0.43
Time to work on presentation in class	40	3.73	0.68
Presenting findings of study	40	2.89	0.95
Peer review of chapters	40	2.64	1.04
Supplemental reading material	40	2.59	0.86
Text: *The Art of Classroom Inquiry*	40	2.37	0.97

[a]1 indicates the item was not useful, 4 indicates it was very useful

The candidates' written responses provided evidence of the professional growth that can occur as the result of engaging in action research. They shared that they had gained new skills in using technology, now recognized the importance of systematically collecting and analyzing data, planned to continue using the interventions they had investigated, and had developed an understanding of the research process. One graduate responded that she learned "how to be a better researcher and be more evaluative of others' research," and another stated, *"I am a more critical thinker and not scared to use data to drive instruction."* Table 5 provides a summary of candidates' responses to the open-ended survey questions.

Table 5: Responses to Survey after Final Course

Project Outcome	Yes	No	Comments
Able to implement intervention that addressed an area of need	39	1	
Observe changes in students	37	1	Moderate changes—1 To some degree--1 **Not such a struggle to get students to read the text
Deeper understanding of one aspect of literacy instruction	38	0	To some degree--1 No response--1 **The lit. review was fascinating and what was learned was very valuable to my teaching practice. **I enjoyed reading about other researchers' programs & taking pieces of theirs to modify my own program that fits my needs.
Continue using intervention	34	4	Undecided--1 No response--1 **Helped with the behavior in my class
Understanding of action research process and its relation to roles as reading specialist	39		No response—1 **Ask questions—seek answers—reflect **Using the IRA standards helped me to realize how the process is vital to teachers & students. **However, most districts probably don't give teachers or specialists an opportunity to do the research—nor would many districts value the conclusions drawn.

Candidates' reflections in the final chapter of their reports addressed the strengths and weaknesses of their projects as well as insights they gained as a result of the action research process. Project strengths included the improvements in students' reading skills and motivation, increased parent participation, positive changes in classroom instruction, attention from colleagues, and the collection of data that would be valuable for future decision-making. Areas of weakness identified by the candidates were the need to make some changes in the implementation of their interventions, better selection or creation of assessment instruments, and the adoption of a more organized and systematic approach to data collection.

As a result of their participation with action research, the candidates noted several insights they had acquired. With regard to the research process, they wrote about being more knowledgeable and confident about researching and now recognizing the value of data collection and analysis. By engaging in a review of the literature for their projects, candidates acknowledged the importance of using strategies supported by research and literature and the need to stay current with developments in the field of literacy. Many also felt that the project enabled them to improve their classroom instruction. In the beginning of this study, when the candidates were directed to connect their research experience with the roles of a reading specialist as stated in the 2003 IRA standards, many of their comments connected more with their current practices as teachers of reading. However, when the directions for the reflections were made more specific and included guiding questions for the candidates, written responses were more focused on the roles of the reading specialists as well as the use of action research, noted in the comments of these candidates.

- *Districts are so quick to bring in "experts" before looking at the strengths and expertise of their own professionals. The reading specialist could promote professional development from the "inside" by convincing teachers that they have the capacities to guide the direction of educational practices through action research.*

- *As a reading specialist, a piece of the job description is to provide professional development and what better way than to have "in-house" professional development in classrooms to reflect and refine one's own practice. The action research project taught the researcher that the questions that need to be investigated and documented happen every day in every classroom.*

Although this study has been able to collect data for twelve months from candidates at different points in their master's programs, some limitations should be noted. First, as with any kind of survey research, the results are based on self-report and the comments reflect the candidates' personal perceptions about the success of their projects, knowledge they have gained, or the impact on colleagues. Second, due to the length of the study, no cohort has been surveyed throughout its entire action research project. However, data have been collected from two cohorts at the beginning and progress check points in their research and from three cohorts at the mid-point and end of their research. Third, although candidates were asked to support their yes/no responses with short explanations for their responses, many did not provide written explanations. These comments would have provided further insights into the outcomes of action research projects.

Conclusions and Implications

The action research component of this reading specialist master's program has the potential to provide the candidates with a process which can empower them to make their own instruction more effective, provide professional development for themselves and their colleagues, and improve student performance and parent relationships. Based on the findings, it can be concluded that the candidates felt that they had positive experiences with their action research projects. But even though the candidates generally responded positively to their action research projects, was it a meaningful experience which enabled them to develop the knowledge, skills, and vision of future reading specialists? Judging from the reflection statements, although some candidates were not yet able to envision themselves in the roles of reading specialists, others were beginning to conceive of ways to utilize the action research process subsequent to the completion of their projects.

Based on the feedback from these surveys, a number of changes have been implemented in the action research courses.

- Course instructors meet with the cohort prior to the first action research class in order to provide information, ideas, and encouragement before starting the class
- A statement has been added to the syllabus of the first course indicating that the inquiry process can and should be utilized by reading specialists
- Adoption of a new text
- Revisions to the action research manual
- Sample projects provided for all instructors
- Presentations of completed action research projects made to candidates in the introductory course
- Revised course sequence in which the two courses will be offered closer to the end of the program and will be back-to-back for a full semester devoted to the action research projects; no other classes will be taken during this time

The results of this study have been shared with the instructors supervising the action research projects so they can view the process from the candidates' perspectives, design instruction to better meet their needs, and continue to impress upon the candidates the importance of applying an inquiry process to their work as reading specialists.

This study has several implications for literacy teacher education programs utilizing the action research process. First, the candidates frequently commented about the numerous contributions of their course instructors. They looked to their instructors to provide support in the form of timely feedback on their working drafts, knowledge and skills on the computer with electronic research and utilization of software, and individual conferences during and outside of class time. The candidates also valued instructors who were able to break down the steps of the research process for them and provide deadlines throughout the project. This helped to keep them on track and minimize stress at the completion of the project. Second, the candidates appreciated instructors who shared their professional materials with the classes, particularly those classes that met off campus. Not only did this provide the candidates with resources for their literature reviews, but they would often purchase texts for themselves as a result, developing their own professional collections. Third, time to work on the computers during class was noted in the surveys for both research classes. Candidates commented that they benefitted from the immediate feedback of the instructor, being able to focus on their research without distractions, and having software available that they may not have on their home computers. Fourth, candidates wanted models—completed action research projects, templates for the organization and writing of the chapters, samples of chapters, and presentations made by candidates finishing their projects. As this master's program has developed, more exemplars have been identified and provided for the candidates. Finally, systematic data collection and analysis are not only elements of action research but are essential components of program evaluation and revision. Teacher education programs can also benefit from engaging in research which guides their program evaluation and development.

Action research need not be viewed by candidates as an arduous assignment required for the completion of a master's program. Rather, it can be presented to future reading specialists as a valuable tool for their own continued professional development, for engaging their colleagues in professional development, and for studying and analyzing literacy issues within an educational setting, thereby bringing about change in themselves and others.

References

Bean, R. M. (2004). *The reading specialist: Leadership for the classroom, school, and community.* New York: Guilford.

Brydon-Miller, M., Greenwood, D., & Maguire, P. (2003). Why action research? *Action Research, 1*(1), 9-28.

Burnaford, G., Beane, J., & Brodhagen, B. (1994). Teacher action research: Inside an integrative curriculum. *Middle School Journal, 26,* 5-13.

Calhoun, E. (2004). *Using data to assess your reading program.* Alexandria, VA: Association for Supervision and Curriculum Development.

Falk-Ross, F., & Cuevas, P. D. (2008). Getting the big picture: An overview of the teacher research process. In C. A. Lassonde & S. E. Israel (Eds.), *Teachers taking action: A comprehensive guide to teacher research* (pp. 15-26). Newark, DE: International Reading Association.

Godt, P. T. (2007). Action research: Putting teachers into the driver's seat when planning classroom research studies. *Illinois Reading Council Journal, 35*(3) 39-43.

Hubbard, R. S., & Power, B. M. (2003). *The art of classroom inquiry: A handbook for teacher-researchers* (Rev.ed.). Portsmouth, NH: Heinemann.

International Reading Association. (2004). *Standards for reading professionals*—Revised 2003. Newark, DE: author.

International Reading Association. (2008). *Standards for reading professionals 2010: Draft 1—November 2008.* Available at http://www.reading.org/downloads/resources/standards2008.pdf.

Lassonde, C. A., Ritchie, G. V., & Fox, R. K. (2008). How teacher research can become your way of being. In C. A. Lassonde & S. E. Israel (Eds.), *Teachers taking action: A comprehensive guide to teacher research* (pp. 3-14). Newark, DE: International Reading Association.

Levin, B. B., & Merritt, S. P. (2006). Guest editors' introduction: Action research for teacher empowerment and transformation. *Teacher Education Quarterly, 33*(3), 3-6.

Mertens, D. M. (1998). *Research methods in education and psychology: Integrating diversity with quantitative & qualitative approaches.* Thousand Oaks, CA: Sage Publications.

Mertler, C. A. (2009). *Action research: Teachers as researchers in the classroom* (2nd ed.). Los Angeles, CA: Sage.

Puig, E. A., & Froelich, K. S. (2006). *The literacy coach: Guiding in the right direction.* New York: Allyn & Bacon.

Rosemary, C. A., Roskos, K. A., & Landreth, L. K. (2007). *Designing professional development in literacy: A framework for effective instruction.* New York: Guilford.

Sagor, R. (2000). *Guiding school improvement with action research.* Alexandria, VA: Association for Supervision and Curriculum Development.

Snow-Gerono, J. L. (2005). Naming inquiry: PDS teachers' perceptions of teacher research and living an inquiry stance toward teaching. *Teacher Education Quarterly, 32*(4), 79-95.

Stark, S. (2006). Using action learning for professional development. *Educational Action-Research*, 14(1), 23-42.

Trotter, Y. D. (2006). Adult learning theories: Impacting professional development programs. *Delta Kappa Gamma Bulletin, 72*(2), 8-11.

Appendix A: Candidate Survey for Introductory Research Course

Survey For EDU6300

Rate the usefulness of the following materials, activities, or resources for EDU6300 on a scale of 1 to 4, with 1 indicating the item was not useful and 4 indicating it was very useful. N/A can be used to indicate that a rating is not applicable to the item.

Text: *The Art of Classroom Inquiry* _____

Text: *Lenses on Reading* _____

Action research manual _____

APA manual _____

PowerPoint on APA style _____

PowerPoint on reading theory _____

Guest speaker—AU electronic sources _____

Samples of chapters or projects _____

Chapter excerpt—writing questions _____

Rubrics for scoring chapters 1 & 2 _____

Access to computers during class _____

Peer editing opportunities _____

Instructor's professional resources _____

Feedback from instructor on rough drafts _____

1. List any materials or classroom activities your instructor used which you considered to be particularly effective.
2. List any struggles you experienced as you began the research process.
3. List any suggestions regarding things that would help you begin your action research project.
4. List any new skills or insights you have gained as a result of this class.

Appendix B: Survey for Mid-point in Research

Research Progress Survey—Candidate
Read the following statements regarding the implementation of your action research project. Rate the implementation of your action research project on a scale of 1 to 4, with 1 indicating the implementation is progressing very poorly and 4 indicating it is progressing very smoothly. N/A can be used to indicate that a rating is not applicable to the item.

1. I have been able to secure parent permission for the students to take part in my action research project. _____
2. I have been able to implement my intervention in my classroom. _____
3. I have been able to collect the different types of data I need for each of my research questions. _____
4. I have been able to make revisions to my rough drafts of chapters 1 and 2. _____
5. I have been able to make progress on writing my chapter 3 (methodology). _____

Answer **Yes** or **No** for each of the following questions; then provide a short explanation for your response.
1. I have been able to implement an intervention that has addressed an area of need I had identified in my classroom. _____
2, I have been able to see changes in my students' reading habits / skills / attitudes as a result of my action research project. _____
3. I have been able to develop a deeper understanding of one aspect of literacy instruction as the result of reading extensively for the literature review and then using that research as a basis for an effective intervention. _____
4. I have noticed interest in my project from colleagues, administrators, or parents. _____

1. List any changes you've had to make in your original research plan.
2. List the biggest obstacles you have faced in the implementation of your action research.
3. List the most rewarding aspects regarding the implementation of your action research.
4. List any suggestions for the improvement of the implementation phase of the action research project.

Appendix C: Survey at End of Research

SURVEY FOR EDU6400

Rate the usefulness of the following materials, activities, or resources for EDU6400 on a scale of 1 to 4, with 1 indicating the item was not useful and 4 indicating it was very useful. N/A can be used to indicate that a rating is not applicable to the item.

Text: *The Art of Classroom Inquiry* (or Sagor text) _____

Text: *Lenses on Reading* _____

Action research manual _____

APA manual _____

Supplemental readings _____

Feedback from instructor prior to 6400 _____

Feedback from instructor during 6400 _____

PowerPoint on *Academic Writing* _____

Activities/readings/examples on how to display data _____

Access to computers during class _____

Samples of chapters or action research projects _____

Time to work on chapters during class _____

Time to work on presentation during class _____

Opportunities for peer review _____

Opportunity to present to colleagues & school officials _____

1. List any materials or classroom activities your instructor used which you considered to be particularly effective.
2. List any struggles you experienced as you completed the research process.
3. List any suggestions regarding things that would help you finish your action research project.
4. List any new skills or insights you have gained as a result of this class.

Answer **Yes** or **No** for each of the following questions; then provide a short explanation for your response.

1. I was able to implement an intervention that addressed an area of need I had identified in my classroom.   _____
2. I was able to see changes in my students' reading habits / skills / attitudes as a result of my action research project.   _____
3. I was able to develop a deeper understanding of one aspect of literacy instruction as the result of reading extensively for the literature review and then using that research as a basis for an effective intervention. _____
4. I plan to continue using this reading intervention in my classroom.

                                                                              _____

5. I developed an understanding about the manner in which the action re search process (identify a need, write the questions you wish to answer, look for support in the literature and previous research, systematically collect and analyze data, draw conclusions from your data) could be useful for me in the role of a classroom teacher or a reading specialist.

                                                                              _____

Follow-up contact—Is there someone (e.g., supervisor, administrator, colleague, volunteer) who would be willing to share his/her response to your action research project, particularly regarding any implications for the building/district?

Name_____ Relationship _____

Phone_____ E-mail_____

MENTORING
CLASSROOM TEACHERS

Mentoring Teachers to Think Outside the Box: Innovations for Struggling Readers and Students with Learning Disabilities

Rebecca P. Harlin

Florida Atlantic University

Rosemary Murray

Mary E. Shea

Canisius College New York

Abstract

This article highlights the impact of teacher educators' mentoring classroom teachers as they identified and implemented innovative literacy approaches for struggling readers and students with learning disabilities. The collaborative action research projects included multimedia projects (iMovies) that improved students' writing; structured heterogeneous groups for literacy centers; practice with reading fluency and word recognition using paired repeated reading along with teacher modeling; and improved reading motivation as an outgrowth of reading aloud episodes and incentive programs. The results of this study show the power of action research in supporting teachers to question current practices and to investigate research-based solutions to their classroom problems. This tool provides teacher educators with the means to empower teachers once more.

"In an era that is rife with social controversies and political difficulties, in which public schooling has increasingly come under attack…we must educate well our teaching force" (Meyer & Manning, 2007, xi).

As literacy educators, we heeded Meyer and Manning's (2007) words and incorporated changes in our teacher preparation programs. These were specifically designed to equip teachers with the substance and the pedagogy to meet the challenges faced in today's public schools. Over time, we discovered that collaborative action research was indeed a powerful tool to educate and empower teachers.

By sharing our own experiences in schools, our first goal was to encourage teacher educators to use action research as a tool to "test" practices in their own classroom and to share the results with colleagues. It is believed this exchange will spark rich discussions, further research, and encourage the implementation of innovative practices in more classrooms. Sparking such teacher-led inquiry on practice is difficult in a climate where much curriculum is assigned, even mandated in situations, because particular programs have been approved as "research-based" practice (Conley, 2005; Garan, 2002; Smith, 2003).

Second, we sought to counter the legacy of No Child Left Behind (NCLB, 2001) on literacy instruction and teachers' beliefs by enabling teachers to question prescribed teaching practices and seek alternative strategies. The testing mandates of NCLB, as well as, the requirements for funding grants have created a climate of control under the seemingly benign cover of consistency. It disregards the reality of diversities found in today's classroom. Teachers who feel their voice diminished by NCLB mandates and prescribed reading programs need a mechanism that testifies to the importance of their ideas and their professional choices (Bracey, 2002; Garan, 2004; Smith, 2003). We discussed the difference between "research-based" and "research-tested" practices with our students. Researched-based can be applied as a label to much that is only loosely connected to valid research, limiting the generalizable, or even connected to questionable research while research-tested practices are ones that have been directly tested in a research study (Garan, 2002: Scanlon, Anderson, & Sweeney, 2010).

We asked teachers to examine the supposedly research-based practices they were using and/or test ones which seemed useful and appropriate but lacked a research-based label. The purpose of this article is to highlight the power some teachers gained through each of the projects. These projects offer insights that can easily be replicated as they are or in an adapted form - one that meets specific needs in a classroom.

Theoretical Framework

Three areas of research provide the theoretical framework for this study: 1) the principles of action research; 2) teacher's self-efficacy and empowerment; and 3) school culture and environment. By integrating these three factors, teacher-researchers can question practices, curriculums, and interactions in the classroom to determine what works and what would be more effective.

Action Research

Ideally, an action research project results from the identification of an authentic problem or situation that affects the immediate educational community (Leedy & Ormrod, 2010), as an authentic problem has more value to the researcher(s). When working in collaboration, researchers have the benefit of multiple perspectives, as well as, an opportunity for division of labor in ways that draw on everyone's strengths. However, communication among team members is critical.

It takes effort to define problems, determine and collect data critically, examine data systematically, and draw conclusions. Despite these obstacles, a small group of researchers engaged in action research to improve the learning environments and instructional practices at a particular school site. The researchers examined the rationale for instructional approaches, the population of students involved, and the classroom setting where identified practices were implemented (Kemmis & McTaggart, 1988).

By design, action research is intended to challenge existing knowledge, advocate for political change, and provide an audience for teachers' voices to be heard (Hendricks, 2009). Yet, the current political climate in American schools has not only narrowed the scope of teachers' work, but has also silenced dissention. Teachers feel a covert pressure to focus on test preparation without complaint (Jones & Egley, 2006; Popham, 2001). Teachers understand that the consequences for not meeting benchmarks can be serious for them and/or their students.

Teacher's Self-efficacy and Empowerment

Whether working alone or collaboratively, the researcher's professional expertise and judgment impacts decisions on the process, data analysis, and the conclusions throughout an action research project. Teachers bring their knowledge from coursework, classroom experiences, self-initiated professional reading, networking with colleagues, and staff development opportunities to the research process. They also bring their philosophical (values) and epistemological (how information is acquired) beliefs to the research process.

Action research deepens this knowledge and beliefs. In addition, it is affected by the researcher's sense of self-efficacy and empowerment. Studies have concluded that teacher self-efficacy (feeling capable) is essential to school change and improvement (Enderlin-Lampe, 2002; Rosenholtz, 1991). Bandura (1977) proposed that when individuals view themselves as highly capable, they are willing to take on difficult tasks, expend considerable effort, and demonstrate persistence in meeting the challenge. Enderlin-Lampe (2002) proposes, "The teacher's competency and self-efficacy...is at the heart of reform and...meaningful change in schools" (p. 146).

Many teachers in courses, workshops, and conferences report feeling diminished, outnumbered, and outmaneuvered by directives from the federal, state, and local governments (Jones & Egley, 2006). The legacies of NCLB, high-stakes testing, and Adequate Yearly Progress (AYP), contradict teachers' beliefs and impose limitations on instructional delivery (Gambrell, Malloy, & Mazzoni, 2007), particularly in literacy programs for struggling students (Allington & Baker, 2007).

School Culture and Environment

For self-efficacy to grow, teachers need to be confident that their instructional decisions have the power to affect students' learning. They need the authority to act on their own informed professional decisions. Empowerment provides the classroom teacher—the person closest to students—the autonomy to make decisions about instruction and curriculum that will meet their needs. Empowerment also demands responsibility for continued professional growth. It requires the teacher to problem-solve how to differentiate efficiently instruction for his/her students (Short, 1994). Teachers who feel entrusted to make decisions typically meet their responsibilities.

Since action research takes place within the school environment, the characteristics and culture of the school affect the outcome. Schools can support or inhibit choice and autonomy, as well as, encourage risk-taking and problem-solving (Allington & Cunningham, 2007). For success, action research requires school communities with collegial relationships where professionals support each other and reflect together about their practice and students' achievement.

Now more than ever before, literacy educators must support teachers by promoting collaborative action research and mentoring classroom teachers throughout the process (Mills, 2007). Collaboration between teachers in the field and college/university researchers holds the promise for a partnership that can build a body of valid researched practices (Buysse, Sparkman, & Wesley, 2003).

Methodology

Setting

There were two settings. The first setting was at an institute of higher learning where the graduate courses were taken. One institute was a large public university in Florida and one was a private college in New York State. The second setting was the participant's individual public school classrooms around the universities.

Participants

There were two groups of participants. The first group included three literacy professors who served as both teachers and mentors to the various graduate students working on their master's degree in reading. This particular course was the last course offered in the reading program. The second group included the graduate students who were currently classroom teachers who were completing a master's degree in reading and had from one to five years of teaching experience in various urban schools. Even though all graduate students participated in the action research project, the four projects presented in this article illustrate the variety of problems that were encountered by all the participants while doing the course work.

- Teacher A is a Caucasian female. Her first grade classroom is culturally diverse—30% Hispanic, 20% African American, and 50% Caucasian. She worked with students who ranged from non-readers to children reading at second grade level. In addition, she had five special needs students.

- Teacher B is a Caucasian female. Her special education class works as a pull-out program. This urban school is predominantly White, but has about 20% of the students on free or reduced lunch.
- Teacher C is a Caucasian female. Her special education classroom is found in a year-round K-5 building. This school is considered a Title I school, as almost 30% of the students are English language learners.
- Teacher D is a Caucasian female. Even though she is a classroom teacher (with special education certification); her research was conducted in the Literacy Center of a private college located in a large urban city in the northeast. The neighbor-hood, which is served by the center, is considered to have a low social economic status. The group of children who attended the Center was composed of six boys and two girls from 5th to 8th grade; all were African American.

Procedure

The college classrooms provided the supportive, collaborative context required for action research studies. The advantage of working in this context is it stimulates inquiry and prompts teachers' examination of current literacy knowledge.

Phase One. At the beginning of the semester, the inservice teachers were introduced to action research and started to brainstorm ideas for the project. The inservice teachers were encouraged to think aloud to identify topics of interest and/ or problems that concerned them in their own classroom. Each teacher selected a problem to investigate either in their own classroom or in the Literacy Clinic. Some inservice teachers identified what was not working in their own classrooms, while others decided to implement something they had only read about, but had never tried. Peer support was essential as a portion of each class was devoted to thinking aloud and sharing ideas about how each project could be designed. Teachers learned to trust one another and their professors as they wondered aloud and shared their problems or concerns. For most teachers, this was a new way of thinking about their teaching and considering decisions for their own classrooms.

Each student investigated the research literature on her reading topic. They had to find and read ten studies in peer-reviewed journals to formulate their questions and design their studies. We called this *reading around in the known* to learn how others had investigated similar problems and what they had discovered. The inservice teachers outlined what they had discovered from their research, listed their research questions, developed a timeline, and planned data collection.

Phase Two. Each inservice teacher met individually with her professor for feedback. This included guidance in broadening or narrowing the scope of the project, revisiting the timeline, and clarifying the intentions of the action research. Then, the action research projects were initiated. Throughout the semester, each inservice teacher was individually mentored by her professor, as well as, supported by her peers, as the projects were designed, revised, and enacted in classrooms.

For the next several weeks, a portion of each class meeting at the university was devoted to thinking aloud, problem-solving, proposing alternative data collection methods, triangulating data, reflecting, and making sense of data results. Inservice teachers shared their concerns, obstacles the faced, classroom observations, and reflections with one another. They reviewed and analyzed data regularly in order to make changes when results weren't helpful in answering their questions. No one was locked in by the plan they had turned in for *Phase One*.

Mid-semester, each inservice teacher turned in a summary paper. First, they wrote the summaries and findings from their required research articles. Second, they described how their own project was progressing, changes that had been made in the timeline or data collection, and findings so far. Each teacher met individually with her professor for additional mentoring and assistance completing the project.

Phase Three. At the end of the semester, the inservice teachers summarized their results in a final paper and presented their findings to their peers and other faculty members. Since peers were aware of each other's projects throughout the semester, they were very interested and invested in learning about the outcomes. The inservice teachers' presentations were creative, interactive, and well received. The inservice teachers felt confident, knowledgeable, and empowered by their work. Many had already engaged their co-workers and administrators in their projects and were seeking ways of continuing their work and becoming change agents in their schools.

The Project

Three of the action research projects are presented here to illustrate the differing approaches each inservice teacher used while designing and completing her investigations. The fourth project is discussed in depth later in this article.

Table: Design of Teacher A's Project

Innovations	• Changing from ability grouping to mixed ability groups for work at literacy centers • Student roles in group alternate between teacher-assigned and self-selected
Data Sources	• Teacher observations • Teacher rubrics for vocabulary and reader response literacy center work • Children's rubrics for group contribution and feelings
Data Analysis	• Children's ratings on self-esteem rubrics recorded daily for each child and charted throughout study by teacher • Children's self-esteem ratings compared for self-selected versus assigned group roles • Scores on rubrics for vocabulary and reading response rubrics recorded for each child's work at centers and charted throughout study by teacher • Children's scores for work prior to heterogeneous grouping compared to work completed during study •Teacher's weekly observations of student participation, effort, and cooperation within groups analyzed for changes in behaviors
Findings	• Higher levels of students' on task behavior • Quality of student work improved as well as completion of assignments • Below average child preferred self-selected roles • Members shared responsibility for keeping group on task
Implications for NCLB	• Peer contexts can influence student values and achievement. • Tendency to use ability grouping to increase test scores may be counterproductive.

Teacher A was a first grade teacher interested in improving the students' interaction and the quality of their individual work during literacy center time. She had usually grouped her students by ability for instruction and literacy center time, but found her students' off-task behavior was causing management problems in her classroom. After investigating the advantages of heterogeneous versus homogeneous grouping, she organized heterogeneous groups comprised of children whose reading levels varied from above to below grade level. In Table 1, the design and outcomes of Teacher A's action research project are presented. Teacher A was interested in the impact of self-selection versus teacher-assigned roles on the quality of students' literacy work. Each week, the students alternated between teacher-assigned and self-selected roles. Finally, she compared students' self-esteem to the production of quality work. Her results showed that the heterogeneous grouping was more successful in terms of classroom management and the quality of her students' work during literacy center time. Teacher A's "a-ha" moment happened during the fourth week of her project when she discovered that not only did all students complete their work, but that their vocabulary and reader response levels had improved!

Table 2: Design of Teacher B's Project

Participants	5 fourth grade Exceptional Education Students • 2 girls and 3 boys • All had a specific learning disability in reading
Innovations	• Group created list of good reader behaviors to emulate • Began daily practice for reading fluency with connected text • Replaced patterned texts with natural language texts • Pairs practiced reading with higher ability peer • End of week two students volunteered to read aloud
Data Sources	• Pre- and post audio-taped reading • Student self-rated daily performance surveys • Student goal setting for each week's paired reading
Data Analysis	• Teacher rated pre and post audiotapes rated on rubric for four dimensions of fluency- expression, phrasing, smoothness, and pace • Teacher compared ratings compared for pre and post audiotapes • Student self-ratings on performance surveys tallied and charted daily by teacher
Findings	• Improved fluency across three dimensions—expression, inflection, and smoothness • Word recognition increased • Student confidence improved: willingness to read for an audience
Implications for NCLB	• Demonstrates the Matthew effect • Word recognition and comprehension improve through real reading, not skill and drill exercises

Teacher B was a special education teacher who worked in a pullout program for fourth graders with specific learning disabilities in reading. She investigated the research on fluency and repeated readings to design her study. She wanted to analyze the effects of repeated readings on students' reading fluency performance, word recognition, and confidence. Her project data is presented in Table 2. Teacher B modeled fluency behaviors such as prosody during her daily read aloud episodes, highlighted how these behaviors affected students' understanding of the texts, and guided the students to generate a list of good readers' behaviors. The class made both a good readers' behaviors chart, as well as, their own bookmarks with a list of good readers' behaviors. The students referred to these as they set weekly goals for their buddy reading. Students engaged in daily buddy reading with pairs changing each week to provide a variety of models. At the end of each week, two students volunteered to perform by reading their book to the group. Students set individual performance goals and self-evaluated their performance daily. Teacher B's "a-ha" moment occurred when she listened to her students' buddy reading during the second week of her study, and heard them imitate her expression and intonation.

Table 3: Design of Teacher C's Project

Participants	5 fifth grade Exceptional Education Students • 2 girls and 3 boys • Reading levels ranged from beginning 3rd to beginning 5th grade • Group included language impaired, health impaired, emotionally-behaviorally disabled, and specific learning disabled students
Innovations	• Created new reading area for quiet reading in classroom • Increased the variety of genres and reading levels available in classroom library and for student check-out • Student choice in book teacher read aloud each week • Class period extended to include 15 minutes for daily silent self-selected reading • Invited parent participation in child's reading
Data Sources	• Motivation to Read Profile (MRP) given pre and post • Student book logs and ratings of their books--too easy, just right, too hard • Parent surveys and comments on students' book logs • Teacher observations during silent reading time
Data Analysis	• Teacher tallied scores for MRP on value of reading and reading self-concept for each student • Teacher compared MRP pre and posttest scores • Teacher read student logs and tracked amount of time spent reading
Findings	• Motivation to Read Profile scores increased for 4 of 5 students in both value of reading and self-perceptions as readers • Students increased amount of time spent reading and shared readily with each other. • Parent involvement was minimal beyond a signature
Implications for NCLB	• Importance of classroom libraries and time for self-selected reading is more valuable than test scores in supporting the reading habit. • Student choice is essential in building positive attitudes toward reading.

Teacher C was a special education teacher in a pull-out program for fifth graders who ranged in reading ability from beginning third to beginning fifth grade. Teacher C's study is shown in Table 3. Her study's goals were to increase the students' motivation to read and their ability to discuss books read aloud to them. Teacher C's study had three components: 1) student choice in the books read to them, followed by open discussions and weekly student ratings of their favorite book; 2) sustained silent reading of self-selected books for buddy reading; and 3) reading self-selected books at home, encouraging parent involvement. Students kept book logs in which they recorded reading time and rated each book as being too easy, just right, or too hard. Although Teacher C was disappointed by the level of parent participation, she was encouraged by the students' increased levels of discussion following her read aloud episodes and their sharing of their self-selected books with each other.

A Closer Look at One Teacher' Study

Teacher D was a classroom teacher (also certified as a special education teacher) and worked at the college's Literacy Center. She worked with struggling readers, ranging from fourth to eighth grade. The College is situated in a high needs, minority community. According to the New York State Department of Education 2004-2005 School Report Card, statistics for the elementary school that serves this neighborhood indicate that 99.4% of students are African American or Hispanic and 92.6% of students are eligible to receive free or reduced lunch. Scholastically, 64% of fourth graders and 93% of eighth graders scored below grade-level standards in English language arts. Many caregivers in this neighborhood also lack basic reading and writing skills, making it difficult for them to provide children with the home support necessary for school success.

After investigating research on teaching writing, Teacher D designed a study to incorporate individual multimedia projects as a means to spark motivation to write and improve students' skills in the writing process. The program promoted literacy through photography and visual media in addition to traditional reading and writing exercises. It incorporated the additional literacy processes of viewing and visually representing messages as identified by the International Reading Association (IRA) and the National Council of Teachers of English (NCTE) (1996).

Teacher D took students on field trips to several cultural destinations. It was the first time many of these students had been to most of these sites. The experiences became a catalyst for verbal, written, and visual expression about the central theme of their hometown. The project provided students with the opportunity to think critically about media messaging, to express themselves through language and visuals, to use digital cameras, computer searches, and iMovie technology, to enhance their awareness of local cultural assets, and to develop self-confidence as successful writers with a voice in their community.

Rationale for the Project

Evidence suggests that photography, video, and other visual mediums are important vehicles for self-expression and language development. "A vast and varied array of media is commonplace in the real world that learners experience" (Shea& Murray, 2003). Learners interact and use these visual components in their daily lives to "read the world." Visual images have a powerful affect on the learners' ability to comprehend texts and to construct an understanding of themselves and society. The IRA and NCTE acknowledged this powerful affect by giving visual processing a level of importance equal to the traditional processes of reading, writing, listening, and speaking (IRA & NCTE, 1996).

Keifer (1995) describes visual literacy as the ability to recognize and interpret what is seen. It involves reading, examining, and understanding images. Balanced instruction in the language arts incorporates simultaneous guided practice in both visual and language literacies (Shea & Murray, 2003). Piro (2002) emphasized, "students live multi-textual lives inside and outside the classroom" (p. 34); this call for versatility in code switching between visual and print sources of information.

When learning in school mirrors learning in the world, students are more motivated to become engaged (Au & Mason, 1983). Our constant challenge as teachers is to keep up with the realities of the world our students live in and the future they need to be prepared to meet. This makes the content and delivery of curriculum ore relevant to them.

The Learning Activities for the Project

The learning activities planned for this program motivated students to fully engage in both areas of literacy (visual and print) in meaningful ways. Compton-Lilly (2007) reminds us that becoming literate involves "learning multiple types of literacy practices that are differentially useful in various contexts" (719).

Today's students come to the classroom from a world where technology is used in so many aspects of their lives. They use computers, text messages, Wiki, Facebook, YouTube, and/or other modern technology. Young people are comfortable with viewing and visually representing as language processes for learning and expressing their knowing. Embracing technology in the classroom in ways that complement learning and the curriculum is critical in making what happens in school relevant for students' life in the world (Tompkins, 2010).

Table 4: Schedule for iMovie Project

Session	Activities
1	•Welcome and Introductions; tour of Learning Center • Discussion of Viewing (getting information from visuals, sharing inferences, supporting inference with evidence • Independently viewing picture and responding to prompts about it (baseline assessment)
2	• Introduction to digital camera; discussion on taking good pictures • Visit to Marina; students takes pictures and notes • Download pictures at Literacy Center (LC); review notes
3	• Web research on Zoo and Delaware Park • Visit to Buffalo Zoo and Delaware Park; take pictures and notes • Download pictures at LC; review notes
4	• Web research on Old Fort Niagara • Visit to Old Fort Niagara; take pictures and notes • Download pictures at LC; review notes
5	• Web research on Griffs (college) Hockey Team • Attend a hockey game; take pictures and notes • Download pictures at LC; review notes
6	• Students draft scripts to narrate pictures for each site visited • iMovie instruction • Students enter pictures into iMovie

7	• Complete draft, revise, edit scripts • Work with artistic effects in iMovie
8	• Rehearsing scripts, recording to iMovie, publishing iMovie
9	• Finishing touches • Premier Day; presentation to family members

The Research Design

The children who participated in this project visited points of interest in Western New York. They photographed images that were interesting or important to them, and wrote about their experiences and feelings. During the program, students:

- Explored the questions and concepts of media literacy (students learned how and why messages are created, the techniques used to attract a viewer/reader's attention, how messages might be interpreted differently, and what values are imbedded in the message);
- Visited local destinations that were important for cultural development;
- Thought critically and creatively about their environment and relationships with others as they worked together;
- Enhanced writing, listening, and communication skills;
- Constructed messages using language, images, photography, video and audio to express their point of view; and
- Built a positive self-image of themselves as successful learners who have a civic responsibility to their community and this region.

Outcomes of the Project

In the culminating activity, students shared their photographs in a narrated iMovie directed and produced under the guidance of Teacher D. Students added artistic and sound effects. They orally rehearsed their written scripts to improve fluency and prosody before recording for the iMovie. A special showing was held for family and friends after each iMovie went through a final edit. Students showcased their experiences, conveying their feelings about each and their hometown, Buffalo. They described sites visited using writing, photographs, and other digital media. The demonstrated growth in students' literacy abilities was far greater than expected.

Through a process of reflecting on a problem, considering possibilities, and trying out one "what if" scenario, Teacher D found that connecting struggling readers and writers with exciting experiences and current formats for expressing reflections positively affected their learning, motivation, and self-concept. Thus, both Teacher D and her students benefited from this innovative action research project.

Table 5: Design of Teacher D's Project

Participants	• Struggling readers, ranging from fourth to eighth grade • Six boys and two girls • All African American from low SES neighborhood
Innovations	• Students learned to examine visual sources of information and make inferences • Students created visual displays of information on local sites using digital camera • Students created narrations (written scripts) for their visual displays • Students directed and produced an iMovie, using newly acquired technology skills to arrange pictures and narrations aesthetically
Data Sources	• Initial writing in response to questions about picture • Notes taken in web search for information on sites visited • Scripts written to narrate pictures; revision and editing of scripts • Improvement of fluency and prosody during practice of narrations • Development of technology skills
Findings	• Writing grew from fragmented, disjointed thoughts to multiple paragraphs • Increased motivation to persist with revision • Increased motivation to practice fluent, expressive reading • Competence in using the computer to search for information • Competence in using digital cameras and iMovie process • Confidence in their ability to produce and present a creative, interesting, useful advertisement for their hometown
Implications for NCLB	• New technologies stimulate interest in learning • Processes and resources used outside of school can be effectively incorporated in the classroom • Allowing learners to take ownership of the task builds motivation • Learning connected to authentic experiences has greater impact • Creating a quality product with a personal signature boosts confidence
Action Research Process Because Action Research must be	• Baseline: analysis of students' initial journal entries (writing sample) and responses to questions related to interest in writing and photography.

participatory and collaborative, (Kemmis and McTaggart, 1988, p.23), the analysis of data was accomplished collaboratively by Teacher D, the two university professors and the students themselves.	• Analysis of students' ability to learn about and use cameras effectively in capturing visual images that present information and/or perspectives. • Analysis of students' ability to gradually take control of iMovie production after initial demonstration. • Analysis of students' ability to compose high interest, well-constructed scripts for iMovie that effectively match photos with messages. Scripts compared to initial journal entries. • Analysis of students' appreciation of writing and technology as tool for expression as reflected in discussion responses on last day.

Conclusion

Today's teachers find their decisions and their professionalism under siege by people outside of the classroom who have become gatekeepers (Bracey, 2002; Garan, 2003; Popham, 2004). The classroom teacher knows her students. She is in the best position to make informed instructional decisions individualized to their interests and needs (Conley, 2005; Cooper & Kiger, 2008). As a trained and certified professional, the classroom teacher is prepared to make informed instructional choices for effective differentiation. Curricular mandates for material and approaches may create consistency, touting a measure of equality as everyone does the same thing - even at the same pace. However, equality is not equity nor does it meet the specific needs of individual learners.

In line with the findings of others, our work with teacher educators yielded research projects that represented a continuum of acceptable to exemplary as expected. Teachers fall along a continuum of growth in becoming researchers (Donoahue, 1996; Smith, 1993). We expect that motivation to examine practices carefully will persist in the face of continuing curricular mandates.

As literacy educators, we find ourselves under assault by those with a political agenda to improve schools (Allington, 2002; Garan, 2003; Bracey, 2002). Intentions may be honorable; but, without a deep understanding of the learning process, actions can be misguided. Educators need to take the first steps in re-establishing themselves as curriculum leaders. Incorporating the tenets of action research into university course work and mentoring teachers in their self-identified inquiry, become the avenues for restoring teachers autonomy.

References

Allington, R. 2002. "Troubling times: A short historical perspective". In R. Allington. 2002. *Big Brother and the National Reading Curriculum: How ideology trumped evidence.* Portsmouth, NH: Heinemann.

Allington, R.L. & Baker, K. (2007). Best practices for struggling readers. In L.B. Gambrell, L.M. Morrow, and M. Pressley (Eds.) *Best practices in literacy instruction* (3rd ed.) (pp. 83-103). New York: Guilford Press.

Allington, R. & Cunningham, P. (2007). *Schools that work: Where all children read and write.* New York, NY: Allyn & Bacon.

Au, K.H., & Mason, J.M. (1983). Cultural congruence in classroom participation structures: Achieving a balance of rights. *Discourse Processes, 6*(2), 145-167.

Bandura, A. (1977). Self-efficacy: Toward a unifying theory of behavioral change. *Psychology Review, 84,* 191-215.

Bracey, G. (2002). *The war against America's public schools: Privatizing schools, commercializing education.* Boston, MA: Allyn & Bacon.

Buysse, V., Sparkman, K.L., & Wesley, P.W. (2003). Communities of practice: Connecting what we know with what we do. *Exceptional Children, 69,* 263-277.

Conley, M. (2005). *Connecting standards and assessment through literacy.* New York, NY: Allyn & Bacon.

Compton-Lilly, C. (2007). What can video games teach us about teaching reading? *The Reading Teacher, 60*(8), 718-727.

Cooper, J.D., & Kiger, N. (2008). *Literacy assessment: Helping teachers plan assessment* (4th ed.). Belmont, CA: Wadsworth Cengage Learning.

Donoahue, Z. (1996). "Collaboration, community, and communication: Modes of discourse for teacher research". In Z. Donoahue, M.A.VanTassell, and L. Patternson (Eds.). *Research in the classroom: Talk, texts, and inquiry* (pp. 91-108). Newark, DE: International Reading Association.

Enderlin-Lampe, S. (2002). Empowerment: Teacher perceptions, aspirations, and efficacy. *Instructional Psychology, 29*(3), 139-146.

Gambrell, L., Malloy, J.A., & Mazzoni, S.A. (2007). Evidence-based best practices for comprehensive literacy instruction. In L.B. Gambrell, L.M. Morrow, and M. Pressley (Eds.) *Best practices in literacy instruction* (3rd ed.) (pp. 11-29). New York: Guilford Press.

Garan, E. (2002). *Resisting reading mandates.* Portsmouth, NH: Heinemann.

Garan, E. (2004). *In defense of our children: When politics, profit, and education collide.* Portsmouth, NH: Heinemann.

Hendricks, C. (2009). *Improving schools through action research: A comprehensive guide for educators.* Boston: Pearson Education.

International Reading Association (IRA) & National Concil of Techers of English (NCTE). (1996). *Standards for the English language arts.* Newark, DE & Urbana, IL: IRA and NCTE.

Jones, B.D., & Egley, R.J. (2006). Looking through different lenses: Teachers' and administrators' views of accountability. *Phi Delta Kappan, 87*(10), 767-771.

Keifer, B. (1995). *The potential of picture books from visual literacy to aesthetic understanding.* Englewood Cliffs, NJ: Merrill.

Kemmis, S., & McTaggart, R. (1988). *The Action Research Planner.* Victoria: Deakin University Press.

Leedy, P., & Ormrod, J. E. (2010). *Practical research: Planning and design.* New York: Pearson.

Meyer, R. J., & Manning, M. (2007). *Reading and teaching.* Mahwah, NJ: Lawrence Erlbaum.

Mills, G. E. (2007). *Action research: A guide for the teacher researcher* (3rd Ed.). Upper Saddle River, NJ: Merrill/Prentice Hall.

Piro, J., (2002). The picture of reading deriving meaning in literacy through image. *The Reading Teacher, 56*(2), 126-134.

Popham, W.J. (2001). *The truth about testing.* Alexandria, VA: Association for Supervision and Curriculum Development (ASCD).

Popham, W.J. (2004). *America's failing schools: How parents and teachers can cope with No Child Left Behind*. New York: Routledge Falmer.

Rosenholtz, S.J. (1991). *Teachers' workplace: The social organization of schools*. New York: Teachers College Press.

Scanlon, D., Anderson, K., & Sweeney, J. (2010 in press). *Early intervention for reading difficulties: The interactive strategies approach*. New York: Guilford Press.

Shea, M., & Murray, R. (2003). Political cartoons: Pictures that speak a thousand words. *Balanced Reading Instruction, 10*, 126-134.

Short, P.M. (1994). Defining teacher empowerment. *Education, 114* (4), 488-492.

Smith, F. (2003). *Unspeakable acts unnatural practices: Flaws and fallacies in scientific reading instruction*. Portsmouth, NH: Heinemann.

Smith, K. (1993). Meeting the challenge of research in the elementary classroom. In L. Patterson, C.M. Santa, K. Short, and K. Smith (Eds.). *Teachers as researchers: Reflection and action*. (pp. 37-42). Newark, DE: International Reading Association.

Tompkins, G. (2010). *Literacy for the 21st century: A balanced approach* (5th ed.). New York, NY: Pearson.

MENTORING PROMOTES QUALITIES THAT LEAD TO TEACHER SATISFACTION

Debra J. Coffey

Kennesaw State University

Abstract

During a university program, graduate students mentored preservice teachers while they were preparing literacy centers for a university field experience. The graduate students initially established positive relationships with the preservice teachers during a Mentoring Extravaganza. Then these preservice teachers and graduate students, who were practicing teachers, exchanged ideas for literacy centers using email and an Internet bulletin board. Throughout this experience, both groups of students developed new appreciation for technology as they established communication networks. Both groups enhanced their creative expertise and developed qualities that lead to teacher satisfaction.

Students enter teacher preparation programs with high expectations. As they complete four or five years of intensive training, they eagerly anticipate teaching in their own classrooms. Teacher education programs provide these preservice teachers with a plethora of ideas and strategies to meet the expectations of their school systems when they enter the world of teaching. During class sessions, preservice teachers describe the ways they will design their classrooms to promote maximum learning, and many develop a zeal for teaching during their field experiences and student teaching. Many of those preservice teachers actually experience the fulfillment of their dreams, but others leave the teaching profession within their first five years of teaching.

This exodus from the teaching profession is not only disappointing to those teachers and their families, but it is expensive for school systems. While school districts invest considerable time and money to recruit over 500,000 new teachers annually, they typically lose over 50% of them during the first five years (Greiner & Smith, 2009; Ingersoll & Kralik, 2004; Wilkins & Clift, 2006). In 2005, the Alliance for Excellent Education reported that the cost of replacing teachers that leave the profession amounts to about $2.2 billion annually, and the cost of replacing public school teachers who transfer among schools brought the total cost to about $4.9 billion. It has become challenging to calculate the annual cost of teacher turnover, as the "revolving door" has escalated (Boe, Cook, & Sunderland, 2008; Carroll, 2007).

Imagine the benefits for the entire educational process if we transformed those statistics into funding for education by building job satisfaction among teachers. This funding could enhance the lives of teachers and students all over the country. When we think of these possibilities, there is deep concern when we realize that in spite of the good intentions of teachers, school systems, and teacher education programs, teacher attrition rates continue to escalate. What can be done to raise job satisfaction and keep teachers from leaving the profession?

Educational communities constantly seek ways to enhance the educational journey and pave the way toward higher levels of exploration and achievement. It has been shown that mentoring relationships with classroom teachers can empower preservice teachers to walk confidently into their own classrooms feeling well prepared to meet the needs of their students (Kent & Simpson, 2009). This comfort level builds satisfaction with the teaching profession and helps teachers to influence the lives of children in positive and meaningful ways. A cycle of success can lead to job fulfillment as teachers experience many levels of mentoring relationships (Marable & Raimondi, 2007). A mentor helps a protégé to feel valued and provides beneficial feedback and companionship (Conderman & Johnston-Rodriguez, 2009). A mentoring relationship based on mutual respect opens new possibilities as social interaction promotes a transfer of learning that helps the mentee to develop new expertise for collaboration and creative teaching.

The term *mentor* can be traced back to *The Odyssey of Homer* (Lattimore, 1999). Homer, the Greek poet, described the ways Mentor, a family friend, shared knowledge with Odyseus' son, Telemachus, as he prepared for a journey to find his father (Bell, 1996; Gow, 2006). During their discussions, Mentor shared knowledge with Telemachus to prepare him for his role as the next king (Whitehead, 1995).

Definitions of mentoring often emphasize the benefits of the reciprocal relationship that develops during this partnership. For instance, Healy and Weichert (1990) defined mentoring as "a dynamic, reciprocal relationship in a work environment between an advanced career incumbent (mentor) and a beginner (protégé) aimed at promoting the career development of both" (p. 17). Bell (1996) described mentoring as a relationship in which "mentors practice their skills with a combination of never-ending compassion, crystal-clear communication, and a sincere joy in the role of being a helper along a journey toward mastery" (p. 6). He noted that "great mentors are not only devoted fans of their protégé; they are loyal fans of the dream of what the protégé can become with their guidance" (p. 6).

The Impact of Mentoring Relationships

International interest in mentoring has rapidly gained momentum in fields such as education, psychology, management, and medicine (Briggs & Pehrsson, 2008; Grindel & Hagerstrom, 2009; Patton, 2009; Riley & Fearing, 2009; Stokking, Leenders, de Jong, & van Tartwijk, 2003). Educational research during the last fifteen years has emphasized the benefits of mentoring in connection to initial teacher education, teacher induction, and professional development (Bey, 1995; Galvez-Hjornevik, 1986; Hagger, Burn, & McIntyre, 1995; King & Bey, 1995; Steadman & Simmons, 2007). Most of these research studies have explored the impact of mentoring relationships between cooperating teachers and preservice teachers (Campbell & Brummett, 2007; Eisenman & Thornton, 1999; Kent & Simpson, 2009; Maltas & McCarty-Clair, 2006; Siebert, Clark, Kilbridge, & Peterson, 2006).

While many studies emphasize mentoring relationships during student teaching, few studies have explored mentoring relationships between graduate students and preservice teachers. Researchers who did explore these relationships noted the positive effects of mentoring. For example, Allen, Cobb, and Danger (2003) found that both preservice teachers and graduate students improved their literacy instruction as a result of mentoring relationships. During a similar study, Boreen and Niday (2000) paired students in their secondary English teaching methods course with four teacher-mentors in Iowa and Arizona. The preservice teachers in this course documented their developmental growth through email conversations. This study demonstrated the ways a mentoring program can be used to break through the isolation which teachers often experience in the classroom. Teachers who leave the classroom often consider this isolation a major factor in their decision to leave the profession (Dillon, 2009).

Planning the Journey

In this article, the metaphor of a road trip is used to describe a qualitative research study in which preservice teachers had the opportunity to form communication networks with experienced teachers. (See Figure 1 in the Appendix.) This research study was designed to determine the impact of a mentoring program on preservice teachers and their mentors, who were practicing teachers. This study was also conducted to explore the question: What can be done to raise job satisfaction and keep teachers from leaving the profession?

During our university program, our graduate students mentored our preservice teachers while they were preparing literacy centers for a university field experience with elementary students. These preservice teachers were enrolled in their final literacy methods course. Thus, the preservice teachers were beginning the final stage of their journey toward a Bachelor's Degree in Elementary and Early Childhood Education and preparing to embark on a new journey as student teachers and full-time teachers. As tour guides, the graduate students became mentors and provided feedback and encouragement to their assigned preservice teacher using email and an Internet bulletin board, which provided ongoing opportunities for discussion as both groups of students signed in with a user name and password.

Mapping the Journey

This mentoring project was designed to build a sense of community between a graduate cohort of experienced teachers and seniors in a university literacy methods course. Armstrong (2007) noted that "a superhighway is being built across today's education landscape. It has been under construction for some time" (p. 16). This mentoring project provided opportunities for the veteran teachers and preservice teachers to take an innovative journey down this superhighway. As they collaborated, the graduate students helped the preservice teachers to create developmentally-appropriate learning centers that matched curriculum standards and focused on the needs and interests of elementary students.

The graduate students planned this research project during the fall. Then they mentored preservice teachers in the spring while they completed a Master of Education program. As graduate students planned this mentoring project, they gleaned ideas from a middle school teaming project (Warner & Coffey, 2004). One of the hallmarks of the contemporary middle school is interdisciplinary teaming, and this article described the ways two teachers used technology to build bridges of communication. As this graduate cohort of experienced teachers mentored undergraduate preservice teachers using an Internet bulletin board and email messages, the undergraduate preservice teachers developed creative units and gained new expertise.

During the planning phase of our mentoring project, graduate students set goals collaboratively, designed research questions, and prepared surveys questions for the project. The Professor's subtle guidance helped them maintain ownership of the project and experience the benefits of shared decision making.

Planning the Mentoring Extravaganza

Graduate students and preservice teachers initially met during a collaborative celebration called a Mentoring Extravaganza. The graduate class met each week in the large media center of an elementary school, so this space provided ample room for presentations and interactions during our initial session. Graduate students chose leadership roles and planned presentations for the evening. Mentoring teams were chosen in relation to personalities, interests, and assigned grade levels (Glesne, 1999). In some cases, groups of three preservice teachers had two graduate students as tour guides since there were 26 university seniors in the literacy methods class and 22 students in the graduate cohort. Collaboration between the two classes was cohesive since all of the students had the same course instructor. Both groups of students chose pseudonyms for themselves as they embarked on a quest to integrate literacy across the curriculum.

The Road Trip

Graduate students shared expectations for the project during the Mentoring Extravaganza. Both groups of students wrote goals for the project on golden paper chains, and then joined the chains at the beginning of this session. As the program unfolded, the Associate Dean and the Professor discussed the mentoring project with both groups, and two graduate students, dressed as chefs, presented a recipe for successful learning centers. After graduate students shared a PowerPoint presentation with ideas for learning centers in the classroom, preservice teachers wrote their own recipes for successful learning centers, including ingredients such as creative materials, flavorful literature, and a touch of innovation.

Then both groups of students discussed their teaching experiences as two graduate students led a scavenger hunt so the preservice teachers could discover unique facts about their mentor teacher(s). Graduate students encouraged preservice teachers to enjoy special refreshments while they considered ideas for learning centers and exchanged email addresses. At the end of the session, preservice teachers gained new ideas as they viewed the learning center presentations created by the graduate students which showed various centers they had used in their own classrooms.

The First Mile of the Journey

The first mile of the journey officially began as the cohort of graduate students and preservice teachers exchanged ideas through email and the Internet bulletin board. Graduate students and preservice teachers kept records of the journey using copies of email messages, reflective notes, and postings on the Internet bulletin board. Both groups also completed survey questions at the beginning and end of the project. (See Figure 2 in the Appendix.)

Pausing for Tune-ups

During this road trip, a few tune-ups were needed to make sure everyone was receiving communication for the mentoring process on a regular basis. Since some email systems deleted messages due to Internet protection, the Professor acted as a mediator to be sure that navigational systems were working. Then preservice teachers could receive feedback from their mentors and build communication networks.

Gaining Momentum and Developing Learning Centers

As graduate students guided the preservice teachers in our study, the goal was to create interactive learning centers that would help elementary students to explore ideas or reinforce concepts relating to lessons taught in elementary classrooms. A learning center is a designated space in the classroom with materials or activities designed to promote independent exploration of topics that are taught in the classroom (Diller, 2003, 2005, 2007; Tomlinson, 1999). This space gives elementary students opportunities to practice "hands-on thinking and see how facts, skills, and strategies relate to broader goals and concepts" (Armstrong, 1994, p. 76). Preservice teachers created display boards to activate students' imaginations. Each display board served as an interactive activity to enhance student knowledge and progress. These display boards were designed to encourage inquiry, independent problem solving, and higher levels of thinking.

Preservice teachers designed these learning centers to give elementary students opportunities to travel across the levels of Bloom's taxonomy and explore multiple intelligences (Bloom, 1956; Gardner, 1993, Noble, 2004). They used creative strategies that aligned with Bloom's taxonomy and Backward Design (Wiggins & McTighe, 2005; See Figure 3 and Figure 4 in the Appendix). These learning centers gave elementary students a special place in the classroom where they could explore significant issues, such as saving the rainforest and protecting our oceans from pollution.

As these project-based learning activities were being developed, (Simkins, Cole, Tavalin, & Means, 2002) graduate students and preservice teachers discussed open-ended activities that would inspire creative thinking in accordance with the perspectives of Piaget (2008/1959) and Vygotsky (1978/1934). Using collaborative innovations, the preservice teachers designed learning centers to help elementary students to reconstruct concepts and build new understanding during their units of study.

Building Communication Networks

During this project, communication through email and the Internet bulletin board transformed an individualized project into a collaborative experience. (See Figure 5 in the Appendix.) As with the middle school teaming project (Warner & Coffey, 2004), technology was the tool that empowered the learning community to overcome the barriers of time constraints and distance so we could establish communication networks. Nicenet, a user-friendly Internet bulletin board, established a forum for exchanging ideas as a community. Each student logged onto the Internet site with a user name and password. Then they introduced themselves and shared information about their schools and their interests.

As graduate students provided instructional leadership and scaffolding, preservice teachers discovered creative ways to convey content, meet the expectations of state standards, and differentiate instruction (Latz, Speirs, Neumeister, Adams, & Pierce, 2009; Rogoff, 1994; Vygotsky, 1978/1934; Walker-Dalhouse & Risko, 2009). This scaffolding was evident when Julia and Vivian (all names are pseudonyms) initiated their road trip and established their communication network. After the Mentoring Extravaganza, Julia, a preservice teacher, sent her mentor, Vivian, a quick email message to establish communication:

> *This is just a short note to say hello. It was nice to meet you the other night, and I am looking forward to a great mentoring relationship. If you have any ideas for my topic, measurement, I would love to have them! I'll talk to you soon.*

Vivian quickly responded to Julia's message with ideas from activities she enjoyed in her own classroom:

> *It was great to meet you too! I have several ideas for your learning center. Measuring Penny is a great picture book about a teacher who gives his class a project on measuring. If you can get a copy of the book, you'll see my train of thought....I would probably read this book to the whole group and use it to*

launch into some whole group measurement concepts. I would have standard and non-standard units of measure that the children could use to measure objects. You would probably need to create some sort of data sheet for them to record information on. You might use a chart that says object/measurement/ unit or something else.

Vivian provided Julia with many options to consider, and Julia was enthusiastic about her collaborating teachers' response to the ideas they discussed. Julia shared:

I hope your week is going well. I made a rough draft of my center and took it to my collaborating teacher today. She loved the ideas and thinks her class will enjoy doing the activities. I showed her the book about measuring Penny, and she thought that would be a good motivation for the lesson. Thanks for the idea!

Throughout this project, preservice teachers and graduate students explored research articles and websites to encourage higher levels of thinking and develop creative activities to bring out the genius in every child.

The Grand Finale

During the final Mentoring Extravaganza, or tailgating party, graduate students and preservice teachers celebrated their success with Hawaiian refreshments. Excitement was in the air as preservice teachers beamed with enthusiasm and displayed their learning centers. When Andrea, a graduate student, described this experience, she said:

At the end of the mentoring project, it was nice to see that my voice was heard during a post mentoring project display. Each preservice teacher displayed a trifold board, along with a brief description and presentation of a learning center. I thought this was a fantastic way for students to demonstrate their knowledge and research on a specific topic. I could tell that each and every student put in a lot of hard work and time to achieve their colorful displays.

Driving to Higher Ground

Graduate students gained new ideas as they viewed 26 learning centers during the Mentoring Extravaganza, and preservice teachers discovered new ideas for their field experience. As preservice teachers displayed their learning centers during the Mentoring Extravaganza, the Associate Dean and the Professor guided them into exploration of additional ways they could use their learning centers to extend opportunities for constructivism and higher levels of thinking. This extended their repertoire of teaching strategies as they prepared to implement their units during a field experience.

Reflecting on the Journey

Preservice teachers were pleased that they learned much about various units of study and clarified their understanding of many aspects of the real world of teaching during their discussions. The benefits of the mentoring project were evident during typological analysis (Hatch, 2002) of surveys, reflective notes, interviews, and information from Internet sources. Typological analysis was used to divide the data into categories that were relevant to the study. Data analysis was conducted throughout the study to look for common themes and extensively review the data.

Following the procedure outlined by the typological model, specific categories were identified, which were designed to incorporate all relevant data. As themes emerged from the data, color-coding with Microsoft Word was used to categorize the data. Finally, the data was analyzed in relationship to emerging patterns. Through additional analysis, the entire data set was examined for internal consistency by searching for any contradictory examples. In the final steps of analysis, themes from the analysis were used as a basis for categorically writing brief summary statements and collecting significant quotes from the interviews to explore relationships in the findings.

Typological analysis revealed interesting relationships and patterns in the research data. The survey questions in Figure 2 of the Appendix were administered at the beginning and end of the study. Ongoing data analysis and extensive analysis at the conclusion of the research process provided insight into the experiences of the participants. Emerging themes from data analysis indicated that preservice teachers and graduate students (1) enhanced the quality of their teaching, (2) found innovative ways to differentiate instruction and promote creativity while meeting educational standards, and (3) gained confidence and ownership of the learning process. The following pages provide a synthesis of results from data analysis, including quotes from surveys, email messages, reflections, and entries on the Internet bulletin board.

Reflecting on Learning Centers

Survey data showed that students were moderately familiar with learning centers before the project. By the time students displayed their own projects, they were highly familiar with learning centers, and they knew how to implement them for differentiation, strategy practice, assessment, and enhancement of understanding. They were confident in their ability to take students' understanding to deeper levels by using innovative learning centers to enhance units of study in elementary classrooms.

Triangulation of the survey data, reflective notes, and Internet sources revealed that both groups of students realized the value of mentoring. Preservice teachers appreciated the gift bags they received from the graduate students during the second Mentoring Extravaganza, but they were even more grateful for the time and ideas these mentors shared with them. Tiffany, a preservice teacher, stated, *"I have been a mentor, and I have also had a mentor. It is crucial to have a support system when learning new information.*"Preservice teachers were grateful for ideas, feedback, and suggestions for effective websites and beneficial books. Bell (1996) described the value of mentoring when he said:

> *Mentoring is an honor. Except for love, there is no greater gift one can give than the gift of growth. It is a rare privilege to help another learn, have the relevant wisdom useful to another, and have someone who can benefit from that wisdom.* (p. 205)

Lessons Learned During the Journey

Graduate students took an active interest in the success of preservice teachers during this project. Preservice teachers enjoyed the supportive assistance of their mentors, and the mentors were glad to share the strategies that worked effectively in their own classrooms. Students in both groups said they would like more time for mentoring, and they wanted to continue their relationships.

The Impact of the Journey

As a result of this mentoring experience, preservice teachers experienced a new level of preparation for teaching. They became more confident in their abilities, as they learned new strategies and skills which empowered them to provide quality instruction. Laura shared her perspective on developing a learning center:

> *It helped me focus on all of the aspects of teaching about the ocean by looking at the required standards for fifth graders, determining what I wanted the students to learn, and developing some hands-on activities that will reinforce their learning. Originally, I looked at centers as just some fun stuff for the students to participate in. After developing these centers, I realize that they are fun activities, but they also incorporate lots of learning.*

Julia described the process of developing a learning center in collaboration with Vivian:

> *My mentor, Vivian, was very helpful because she teaches third grade and has designed many learning center activities. In our emails, we discussed learning center ideas for activities as well as the design process. She recommended a book called Measuring Penny that I chose as a theme and motivation for my learning center. I would not have known about the book otherwise.*

Benefits of this collaboration were evident when Julia presented her learning center during our Mentoring Extravaganza. Julia's learning center featured innovative ideas from the book *Measuring Penny* (Leedy, 2000) and open-ended activities to encourage creative thinking. (See Figure 6 and Figure 7 in the Appendix.) Julia summarized statements of many participants when she said, *"The learning centers were designed with confidence because we had such great help."*

Connections with Educational Issues

Mentoring relationships gave preservice teachers tools to enhance the quality of their teaching and their future job satisfaction. Benefits of this network of communication resonate with major issues in education. For instance, these preservice teachers found innovative ways to differentiate instruction and promote creativity while meeting educational standards (Ballantyne & Hansford, 1995; McTighe & Brown, 2005; Tomlinson, 1999). They gained confidence and ownership of the learning process in ways that promote teacher retention and job satisfaction (Maltas & McCarty-Clair, 2006; Moffett, 2000).

Preservice teachers enhanced the quality of their teaching, used technology in practical ways, and added new ideas to their teaching repertoire through their collaborative networks. This collaboration will encourage both groups of students to maintain and develop communication networks wherever they teach, and this will help them to avoid the sense of isolation that occurs in many schools today (Boreen & Niday, 2000).

As Gayle, a preservice teacher, reflected on her collaborative experience, she expressed a common theme among the preservice teachers:

There have been many times in my life that I began something new, and it would have been great to have someone there to guide me through the process. Unfortunately, it is not always possible to have mentors throughout the experiences of our lives. Fortunately, however, I had the opportunity to be mentored during this experience.

Laura, a preservice teacher, was grateful for the opportunity to enjoy a mentoring relationship, and she reflected on her mentoring experience with Becky:

The mentoring project has been a very enriching experience. I have enhanced my circle of friends both professionally and personally. Through various emails, I have come to appreciate the wealth of experience that these teachers possess and how much I can learn from each one of them. These relationships have helped me gain insight into the day-to-day lives of working teachers. It has also helped me develop positive, reciprocal relationships with this group of teachers. These relationships allow each one of us to reach out to each other for support, feedback, and friendship.

Future Directions

Preservice teachers felt well-prepared to enter the classroom after their opportunities for collaboration and growth. Brooke told her mentor, *"It was wonderful having you as a mentor, and I hope to continue our friendship. It is good to know that there are teachers out there who are willing to help new teachers!"*

When Susan, a mentoring teacher, discussed the middle grades teaming project (Warner & Coffey, 2004), she concluded, "Studies have shown that when students take the information they have learned and apply it to new situations, true learning has occurred. It is my belief that a whole lot of learning occurred with this class" (p. 17).

Our mentoring project demonstrated ways that mentoring relationships multiply learning opportunities. Through collaboration, preservice teachers developed a deeper appreciation for learner diversity and felt more equipped to meet students' needs. They were excited about using their learning centers during their field experience and future teaching.

This mentoring project has many implications for professional development. Mentoring relationships can build job satisfaction and increase teacher retention. Maybe the students who participated in this mentoring project will have an impact on the ways student teachers are mentored. After successful mentoring experiences, many of the graduate students, who participated in this study, shared their knowledge and expertise with their own student teachers. Julia, a preservice teacher who won the award for Outstanding Student Teacher in the College of Education, wrote:

The mentoring project helped me to better understand how valuable experienced teachers are to preservice teachers. I'm sure that the first few years of teaching will be a time of growth and discovery for me. I will certainly need and welcome a mentor during those years. Mentors can provide guidance and direction with projects, like the learning center I designed....I hope that I will be able to mentor a student or a new teacher some day. I will remember how comfortable this process was for me and try to duplicate that in the future.

Julia's collaborating teacher was chosen as the Outstanding Collaborating Teacher in the College of Education during that year, and her mentor, Vivian, was chosen as the Teacher of the Year in her elementary school.

During this mentoring project, preservice teachers began to think like veteran teachers as they worked on a mutual project, and the graduate students fine-tuned their leadership skills during their interactions. Preservice teachers described many ways in which this project made them feel better prepared to walk into their own classrooms and make a difference in students' lives. A mentoring relationship helps preservice teachers to view the classroom as a comfort zone and prepares them to face the inevitable challenges of classroom teaching with enthusiasm.

References

Allen, D. D., Cobb, J. B., & Danger, S. (2003). In-service teachers mentoring aspiring teachers. *Mentoring and Tutoring, 11*(2), 177-182.

Alliance for Excellent Education. (2005). Teacher attrition: A costly loss to the Nation and to the states. (Issue Brief). Retrieved May 20, 2007 from http://www.all4ed.org/publications/TeacherAttrition.pdf.

Armstrong, T. (1994). *Multiple Intelligences in the classroom*. Alexandria, VA: Association of Supervision and Curriculum Development.

Armstrong, T. (2007). The curriculum superhighway. *Educational Leadership, 64*(8), 16-20.

Ballantyne, R. & Hansford, B. (1995). Mentoring beginning teachers: A qualitative analysis of process and outcomes. *Educational Review, 47*(3), 297-307.

Bell, C. (1996). *Managers as mentors: Building partnerships for learning.* San Francisco: Berrtett-Koehler Publishers.

Bernstein, L. (2007) Is there a mentor in your future? *Career World, 35*(4), 9-11.

Bey, T. (1995). Mentorships: Transferable transactions among teachers. *Education and Urban Society, 28*(1), 11-19.

Bloom, B. (1956). *Taxonomy of educational objectives, handbook 1: Cognitive domain.* Boston, MA: Addison-Wesley Publishing Company.

Boe, E. E., Cook, L. H., & Sunderland, R. (2008). Teacher turnover: Examining exit attrition, teaching area transfer, and school migration. *Exceptional Children, 75*(1), 7-31.

Boreen, J. & Niday, D. (2000). Breaking through the isolation: Mentoring beginning teachers. Journal of Adolescent & Adult Literacy, 44(2), 152-163.

Briggs, C., & Pehrsson, D. (2008). Research mentorship in counselor education. Counselor *Education & Supervision, 48*(2), 101-113.

Carroll, T. G. (2007). Policy brief: *The high cost of teacher turnover.* Washington, D.C.: National Commission on Teaching and America's Future.

Campbell, M., & Brummett, V. (2007). Mentoring preservice teachers for development and growth of professional knowledge. *Music Educators Journal, 93*(3), 50-55.

Conderman, G., & Johnston-Rodriguez, S. (2009). Beginning teachers' views of their collaborative roles. *Preventing School Failure, 53*(4), 235-244.

Diller, D. (2003). *Literacy work stations: Making centers work.* Portland, ME: Stenhouse.

Diller, D. (2005). *Practice with purpose: Literacy work stations.* Portland, ME: Stenhouse.

Diller, D. (2007). *Making the most of small groups: Differentiation for all.* Portland, ME: Stenhouse.

Dillon, N. (2009). Pay attention to retention. *American School Board Journal, 196*(9) 26-29.

Eisenman, G., & Thornton, H. (1999). Telementoring: Helping new teachers through the first year. *THE Journal, 26*(9), 79-82.

Galvez-Hjornevik, C. (1986). Mentoring among teachers: A review of the literature. *Journal of Teacher Education, 37*(1), 6-11.

Gardner, H. (1993). *Frames of mind: The theory of multiple intelligences.* New York: Basic Books.

Glesne, C. (1999). *Becoming qualitative researchers: An introduction.* New York: Longman.

Greiner, C. S., & Smith, B. (2009). Analyses of selected specific variables and teacher attrition. *Education, 129*(4), 579-583.

Grindel, C., & Hagerstrom, G. (2009). Nurses nurturing nurses: Outcomes and lessons learned. *MEDSURG Nursing, 18*(3), 183-194.

Gow, P. (2006). Admirable faculty: Recruiting, hiring, and retaining the best independent school teachers. *Independent School, 65*(4), 50-54.

Hagger, H., Burn, K., & McIntyre, D. (1995). *The school mentor handbook: Essential skills and strategies for working with student teachers.* London: Kogan Page.

Hatch, J. A. (2002). *Doing qualitative research in education settings.* Albany, NY: State University of New York Press.

Healy, C. C., & Weichert, A. J. (1990). Mentoring relations: A definition to advance research and practice. *Educational Research, 19*(9), 17-21.

Ingersoll, R.M. & Kralik, J. (2004). *The impact of mentoring on teacher retention: What the research says.* Denver, CO: Education Commission of the States. Retrieved May 22, 2007 from http://www.ecs.org/clearinghouse/50/36/5036.htm.

Kent, A., & Simpson, J. (2009). Preservice Teacher Institute: Developing a model learning community for student teachers. *College Student Journal, 43*(2), 695-704.

King, S. & Bey, T. (1995). The need for urban teacher mentors: Conceptions and realities. *Education and Urban Society, 28*(1), 3-10.

Latz, A., Speirs Neumeister, K., Adams, C., & Pierce, R. (2009). Peer coaching to improve classroom differentiation: Perspectives from Project CLUE. *Roeper Review, 31*(1), 27-39.

Lattimore, R. (1999). *The Odyssey of Homer.* New York: Harper Perennial Modern Classics, Reprint Edition.

Leedy, L. (2000). *Measuring Penny.* New York: Henry Holt and Company.

Maltas, C., & McCarty-Clair, J. (2006). Once a student, now a mentor: Preparing to be a cooperating teacher. *Music Educators Journal, 93*(2), 48-52.

Marable, M., & Raimondi, S. (2007). Teachers' perceptions of what was most (and least) supportive during their first year of teaching. *Mentoring & Tutoring: Partnership in Learning, 15*(1), 25-37. doi:10.1080/13611260601037355.

McTighe, J., & Brown, J. (2005). Differentiated Instruction and Educational Standards: Is Detente Possible? *Theory Into Practice, 44*(3), 234-244.

Moffett, C. A. (2000). Sustaining change: The answers are blowing in the wind. *Educational Leadership, 57*(7), 35-38.

Noble, T. (2004). Integrating the revised Bloom's taxonomy with multiple intelligences: A planning tool for curriculum differentiation. *Teachers College Record, 106*(1), 193-211.

Patton, L. (2009). My sister's keeper: A qualitative examination of mentoring experiences among African American women in graduate and professional schools. *Journal of Higher Education, 80*(5), 510-537.

Piaget, J. (2008/1959). *Language and thought of the child.* New York: Routledge Classics.

Riley, M., & Fearing, A. (2009). Mentoring as a teaching-learning strategy in nursing. *MEDSURG Nursing, 18*(4), 228-233.

Rogoff, B. (1994). Developing understanding of the idea of communities of learners. *Mind, Culture, and Activity, 1*(4), 209-229.

Siebert, C., Clark, A., Kilbridge, A., & Peterson, H. (2006). When preservice teachers struggle or fail: Mentor teachers' perspectives. *Education, 126*(3), 409-422.

Simkins, M., Cole, K., Tavalin, F., & Means, B. (2002). *Increasing student learning through multimedia projects.* Alexandria, VA: Association for Supervision and Curriculum Development.

Steadman, S. C. & Simmons, J. S. (2007). The cost of mentoring non-university-certified teachers: Who pays the price? *Phi Delta Kappan, 88*(5), 364-367.

Stokking, K., Leenders, F., de Jong, J., & van Tartwijk, J. (2003). From student to teacher: reducing practice shock and early dropout in the teaching profession. European *Journal of Teacher Education, 26*(3), 329-350.

Tomlinson, C. (1999). The differentiated classroom: Responding to the needs of all learners. Alexandria, VA: Association for Supervision and Curriculum Development.

Vygotsky, L. (1978/1934). Mind in society: *The development of higher psychological processes.* (M. Cole, V. John-Steiner, S. Scribner, & E. Sourberman, Eds. and Trans.). Cambridge, MA: Harvard University Press.

Walker-Dalhouse, D., & Risko, V. (2009). Crossing boundaries and initiating conversations about RTI: Understanding and applying differentiated classroom instruction. *Reading Teacher, 63*(1), 84-87.

Warner, M., & Coffey, D. (2004). Technology facilitates teamwork among middle grades teachers. Connections: *Georgia Language Arts, 42*(2), 11-18.

Whitehead, J. (1995). Mentoring. *British Journal of Sociology of Education, 16*(1), 129-133.

Wiggins, G., & McTighe, J. (2005). *Understanding by design* (2nd ed.). Upper Saddle River, New Jersey: Prentice Hall.

Wilkins, E. A., & Clift, R. T. (2006). Building a network of support for new teachers. *The Journal of the Association of Teacher Educators, 28*(4), 25-35.

Appendix

Figure 1: Components of the Mentoring Journey

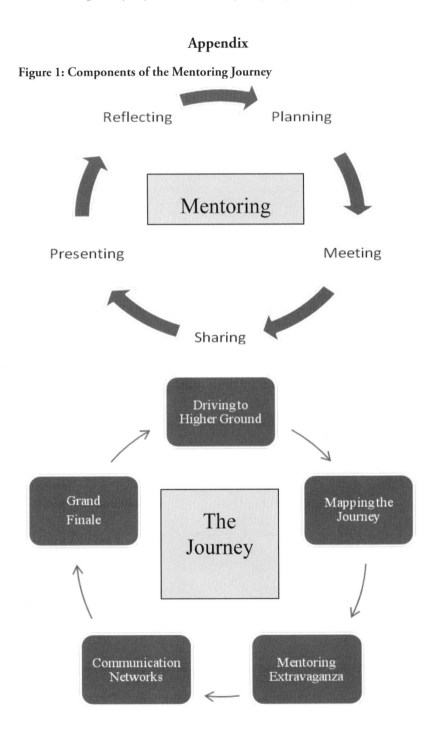

Figure 2: Survey Questions

1. What is a learning center?

2. What is the main objective of a learning center?

3. How do you create a learning center?

4. How do you assess a learning center?

5. How do you reach all learners through learning centers?

6. What do you think about learning centers?

7. Have you seen learning centers being used in elementary classrooms? If so, what types of materials or activities did you see in the learning centers?

8. What materials are available to you for designing learning centers?

9. Would you like some help finding ideas or materials for learning centers?

10. Have you used the Internet as a means of communication for a collaborative educational experience? If so, what limitations or benefits have you experienced with Internet communication?

Figure 3: Laura's Learning Center Aligns with Bloom's Taxonomy

Oceanographic Learning Center	
Bloom's Taxonomy	**Oceanographic Activity**
Knowledge The first activity gives students an opportunity to enhance their *knowledge* of the ocean through research.	**Animals of the Ocean:** The students select a card that identifies an animal in the ocean (a nurse shark, jelly fish, sea scallop, etc.). They will research the animal and tell four major facts about the animal: what ocean it is typically found in, where it lives in the ocean (what zone), and one fact that is interesting that they do not think many people know. They will complete that information on an index card. **Materials:** 3x5 index cards of various ocean animals, access to the Internet, encyclopedias, and books on the ocean, pencils, pens, blank 3x5 index cards for facts about the animals
Comprehension The Mapquest Activity gives elementary students opportunities to demonstrate their *comprehension* of geographical terms using various maps.	**Mapquest:** The students read and label oceans, seas, and continents on laminated maps the world, North America, and the United States. They have specific opportunities to apply their reading comprehension skills. Since these maps are designed in various formats, the students see how the same information can be presented in various ways. **Materials:** Laminated maps of North America, the United States, and the world
Application Students *apply* their knowledge of math by planning a trip to a seafood restaurant.	**Order Up!** The students are given a specified amount of money ($62.50) to take their best friend to a seafood restaurant. Several seafood restaurant menus are included, and they select a restaurant and make dinner selections for two. Then they calculate how much it will cost and how much change they will get back. This is a lesson on adding and subtracting decimals, money, and decision-making. **Materials:** Various laminated menus, a notepad for orders and calculations, markers, and calculator for self-checking

The Monsterjob.com Activity gives students an opportunity to *analyze* various jobs associated with the ocean.	various jobs associated with the ocean, and write a brief description of "A Day in the Life of a/an _____." (This encourages students to look beyond the normal jobs and explore new horizons.) Students may choose among careers such as a marine biologist, aquatic botanist, physical scientist, oceanographer, etc. They may also choose other careers related to the ocean. (Our elementary school is currently having various people come in and talk to the students about their jobs, and this activity will enhance their knowledge of jobs related to the ocean.) **Materials:** Writing materials, books, Internet access
Synthesis After students learn a great deal about the ocean, they have the opportunity *synthesize* their knowledge and create a fish. Before they create their own fish, students look through a porthole to see an ocean scene.	**Build-A-Fish:** The students create a 3 dimensional picture of the fish. They will cut out two images of the fish they draw, stuff it with newspaper, and staple the two sides together. They will color it and decorate it appropriately. At the conclusion of this project, students will present facts about the fish to the class, show the 3D picture, and place the fish in the proper zone on the interactive bulletin board. We will pin the cards that they completed next to the fish, and this will extend the learning for all of the students. **Materials:** Butcher paper, stapler, crayons, paint, markers, glitter, tissue paper, glue, yarn, and eyes
Evaluation Students *evaluate* the characteristics of specific jobs and choose the ones they find most appealing.	**Monsterjob.com:** In this research activity that was described previously, students have the opportunity to consider oceanic jobs and choose their favorites.

Figure 4: Laura's Oceanographic Learning Center

Figure 5: Kim's Entry on the Internet Bulletin Board

Kim shared these beneficial ideas with the entire group on the Internet bulletin board: Here are some ideas I wish I'd thought of during my first year as a teacher. These were things that came up during the year that seemed obvious, but had totally slipped by as I'd prepared to start the year. Some of the things should be done before you even start teaching, so I thought I would share them...

1. When you have time before the year begins, die cut several alphabet sets in several colors. I cut out 6 of each letter in each color. It's much easier to cut out lots of letters at once than cutting out individual phrases for bulletin boards.

2. Whatever you make/buy for your students at the beginning of the year (name tags, job tags, desk labels, birthday signs, parent notes, handbooks, etc) go ahead and make/buy at least 10 extra and put them in a folder labeled "New Students." When new students enroll throughout the year, it's so nice to have that all ready to go. It really makes them feel welcome if it doesn't take you two weeks to make things for them.

3. Go ahead and make a file folder for each unit/story/theme/holiday that you will be teaching for the year. Even if they are empty when the year starts, it will give you a place to drop extra copies, resources that other teachers give you, or notes about ideas you want to do next year. Don't start a "file pile" and think you'll get around to it!

4. Make a file for each student and start dropping in copies of work samples/notes about the student from day one in all subjects. If you need to start an SST/504/IEP, this makes it so easy to gather work samples. If you don't ever need it for that, it is so nice to have samples from the first few weeks of school to compare to later.

6. Start a parent contact binder and keep a record of all phone calls, emails, and notes from home.

    *I keep the info from ideas 5 and 6 for one year after my kids leave my room, and that's been a real lifesaver. I've been asked to attend several meetings once my kids have moved on to fifth grade to talk about what worked for that child in my room. It's so helpful to have all the communication between you and the parents as well as work samples from the previous year to refresh your memory and document your statements!

7. Take lots and lots of pictures! Pictures from the first day of school make a great addition to reflective activities at the year's end. I always make a class scrapbook of pictures, and the kids love it. It's also great to put out at Open House/Parent Night the next year!

8. Think about how you want your classroom to run from the smallest routine, like turning in papers, to the biggest. Plan and practice them during the first days of school! The way your classroom runs on the first day sets the tone and predicts the whole year.

Figure 6: Julia's Entry on the Internet Bulletin Board
An Overview of Julia's Learning Center Based on the Book Measuring Penny:

Learning Center Activities:

Measuring with Penny's Bones
The student will use dog biscuits to measure a variety of items that are easy to access. They will choose two other items that are not listed to measure. Before they measure, they must estimate how many dog biscuits long the object is. The student will then calculate and record the difference between the estimated and actual measurements.

The Earlier and Later Game
This is an activity for two students. The students will take turns and spin a spinner to select a time. They will then spin another spinner and change the clock to reflect the new time. For example, player 1 spins 10:15, and player 2 spins ½ hour later. The new time will be 10:45. The students will record the before and after times on a sheet with blank clock faces on it.

Guess the Time Game
This is an activity for two students. Student 1 will draw a card from the time card box and set the mini-clock to that time. Student 2 will then have to guess the time by asking questions like: Is it after 12:00? The students will use a sheet with blank clock faces to record their times.

The Beanstalk Caper
The story of Jack and the Beanstalk is the theme behind this activity. The student will read a summary of the story and then use problem solving skills to determine what objects Jack should bring back down the beanstalk. The weight and value of each item is listed on a card. The student will record the number of items, the weight of the items, and the value of the items on a sheet.

Square Shuffling
The student is learning how to find the shortest and longest perimeter in this activity. The student will select eight colored tiles and arrange them side by side to find the longest and shortest perimeter. Once they have done this, they will use grid paper to draw what they have come up with.

Ribbons of Rivers
The student will locate five major rivers on a map of the United States. Then they will read about the length of these rivers and create a model with a piece of yarn. The yarn will be measured using proportionate units of length. (1 inch = 100 feet). They will create a graph by ordering the longest piece of yarn to the shortest. The yarn will be glued onto a piece of paper and labeled with the correct name.

Figure 7: Julia's Measurement Center

Teachers' Perceptions of the Influence of Professional Development on Their Knowledge of Content, Pedagogy, and Curriculum

Aimee L. Morewood

West Virginia University

Julie W. Ankrum

University of Pittsburgh at Johnstown

Rita M. Bean

University of Pittsburgh

Abstract

As professionals, teachers must continue to move toward becoming experts in the field (Bransford & Schwartz, 1999). Research indicates that the teacher plays a primary role in student learning (Darling-Hammond, 2000; International Reading Association, 2000; Mosenthall, Lipson, Torncello, Russ, & Mekkelsen, 2004); therefore teachers must participate in effective professional development that strengthens their teaching. An interview was used in this study to better understand teachers' perceptions of the influence that professional development had on their knowledge of content, pedagogy, and curriculum. Shulman's (1986) work in teacher knowledge was used as the framework for this study. Overall, the teachers indicated that professional development did influence their understanding of content, pedagogy, and curriculum. A discussion about these findings and implications of this research are presented.

Teachers must be life-long learners. Reform initiatives continually change education, therefore it is necessary for teachers to learn about, understand, and implement these changes to improve instruction. Because life-long learning is crucial to educational change, quality professional development opportunities must be available for teachers. Professional development is required in most school reform guidelines because policy makers recognize that schools will not improve if teachers do not continue to learn (Guskey & Sparks, 2002).

A teacher's commitment to life-long learning more deeply develops his/her knowledge of content, pedagogy, and curriculum (Shulman, 1986). A deep understanding of these three areas coupled with how these areas connect creates an environment where effective instructional practices occur. As teachers begin to better understand connections among the content they teach, the pedagogy they choose to implement, and the curriculum to which they adhere they may begin to alter their teaching. Since current reading research indicates it is the teacher that influences student learning the most, (Darling-Hammond, 2000; International Reading Association, 2000; Mosenthall, Lipson, Torncello, Russ, & Mekkelsen, 2004) teacher learning through effective professional development is necessary.

Professional development may be perceived differently by individual teachers. It is important to gain a better understanding of teachers' perceptions about the influence professional development has made on their knowledge of content, pedagogy, and curriculum before a link can be drawn between teachers' knowledge and student learning. This study specifically focused on the teachers' perceptions of the influence of professional development on their content, pedagogical, and curricular knowledge. The following research question guided this study: How do teachers perceive professional development to influence their knowledge of content, pedagogy, and curriculum?

Literature Review

There are connections among teachers as life-long learners, effective professional development, teacher beliefs, and the deepening of content, pedagogical, and curricular knowledge. All of these topics can be discussed and researched in isolation; however each of these topics becomes more definitive when the connections among them are closely examined.

Teachers as Life-long Learners

Effective professional development is necessary for teachers to have opportunities to improve (Bean & Morewood, 2007). The National Staff Development Council (NSDC) is a professional organization that encourages teachers and administrators to participate in professional development and become life-long learners. The NSDC (2001) recognizes that teachers and administrators need to allot time to participate in professional development. Research by NSDC (2001) suggests professional development opportunities should account for 25% of a teacher's work week; this emphasizes how vital effective professional development is for advancing the field of education. The American Educational Research Association (AERA, 2005) and Doubek and Cooper (2007) also indicate that teachers must be provided time to engage in professional development. Hopefully, as teachers and administrators perceive the importance of participation in effective professional development, more time will be provided for life-long learning opportunities.

Effective Professional Development

Many educational conversations involve the topic of high-quality teaching. These conversations should be deeply entrenched in the discussions around effective professional development. All teachers need effective professional development when working to become high quality teachers. Novice and veteran teachers need effective professional development to provide them with experiences and examples of effective practices to move them on "the trajectory toward expertise" (Bransford & Schwartz, 1999, p. 68)

Professional development is deemed "effective" when positive changes to instruction occur because of participation. The ultimate goal of professional development is to deepen teachers' knowledge and pedagogy. Deeper understanding will lead to more effective instruction and ultimately lead to improved student learning (Guskey, 2000). Research outlines connections between high-quality teaching and student learning thus supporting teacher learning through effective professional development opportunities (American Education Research Association, 2005; Au, 2002; Darling-Hammond, 2000; Guskey, 2000; Joyce & Showers, 2002; Rosemary, 2005; Taylor, Pearson, Peterson, & Rodriguez, 2005). Since educational research indicates that high-quality teaching does influence student learning it is necessary to review key components of effective professional development.

Research indicates that specific criteria help to define effective professional development. These criteria identify effective professional development as job embedded, relevant to teachers' needs, and occurring over time. (American Educational Research Association, 2005; Bean, Swan, & Morris, 2002; Desimone, Porter, Garet, Yoon, & Birman, 2002; International Reading Association, 2000; National Staff Development Council, 2001; Taylor, Pearson, Clark, & Walpole, 2000). As teachers participate in professional development that incorporates these characteristics they are likely to become actively engaged in their learning. Teachers who actively participate in effective professional development sessions are more likely to positively influence student learning.

Teacher Beliefs

Although research outlines the criteria of effective professional development, teacher beliefs also influence their perceptions of professional development opportunities. Research indicates that teachers perceive professional development to be effective when their engagement in professional development has a link to student improvement (Commeyras & DeGroff, 1998; Doubek & Cooper, 2007). Teachers need to have choice in what sessions to attend so that the professional development opportunity best suits their learning needs (American Educational Research Association, 2005; Bean et al., 2002; Desimone et al., 2002; IRA, 2000; NSDC, 2001; Taylor et al., 2005; Taylor et al., 2000). When teachers are given professional development choices they are more likely to align student learning needs with their professional learning needs; thus influencing student achievement

(Morewood & Bean, 2009). Furthermore, teachers who are granted choice in their professional development opportunities may be more likely to participate in continued life-long learning; this deepens their knowledge of content, pedagogy, and curriculum which allows them to gain more expertise in the field (Bransford & Schwartz, 1999, p. 68).

Knowledge of Content, Pedagogy, and Curriculum

Knowledge of content, pedagogy, and curriculum is necessary for literacy educators. Teachers must have both substantive (i.e. the way information is organized) and syntactic (i.e. evidence that supports the information as being true or false) content knowledge (Shulman, 1986). Literacy teachers must possess a deep understanding of how to teach literacy skills and what makes learning easy or difficult (Shulman). Finally, curricular knowledge is necessary because literacy teachers must understand how literacy instruction aligns across grade levels (e.g. vertical curriculum) and across content areas within a grade level (i.e. horizontal curriculum) (Shulman). The IRA (2000) reiterates the need for content, pedagogical, and curricular knowledge. "They [effective teachers] have strong content and pedagogical knowledge, manage classrooms so that there is a high rate of engagement, use strong motivation strategies that encourage independent learning, have high expectations for children's achievement, and help children who are having difficulty" (IRA, 2000, p.1).

Because the link between teacher perceptions and involvement in professional development seems vital to increasing expertise, this study focused on teachers' perceptions of how professional development influenced their knowledge of content, pedagogy, and curriculum.

Methods

Context

This study occurred in a small city in southwestern Pennsylvania. Approximately 50% of the people in this city lived at or below the poverty rate. The school, Clemons Elementary School (CES) (pseudonym), was a Title I school with 71% of the students identified as White/Other and 29% Black. CES was one of three primary centers (grades 1-3) in the school district; kindergarten classes were held in a nearby kindergarten center. CES had 270 students and 19 teachers; 15 general education teachers, a special education teacher, a gym teacher, a music teacher, and a computer teacher in the 2006-2007 school year.

CES was a recipient of Reading First funds and also demonstrated improving student achievement on statewide tests. This school had a full-time reading coach and a part-time reading coach. Also, CES administered the Dynamic Indicator of Basic Early Literacy Skills (DIBELS) (Good & Kaminski, 2002) to students in grades 1-3. Student scores in the spring of 2006-2007 school year, on the Oral Reading Fluency (ORF) component of the DIBELS assessment (Good & Kaminski) indicated that 9% of first graders, 20% of second graders, and 23% of third grade students scored "at-risk"; all grade levels had an improving score on this assessment. CES was also mandated by the state to give all third grade students the state assessment; in the spring of 2005-2006 school year 57% of third grade students were "on-grade level"; this marked an improvement on the state reading assessment for three consecutive years. In addition to the DIBELS assessment and the statewide reading assessment, the students at CES were also assessed quarterly with instruments that aligned with *Success For All* (SFA) (Madden, Slavin, Farnish, Calderon, & Gwaltney, 2001) (e.g. the core reading program).

Sample

The researchers established two criteria for the sample before the onset of the study, thus creating a purposeful sample: improving student achievement scores and a Reading First School. The seven teachers who participated in this study volunteered; therefore, the sample was convenient. The teacher volunteers were recruited at grade level meetings by the researchers and had a range of years of experiences from a minimum of 4 years to a maximum of 10 years. All of CES's grade levels and special education were represented in the study's sample (i.e. 1 first grade teacher, 1 second grade teacher, 4 third grade teachers, and 1 special education teacher).

The educational experiences and certifications of the seven teachers in the study also varied. The majority of the teachers held initial certification in elementary education, while the remaining teachers had initial certification in elementary and special education. The teachers had different educational experiences beyond their initial certifications as well. For example, two teachers completed a master's degree program and were currently enrolled in additional graduate courses. The study was completed by all teachers who initially volunteered.

Procedures

All teachers participated in a pre-observation interview, a classroom observation of a literacy lesson, and a post-observation interview. Each teacher's interview was audio-taped and transcribed. The portion of the post-observation interview that is the focus of this article can be found in the Appendix.

The section of the post-observation interview for this article required teachers to reflect on the literacy professional development that they had participated in over the past year. The interview questions focused on content, pedagogy, and curriculum (Shulman, 1986). Each teacher was asked two questions for each of these categories (See Appendix). For example, the first question each teacher answered was, "How do you decide what you should incorporate from the professional development activity into your teaching?" This question focused on content knowledge. Each of the six general questions about effective professional development that focused on literacy was answered by each of the seven teachers.

Data Analysis

The framework for this study was based on Shulman's (1986) definitions of content, pedagogy, and curricular knowledge. By using this framework of knowledge, the teachers' utterances were coded in a two-phase process. In the first phase, the teachers' responses were coded to better understand how teachers' perceived their participation in professional development to influence their literacy knowledge of content, pedagogy, and curriculum. In addition to the three areas of knowledge, two other categories emerged from the teachers' responses. The two additional categories that were added were teacher learning and experiences. Although the teachers were asked to provide information about their learning through professional development, several responses also included information about how they perceived themselves as gaining a deeper understanding of literacy instruction through teacher learning (e.g. reflective practice) and experience (e.g. teacher wisdom). Table 1 provides the definitions for the phase one codes.

Table 1: Phase One Codes

Knowledge of Content	Understanding both the substantive and syntactic structure of content. Substantive was the way the facts are organized (i.e., reading instruction had multiple categories: comprehension, vocabulary, phonics, phonemic awareness, and fluency). Syntactic was what governs the information as true or false (i.e., evidence that supports claims in reading instruction; research states that repeated reading increases reading rate or fluency) (Shulman, 1986).
Knowledge of Pedagogy	The most effective ways (i.e., scientifically-based reading research) to teach reading and understanding what makes learning difficult or easy (Shulman, 1986).
Knowledge of Curriculum	Understanding vertical (e.g., grade level) curriculum and horizontal (e.g., content area) curriculum; variety of materials used to teach different curriculum; why certain curriculums are appropriate for certain instruction (Shulman, 1986).
Experience (i.e., Teacher Wisdom)	Based on teachers' personal experiences of teaching reading (i.e., it was not based on scientifically-based reading research).
Teacher Learning (i.e., Metacognition)	Teachers' metacognitive reflections that guided their reading instruction (Harris & Hodges, 1995).

In the second phase of coding the teachers' responses were coded more specifically within each of the five phase one codes. The phase two codes emerged from the teachers' responses and were not predetermined before coding began. Tables 2-5 provide the codes and definitions used in the second phase of coding.

Table 2: Phase Two Content Codes

Phase One Code	Phase Two Code	Definition
Content	Knowledge of literacy	Teachers' general understanding of literacy/literacy instruction.
	Comprehension	Teachers' discussion of understanding comprehension instruction.
	Fluency	Teachers' discussion of understanding fluency instruction.
	Vocabulary	Teachers' discussion of understanding vocabulary instruction.
	Writing	Teachers' discussion of understanding elements of writing instruction.
	Grammar	Teachers' discussion of teaching writing conventions.
	Assessment	Teachers' discussion of specific assessments (i.e., assessment guides the instruction).
	Motivation	Teachers' discussion of developing interest in reading or reading related activities.
	Reading and writing connection	Teachers' discussion of the links between reading and writing.
	Complexity of reading	Teachers' discussion about the many components or elements of reading instruction.
	Programs	Teachers' discussion of their understanding of specific published programs.

Table 3: Phase Two Pedagogy Codes

Phase One Code	Phase Two Code	Definition
Pedagogy	Knowledge of learners	How teachers' understanding of student needs affected their instruction.
	Differentiation	Specific mention of changing student instruction based on needs of students.
	Grouping	Teachers' references as to how students were grouped for instructional purposes.
	Scaffolding	Teachers' discussion about modeling or explaining expectations to students.
	Set instructional goals	Teachers' use of assessment data to plan instruction for the current year.

Table 4: Phase Two Curriculum Codes

Phase One Code	Phase Two Code	Definition
Curriculum	SFA (2001)	The scripted program implemented at CES.
	Sequence of curriculum	References to vertical curriculum (i.e., curriculum between grade levels).
	Impact of reading on all subjects	Influence reading has across student achievement.

Table 5: Phase Two Teacher Learning and Experience Codes

Phase One Code	Phase Two Code	Definition
Teacher Learning	Metacognition	"Awareness and knowledge of one's mental processes such that one can monitor, regulate, and direct theme to a desired end: self-mediation" (Harris & Hodges, 1995, p. 153).
Experiences	Teaching wisdom	Personal feelings, perceptions and experiences that guide reading instruction.

The two-phase process allowed the researchers to first analyze the teachers' responses from a general perspective. The second phase provided the researchers the opportunity to gain a better understanding about the specific topics that the teachers discussed in each of the Phase One categories. By analyzing the data in a two-phase process the researchers were able to see how teachers' perceived professional development to influence their learning from a general perspective and to better understand the intricacies nested within each of the topics as it related to professional development. Since the teachers' responses were complex at times, more than one code may have been assigned to an utterance in order to capture all of the information provided in the response. For example, Teacher 6's response was coded as writing and assessment because the teacher discussed the 4-Sight Benchmark writing assessment (Madden, Slavin, Farnish, Calderon, & Gwaltney, 2001) and how she learned about writing rubrics in a professional development session. This response indicated that this teacher had a better understanding of the statewide writing expectations because of her participation in a professional development session.

> *It [4-Sight] is their [the state's] checking system to see how well we [the school] are doing or how we'll do on the PSSA[the statewide assessment]; it is like a pretest. And what they [the professional development providers] did was they went over, they had a score and then they had another teacher score the same thing to see how, how far, you know, together we are on our scoring. Because it could be ... it is subjective grading so they give a rubric of how to do that. So that was very helpful to keep us all on the same page.*
> (Teacher 6, personal interview, April 3, 2007)

Two raters read the teacher interview responses to ensure reliability in the coding of this study. First, one teacher interview was randomly selected for both of the raters to read. After an initial read, the two raters reread the transcript and coded the document for Phase One. As they read the transcript for the second time, they each noted emerging codes, many of which eventually became the Phase Two codes. The two raters discussed their Phase One codes and the emerging Phase Two codes that they had independently documented. The raters recorded the Phase One and Two codes that were identified in this initial transcript reading and continued this same process for the next two transcripts that were read independently. While reading the second round of transcripts, the raters clarified their understanding by discussing the codes each rater identified in the transcript. These two raters established 80% inter-rater reliability using these two transcripts. The additional transcripts were then coded by the primary researcher.

Results

The following is a description of results based on the respondents' answers to the six questions regarding the role professional development played in their learning.

Phase One

All of the teachers responded to the questions about their knowledge of content, pedagogy, and curriculum. Overall, teachers' responses were most frequently coded as content (38.4%). Knowledge of pedagogy was coded in 20% of the teachers' responses, while 23.7% of the responses were coded as curricular knowledge. Some of the teachers' responses included experiences and teacher wisdom; these teachers indicated that their knowledge was deepened by these areas in addition to the provided professional development. The two additional codes for the initial phase accounted for 17.3% of the coding (i.e. experience was 12.6% and teacher learning was 4.7% of the codes). Figure 1 represents this data. When reviewing this data, it is necessary to consider that the number of codes varied per category and per teacher. For example, Teacher 6's responses were coded more frequently for content (e.g. 19 content codes were assigned to this teacher's responses) than Teacher 2 (e.g. 4 content codes were assigned to this teacher's responses).

Figure 1: Phase One Codes

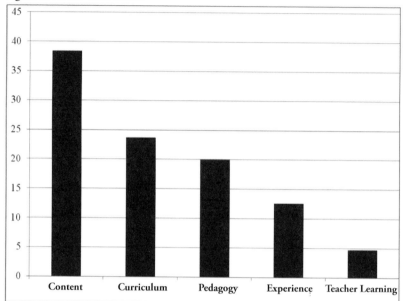

Phase Two

   Content Codes. During phase one of the analysis, content was coded the most frequently in the teachers' responses (38.4%). In order to better understand the "content" that teachers referred to, this category was coded again in phase two to specifically break down the teachers' response. Eleven phase two content codes (Table 6) emerged. There was a range in the percentage of times these codes were assigned in the teachers' responses; for example, assessment was coded most frequently (11.6%) while the complexity of reading was coded least frequently (1%). Again, there was a range of responses among the teachers as well; Teacher 6's responses were coded 19 times in this area while Teacher 2's responses were coded four times. It is important to recognize that the number of teachers represented in each of these categories differed. For example, writing instruction accounted for 5.8% of the coding in this area; however only three teachers' responses were assigned the writing code. Therefore, the codes assigned to writing only represent three of the seven teachers' perspectives.

Table 6: Content Codes

Code	Teacher 1	Teacher 2	Teacher 3	Teacher 4	Teacher 5	Teacher 6	Teacher 7	# of Responses	% of Responses
Content (Total)	13	4	8	17	6	19	7	73	38.4
Assessment	0	0	3	9	2	6	2	22	11.6
Writing	4	0	0	3	0	4	0	11	5.8
Fluency	1	2	0	3	3	0	1	10	5.3
Motivation	1	0	1	0	0	1	3	6	3.2
Knowledge of literacy	1	0	3	0	0	1	0	5	2.6
Comprehension	1	0	1	0	1	1	1	5	2.6
Vocabulary	0	2	0	2	0	1	0	5	2.6
Grammar	1	0	0	0	0	3	0	4	2.1
Reading and writing connection	2	0	0	0	0	0	0	2	1.1
Complexity of reading	0	0	0	0	0	1	0	1	1.0
Programs	2	0	0	0	0	1	0	3	1.6

Assessment was the most frequently coded phase two topic. Teachers' responses included information on learning about rubrics for writing evaluation, and reviewing both progress monitoring and standardized assessment data. The following excerpt provides an example of how professional development provided a teacher with deeper content knowledge about assessment. This will also provide insight into how the content codes were assigned.

Initially during the post observation interview, Teacher 4 indicated that her content knowledge was influenced by the professional development sessions that focused on assessment. Later in the interview, Teacher 4 reiterated that because professional development at CES focused on teachers' understanding of assessments, reading instruction overall had changed at this school. She also indicated that she recognized that her reading instruction was influenced by the professional development that was provided.

> *I think I have to always go back and say our test results because that I think is our most important tool because, I hate to repeat myself, but if that is what we have to work harder with and that is where we have to work harder. PSSA, you know discussing that. But I would always mostly say the PSSA and the Terra Nova are most important.*
>
> (Teacher 4, personal communication, April 2, 2007)

Teacher 6 began to think about literacy and literacy instruction through a more critical lens as a result of professional development opportunities. *"I am going to make a statement… not one size fits, not all programs are going to work and that is what I know"* (Teacher 6, personal communication, April 3, 2007). Professional development sessions deepened this teacher's knowledge of literacy and therefore her instruction began to change, based on her evolving knowledge.

Curriculum Codes. The teachers' responses were analyzed for phase two codes in the area of curricular knowledge. According to teachers, professional development influenced their knowledge of curriculum, which was coded in almost 24% of the responses. The topics that emerged as phase two codes pertaining to curriculum were: SFA (2001), impact of reading (all subjects), and sequence. Again there was a range among teachers' responses. For example, 14.7 % of the responses focused on SFA while 3.7% of the responses focused on the sequence of the curriculum, Teacher 7 had 7 responses coded as curriculum whereas Teacher 1 had only one response coded as curriculum, and Teacher 6's response was coded for sequence four times, however Teacher 3's response was not assigned this code in the second phase of analysis.

Each teacher's response indicated that professional development had deepened their knowledge of curriculum in some way. It was not surprising that SFA (2001) was frequently coded in the teachers' responses; this was the core curriculum at CES. Although SFA was coded the most often, most teachers also discussed vertical (e.g. sequence) and horizontal (e.g. impact of reading: all subjects) curriculum (Table 7). Interestingly most teacher's discussion about vertical and horizontal curriculum was embedded in their knowledge of the SFA program.

Table 7: Curriculum Codes

Code	Teacher 1	Teacher 2	Teacher 3	Teacher 4	Teacher 5	Teacher 6	Teacher 7	# of Responses	% of Responses
Curriculum (Total)	1	7	5	3	10	8	11	45	23.7
SFA (2001)	0	4	3	3	7	2	9	28	14.7
Impact reading has across all subjects	1	2	2	0	2	2	1	10	5.3
Sequence	0	1	0	0	1	4	1	7	3.7

Many of the teachers' responses indicated that their knowledge of curriculum was developed through sessions that focused on the SFA (2001) reading program. An example of this is provided in an excerpt from Teacher 2's interview.

Teacher 2 indicated that the SFA (2001) program dictated his reading instruction. He related his knowledge of the SFA program directly to professional development opportunities, although these opportunities occurred prior to the 2006–2007 school year.

Everything for us is pretty much structured; SFA, Success For All. It tells us what to say, when to say it, how to say it, and at what time to say it.... When I first came to here, to this district, no one knew about SFA, but through training and in-services and things like that, we are taught how to teach this.
(Teacher 2, personal communication, March 31, 2007)

The following example from Teacher 5 suggests how professional development created a space for her to connect her literacy instruction to students' achievement in different content areas. *"It is very important for kids to learn how to read. Well, basically if they struggle with reading and the teacher is not putting enough emphasis on their reading, then every other subject is going to suffer"* (Teacher 5, interview, April 3, 2007).

Pedagogy Codes. Teachers' responses indicated that they viewed professional development to be the least influential in their knowledge of pedagogy. In phase one, pedagogy was coded in 20% of the teachers' responses. Phase two included six specific pedagogical codes (Table 8). The phase two codes for pedagogy also indicated a range of responses by the teachers. For example, knowledge of learners was coded in almost 8% of the responses, while differentiation was coded in just over 1% of the teacher responses. All of the teachers' responses indicated that professional development did influence their knowledge of pedagogy; however, there was a range of responses. Teacher 3 discussed elements of pedagogical knowledge eight times, whereas Teacher 1's responses were coded only once. When viewing this data it is important to consider the different perspectives of the teachers. For example, Teacher 3 spoke more often about additional resources (e.g. 5 codes) than Teacher 7 (e.g. 0 codes); this demonstrates that teacher beliefs, needs, and value of professional development differ among teachers.

Table 8: Pedagogy Codes

Code	Teacher 1	Teacher 2	Teacher 3	Teacher 4	Teacher 5	Teacher 6	Teacher 7	# of Responses	% of Responses
Pedagogy (Total)	1	5	8	6	5	6	7	38	20.0
Knowledge of Learners	0	3	2	2	2	3	3	15	7.9
Additional Resources	1	0	5	2	1	1	0	10	5.3
Grouping	0	0	1	1	2	0	1	5	2.6
Differentiation	0	1	0	0	0	0	1	2	1.1
Scaffolding	0	1	0	0	0	1	1	3	1.6
Set instructional goals	0	0	0	1	0	1	1	3	1.6

The teachers' responses indicated that professional development influenced their knowledge of pedagogy. According to teachers, the professional development sessions focused on a variety of instructional topics such as gaining a better understanding of students, implementing different resources into reading instruction, focusing on grouping students for more effective instruction, and differentiated instruction.

The teachers in this study also acknowledged that the professional development that they engaged in provided them opportunities to better understand their students' needs; they gained a deeper knowledge of their students. Teacher 2 described how he applied information from professional development sessions based on his students' needs. *"Again, it [using information from the professional development session] depends on the students. I do try to use what I have been taught or what I have seen that looks good and so that I can use it"* (Teacher 2, personal communication, March 31, 2007).

Later in the interview, Teacher 2 further explained how his participation in professional development deepened his pedagogical knowledge about understanding his students and differentiated instruction. Professional development guided Teacher 2's learning which lead to a change in his instructional practice.

> *I have learned so much. Not every child learns how to read the same way, and I think I learned in that some are more visual and that is just with learning; in general, some can learn by just watching you do it and some have to do it themselves, and some have to be shown more than one time how to do it. So what I learned about literacy is that no one way is the correct and only way. I have to adapt to what best meets the students' needs. Not all 15 kids are going to learn just this way.*
>
> (Teacher 2, personal communication, March 31, 2007)

Experiences and Teacher Learning. Some of the teachers' responses included the codes experiences (e.g. 12.6%) and teacher wisdom (e.g. 4.7%). These two categories emerged from the data during analysis and were included because teachers' responses indicated that their knowledge of content, pedagogy, and curriculum was deepened through their participation in professional development. The teachers specifically described how the professional development connected to their teaching experiences and required reflective practice that created instructional awareness and ultimately changed their reading instruction.

There was a range in the number of codes assigned to each teacher for these two categories. For example, Teacher 6's responses were coded 7 times for experience, while Teacher 1 did not have any experience codes assigned to her responses. Table 9 provides the number of teacher responses per category.

Table 9: Experience and Teacher Leearning

Code	Teacher 1	Teacher 2	Teacher 3	Teacher 4	Teacher 5	Teacher 6	Teacher 7	# of Responses	% of Responses
Experience: Teaching Wisdom (Total)	0	6	5	2	2	7	2	24	12.6
Teacher Learning: Metacognition (Total)	4	3	0	1	1	0	0	9	4.7

Almost all of the teachers' responses suggested that they were able to connect their teaching experiences with information from the professional development that they participated in to guide their reading instruction. The following excerpt from Teacher 5 demonstrates how this teacher connected her teaching experiences to professional development to change her reading instruction.

Well, you know what applies to what you need. You take from the in-service what you could utilize in your class.... I think it [professional development] just touches base to refresh you. You know year to year.... Well, you apply it [professional development] as needed. You take what you need. If they [professional development providers] tell you how to increase fluency, and you have a child who is struggling in fluency, you are going to target that.

(Teacher 5, personal communication, April 3, 2007)

The teachers' responses that were coded as teacher learning discussed how their reading instruction changed because their participation in professional development required them to become a more reflective practitioner. In the following example Teacher 1 described how she provided additional instructional support for a student in her classroom because of her participation in a graduate course. She indicated in the interview that she continued to provide this additional academic support because of her student's academic improvement.

I have always wanted to see an improvement in his [the student's] reading, in his fluency, and comprehension. And I never wanted to see it, but I never made the time to do it [additional instructional time] and then I had to make the time for my class, so now I am continuing to do that...

I think I become more aware of what I am doing. At times, I assumed that they know what I am talking about and the tutoring [for the graduate course assignment] and the suggestions I got, I thought, "well he didn't know how to do this."... Now, I am concentrating on that, to make sure that they understand... (Teacher 1, personal communication, March 31, 2007

Teacher 2 also spoke about how professional development opportunities have enabled him to be more reflective in his teaching. "It [professional development] has made me more aware of what I need to do to get them [his students] to where they need to be" (Teacher 2, interview, March 31, 2007). Both of these teachers adopted a more reflective teaching stance because of professional development opportunities.

Discussion

This study focused on teachers' perceptions of how professional development influenced their knowledge of content, pedagogy, and curriculum. Research has indicated that high-quality teaching does influence student achievement (Darling-Hammond, 2000; International Reading Association, 2000; Mosenthall et al., 2004). Educators must participate in life-long learning to better understand the links among content, pedagogy, and curriculum. Teachers' deep knowledge of content, pedagogy, and curriculum allows them to provide more effective instruction; moreover, this knowledge may influence student learning (Doubek & Cooper, 2007). The following conclusions can be drawn from the results of this study which provide important insights for research that focuses on teacher beliefs and professional development.

First, all of the teachers indicated that professional development did influence their knowledge of content, pedagogy, and curriculum (Commeyras & DeGroff, 1998; Shulman, 1986). However, there was a range in teachers' coded responses for each of these categories. For example, the area of content code range was between 4 and 19, indicating the different perceptions of the teachers in the sample. A range in responses such as this suggests that each of these categories be considered on an individual basis when planning for effective professional development.

Second, although this study indicated that in general teachers most often perceived professional development to influence content knowledge, there was a range of responses with each of the categories. This range of responses indicates that teachers have diverse professional learning needs and these must be addressed through professional development choices (American Educational Research Association, 2005; Bean et al., 2002; Desimone et al., 2002; IRA, 2000; NSDC, 2001; Taylor et al., 2005; Taylor et al., 2000). When teachers are provided choice they are more likely to participate in professional development that aligns with their life-long professional learning goals.

Finally, most of the teachers in this study indicated that their participation in professional development influenced their knowledge of content, pedagogy, and curriculum because it connected to their teaching experiences and teacher learning. This suggests that teachers do connect the information provided in professional development sessions to their previous teaching experiences and teacher learning to provide high-quality reading instruction.

Limitations

Teachers did perceive professional development to influence their knowledge of content, pedagogy, and curriculum. However, given that the research was conducted with half of the faculty at one Reading First school not all teachers at CES had their perceptions captured. Because of this limitation, the results of this study should be generalized with caution. Another limitation of the study is embedded in the duration of the study. The data for this study focused on one school year which may influence the results.

Implications for Professional Development

All professionals need to continue to learn about their field, education is no different (Desimone et al., 2002; Guskey, 2000; NSDC, 2001). The data from this study indicates that teachers did perceive professional development to influence their reading instruction. The implications for this finding are cyclical.

Teachers need professional development choices that fit their learning needs (Bean et al., 2002). Once teachers are able to align their learning needs with professional development opportunities and student achievement they may perceive the professional development to be more valuable (Commeyras & DeGroff, 1998; Doubek & Cooper, 2007). As teachers begin to perceive the value of professional development they may begin to participate in more professional development sessions. Teachers who participate in more professional development opportunities will develop a deeper knowledge of content, pedagogy, and curriculum (Shulman, 1986). A deeper understanding of the connections among content, pedagogy, and curriculum may change their instruction (i.e. Teacher 4's response of learning about assessment leading to a change in her instruction and Teacher 2's discussion about gaining a better understanding of his students and differentiating instruction because of this), leading to higher-quality teaching. Higher-quality teaching will improve student achievement. This will reinforce teachers' positive beliefs about the value of professional development and continue life-long professional learning cycle. Figure 2 represents the life-long professional learning cycle.

Figure 2: Life-Long Professional Learning Cycle

Given that professional development is embedded in the cycle of teachers' professional life-long learning it is important to consider the following questions that emerged from the findings of this study. First, how can professional development providers offer varied opportunities that better suit individual teacher needs? Another suggestion for future research would be to examine how effective professional development can be better understood through aggregated data and through a case study approach? And finally, in order for teachers to glean as much information from a professional development opportunity, how can professional development providers facilitate the connections among professional development and high-quality teaching?

References

American Educational Research Association. (2005). Research Points. *Teaching teachers: Professional development to improve student achievement* (Vol. 3, Issue 1) [Brochure]. Washington, DC: American Educational Research Association.

Au, K.H. (2002). Elementary Programs: Guiding Change in a Time of Standards. In S.B. Wepner, D.S. Strickland, & J.T. Feeley (Eds.), *The Administration and Supervision of Reading Programs* Vol. 3 (pp.42-58). New York, NY: Teachers College Press.

Bean, R.M. & Morewood, A.L. (2007). Best practices in professional development for improving literacy instruction. In L.B. Gambrell, L. Mandel Morrow, & M. Pressley (Eds.), *Best practices in Literacy Instruction Vol. III*. New York, NY: Guilford Publications, Inc.

Bean, R., Swan, A., & Morris, G.A. (2002). *Tinkering and transforming: A new paradigm for professional development for teachers of beginning teachers*. New Orleans, LA: Annual Meeting of the American Educational Research Association. (ERIC Document Reproduction Service No. ED 465983).

Bransford, J. D., & Schwartz, D. L. (1999). Rethinking transfer: A simple proposal with multiple implications. In A. Iran-Nejad & P. D. Pearson (Eds.), *Review of Research in Education 24*, 61-100. Washington, DC: American Educational Research Association.

Commeyras, M., & DeGroff, L. (1998). Literacy professionals' perspectives on professional development and pedagogy: A united states survey. *Reading Research Quarterly, 33*(4), 434-472.

Darling-Hammond, L. (2000). *Teacher quality and student achievement: A review of state policy evidence*. Tempe, AZ: Education Policy Analysis Archives.

Desimone, L., Porter, A.C., Garet, M.S.,Yoon, K.S., & Birman, B.F., (2002). Effects of professional development on teachers' instruction: Results from a three-year longitudinal study. *Educational Evaluation and Policy Analysis. 24*(2), 81-112.

Doubek, M. B. & Cooper, E. J. (2007). Closing the gap through professional development: Implications for reading research. *Reading Research Quarterly. 42*(2), 411-415.

Good, R. H., & Kaminski, R. A. (Eds.). (2002). *Dynamic Indicators of Basic Early Literacy Skills* (6th ed.). Eugene, OR: Institute for the Development of Educational Achievement.

Guskey, T. (2000). *Evaluating professional development*. Thousand Oaks, CA: Corwin Press.

Guskey, T., & Sparks, D. (2002). *Linking professional development to improvements in student learning*. New Orleans, LA: Annual Meeting of the American Educational Research Association. (ERIC Document Reproduction Service No. ED464112).

Harris, T.L. & Hodges, R.E. (1995). *Literacy dictionary*. Newark, DE: International Reading Association.

International Reading Association. (2000). *Excellent reading teachers: A position statement of the International Reading Association*. [Brochure]. Newark, DE: Author.

Joyce,B. & Showers, B. (2002). *Student achievement through staff development* (3rd Ed.). Alexandria, Virginia: Association for Supervision and Curriculum Development.

Madden, N.A., Slavin, R. E., Farnish, M. A., Calderon, M., & Gwaltney, C. (2001). *Success For All*. Baltimore, MD: Success For All Foundation, Inc.

Madden, N.A., Slavin, R. E., Farnish, M. A., Calderon, M., & Gwaltney, C. (2001). *4Sight Benchmarks*. Baltimore, MD: Success For All Foundation, Inc.

Morewood, A.L. & Bean, R. M. (2009). Teachers' perceptions of professional development activities in a case study school. In F. Falk-Ross, S. Szabo, M. B. Sampson, & M. Foote, (Eds) *Literacy Issues During Changing Times: A Call to Action*, (pp-248-263). Commercer, TX: College Reading Association.

Mosenthall, J., Lipson, M., Torncello, S., Russ, B., & Mekkelsen, J. (2004). Contexts and practices of six schools successful in obtaining reading achievement. *Elementary School Journal, 104*(5), 343-367.

National Staff Development Council. (2001). *2001 Member survey results*. Retrieved Feb. 01, 2006, from www.nsdc.org.

National Staff Development Council. (2001). NSDC Standards for Staff Development Retrieved Feb. 01, 2006, from http://www.nsdc.org/standards/index.cfm.

Rosemary, C.A. (2005). Teacher learning instrument: A metacognitive tool for improving literacy teaching. In S.E. Israel, C.C. Block, K.L. Bauserman, & K. Kinnucan-Welsch (Eds.), *Metacognition in literacy learning* (pp. 351-369). Mahwah, NJ: Lawrence Erlbaum Associates.

Shulman, L.S. (1986). Those who understand: Knowledge growth in teaching. *Educational Researcher, 15*, 4-14.

Taylor, B.M., Pearson, P.D., Clark, K., & Walpole, S. (2000). Effective schools and accomplished teachers: Lessons about primary-grade reading instructions in low-income schools. *The Elementary School Journal, 101*,121-165.

Taylor, B. M., Pearson, P.D., Peterson, D.S., & Rodriguez, M.C. (2005). The CIERA school change framework: An evidence-based approach to professional development and school reading improvement. *Reading Research Quarterly. 40*(1), 40-69.

Appendix: Teacher Interview Protocol

Post-observation interview
General PD

1. How do you decide what you should incorporate from the professional development activity into your teaching? (content)
2. How does this new information from the professional development activity fit into what you already know about reading? What did you learn about literacy? (content)
3. How do you incorporate this newly learned information into your teaching? (pedagogy)
4. How does this new information fit into what is currently taught at other grade levels? (curriculum content-vertical)
5. How does this new information fit with what is currently taught in other content areas? (curriculum content-horizontal)
6. What did you learn about teaching literacy? (pedagogy)

How and Why Teachers Adapt Their Literacy Instruction

Seth A. Parsons

George Mason University

Stephanie G. Davis

University of North Carolina at Greensboro

Roya Q. Scales

Western Carolina University

Baxter Williams

University of North Carolina at Pembroke

Kathryn A. Kear

Binghamton University, SUNY

Abstract

Researchers have suggested that reading teachers must adapt their instruction to meet students' individual needs. However, the empirical base for adaptive teaching is limited. To address this gap in the research literature, this collaborative, longitudinal study used observations and interviews to examine how and why teachers adapt their literacy instruction. The coding systems created through this study demonstrated that teachers adapt their instruction in a variety of ways and for a variety of reasons. The results indicated that teachers' adaptations might not be as thoughtful as researchers have previously suggested. Implications for future research and for teacher education are discussed.

In their recent review of research on effective literacy teachers, Williams and Baumann (2008) stated,

> Excellent teachers demonstrated instructional *adaptability*, or an ability to adjust their instructional practices to meet individual student needs. For successful teachers, this flexibility appeared to be second nature; they

were able to sense and respond to diverse students and their changing needs. (p. 367; italics original)

These researchers were not the first to claim that teachers must be thoughtfully adaptive. Anders, Hoffman, and Duffy (2000) noted that reading teachers must be "thoughtful opportunists" who adapt their instruction to meet students' needs. Gambrell, Malloy, and Mazzoni (2007) expressed the idea that effective teachers of reading "are empowered to identify and select evidence-based literacy practices to create an integrated instructional approach that adapts to the differentiated needs of students" (p. 17).

Similarly, research on exemplary reading teachers has repeatedly identified adaptive instruction as a characteristic of highly effective teachers. For example, Allington and Johnston (2002) wrote, "Although they plan their instruction well, they also take advantage of teachable moments by providing many apt mini-lessons in response to student needs throughout the school day" (p. xiii). Pressley, Allington, Wharton-McDonald, Block, and Morrow (2001) wrote the following about the effective teachers in their studies: "Rather than adapt children to a particular method, teachers adapted the methods they used to the children with whom they were working at a particular time" (p. 208).

Purpose of Study

Researchers agree that reading teachers must be adaptive to meet students' diverse and individual needs (Anders et al., 2000; Duffy, 2005; Gambrell et al., 2007; Hoffman & Pearson, 2000; Snow, Griffin, & Burns, 2005; Williams & Baumann, 2008). However, in our literature review we found that empirical research on adaptive teaching is limited. Therefore, little is known about how teachers adapt their literacy instruction, the rationales teachers offer for adapting their literacy instruction, or the thoughtfulness of teachers' adaptations or rationales. To address this gap in the research literature, we engaged in a longitudinal research agenda examining teachers' adaptive instructional actions. The following research questions guided this project:

1. How do teachers adapt their literacy instruction, and what is the thoughtfulness of their adaptations?
2. Why do teachers adapt their literacy instruction, and what is the thoughtfulness of their rationales?

For the purposes of this research, an adaptation was operationally defined as a teacher action that (a) was non-routine, proactive, thoughtful, and invented; (b) included a change in professional knowledge or practice; and (c) was done to meet the needs of students or instructional situations. Rationales were defined as teachers' responses to the following interview question regarding adaptations: "Why did you make that change?" The thoughtfulness of teachers' adaptations and rationales was defined as the degree to which they were related to the goals of the instruction and the quality of the pedagogy used in the adaptations (see Appendix A).

Theoretical Framework

A social constructivist perspective informed this study. Social constructivism is based upon theories of teaching and learning presented by Dewey (1938) and Vygotsky (1978). Central to social constructivism are the ideas that (a) learners actively construct knowledge based upon what they already know and (b) the construction of knowledge occurs through experiences and social interactions within a particular context (Au, 1998; Guba & Lincoln, 1994; Oldfather, West, White, & Wilmarth, 1999). Moreover, social constructivism highlights the concepts of Zone of Proximal Development (ZPD) and scaffolding. Vygotsky presented the ZPD as the zone between what students can accomplish alone and what they can accomplish with assistance. Scaffolding is the assistance offered to students within their ZPD that helps them accomplish something that alone they could not do. Adaptive instruction parallels these concepts. That is, to scaffold students' learning within their ZPD, teachers must adjust their instruction based upon the particular student(s) with whom they are working and upon the particular situations in which they find themselves.

While social constructivism suggests learning is a social process, it also acknowledges the individual's awareness and control of his or her cognitions. This understanding is evident in a fundamental principle of constructivism: individuals actively construct knowledge based upon what they already know (Bransford, Brown, & Cocking, 1999; Dewey, 1938). This perspective, as it relates to this study, indicates that (a) teachers are aware of their cognitions, (b) their actions are a result of their cognitions, and (c) they are able to articulate how their cognitions influenced their behavior.

For the purposes of this paper, which analyzes the thoughtfulness of teachers' pedagogical moves, it is important that we explain our view of effective literacy instruction. In addition to the social constructivist perspective outlined above, it is our stance that effective literacy instruction embodies what is commonly referred to as a balanced approach to literacy instruction (Pearson, Raphael, Benson, & Madda, 2007; Pressley, 2006). That is, effective literacy instruction balances authentic purposes for reading and writing with explicit skill and strategy instruction. This balanced approach to teaching reading (a) motivates students to engage in real-world literacy experiences (Pearson et al.) and (b) allows teachers to differentiate their instruction providing explicit skills and strategy instruction to students who demonstrate the need (Duffy, 2003; Tomlinson, 2001).

Methodology

The research reported here describes the combined results of a collaborative, longitudinal project. In the early phases of this research agenda, we used a grounded theory process (Glaser & Strauss, 1967) to establish data collection and analysis procedures (Duffy, Miller, Kear, Parsons, Davis, & Williams, 2008). Therefore, we refined definitions, created a coding system for how teachers adapted, created a coding system for why teachers adapted, and created a rubric for rating the thoughtfulness of teachers' adaptations and rationales. The results of our early research are reported elsewhere (Duffy et al.). As we continued working on this research agenda, we used these established procedures to further investigate how and why teachers adapted their instruction. The results reported here combine our early findings with our more current results to provide the most up-to-date picture of what we have learned about thoughtfully adaptive literacy instruction.

Research Design

In this research, we employed instrumental case studies to examine the phenomenon of adaptive teaching. This type of case study differs from intrinsic case studies, which examine cases because the cases themselves are of interest (Barone, 2004). Our research focused on the act of teaching, as we looked at the adaptations teachers made and their rationales for changing what was written in their lesson plans. Therefore, we used collective case studies (Stake, 2005) to address our research questions, looking across cases to describe better the phenomena we investigated.

Participants and Setting

This collaborative, longitudinal project included 24 participants: one kindergarten teacher, five first-grade teachers, seven second-grade teachers, five third-grade teachers, three fourth-grade teachers, one fifth-grade teacher, and two sixth-grade teachers. All but the sixth-grade teachers taught in self-contained elementary school classrooms. The two sixth-grade teachers taught in non-self-contained, language arts classrooms in a middle school. All the teachers taught at Title I schools in an urban Southeastern city and had varying levels of teaching experience, ranging from a first-year teacher to a 27-year veteran. All teachers were female. The participants were selected using convenience sampling. These classroom teachers taught in schools where we placed our preservice teachers and verbally agreed to participate in our research, allowing us to observe their teaching. It is important to note that two of the schools were using restrictive literacy programs. Therefore, seven of the teachers were required to teach reading by following an adopted literacy program, which limited teachers' instructional moves. Although our convenience sampling technique was in no way all-inclusive, we did strive to be representative (e.g., teachers from all elementary grade levels, novice and veteran teachers, etc.). Therefore, we saw these teachers using programmatic instruction as beneficial in that regard.

Data Collection

In this research study, we triangulated our data by collecting teachers' lesson plans, observing their literacy instruction, and interviewing teachers:

Lesson Plans

We collected teachers' lesson plans to help us identify adaptations. The lesson plans varied in their format as we collected whatever the teacher used as a lesson plan. One way we identified adaptations was if the teacher deviated from the lesson plan.

Classroom Observations

Observations of instruction enabled researchers to identify the adaptations teachers made. Most observations were audiotaped, so the researchers could revisit classroom proceedings as needed. We were aware of the teachers' plans because we obtained a copy of the teachers' lesson plans before each observation. When we observed what we perceived to be an adaptation—recognized as teacher actions that were responses to unanticipated student contributions, diversions from the lesson plan, or public statements of change—we recorded the adaptation in our notes. We conducted 154 observations on the 24 participants' literacy instruction. Due to the convenience sampling and variations across school sites, the number of participants at each level and the number of observations varied. Table 1 outlines the number of observations.

Table 1: The number of observations at each grade level

Number & level of participants	Number of observations
One kindergarten	6
Five 1st grade	33
Seven 2nd grade	40
Five 3rd grade	44
Three 4th grade	13
One 5th grade	8
Two 6th grade	10
Total = 24 teachers	Total = 154

Teacher Interviews

After each observed lesson, the researcher interviewed the teacher for a total of 154 interviews. Interviews occurred on the same day as the observation. All interviews were audiotaped and transcribed for analysis. During the interviews, we verified whether the adaptations were indeed spontaneous changes by asking, "When I saw you (describe adaptation) during the lesson, was that a spontaneous change, something you had not planned?" If the teacher indicated it was an adaptation, we asked, "Why did you make that change?" The teacher's response to this question demonstrated her rationale for adapting.

The Role of the Researchers

As noted above, this research took place in schools where we placed our preservice teachers. The researcher collecting the data in each school was the university supervisor for that particular school. Therefore, the researchers had previous relationships with the participants, in varying degrees depending upon the school and the teacher. The researchers were present and visible in the school, and in some cases, they had conducted professional development in the school or had worked with teachers as they acted as the cooperating teachers for teacher candidates.

Data Analysis

In this research, we used previously established coding systems to analyze the adaptations teachers made and the rationales they offered for adapting (Duffy et al., 2008). We also used a previously established rubric to analyze the thoughtfulness of adaptations and rationales (Duffy et al., 2008).

Coding Adaptations and Rationales

We used coding systems created in previous studies to code our data (Duffy et al., 2008). As we coded the data, we used constant comparative analysis to refine the codes. That is, we evaluated the appropriateness of codes in light of new data, adjusting codes to ensure that they reflected the data (Glaser & Strauss, 1967).

To ensure reliability, at least three members of the five-person research team coded all adaptations and rationales together by reading each adaptation and rationale aloud and assigning a code for each. For an adaptation or rationale to be coded, all researchers had to agree on the code, thereby promoting reliability in coding. Following constant comparative method, discrepancies in codes were discussed and codes were refined as needed. The coding systems are presented in Appendixes B and C.

Rating the Thoughtfulness of Adaptations and Rationales

In previous studies, our research team created a rubric to rate the thoughtfulness of teachers' adaptations and rationales as considerably thoughtful, thoughtful, or minimally thoughtful (Appendix A; Duffy et al., 2008). To be rated as *considerably thoughtful*, an adaptation or rationale must have demonstrated an exemplary or creative use of professional knowledge or practice and have been clearly associated with a larger goal the teacher holds for literacy growth. An adaptation or rationale was rated as *thoughtful* if it was tied to the specific lesson objective or larger goal and did not meet any of the criteria for minimally thoughtful. An adaptation or rationale was rated as *minimally thoughtful* if it met any of the following criteria: it required minimal thought; it was fragmented, unclear, or demonstrated incorrect use of professional knowledge or practice; or it did not contribute to a lesson objective or goal.

To ensure reliability, at least three members of the research team rated the thoughtfulness of all adaptations and rationales together. We read each adaptation and rationale aloud and rated its thoughtfulness using the rubric. For the thoughtfulness of an adaptation or rationale to be rated, all three researchers had to agree on the code, thereby promoting reliability in rating the thoughtfulness of adaptations and rationales.

Findings

In this section, we first describe the overall findings of this study, describing how teachers adapted their instruction, the rationales they offered for adapting as they did, and the thoughtfulness of both their adaptations and their rationales. We then provide several classroom examples from our data to illustrate the codes and thoughtfulness ratings of teachers' adaptations and rationales.

Findings for Research Question 1

The first research question asked *how* teachers adapted their literacy instruction. The 24 teachers in this research adapted their instruction 353 times during our 154 observations. These teachers adapted in a variety of ways. The most common codes describing how teachers adapted were "invents an example of analogy" (N = 130), "changes the means by which objectives are met" (94), "omits a planned activity or assignment" (46), and "suggests a different perspective to students" (42). The least common codes included "modifies the lesson objective" (N = 4) and "changes the planned order of instruction" (9). A majority of the adaptations (N = 218; 62%) were rated as minimally thoughtful. Another 125 (35%) were rated as thoughtful. Only 10 (3%) were rated as considerably thoughtful. Table 2 displays these data.

Table 2: The number and thoughtfulness rating of each adaptation across teachers

Adaptation	N	min	thought	consid
1. Modifies the lesson objective	4	1	3	0
2. Changes means by which objectives are met	94	71	21	2
3. Invents an example or analogy	130	77	52	1
4. Inserts a mini-lesson	28	3	23	2
5. Suggests a different perspective to students	42	25	14	3
6. Omits a planned activity or assignment	46	33	11	2
7. Changes the planned order of instruction	9	8	1	0
Total	353	218	125	10

Few patterns emerged in the thoughtfulness of adaptations within individual codes. That is, a majority of adaptations within codes followed the same pattern as the overall results, with a majority being rated as minimally thoughtful. As seen above, an exception was adaptations where teachers "inserted a mini-lesson" (number 4). Teachers adapted their lessons this way 28 times, and only three of these adaptations were rated as minimally thoughtful. Therefore, nearly 90% of their adaptations within this code were rated as thoughtful or considerably thoughtful.

Findings for Research Question 2

The second research question asked *why* teachers adapted their instruction. The

24 teachers in this study offered a rationale for each of the 353 adaptations they made while we observed their instruction. These teachers offered a variety of rationales for their adaptations. The most common codes to describe teachers' rationales included "because the objectives were not met" (N = 97), "to help students make connections" (64), "uses knowledge of student to alter instruction" (45), "to challenge or elaborate" (32), and "anticipation of upcoming difficulty" (31). The least common code to describe teachers' rationales for adapting was "to manage behavior" (N = 5). Like adaptations, the majority of rationales were rated as minimally thoughtful. Of the 353 rationales, 229 (65%) received the lowest thoughtfulness rating. An additional 121 rationales (34%) were rated as thoughtful. Only three rationales (1%) were rated as considerably thoughtful. Table 3 displays these data.

Table 3—The number and thoughtfulness rating of each rationale across teachers

Rationale	N	min	thought	consid
A. Because the objectives are not met	97	76	21	0
B. To challenge or elaborate	32	15	16	1
C. To teach a specific strategy or skill	24	14	9	1
D. To help students make connections	64	38	26	0
E. Uses knowledge of student(s) to alter instruction	45	22	22	1
G. To check students' understanding	12	4	8	0
H. Anticipation of upcoming difficulty	31	19	12	0
I. To manage behavior	5	4	1	0
J. To manage time	21	21	0	0
K. To promote student engagement	22	16	6	0
Total	353	229	121	3

Few patterns emerged in the thoughtfulness of teachers' rationales within individual codes. That is, a majority of rationales within codes followed the same pattern as the overall results, with a majority being rated as minimally thoughtful. As seen above, two exceptions occurred. One was when teachers adapted "to challenge or elaborate" (statement B). Teachers adapted for this reason 32 times. Fifteen of these rationales were rated as minimally thoughtful, 16 were rated as thoughtful, and one was rated as considerably thoughtful. Therefore, more than half of these rationales were rated as thoughtful or considerably thoughtful. The other exception was when teachers adapted "using their knowledge of students to alter instruction" (statement E). Teachers adapted for this reason 45 times. Twenty-two of these rationales were rated as minimally thoughtful, 22 were rated as thoughtful, and one was rated as considerably thoughtful. This rationale, then, also had more thoughtful and considerably thoughtful ratings than minimally thoughtful ratings. Another salient finding was that all adaptations that teachers made "to manage time" (statement J) were rated as minimally thoughtful.

Classroom Examples Illustrating Codes and Thoughtfulness Ratings

In this section, we present classroom examples from our data. We describe four adaptations and their accompanying rationales, explaining how they were coded and the thoughtfulness rating they received. We provide examples of minimally thoughtful, thoughtful, and considerably thoughtful adaptations and rationales. These scenarios (a) provide concrete examples of our coding and rating systems and (b) illustrate the variety in teachers' adaptations and rationales.

First Scenario: In a second-grade classroom, students were competing to see who could cut out and glue down the most words from the newspaper that had the long /i/ sound. The spelling patterns could include i, ie, y, or igh. In this lesson, the teacher adapted her instruction by asking two students to work together instead of working independently. This adaptation was coded as "changes means by which the objective is met" because the teacher altered how these students completed the task. The adaptation was rated as minimally thoughtful because it did not require extensive thought or illustrate informed pedagogy. In the post-lesson interview, the teacher explained that she adapted in this way because "when I planned I didn't think about Frank, but he's just so…so low that I thought it wouldn't be fair for him to have to compete on his own." This rationale was coded as "anticipates student learning needs" because she changed the task in anticipation of future difficulty. It was rated as minimally thoughtful because instead of differentiating competitive instruction for a struggling learner, she simply paired him with a higher-performing student (Tomlinson, 2001).

Second Scenario: In a first-grade classroom, students were sequencing picture cards in a group. A card picturing pulp from a pumpkin confused the students. The teacher adapted the lesson by explaining that it was "the ooey gooey stuff that you guys didn't want to touch when we cut the pumpkin last week." This adaptation was coded as "providing an example or analogy." It was rated as thoughtful because the example demonstrated sound pedagogy by building upon students' previous experiences (Bransford et al., 1999; Dewey, 1938). The teacher's rationale for adapting in this way was that she wanted students to make the connection to their prior knowledge because she knew they had just carved a pumpkin the prior week. This rationale was coded as "making connections" and was rated as thoughtful because she demonstrated professional pedagogy by using students' experiences to clarify meaning (Bransford et al., 1999; Dewey, 1938).

Third Scenario: In a fourth-grade guided reading lesson, the teacher taught a mini-lesson on making inferences. After this mini-lesson as she listened to a student read aloud, the teacher noticed that the student did not understand the concept of making inferences. She asked the student if he knew what an inference was. He replied that he did not. At this point, the teacher adapted her instruction by conducting another mini-lesson on making inferences, defining the concept, and modeling it again for the student. She modeled from the student's book where he had left off reading. This adaptation was coded as "inserting a mini-lesson." It was rated as thoughtful because she demonstrated professional pedagogy by using explicit instruction to clarify a student's confusion (Duffy, 2003). The teachers' rationale for this adaptation was that she saw that he was not reading his book and she knows that he will rarely ask for help. Therefore, she asked him if he understood. This rationale was coded as "uses knowledge of student to alter instruction" because she adapted based upon her knowledge that this student rarely asked help. It was rated as thoughtful because it demonstrated extensive knowledge of her students and the ability to use this knowledge to guide instruction (Tomlinson, 2001).

Fourth Scenario: In a first-grade classroom, a guided reading group was taking a "picture walk" before reading a text. Students' predictions indicated that the main character in the story was a boy. The teacher announced that she would read the first page and allow students to check their predictions. As she read the words "Jessica" and "she," the students realized that the main character was a girl. At this point, the teacher adapted her instruction by discussing the concept of stereotyping and describing how they had stereotyped the character in the story. This adaptation was coded as "suggests a different perspective to students" because the teacher provided an alternate perspective to the students. It was rated as considerably thoughtful because it demonstrated exemplary use of professional knowledge and was related to a larger goal the teacher had for her students. The teacher's rationale for adapting in this way was that she realized the students were stereotyping and wanted to make them aware that stereotyping can have negative consequences. This rationale was coded as "to challenge or elaborate" because she wanted to compel students to be metacognitive about their actions. It was rated as thoughtful because it was connected to the larger goal she had for her students: to be aware of one's prejudgments of others.

These classroom examples demonstrate the coding and rating systems we used in this research. These examples also illustrate the variation in teachers' adaptations and rationales. Teachers adapted in a variety of ways, provided a variety of rationales for adapting as they did, and the thoughtfulness of these adaptations and rationales exhibited variation.

Limitations

There are several limitations to this study. The first limitation is the sample size and the number of observations that occurred. Other limitations of this study are related to our sampling technique and to our thoughtfulness rating system. We selected our participants using convenience sampling. The research literature suggests that effective teachers are thoughtfully adaptive, yet our sampling was unrelated to the quality of the teachers' instruction. Similarly, our participants all taught in the same large, urban school system that emphasized raising test scores. This emphasis certainly influenced teachers' instructional practices. While these aspects of our sampling limit the generalizability of our findings, they also strengthen our study because our findings are based upon the type of instructional practices taking place in schools, which increasingly emphasize raising high-stakes test scores. Therefore, the setting of this study is likely similar to that of other teachers who are working in Title I schools in large, urban school districts.

Another limitation is the protocol we used to rate the thoughtfulness of adaptations and rationales. Based upon the criteria we used for documentation, teachers' instructional actions had to demonstrate some degree of thoughtfulness to be identified as an adaptation. Therefore, the ratings of minimally thoughtful, thoughtful, and considerably thoughtful accurately rate all adaptations. In some cases, however, the rationale was rated as minimally thoughtful when the rationale was not thoughtful at all. Therefore, perhaps another category, such as no thoughtfulness, might be necessary to represent accurately these instances.

Discussion

There appears to be substantial agreement that reading teachers must thoughtfully adapt their instruction to meet the needs of the students they teach (Anders et al., 2000; Duffy, 2005; Gambrell et al., 2007; Hoffman & Pearson, 2000; Snow et al., 2005; Williams & Baumann, 2008). However, little research has examined how teachers adapt their literacy instruction, the rationales teachers offer for adapting their instruction, or the thoughtfulness of teachers' adaptations and rationales. Our research team has engaged in a collaborative, longitudinal research project to examine this gap in the research literature. Our research demonstrated that teachers adapt their literacy instruction in a variety of ways and for a variety of reasons.

This collection of studies adds to the research literature by collecting empirical data describing how teachers adapt their literacy instruction, why teachers adapt their instruction, and the thoughtfulness of their adaptations and rationales. Through this research, we identified patterns in how teachers adapted their literacy instruction. For example, teachers frequently altered their instruction "*on the fly*" to provide examples for students, to change the activity students were completing, and to suggest different perspectives to students. We also identified patterns in teachers' rationales for adapting. Teachers often adapted because students were not understanding the content being taught, because they wanted to help students make connections, or because they had extensive knowledge of their students. The coding systems we created for adaptations and rationales help build the construct of adaptive teaching because we have a better idea of what teachers do when they adapt their literacy instruction and a better idea of why they do it.

Although the coding systems describing adaptations and rationales add to the research literature on adaptive teaching, the results describing the thoughtfulness of teachers' adaptations and rationales were quite surprising. A majority of the adaptations and rationales identified in this study were minimally thoughtful. That is, most of the time adaptations and rationales demonstrated minimal thoughtfulness or displayed fragmented pedagogy. The prevalence with which thoughtfully adaptive teaching is discussed in the research literature indicates that effective reading teachers adapt their instruction in thoughtful ways. However, this longitudinal research studying a convenience sample of 24 teachers did not find an abundance of thoughtfully adaptive teaching. This finding has implications for policy and for teacher education.

In this study, some teachers were more thoughtfully adaptive than others were. However, there was little indication *why* some teachers were more adaptive than others. A teacher's classroom experience was not related to how thoughtfully adaptive teachers were. For example, one of the teachers who adapted her instruction in the most thoughtful ways was a fourth-year teacher. On the other hand, a 19-year veteran's adaptations were almost entirely rated as minimally thoughtful. Two factors that seemed particularly salient in affecting the frequency and thoughtfulness of teachers' adaptations were the context in which they taught and their knowledge, which we discuss below.

All of these studies took place in diverse Title I schools in an urban Southeastern city. Although we did observe good teaching, too often we observed restricted forms of literacy instruction as well as scripted instruction. Some of the schools in which we observed used restrictive literacy programs where principals instructed their teachers, "If it doesn't look like the standardized test, don't do it." It is not surprising that in these settings we saw very few thoughtful adaptations. When teachers' autonomy and professional decision-making are limited, their ability to adapt their instruction to best meet students' needs is removed.

It is our stance that effective literacy instruction is provided by teachers who are given "professional prerogative" (Pearson, 2007) to adapt their instruction using their knowledge of pedagogy and their students. Unfortunately, some of the Title I elementary schools in which we worked did not give teachers professional prerogative. In future studies of thoughtfully adaptive teaching, researchers need to be selective in choosing schools to ensure that teachers have the freedom to adapt their instruction. Likewise, schools and school systems interested in providing optimal literacy instruction to students should give teachers the autonomy to meet their students' needs in the best way possible. Researchers have long demonstrated that the teacher, not the program, is the important factor influencing students' literacy learning (Duffy & Hoffman, 1999). Therefore, schools and school systems would be best served by investing in teachers rather than in programs (Parsons & Harrington, 2009).

Implication

The finding that a majority of teachers' adaptations demonstrated minimal thoughtfulness should serve as an impetus for those in teacher education and professional development. When teachers adapted their literacy instruction in thoughtful ways, they demonstrated extensive knowledge about teaching reading and about effective pedagogy—or in Shulman's (1987) terms, they displayed strong "pedagogical content knowledge." For example, the teacher who adapted by inserting a mini-lesson on making inferences knew that explicit explanations with modeling is effective for teaching comprehension strategies. It follows, then, that increasing teachers' knowledge of effective literacy practice would further enable teachers to adapt thoughtfully their literacy instruction to meet the demands of the students with whom they are working and of the situations in which they find themselves. Unfortunately, the research literature is incredibly thin regarding teacher education practices that develop teachers' ability to adapt thoughtfully their instruction. This area of research certainly requires more attention from teacher educators interested in developing effective teachers of reading.

References

Allington, R. L. & Johnston, P. (2002). *Reading to learn: Lessons from exemplary fourth-grade classrooms.* New York: Guilford Press.

Anders, P. L., Hoffman, J. V., & Duffy, G. G. (2000). Teaching teachers to teach reading: Paradigm shifts, persistent problems, and challenges. In M. L. Kamil, P. B. Mosenthal, P. D. Pearson, & R. Barr (Eds.), *Handbook of reading research* (Vol. III, pp. 719-742). Mahwah, NJ: Lawrence Erlbaum Associates.

Au, K. (1998). Social constructivism and the school literacy learning of students of diverse backgrounds. *Journal of Literacy Research, 20,* 297-319.

Barone, D. M. (2004) Case-study research. In N. K. Duke & M. H. Mallette (Eds.), *Literacy research methodologies* (pp. 7-27). New York: Guilford.

Bransford, J. D., Brown, A. L., Cocking, R. R. (Eds.). (1999). *How people learn: Brain, mind, experience, and school.* Washington, DC: National Academy Press.

Dewey, J. (1938). *Experience and education.* New York: Touchstone.

Duffy, G. G. (2005). Developing metacognitive teachers: Visioning and the expert's changing role in teacher education and professional development. In S. E. Israel, C. C. Block, K. L. Bauserman, & K. Kinnucan-Welsch (Eds.), *Metacognition in literacy learning: Theory, assessment, instruction, and professional development* (pp. 299-314). Mahwah, NJ: Lawrence Erlbaum.

Duffy, G. G. (2003). *Explaining reading: A resource for teaching concepts, skills, and strategies.* New York: Guilford Press.

Duffy, G. G. & Hoffman, J. V. (1999). In pursuit of an illusion: The flawed search for a perfect method. *Reading Teacher, 53*(1), 10-17.

Duffy, G. G., Miller, S. D., Kear, K. A., Parsons, S. A., Davis, S. G., & Williams, J. B. (2008). Teachers' instructional adaptations during literacy instruction. In Y. Kim, V. J. Risko, D.L. Compton, D. K. Dickinson, M. K., Hundley, R. T. Jimenez, K. M. Leander, & D. W. Rowe (Eds.), *57ᵗʰ Yearbook of the National Reading Conference* (pp. 160-171). Oak Creek, WI: National Reading Conference.

Gambrell, L. B., Malloy, J. A., & Mazzoni, S. A. (2007). Evidence-based best practices for comprehensive literacy instruction. In L. B. Gambrell, L. M. Morrow, & M. Pressley (Eds.), *Best practices in literacy instruction* (3ʳᵈ ed., pp. 11-29). New York: Guilford Press.

Glaser, B. J. & Strauss, A. L. (1967). *The discovery of grounded theory: Strategies for qualitative research.* Hawthorne, NY: Aldine de Gruyter.

Guba, E. G. & Lincoln, Y. S. (1994). Competing paradigms in qualitative research. In N. K. Denzin & Y. S. Lincoln (Eds.), *Handbook of qualitative research* (pp. 105-117). Thousand Oaks, CA: Sage.

Hoffman, J. V. & Pearson, P. D. (2000). Reading teacher education in the next millennium: What your grandmother's teacher didn't know that your granddaughter's teacher should. *Reading Research Quarterly, 35*(1), 28-44.

Oldfather, P., West, J., White, J., & Wilmarth, J. (1999). *Learning through children's eyes: Social constructivism and the desire to learn.* Washington, DC: American Psychological Association.

Parsons, S. A. & Harrington, A. D. (2009). Reading the script. *Phi Delta Kappan, 90,* 748-750.

Pearson, P. D. (2007). An endangered species act for literacy education. *Journal of Literacy Research, 39,* 145-162.

Pearson, P. D., Raphael, T. E., Benson, V. L., & Madda, C. L. (2007). Balance in comprehensive literacy instruction: Then and now. In L. B. Gambrell, L. M. Morrow, & M. Pressley (Eds.), *Best practices in literacy instruction* (3rd ed., pp. 30-54). New York: Guilford Press.

Pressley, M. (2006). *Reading instruction that works: The case for balanced teaching* (3rd ed.). New York: Guilford Press.

Pressley, M., Allington, R. L., Wharton-McDonald, R., Block, C. C., & Morrow, L. M. (Eds.). (2001). *Learning to read: Lessons from exemplary first-grade classrooms.* New York: Guilford.

Shulman, L. S. (1987). Knowledge and teaching: Foundations of the new reform. *Harvard Educational Review, 57*(1), 1-22.

Snow, C. E., Griffin, P., & Burns, M. S. (Eds.). (2005). *Knowledge to support the teaching of reading: Preparing teachers for a changing world.* San Francisco: Jossey-Bass.

Stake, R. E. (2005). Qualitative case studies. In N. K. Denzin & Y. S. Lincoln (Eds.), *The Sage handbook of qualitative research* (3rd ed., pp. 443-466). Thousand Oaks, CA: Sage.

Tomlinson, C. A. (2001). *How to differentiate instruction in mixed-ability classrooms* (2nd ed.). Alexandria, VA: ASCD.

Vygotsky, L. S. (1978). *Mind in society: The development of higher psychological processes* (M. Cole, V. John-Steiner, S. Scribner, & E. Souberman, Trans.). Cambridge, MA: Harvard University Press.

Williams, T. L., & Baumann, J. F. (2008). Contemporary research on effective elementary literacy teachers. In Y. Kim, V. J. Risko, D. L. Compton, D. K. Dickinson, M. K. Hundley, R. T. Jimenez, K. M. Leander, & D. W. Rowe (Eds.), *57th Yearbook of the National Reading Conference* (pp. 357-372). Oak Creek, WI: National Reading Conference.

Appendix A: Rubric for Rating Thoughtfulness of Adaptations and Rationales

Considerably Thoughtful (must meet both criteria)

The teacher is showing exemplary or creative use of professional knowledge or practice

The adaptation or rationale is clearly associated with a larger goal the teacher holds for literacy growth (i.e., the adaptation or rationale is motivated by a desire to develop a deep or broad understanding or a conceptual or attitudinal goal).

Thoughtful

Must be tied to the specific lesson objective or to a larger goal the teacher wants to develop

Must not meet any of the criteria for "minimally thoughtful."

Minimally Thoughtful (if it meets any of the following criteria)

The adaptation or rationale requires minimal thought

The teacher's use of professional knowledge or practice is fragmented, unclear, or incorrect

The adaptation or rationale does not contribute to the development of either a larger goal or a specific lesson objective.

Appendix B: Coding System for Adaptations

1. The teacher modifies the lesson objective

2. The teacher changes means by which objectives are met (e.g., materials, strategy, activity, assignment, procedures, or routines)

3. The teacher invents an example or an analogy

4. The teacher inserts a mini-lesson

5. The teacher suggests different ways students could deal with a situation or problem

6. The teacher omits certain planned activities or assignments (for reasons other than lack of time) or inserts an unplanned activity or assignment

7. The teacher changes the planned order of instruction

Appendix C: Coding System for Rationales

A. Because the objectives are not met

B. To challenge or elaborate

C. To teach a specific strategy or skill

D. To help students make connections

E. Uses knowledge of student(s) to alter instruction

G. To check students' understanding

H. In anticipation of upcoming difficulty

I. To manage behavior

J. To manage time

K. To promote student engagement

An Investigation of Teacher Talk during the Administration of an Informal Reading Inventory

Marie F. Holbein

Kennesaw State University

Donna M. Harkins

University of West Georgia

Abstract

Research suggests that classroom dialogue characterized as teacher-talk is an important teaching tool and it can influence student learning (Palincsar cited in Berry, 2006; Culican, 2007). Teachers may use a variety of teacher-talk patterns for different purposes and in varying contexts. What is important is how teachers "make skillful use" of their dialogue (Viiri & Saari, 2006, p. 350). Teacher dialogue that occurs during the administration of an informal reading inventory is socially interactive. To engage effectively in the strategic assessment of learning, teachers must be aware of the impact their teacher-talk has on students' ability to process aural language. The purpose of this study was to determine the extent to which teachers vary teacher-talk when administering an informal reading inventory to clients who receive tutoring services from a reading clinic at a southeastern regional university.

Learning flourishes in a social environment where sociocultural and mental processes can be linked to work together through dialogue (Palincsar cited in Berry, 2006; Vygotsky cited in Berry; Vygotsky, 1962). Dialogue as a component of social interaction takes place both in exchanges with others, as well as, within each individual's mind (Vygotsky cited in Wilson, 2008). Research suggests that classroom dialogue can be characterized as teacher-talk, is a teaching tool, and can influence student learning (Palincsar cited in Berry; Culican, 2007).

Classroom dialogue can be described in patterns and can be analyzed. These patterns are "habitual, intuitive, and largely unconscious" (Culican, 2007, p. 11). Teachers and students hold identities that are historically and culturally linked to patterns of teacher-talk, and unless we study those patterns, we will remain unaware of the impact of dialogue on academic success or possibly, the exclusion of students in the learning process (Culican, 2007).

Dialogue can be segmented into five conversational elements: promotion of discussion; responsivity to student contributions; connected discourse; a challenging, but nonthreatening atmosphere; and general participation including self-selected turns. The impact of these elements of conversation on students with disabilities is particularly important in that those students may struggle with linguistic forms and appropriate word-choice (Morocco cited in Berry, 2006; Palincsar, Magnusson, Cutter & Vincent; cited in Berry, 2006).

According to Berry (2006), discourse strategies can be characterized as either procedural or involvement. The procedural strategies are aiming and modeling (explanations), overlapping and directing (repeating, paraphrasing, providing feedback, informing next steps and transitions, managing students' behavior, and directing attention to the task). Involvement strategies are orchestrating (facilitating), sharing ownership (transfer of control), and scaffolding (allowing participation by proxy).

According to Wells (cited in Culican, 2007), the most common pattern of talk is triadic dialogue. Sometimes referred to synonymously in the literature as either the IRF pattern (Initiate, Response, Follow-Up), the IRE pattern (Initiate, Response, and Evaluate), or the Q & A pattern (Question and Answer), triadic dialogue can be attributed to as much as 70% of the classroom interactions between students and teachers (Lemke cited in Culican, 2007; Wells cited in Culican, 2007; Nassaji & Wells cited in Culican, 2007).

In a triadic dialogue, the initiation is usually a question that requires the student to access information from previous experiences and learning. The student tries to respond and the teacher provides necessary feedback. Reluctant or struggling readers are often disadvantaged in the dialogue exchange as they lack the skills to predict and recall patterns. These difficulties coupled with their lack of experience and prior knowledge creates stressful situations where it is difficult for struggling readers to be successful in the dialogue exchange (Rose cited in Culican, 2007).

The scaffolding interaction cycle, a variation on the triadic pattern, attempts to lessen this disadvantage through prompting and elaborating (Rose cited in Culican, 2007). Wilson (2008) suggests that to optimize learning, teachers should scaffold students' responses by "exploring and elaborating" (p. 368) on them. Wilson proposes an economical application of what she terms "teacher-talk time" (p. 369). Walsh (cited in Wilson, 2008) proposes, "teacher-talk can both facilitate and obstruct learning" in that the teacher becomes the "controlling pivot and mediator of classroom talk" (p. 368). For example, the following dialogue exchange derived from verbatim transcripts extracted from the administration of an informal reading inventory shows a knowledge gap between the question posed by the tutor and the student client during the administration of the QR I-4 (Leslie & Caldwell, 2005). The tutor appears to intuitively move into what Rose calls "prompting and elaborating" (cited in Culican, 2007) to bridge the knowledge gap. The teacher-talk involved in the process may be construed as effective or ineffective (Casa &

DeFranco cited in Viiri & Saari, 2006) depending on the purpose of the question, in this case to establish prior knowledge, and may impact the cognitive load (Rose, cited in Culican, 2007) as represented by elaborations on the tutor's personal experience which may or may not be meaningful to the student.

Tutor: *Have you ever heard of Johnny Appleseed? (Question from IRI administration)*

Student: *No.*

Tutor: *You've never heard of Johnny Appleseed? When I was growing up, we have a song about Johnny Appleseed. I can't remember it, but I remember it being a song about Johnny Appleseed. Well, this story is going to be about a guy named Johnny Appleseed.*

Tutor: *Why do you think people plant apple seeds?*

Teachers may use a variety of teacher-talk patterns for different purposes and in varying contexts. What is important is how teachers "make skillful use" of the triadic model (Viiri & Saari, 2006, p. 350). In their study of teachers and student teachers, Viira & Saari (2006) gathered data on classroom talk through videotaped sessions. Six categories of teacher-talk emerged: (a) teacher presentation, (b) teacher-guided discussion, (c) authoritative discussion, (d) dialogic discussion, (e) peer discussion, and (f) other. Findings from their study revealed varying patterns of talk ranging from simple and monotonous to interactive patterns that were strategically focused. Implications from their work suggest that teachers should be able to understand their talk patterns and vary them if necessary, but they must be taught to do so.

Nystrand (2006) suggests that both qualitative and quantitative research methodologies offer promising possibilities for analyzing teacher discourse with respect to both educational outcomes and cultural contexts. The findings from such research provide insights into "ecologies of speaking and listening in everyday life" (Erickson, cited in Nystrand, p. 404).

The impact of classroom dialogue is particularly important to students with learning disabilities. Berry (2006) examined involvement strategies used by teachers with learning disabled students in whole class discussions. The implications from her study suggest that "when teachers make use of a more conversational method, they must support and scaffold student entry into the conversation" (p. 229). Berry further suggested that teacher education programs should provide an intentional focus on promoting student interaction and involvement strategies such as prompting, cueing, and cognitive modeling for students with learning disabilities.

According to Wilson (2008), the impact of talk is particularly important in reading classes as it "encourages students to engage in direct dialogue with texts, allowing them to construct meanings for themselves rather than relying on the teacher as arbiter of meaning" (2007, p. 373). A particular example of teacher student interaction and conversation dialogue is the one-on-one administration format of an informal reading inventory that measures students' oral and silent reading comprehension (Leslie & Caldwell, 2005). The administration of these inventories occurs in an oral and aural environment where teachers have a great deal of flexibility in language usage. The dialogue exchanges that occur during those administrations become increasingly important in terms of economy of teacher-talk, use of conversation elements, and implementation of various strategies.

The teacher dialogue that occurs during the administration of an informal reading inventory is embedded within the environment of social interaction. To engage effectively in strategic assessment, teachers must be aware of the impact of social interaction and dialogue in the learning process (Berry, 2006; Wilson, 2008).

Purpose of Study

The purpose of this study was to determine the extent to which teachers vary teacher-talk when administering an informal reading inventory to clients who receive tutoring services from a reading clinic at a southeastern regional university. As part of the diagnostic process, these clients participated in a number of assessment procedures whose major purpose is to determine their areas of tutorial needs. Communication between client and assessor is critical to obtain accurate results and relies heavily on clarity, which is defined as the ability to communicate expectations clearly (Cruikshank, Jenkins, & Metcalf, 2005).

Research Questions

The research questions that propelled the study focused on the variability of applications in teacher-talk. More specifically the investigators guided their research by asking the following questions:

1. How do tutors employ teacher-talk beyond structured questions during the administration of a reading inventory?
2. How does teacher-talk vary among tutors during the administration of a reading inventory?
3. How does teacher-talk vary between tutors and clients during the administration of a reading inventory?

Methods

Setting

The reading clinic is housed in the College of Education. Approximately 35 clients are tutored each semester by undergraduate enrolled in an elementary education program and graduate students enrolled in a master's level reading education program. Undergraduate and graduate students work in the clinic to fulfill field experience and clinical requirements for the courses required in their respective undergraduate and graduate programs of study. The director of the clinic manages and supervises the entire process. Clinic clients are tutored weekly for one hour throughout the sixteen-week semester.

The clinic employs certificated teachers to administer and interpret an informal reading inventory to the clients upon enrollment for the clinic services. The purpose of the informal reading inventory assessment and interpretation is to establish a baseline for client performance and to facilitate the development of a tutoring plan for each client developed by the tutors. These certificated teachers hold a master's degree in Reading Education and have experience administering and interpreting the informal reading inventory diagnostic instrument.

Participants

The participants in this study are two certificated teachers who administered and interpreted the informal reading inventory and four clinic clients. Each teacher had at least two semesters of previous experience employed by the clinic in assessing clients. Their participation in the study was voluntary. The teachers are Selene, an African-American female with 20 years teaching experience at the middle school (4-8) level, and Andrea, a white female with fewer than five years teaching at the elementary level.

The clients, Paul, Sam, Mark, and Will, were all fourth grade white males, ages 10 and 11, seeking clinic services. The clients were brought to the clinic by their parents for enrichment and academic support. All participating teachers and clients in the study were given pseudonyms.

The two researchers are instructional faculty in the College of Education. One was a former director of the clinic and the other, at the time of the study, was the current director of the clinic. Both have more than 8 years experience working with literacy.

The undergraduate and graduate students were not participants in the study. Their roles as tutors have been described to provide context for the setting.

Procedures

The sessions were conducted during the first few weeks of the fall semester's tutoring sessions. The informal reading inventories were administered to each of the four clients in one-on-one tape-recorded sessions in a closed environment. Verbatim transcripts were coded and analyzed to determine categories and patterns of responses.

Informal Reading Inventory Instrument

The *Qualitative Reading Inventory 4* (Leslie & Caldwell, 2005) was used for the informal reading inventory assessment. Paul, Sam, and Mark all read the same three stories: (Level Two) "What Can I Get for My Toy?", (Level Three) "The Trip to the Zoo," and (Level Three) "Johnny Appleseed." Will read two stories: (Level One) "Mouse in a House" and (Level Two) "What Can I Get for My Toy? (see Appendix A). In accordance with guidelines for administering the informal reading inventory, stories were selected based on word list performance. Reading ended when clients demonstrated fatigue or frustration, or if they asked to stop. Leslie and Caldwell (2005) define frustration-level text as a level at which "the student is completely unable to read the material with adequate word identification or comprehension" (p. 26).

Data Analysis

The researchers applied qualitative case study methodology (Creswell, 2006) to investigate the impact of teacher-talk among clinic clients and the teacher (certificated teacher) who administers the informal reading inventory. The transcribed data were analyzed within Vygotsky's (1962) grounded theory of social interaction. Coding was developed from a synthesis of the literature on teacher-talk and dialogue (Roskos et al. cited in Berry, 2006; Rose cited in Cucilan, 2007; Weeks cited in Culican, 2007).

Results

Four major categories of responses surfaced from an analysis of the dialogue transcripts: Overlapping & Directing (OD); Feedback (FD); Prompting (PRO); and Teacher-Talk Time (3T).

- *Overlapping and Directing:* These strategies were broken down into subcategories: Transition/Next Steps (T); Managing Behavior (BH); and Directing Attention to Task (DA).
- *Prompting:* Prompting was generated from Unstructured Dialogue (UD) or from Structured Questions (SQ). Prompting included repetitions, restatements, and rewordings. Prompts were determined to either change (CH) or not change (NC) meaning.
- *Feedback:* These strategies consisted of Encouraging Comments (EC); Acknowledging & Accepting Efforts (AA); Praising and Accepting Efforts (PR); and Clarification (CL).
- *Teacher-Talk Time (3T):* Teacher-Talk Time referred to dialogue that was either tangential or not related to the task at hand. Teacher-Talk Time was determined to be either conversational with some relevance to the task or distracting and completely irrelevant to the task.

The findings suggest that teachers do employ a variety of dialogue strategies during the administration of informal reading inventories. Interestingly, the number of those dialogue events tended to diminish as the stories progressed with more and lengthier ones occurring during the first story and fewer and shorter ones occurring during the last story.

Overlapping and Directing. Most notable was that Overlapping and Directing strategies tended to be more extensive during dialogue segments where the tutor was providing directions for introducing the session, predicting, and retelling renditions.

Tutors demonstrated similar numbers of events for Directing and Overlapping: with Paul, 40; with Sam, 47; with Mark, 42; and with Will, 27 (See Appendix B). The discrepancy for Will can be explained by his reading two stories instead of three stories. Examples for Overlapping and Directing strategies were:

- *"I want you to think about the story that you just read. And I want you to tell me everything that you can remember from that story. Everything that happened, everything that you can remember."*
  (Andrea to Paul: Directing attention to task for retelling):
- *"So, I have to write everything down. So, this doesn't mean that you're missing anything, it just means that I have got to write everything down. And when you give me answers to questions, it's just so I can remember things, okay?"*
  (Andrea to Sam: Directing attention to task for initiating the session)
- *"Okay, Mark, I'm going to start with having you go over some words in a list. And I will tell you when to stop and when you get finished just go on to the next row I tell you. Just pronounce them. If you get to a word that you don't know, say 'don't know' and go on to the next one after it, okay? Um, then I'm going to have you read stories and I need you to read. Do your best reading for me. But, I need you to read so that you remember what you've read, because I'm going to ask you questions about what you just read. And you're going to have to remember as many details as you can like the beginning, the middle, and the end, and then some details in between."*
  (Selene to Mark: Directing attention to task for initiating the session)
- *"Okay, alright, okay, again the name of the story is 'What Can I Get for My Toy.' What do you think this story is going to be about? That's your prediction. That's the word we call prediction. We are going to predict, based on the questions that I ask you and the title 'What Can I Get for My Toy?' What do you think this story is going to be about? Before we even read it."*
  (Selene to Will: Prediction)

Prompting. During direct questioning which was coded as Structured Questions (SQ) there was little evidence that any dialogue deviated from the prescribed wording in the text. There was some evidence of restatements, rewordings, and repetitions, but little change in meaning. This finding would be consistent with the questions being standardized across all stories. Prompting elements (PRO) for Structured Questions were for the most part uniformly distributed across tutors with the exception of one tutor who engaged in some extended irrelevant prompting. Most prompts were short and directly related to the content of the story; however, some were extensive and some seemed to probe beyond the boundaries of the questions. Promptings that occurred following structured questions taken directly from the IRI were, for the most part, brief and limited in scope; however, some were more extensive. Unstructured dialogue resulted in a mixture of short and extended prompts with short predominating. Elements of unstructured dialogue (UD) also were fairly uniform across all tutors' talk considering the number of stories read: Paul, 37; Sam, 47; Mark, 51; and Will, 19 (see Appendix B). Examples of unstructured dialogue were:

- *"What kind of toys?"*
  (Andrea to Sam's initial response, "toys" to the SQ "In the future what must both boys have for trading to make them both happy?")
- *"You like being by yourself? You like to play with your buddies all the time. Can you play by yourself? What do you do when you play by yourself?"*
  (Andrea to Sam's initial response, "Alone" to the SQ "What does being by yourself mean?")
- *"And locating where they are going. Is that what you are saying?"*
  (Selene to Mark's initial response, "Where they're going and locating." to SQ "Why do people use maps?")
- *"The ice cream? Shop or stand?"*
  (Selene to Will's initial response, "To find how to get ice cream" to the SQ "Why did Carlos go to get a map from the zoo entrance?")
- *"Why would you trade your toy?"*
  (Andrea to Paul's initial response, "About trading…your toy" to the UD prediction, "What do you think this story might be about"?)
- *"Okay, what else can you remember about the story?"*
  (Andrea to Sam's initial response, *"Um. John and Chris traded…and…they, I mean, his mother said that, they, they did not have enough money to buy him some new toys"* to the UD request for retelling)
- *"An old house for sale. You see a sign out there that says 'old house for sale.' What does that make you think of? What do you think that's about?"*
  (Selene to Mark. Rewording of SQ "What does an 'old house for sale' mean to you?")
- *"Getting something for the toy. So you mean trading or what do you mean?"*
  (Selene to Will's initial response, "Getting something for your toy." to the UD request for prediction, "What do you think this story is going to be about.?")

In some instances, prompts were leading the clients to responses rather than allowing the clients to generate independent responses. In addition, the length of some of the prompting tended to leave the dialogue open to seemingly unnecessary repetitions and rewordings. Numbers of prompts that tended toward leading clients ranged from a low of 2 to a high of 15: Paul, 15; Sam, 2; Mark, 11; and Will, 3 (see Appendix B). Examples of prompting were:

- *"Okay, think about what you said. What his other friend wants and what his friend wants. Think about that again. I don't think you're saying it right."*
(Andrea to Paul's response, *"They have, they will have to have what his other friend wants and umm what his friend wants"* to the Structured Question SQ *"In the future, what must both boys have for trading to make them both happy?"*

- *"Okay, think about the questions that I ask you, about the class trip, taking notes being by yourself, using maps."*
(Andrea to Paul. Request for UD Prediction, "What do you think this story is going to be about?")

- *"Okay, based on the story, and the predictions that I just gave you, and the name of the story, 'What Can I Get for My Toy?' What do you think this story might be about? We've talked about new toys, we've talked about trading toys, we've talked about toys that you've had a long time, and then the title of this story is 'What Can I Get for My Toys?' What do you think this story might be about?"*
(Andrea to Paul: Request for UD Prediction, "What do you think this story might be about?")

- *"Okay, the name of this story. I want you to read the story the very best you can. The name of the story is 'What Can I Get for My Toy?' Now before you start reading, I'm going to ask you some questions and then I'm going to ask you to predict what you think the story is going to be about. But first, I'm going to ask you some questions. What does new toys mean to you? What does it mean when you buy new toys, what are you talking about?"*
(Selene's request to Will for UD Retelling)

- *"I already have a pencil. So, why would I want to trade you for yours unless I like yours better? In a trade, Mark, you have to give somebody something. They have to give you something. You can't do just one thing. Do you see what I'm saying? If I give you a pencil, you're going to have to give me something for it to be a trade. Otherwise it's a gift. And you don't get anything in return. You see the difference? Okay. So this question says, 'What are reasons for trading toys?' What are some reasons for trading toys? Why would you trade toys? With your best friend next door or down the street, or whatever."*
(Selene to Mark's response *"What are reasons for trading toys?"* to Structured Questions SQ *"What are reasons for trading toys?"*)

In some instances, probing was only marginally related to the content of the story. These prompts tended to be more conversational and incidental than probing.

- *"Oh, you'd trade a skateboard for a skateboard. Okay, would you trade it with a friend, or would you try and get a new one?"*
(Andrea to Paul: UD Prediction *"What do you think this story might be about?"*)

- *"What do you do on a field trip?"*
(Selene to Sam: Structured Question SQ *"What is a field trip?"*)

Feedback Strategies. Interestingly, while tutors' dialogue did provide evidence of feedback and with the exception of one tutor's interaction with one client, little was in the form of encouragement. Praising or reinforcing statements were more evident for one tutor and across both tutors; the evidence was derived from unstructured dialogue rather than direct questioning. Praise from both tutors across all clients was short and for the most part was characterized by "good job" or "very good." Total feedback events ranged from 10-26: (Paul, 26; Sam, 10; Mark, 21; and Will, 19 (see Appendix B). Encouraging comments included:

- *"You can do it. I know you can do it."* (Andrea to Sam)
- *"If you don't know the word, it's okay. I just want you to tell me the best that you can. Try and figure out what that word is, okay?"* (Andrea to Paul)
- *"Don't know? Okay. Thank you."* (Selene to Mark)
- *"Thank you so much, Will, for helping us out here. And you continue that and you are going to be doing very well in school. Thank you very much."* (Selene to Will)

On some occasions, the situation called for some form of clarification. Those events were few, were typically short, and were initiated by Selene: Mark, 10 and Will, 4 (see Appendix B).

- *"Okay, we're getting a little confused here. What did John have? Did he have a car or did he have a truck?"* (Selene to Mark)
- *"Ah, so now tell me about it, now that we got that straightened out, because you had them confused. I think you know the details, but you just had the name confused, so tell me again about this."* (Selene to Mark)
- *"Oh, what was that? I'm sorry, did you say that?"* (Selene to Will)

The use of "Okay" as a pause, pacing, or feedback mechanism was high for both tutors across all four clients: Paul, 57; Sam, 37; Mark, 66; and Will, 43 (See Appendix B).

Teacher-Talk Time (3T): Another notable finding was that Teacher-Talk Time (3T) exchanges were typically few in number, were largely associated with managing tasks, and were derived predominantly from one teacher. Those events were not restricted to any particular dialogue strategy, were largely conversation, and were unrelated to the task: Paul, 15; Sam, 20; and Mark, 1 (see Appendix B).

- *"I've got to change my paper so give me a second."* (Andrea to Paul)
- *"Okay, I have to write down what I'm saying, that's why it's taking me a few minutes."* (Andrea to Paul)
- *"I'm missing some sheets here. Hold on."* (Andrea to Sam)
- *"Sorry, I broke your chain of thought by talking to you. Start again."* (Selene to Mark)

Implications Leading to Next Steps for Teacher Education

Findings from this study suggest that discourse varies among teachers and among teacher/client pairs. Dialogue elements were not uniformly applied across each session for each client. Praise and encouragement statements were overall limited, short, and fairly consistent in the form of "Okay" or "Good job." Those findings suggest the need to investigate the extent to which extraneous dialogue and some forms of prompting can be distracting or misleading. Can over-using a pause element such as "Okay" desensitize students to language interaction and possibly in some cases cause them to simply tune out the teacher? Can prompting, leading questions, and irrelevant dialogue contaminate the interpretations? The variability in dialogue found among tutors in this study suggests that teachers may not be equally prepared to administer informal reading inventories.

Casa and DeFranco (cited Viiri & Saari, 2006), assert that the effectiveness of dialogue patterns depends on the use. Thus, by extension can we assume that used poorly, dialogue may promote interference to credible assessment? Schools and districts that use informal reading inventories to diagnose students' needs develop intervention strategies, and monitor progress must confront serious reliability and validity issues related to the flexibility and subjectivity of diagnostic implementation and interpretation.

Language interference may have a more profound effect on students with learning disabilities (Wilson, 2008). Many students who need academic support in literacy are diagnosed with learning disabilities, and they may have problems with responding and making appropriate word choices, making links to referents (e.g. pronoun referents) and attending to elements of cohesion (Wilson, 2008). For example, the inability to establish linkages between and among concepts may interfere with comprehension. Berry's (2006) study of dialogue in inclusive settings proposes that teacher education provide more support for developing teachers in using prompting, cueing, and cognitive modeling. The use of prompting and cueing techniques in the administration of an informal reading inventory suggests a need for deliberate intentional training for developing and veteran teachers.

Accepting the notion that learning is social and that dialogue patterns impact student and teacher interactions, developing and veteran teachers would benefit from analyzing their dialogue (Cullican, 2007). Such an analysis optimally should rest on the foundation of social learning elements of conversation, patterns of talk, scaffolding techniques, and clarity (Berry, 2006; Lemke cited in Cullican, 2007; Rose cited in Cullican, 2007; Viiri & Saari, 2006; Vygotsky, 1962; & Wilson, 2008). For practicing teachers, the findings from this study suggest a need for a developing awareness of the importance of discourse between student and teacher. Developing teachers would benefit from preparation programs that focus on facilitating their understanding patterns of discourse and helping them develop strategies for using dialogue to promote learning for all students.

Future Research

The small numbers in the study limits generalizations to other settings; however, the results may suggest paths for future inquiry. Contributions to the body of knowledge of the impact of dialogue and awareness of dialogue discourse during the administration of informal readings inventories could better inform teacher preparation and professional learning programs. Teachers in this study were not asked to reflect on their dialogue beyond the member checking that was a component of the qualitative methodology. Subsequent investigations of teachers' reflections on their discourse may illuminate possible links between perceived and actual practice.

Research that explores how dialogue patterns are culturally embedded (Culican, 2007) and to what extent learning disabilities impact diagnostic assessment results (Wilson, 2008) would add another dimension to the exploration of the impact of dialogue interactions in the learning process. Participant demographics should be extended to include students from various language, cultural, and socio-economic backgrounds.

The findings from this study are consistent with the literature in that dialogue is a factor in student and teacher interactions, and it merits further study. An examination of patterns of dialogue reveals that teacher-talk can either facilitate or obstruct learning. The flexibility in the administration of informal reading inventories also may limit the retrieval of credible and useful information about student learning needs. Educators should strive to ensure that diagnostic assessment is based on student renditions that accurately reflect skill level and is not confounded by communication barriers.

References

Berry, R. (2006). Teacher talk during whole-class lessons: Engagement strategies to support the verbal participation of students with learning disabilities. *Learning Disabilities Research & Practice, 21*(4), 211-232.

Creswell, J. W. (2006). *Qualitative inquiry and research design: Choosing among five approaches.* Thousand Oaks, CA: Sage Publications, Inc.

Cruikshank, D., Jenkins, D., & Metcalf, K. (2005). *The act of teaching* (4th ed). Boston, MA: McGraw-Hill.

Culican, S. J. (2007). Trouble teacher talk: The challenge of changing classroom discourse patterns, *The Australian Educational Researcher, 34*(2), 7-27.

Leslie, L. & Caldwell, J. S. (2005). *Qualitative reading inventory 4* (4th ed.). Upper Saddle River, NJ: Allyn and Bacon.

Nystrand, M. (2006). Research on the role of classroom discourse as it affects reading comprehension. *Research in the Teaching of English, 40*(4), 392-412.

Viiri, J. & Saari, H. (2006). Teacher talk patterns in science lessons: Use in teacher education. *Journal of Science Teacher Education, 17*((4), 347-365

Vygotsky, L. (1962). *Thought and language.* Cambridge, MA: MIT Press.

Wilson, K. (2008). Facilitator talk in EAP reading classes. *ELT Journal, 62*(4), 366-375.

Appendix A: Material Coverage and Teacher Dialogue Exchanges

	Paul	Sam	Mark	Will
Grade	4	4	4	4
# of Stories Read	3	3	3	2
Mouse in a House				xx
What Can I Get for My Toy?	xx	xx	xx	xx
The Trip to the Zoo	xx	xx	xx	
Johnny Appleseed	xx	xx	xx	
# of Teacher Comment Exchanges	97	101	126	52

Appendix B: Composite of Talk Strategies

	Andrea		Selene	
Clinic Client	Paul	Sam	Mark	Will
Talk Strategy:				
Directing and Overlapping Language	40	47	42	27
Transitioning/next steps	6	9	13	7
Managing behavior	11	12	3	3
Directing attention to Task	23	26	26	17
Irrelevant dialogue (Prompting + 3T)	28	11	8	0
Feedback	26	10	21	19
Encouraging	16	4	1	0
Acknowledging & accepting efforts	5	5	3	5
Praising or reinforcing outcomes	5 (UD)	1 (UD)	10 (6 UD)	10 (6 UD)
Clarifying	0	0	10	4
Elements of Questioning and Dialogue	72	82	81	49
# of Structured Questions (SQ)	35	35	30	30
SQ restated w/change in meaning	(2)	(5)	0	(7)
# of elements of Unstructured Dialogue (UD)	37	47	51	19
Prompting from SQ	23	25	20	14
Related to content	3	6	6	0
Unrelated to content	7	0	0	1
Leading	6	2	7	3
Prompting from UD	17	8	18	4
Related to content	3	0	0	0
Extensive and unassociated with content	3	0	0	0
Leading	9	0	4	0
Decoding Assistance	0	0	16	0
Teacher Talk Time (3T)	15	20	1	0
Use of "Okay"	57	37	66	43

MENTORING
PRESERVICE TEACHERS

Language Experience Stories Gone Digital: Using Digital Stories with the LEA Approach

Donna Glenn Wake
University of the Ozarks

Virginia B. Modla
La Salle University

Abstract

This article discusses a study conducted with preservice teachers at two universities. Under collaborative faculty direction, preservice teachers created digital stories based on the language experience approach protocol with early elementary students. Data was collected using 1) a pre-/post- survey designed to measure content knowledge and affect toward teaching writing with children, 2) a rubric-based assessment of the lessons and reflections, and 3) a descriptive response form. Results indicated that these preservice teachers increased their knowledge of writing instruction and increased their comfort level with their ability to teach emergent writing.

At a recent literacy conference, a presentation speaker shared his metaanalysis of popular topics in literacy journals over the past fifty years. According to his research, writing was the topic that had experienced the most dramatic decrease of attention in recent years (Morrison, Wilcox, & Wilcox, 2008). He asserted that while the topic of writing had been in moderate favor throughout the middle decades of the 20th century, writing as a topic had received almost no attention in the last two decades.

If writing is not a topic of interest to the research, then it is presumably not an important topic in the classroom practice. Thus, if appears that writing has been put on the back burner as teachers face pressures to teach an overwhelming amount of material. Additionally, some teachers feel uncomfortable teaching writing, as they have had either limited or negative experiences with writing while they were gong to school (Pardo, 2006).

Preservice teachers' writing abilities over the last decade has declined. A study by Moss and Bordelon (2007) and Delpit (1995) found that students entering college were under-prepared to meet the challenges of writing at the college level. Wallace, Pearman, Hail, and Hurst (2007) asserted that students and educators are not using writing, as a learning tool, to its fullest potential. Because of these findings and our own experiences, the authors of this article decided that writing was a topic that must receive more attention in our work with preservice teachers, as it is feared what less writing ability means for their ability to teach writing to their future students. Thus, we set out to more explicitly and forcefully include writing instruction in our reading foundations coursework. The purpose of this study was to support preservice teachers in their acquisition of content about literacy and about teaching writing to elementary students. We also hoped to increase preservice teachers' confidence and willingness to teach writing.

Literature Review

Teaching Children to Write

Many researchers feel a reciprocal relationship exists between student acquisition of reading and writing skills (Pearson, 2002; Shanahan, 1988). Pearson argues that writing is helpful in acquisition of language because it forces the author to slow down and examine the language. Pearson recommends that all early elementary language arts programs include writing time every day and that their writing includes various forms, formats, and audiences. In this way, writers in the primary grades can see the connections between sounds and letters. This connection becomes evident because in writing, sounds become captured on a page as students' oral language is transcribed. Furthermore, students can reinforce this connection because they can then practice reading what they have written. The opportunity for expressive writing should be frequent, particularly for young students, and should draw from many models to include modeled, shared, interactive, guided, and independent writing, and writing for reading instruction.

Language Experience Approach

Educators of elementary students have been assisting their students to tell and write stories using the Language Experience Approach (LEA) for decades. LEA integrates the teaching of reading with the other language arts as children listen, speak, write, and read about their own personal experiences and ideas (Hall, 1999). The language experience approach is based on the theory that students learn to read most easily if what they are reading sounds like the language they speak (Linek, & Nelson, 1999). In the LEA approach, a student dictates a story about his or her experience and the teacher writes down what the child says. The student has a better chance of reading the resulting story successfully than if the language and topic are unfamiliar.

The Language Experience Approach has long been recognized as a powerful strategy for providing students with unique and highly contextualized occasions for literacy development (Stauffer, 1969). In the LEA approach, teachers, and students move through a process where they discuss the presented story topic, students dictate their story so that the teacher can record their words, students read and re-read their work, and take part in literacy activities based on their work, and mini-lessons are taught on embedded literacy skills. LEA values the connections between experience and education and the connections between visual, oral, and textual forms of communication (Labbo, Eakle, and Montero, 2002). Teachers can use LEA successfully with one child or a small group.

Shared Writing

Shared writing, an additional layer used at one site, is an approach similar to LEA in that the teacher acts as a scribe and the students dictate their composition. Most often, this model is explicitly enacted in a small group setting. The premise underlying this approach is that emergent learners can see their ideas and words being recorded on paper. This then makes them co-writers or co-composers in the process without the physical pressure of forming letters. This allows students to focus more fully on developing their ideas and allows emergent learners to develop concepts about print, such as directionality and one-to-one matching (Tompkins, 2006).

The recommended sequence for a shared writing lesson is as follows: the teacher decides on a writing focus based on the students' experiences and needs; the teacher cues student prior knowledge through discussion and manipulation of materials; the teacher guides students in writing the text through thinking out loud, transcribing students' words, reading, re-reading, and revising. Follow-up lessons can be designed to reinforce new skills-based concepts encountered in the writing session. A shared writing composition can represent many different forms, purposes, and genres. Possible topics could include a narrative describing a recent event in class, a letter thanking a guest speaker, a retelling of a story, or an account of a project. The process may be completed in one session or extended over several days.

Digital Storytelling

Digital storytelling is a critical extension to the LEA and shared writing models. Bedenbaugh (2007) explains digital storytelling as the art of telling stories with any of a variety of available multimedia tools, including graphics, audio, video animation, and Web publishing. As students and teachers create digital stories, progressing from idea to final product, they use the writing process and students' progress from pre-writing through the final step of publication (Robin, 2005).

The process and product of digital storytelling involves all the modalities of literacy instruction, including listening, speaking, reading, writing, viewing, and representing (Primary Resources, 2008). This is in line with the IRA (2004) and NCTE (1996) requirements that students engage in meaningful interactions with print and non-print texts. For this reason, digital storytelling is particularly suited to young children involved in learning emergent literacy content and skills. This approach allows young students to rely on visual and oral forms of communication while at the same time encouraging them to begin making visual-oral-textual connections.

Methods

Participants and Settings

University #1 (southern, rural): Nine preservice teachers participated in the project at the rural, southern university: eight women and one man. All participants were of European-American descent. Seven of the participants were traditional undergraduates and were approximately 20 years of age. Two nontraditional female students were in their late 20s and had returned to college after having established their families. Seven of the students were first semester juniors while two students were first semester seniors. All students had experienced a program of study that included two education psychology classes, a special needs class, a foundations of education class, and an instructional methods class. All students were working on their P-4 certification.

All students were enrolled in the required *Foundations of Reading class*. This was the first literacy course in their program of study. The purpose of this class, the first in a two-class sequence, is to present an overview of the components of balanced, comprehensive literacy instruction, and the research basis for the provisions of effective literacy teaching and learning. As this class focuses on the needs of emergent literacy learners in kindergarten and first grade, the curriculum is on early writing and spelling development, phonics, phonemic awareness, fluency, modeled, shared, and interactive reading and writing. Practicum experiences at the local primary (K-1) school are integrated in the class experiences. The LEA project occurred in this placement. One text used for this course is *Literacy for the 21st Century: A Balanced Approach* (Tompkins, 2006).

University #2 (northeast, urban): Sixteen female preservice teachers participated in the project at the urban, northeastern university. Fourteen participants were of European-American descent, one was African-American, and one student emigrated from Africa. All participants were considered traditional undergraduates who were approximately 20 years of age. Eleven of the students were first semester juniors while five were second semester juniors. All students were obtaining licensure in elementary and special education. For the first semester juniors, this was the first literacy course in their program of studies. For second semester juniors, it was their second literacy course.

All students were enrolled in a course entitled: *Expository Reading and Writing for Elementary and Special Education Students*. The purpose of this class is to prepare regular and special education teachers to meet the needs of students who demonstrate significant problems in reading and writing. These students were each assigned a child with special needs. Throughout the semester, all course assignments were linked to their field experience, and the culminating project was a case study for each undergraduate's focus child. Students learned about the components of a comprehensive literacy program with emphasis on shared and interactive reading and writing. They learned the steps in creating language experience stories with students and learned how to use these stories as reading material. Two texts were used for this course: *Teaching Literacy to Students With Significant Disabilities* (Downing, 2005), *Word Identification Strategies: Building Phonics into a Classroom Reading Program* (Fox, 2008), and one informal assessment—*The Critical Reading Inventory* (Applegate, Quinn & Applegate, 2007).

Data Collection Instruments

Data collection at each university included two artifacts. At the southern, rural university, data was collected from the pre/post survey and a rubric-based assessment of the preservice teachers' lessons and reflections. At the northeast, urban university, data was collected for the same pre/post survey and a descriptive response form.

Pre/Post Survey: The pre/post survey was designed to measure content knowledge and affect toward writing with children. It was adapted from a tool developed and published by Hayes & Robnolt (2007) and has twelve questions measuring preservice teachers' knowledge of and comfort with writing instruction, process writing, shared writing, the Language Experience approach, language acquisition, writing assessment, and technology integration. The responses were rated on a Likert scale as follows: 1=seldom, 2=sometimes, 3=frequently, and 4=most of the time (Appendix A).

Lesson Plans: The lessons and reflections the preservice teachers developed for their work with their students on this project were the second data point for the southern, rural university. These lessons and reflections were assessed with a rubric developed by the authors/researchers (Appendix B).

Descriptive Response Form: At the urban, northern university, a descriptive response form was used. It was comprised of ten open response questions inquiring into the preservice teachers' experiences and responses to the curriculum project. The questions were designed to assess knowledge, skills, and disposition toward shared writing and use of digital stories (Appendix C).

Procedures

University #1 (southern, rural): First, students in the required reading course completed the pre-survey. While learning about writing in their university classroom, the preservice students also worked in pairs to design a shared writing lesson using the language experience approach protocol for small groups of K-1 students at a local primary school. After implementing the lessons in small, guided writing groups with the primary students and assessing the results, the preservice teachers individually wrote reflections on their experiences. Finally, the preservice teachers completed the post-survey two weeks after their K-4 classroom experiences ended.

University #2 (northeastern, urban): First, while attending one of the required reading courses, the preservice teachers completed the pre-survey. While these preservice teachers were learning about writing and writing assessment in their university classroom, they were also working with K-6 special education children every Friday throughout the semester. While working with their assigned child or a group of small children, each preservice teacher created a digital story using PowerPoint. At the end of the semester the preservice teachers wrote reflections on their experiences with creating digital stories with children, took the post-survey, and completed the descriptive response form.

The Curriculum

University #1 (southern, rural): The curriculum at the university was structured sequentially. First, the preservice teachers examined the writing development in young students including the stages of writing development: scribble, isolated letter, transitional, stylized sentence, and writing. Second, the relationship of reading and writing was discussed. Third, the writing process was covered; instruction began with the preservice teachers' own knowledge of and experience with process writing. Finally, various models of writing instruction were discussed and simulated to include modeled writing, interactive writing, shared writing, and the language experience approach model.

The preservice teachers were then presented with their assignment for this section of the curriculum. They were given two weeks to work in pairs to design and implement a shared writing lesson using the language experience approach protocol. The lesson would include three, thirty-minute sessions. Four preservice teachers (two pairs) worked with small groups of 5-6 kindergarten students each. Five of the preservice teachers (two pairs and one alone) worked with small groups of 5-6 first grade students each.

The preservice teachers were required to build an experience with their student groups in their first session. In large part, this consisted of bringing in an object to share with the students related to the season (fall, Halloween). Student groups first handled and discussed the object. They were then asked to begin writing a story about their object with the preservice teachers. As a prewriting activity, the groups made spider maps or outline charts of ideas for their stories. Each student was asked to contribute one point to the map or outline in the form of a supporting detail. For example, if the object was a pumpkin, the students were encouraged to contribute a detail about the pumpkin (it is orange, it is round, the surface of the pumpkin is smooth, and so forth). In another group, the students actually took a slightly different approach and decided to write their story about the steps used to take a pumpkin and carve it into a jack-o-lantern. In this story the preservice teachers stressed the use of signal words (i.e. first, next, then, finally) as important to the story.

In the second session with the groups, the preservice teachers led the groups to author their stories' titles and topic sentences in a group, collaborative effort. Each student was then asked to construct their own sentence as a supporting detail of the story based on their work in the prewriting activity concluded in the first session. The preservice teachers recorded the students' words on large chart paper maintaining the students' use of language at all times. The groups then re-read the story in a shared reading experience and made any changes they wished. Finally, the students created captioned drawings of their sentences.

In between the second and third sessions, the preservice teachers scanned the students' captioned drawings and began building the digital stories in Microsoft Photostory 3. In the third session, the students started with a shared reading of their story. They then previewed the unfinished digital stories and worked to rehearse and add oral narration. The shared reading, rehearsal of lines, and oral narration added a fluency component to the lesson. Student groups also selected and added music to their stories. In the week following this session, multiple copies of all stories were burned to disc. Each student and all teachers and preservice teachers involved received a copy of all the digital stories.

University #2: This project began with preservice teachers interviewing their focus child and determining their interests. Based on each child's interest, during the next field experience, the university students selected a stimulus activity. For example, Marianne (all names have been changed) worked with a focus child, Shakiah, who loved the color red. Marianne led Shakiah in a brainstorming session and Shakiah dictated red things that she liked and why she liked them. Marianne, as Shakiah watched, developed a semantic web using Shakiah's ideas.

Shakiah was asked to wear something red on the next field experience day. Marianne also dressed in a red outfit, brought pictures of the red things loved by Shakiah, or found red objects. She took digital pictures of Shakiah holding the pictures or objects and had someone take a picture of her focus child with her.

Before returning to the school on the following week, Marianne imported the pictures into PowerPoint slides. Viewing each slide, Shakiah dictated sentences about each picture. Marianne guided Shakiah in thinking of a title for her story.

During the week, Marianne typed each of Shakiah's sentences on appropriate slides, using the PowerPoint call out feature to form speech bubbles. When she brought the PowerPoint to the field experience, Shakiah was thrilled. Marianne helped Shakiah record her sentences using a microphone with a laptop. A step that Marianne and most of her classmates skipped is to reread the dictated sentences to Shakiah to check if ideas were stated appropriately and if not, assist the children in making revisions.

What Marianne and her fellow undergraduates did do is create the first of several reading lessons adding before, during, and after activities to guide Shakiah in re-reading her story.

Research Questions

The researchable questions framing this study were as follows:

1. Will the use of digital storytelling paired with the language experience approach to reading and writing increase preservice teachers'

knowledge of the writing process, knowledge of shared writing, and knowledge of assessment of reading and writing?

2. Will the use of digital storytelling paired with the language experience approach to writing increase preservice teachers' comfort with teaching writing as an emergent literacy skill?

3. Will the use of digital storytelling paired with the language experience approach to reading and writing increase preservice teachers' comfort in using technology to support literacy instruction?

4. Will preservice teachers find digital storytelling to be a viable approach for reading and writing instruction with emergent literacy learners?

Data Analysis

Results: Pre-/Post-Survey

The results of the pre-/post-survey from the southern, rural university comparison yielded significance on seven of the twelve questions – questions 3-9. Two of these questions (#3 and #6) focused exclusively on the preservice teachers' perceived level of knowledge of the steps of writing process and of the LEA protocol (p>.05 and p>.022). The remaining five questions involved the comfort level of the preservice teachers in teaching shared writing and teaching using the LEA approach.

Five of the questions in the survey did not yield significant results – questions 1-2 and questions 10-12. Questions 1-2 focused on the preservice teachers' perceived comfort level in teaching writing using the process approach. Ironically, this finding indicated that the preservice teachers' did not seem to see the relationship between using the LEA approach and teaching using the writing process approach. Questions 10-12 focused on issues of technology integration and assessment and indicated the preservice teachers still felt uncertain about their ability to assess their students' writing and their ability to integrate technology into their classroom literacy instruction practice.

The results of the pre/post survey from the northeast, urban university yielded significance on only four of the twelve questions. According to the findings, these students felt knowledgeable about the steps for teaching writing using the process approach (p>.0001). They felt comfortable talking about and teaching using a shared writing approach (p>.0001). Students also felt comfortable talking about and using assessments to inform their literacy instruction (p>.0014).

Table 1: Pre-/Post-Survey Data from University #1 and #2

U #1 Pre-Survey	U #1 Post-Survey	*U#1 p*	Full statements can be found in appendix A.	U#2 Pre-Survey	U#2 Post-Survey	*U#2 p*
2.7	3.1	.34	Question #1: I feel comfortable talking about and teaching writing as a content area or skill to students.	2..4	2.9	.07
2.4	3.0	.17	Question #2: I feel comfortable talking about and teaching writing using the writing process.	1.9	3.2	1.65
2.1	2.0	.05*	Question #3: I feel knowledgeable about the steps for teaching the writing process	1.7	3.3	.0001***
2.2	3.4	.009**	Question #4: I feel comfortable talking about and teaching with shared writing	1.8	3.1	.0001***
1.5	2.5	.008**	Question #5: I feel comfortable talking about and teaching with the LEA approach	1.6	3.6	1.43
1.5	2.3	.02*	Question #6: I feel knowledgeable about the guidelines for using the LEA approach	1.4	3.3	2.12
1.4	2.6	.009**	Question #7: I feel comfortable talking about and teaching the acquisition of language using the LEA approach to writing instruction.	1.4	3.3	2.06
1.5	2.7	.01*	Question #8: I feel comfortable talking about and teaching the formation of basic literacy concepts using the LEA approach	1.5	3.6	8.9
1.6	2.6	.009***	Question #9: I feel comfortable talking about and teaching the development of reading skills using the LEA approach	1.6	3.6	2.67
2.5	3.2	.09	Question #10: I feel comfortable talking about and teaching using technology	1.5	3.3	1.16
2.5	2.9	.34	Question #11: I feel comfortable talking about and using assessments to inform my literacy instruction.	2.1	3.4	.0014**
2.3	2.9	.11	Question #12: I know what assessments are appropriate to use in assessing writing.	2.6	3.6	.016*

*p < .05; **p < .01; ***p < .001*

When comparing the survey results for students in the two universities, there were only two survey items common to both schools: Questions 3 and 4. It appears that students at both universities feel knowledgeable about the steps of the process approach and felt comfortable talking and teaching using shared writing.

Results: Lessons and Reflections—University #1

The lessons and reflections created by the preservice teachers in their work with the K-1 students were also used as a data collection point in the southern, rural university. The rubric used to score the preservice teachers in their work on this project was shared with them when the project was introduced. In addition, the preservice teachers' lessons were submitted to the instructor before the implementation of the lessons and formative feedback was offered to the preservice teachers who had the choice to adapt their lessons or leave them as originally authored. The preservice teachers then submitted the final lesson plans and lesson reflections one week following their work with the K-1 students on this project. They were scored on this final submission. Possibly a more "accurate" snapshot of the preservice teachers work on this project would have been yielded in scoring their initial (not final) submissions or in scoring both the initial and final submissions. This would be a recommendation if replicating this study in order to observe preservice teachers' initial lessons and any growth they made over the course of the project upon receiving feedback and working with their emergent learners.

Table 2: University 1: Lessons and Reflections

	Distinguished	Proficient	Basic	Unsatisfactory	*Mean*
Topic/Content	10*	0	0	0	4.0
Student Development	3	4	2	1	2.9
Student Diversity	2	0	6	2	2.2
(learning styles, sociocultural, , etc)					
Planning Skills	7	3	0	0	3.7
Objectives	10	0	0	0	4.0
Procedures	5	5	0	0	3.5
Assessment	6	2	0	2	3.2
Reflection	4	3	1	2	2.9

* indicates simple frequency count

Results: Descriptive Response Form—University #2

University #2, did not do the lesson plan and reflection assignment. However, they completed a descriptive response form. When asked about their focus child's response to the digital story, the preservice teachers at the urban university responded either that their student loved (13) or liked (2) the digital stories. The reasons they gave for this very positive response were: (1) the children enjoyed recording and hearing their voices played back; (2) they enjoyed viewing the PowerPoint; (3) they were very proud of their stories and asked to take them home to show their family; (4) the children enjoyed the process of creating their own story and were amazed at how their pictures and words formed a story; (5) they loved getting their pictures taken in association with something of interest to them. More of their qualitative data is included in the discussion section.

Discussion

University #1

Pre-/Post-Survey: Data collected at the rural, southern university yielded some positive and some negative findings. In response to survey questions #3 and #6, data results indicated that the preservice teachers experienced a perceived, improved level of content knowledge. The results indicated that the preservice teachers felt they had a better grasp on teaching the writing process approach and had a better grasp for using the LEA protocol in classroom instruction. In response to survey questions #4-5, #7-9, the results indicated that the preservice teachers were more confident in their ability to teach using shared writing and LEA approaches. They were also more confident in their ability to use the LEA approach to promote the acquisition of language, form basic literary concepts, and develop reading skills.

In response to survey questions #1-2, results indicated that the preservice teachers still felt insecure in their ability to teach writing as a content area. Indeed, the results on question #2 seemingly contradict the results of question #3 indicating that the preservice teachers felt comfort in their knowledge of the steps of the writing process, but that they still were uncomfortable with the idea of teaching writing in general.

The results in response to questions #10-12 were disappointing. Despite a highly structured technology integration environment with plenty of support and scaffolds, the preservice teachers still did not feel comfortable using technology in their instruction. Unfortunately this finding is aligned with the research in teacher education on preservice teacher's use of and comfort level with technology in the classroom (Groth, Dunlap, & Kidd, 2007; Labbo, Eakle, and Montero, 2002). These researchers found that even though teachers can and should integrate technology to support their students' literacy development when appropriate, many teachers still shy away from using technology to support instruction.

The preservice teachers also clearly did not feel comfortable with choosing or implementing assessments for writing and may not have seen the connection between the process and product of this curriculum and opportunities for assessment even though their lessons required embedded assessment of both process and product. This is certainly an area for increased attention in refining this curriculum.

Lessons and Reflections: Results of the lesson and reflections gathered at the rural, southern university indicated that the preservice teachers scored at the distinguished level in two categories: topic and objectives. First, they showed strong ability to articulate why this content was critical to teach for the intended student population. The score for this section of the rubric is taken from the written rationales for the lesson plan where the preservice teachers are asked to justify why they are teaching the content and their choices for how they present the content. In this section of the rubric, they are asked to place their lesson within the context of the larger curriculum requirements. The preservice teachers also showed an advanced ability to fashion specific, measurable objectives. The preservice teachers also scored well in the following five categories: student development, planning skills, procedures, assessment, and reflection.

Finally, the lessons indicated one area of concern in the preservice teachers' consideration of student diversity yielding a low basic result. Consideration of student diversity is a key aspect of instructional planning. As such, a low result on this indicator indicates a need for curriculum revision and refocusing of preservice teacher attention on the needs of individual students and students from diverse backgrounds.

University #2

Pre-/Post-Survey: Data collected at the urban, northeast university also had both positive and negative findings. In response to survey questions #3 and #4, data results indicated that the preservice teachers experienced a perceived, improved level of content knowledge. The results indicated that the preservice teachers felt they had a better grasp on teaching using the writing process approach and teaching using shared writing in the classroom. In response to survey questions #11 and #12, the results indicate that the preservice teachers were more confident in talking about and using assessments including those in writing to inform their literacy instruction.

Interestingly, as with their southern peers, their response to survey question #1, results indicate that the preservice teachers were less confident in their ability to teach writing and writing process even though they were more confident about their ability to ability to teach shared writing and to teach using the LEA. Based on the results of question #2 one can infer that the preservice teachers felt confident in their knowledge of the steps of the writing process, but that they were less confident in applying their knowledge. The results in response to questions #5-10 were unexpected. After spending much time in studying the LEA Approach, they remained unsure about using it in the classroom. Responses to #10 were surprising because despite the impressive digital stories they created with their students and after a significant amount of time in the computer lab with the support of their instructor and fellow students, they indicated that they did not feel comfortable using technology in their instruction.

Descriptive Response Form: As seen in the result section, the preservice teachers noted a number of positives related to the experience of creating a digital story. They described how motivated the children were to improve their sentences and to improve their ability to read fluently because they took pride in the product. The children felt special and more in charge during the process. Both the preservice teachers and elementary students had fun working together. The preservice teachers learned more about the children with whom they were working. One student remarked, "Digital stories allow the individual to be creative and talk about what they would like to talk about. It also allows them to use different types of technology to bring the story to life with their own pictures and voice recordings." The preservice teachers admitted that they relearned how to use the PowerPoint program.

They also noted three negatives of the experience. These included making the other students in the class feel left out when the focus child returned with his digital story. The preservice teachers also were not sure about whether or not they should correct nonstandard English and some of the children had difficulty reading what they had dictated. Finally, the preservice teachers also mentioned difficulties with technology mostly related to recording the sound.

The preservice teachers, when asked to describe times when their assigned student knew more or less than they thought they would know, responded that their students were able to dictate much more complex sentences than expected. Some of them also mentioned "grammar" problems exhibited by students who had features of nonstandard English in their speech.

The preservice teachers mentioned a number of ways they assessed what students learned while creating and reading the digital stories. They observed their focus children applying skills they were taught during the digital story experience at other times. They noticed how well students read with expression attending to punctuation.

The preservice teachers mentioned a number of ways the digital language experience approach could be adapted for different learners. Because the approach is unique to each learner, it can be modified and adapted based on what the student likes or dislikes and what the student's strengths and needs are. They observed that children who are more linguistic learners can utilize this learning style in their story by using more words or a longer story. In contrast, students who have strengths in the auditory area can listen to the story being read as they read it. They also learned how mini-lessons accompanying the stories can be individualized. The preservice teachers mentioned that they learned how the process can be designed for different learners when they viewed the digital stories of their classmates.

The preservice teachers identified a number of positives about the LEA approach as a writing strategy. First, the children will enjoy reading what they wrote because they created the story and it is familiar to them. Second, the LEA allows for an integration of all areas of literacy. The LEA approach motivates students to stay on task. Third, the approach is an excellent way to get students interested in reading and writing. They also mentioned some negatives. The approach might be difficult to implement in a classroom because it is time-consuming and requires much one-on-one instruction.

Would the preservice teachers use the digital LEA in their future classroom reading instruction? Eleven of the sixteen students said they would because the approach is comprehensive, engages students and is fun for them. It motivates children to read even more challenging text because it focuses on their interests. It individualizes instruction.

Several thought they might use it depending on the grade level they were assigned and how many students they were assigned. They were daunted by the time consuming aspect of the approach.

Limitations

While the results of this action research intervention were encouraging, a limitation of this study was the exclusive focus on the preservice teachers as well as the small number of participants (n = 25). Self-perception of the teachers varied significantly in terms of their comfort with content and their feelings of efficacy in teaching that content. Moreover, participant's unease with assessment was problematic. If an assessment of the student acquisition of language had been embedded, perhaps the preservice teachers would have been better able to see the connection between process, product, and assessment in their lessons and better able to measure impact on student learning. Another limitation of the study was discovery of the preservice teachers' lack of knowledge of the writing process and the fact that they themselves did not use the writing process in their own writing. More time should have been spent with these preservice teachers discussing their experiences writing and learning how to be writers. In addition, related to this, were the problems some of the preservice teachers had in failing to notice their own spelling mistakes and lack of intervention when the oral language of their assigned students needed polishing. Another limitation of this study was the inability of the researchers to conduct this action research as a more controlled experimental design. Finally, assessment and protocol differences between the two sites may have clouded some comparative data, and the study locations could be brought closer into alignment.

Implications for Further Study

Further research is needed to identify ways to increase preservice teachers' knowledge of writing instruction and their comfort level in teaching writing. Using the digital Language Experience Approach seems to hold promise in assisting preservice teachers to (re)learn writing content including key tenets of the writing process, shared writing, the relationship of reading to writing, writing assessment, and the use of technology to support literacy instruction.

Conclusion

This action research project with preservice teachers described the implementation and results of a curriculum designed to teach the instruction of writing to elementary students. This article shared the details of the developed curriculum and the results obtained on two separate assessment measures as the instructor attempted to determine (a) preservice teacher knowledge of writing process and writing instruction for elementary students and (b) preservice teacher self-efficacy toward teaching writing and their own ability to teach writing.

The researchable questions framing this study and the success of the study in meeting these questions were as follows. Question #1 inquired if the use of digital storytelling paired with the language experience approach to reading and writing increased preservice teachers' knowledge of the writing process, knowledge of shared writing, and knowledge of assessment of reading and writing. Without a doubt the preservice teachers' knowledge in these areas improved; however, the answer to research question #2 indicates an area of continued development. While the preservice teachers' felt their knowledge of writing process, shared writing, and LEA was increased, they still indicated discomfort in teaching these aspects of literacy

Research question #3 asked if the use of digital storytelling paired with the language experience approach to reading and writing would increase teachers' comfort in using technology to support literacy instruction. Unfortunately, at both locations, the preservice teachers still felt uncomfortable with their ability to integrate technology into their instructional practice. Finally, question #4 asked if preservice teachers would find digital storytelling to be a viable approach for reading and writing instruction with emergent literacy learners. Fortunately, preservice teachers at both universities found digital storytelling to be a powerful approach to support emergent learners' writing development; however, the time and support needed for technology caused some concern.

Results show that the preservice teachers at the rural, southern university better understood process writing, writing instruction, and the language experience approach. However, results also showed that these preservice teachers were still uncertain of their ability to teach writing outside of the parameters of this study and were still uncertain of their ability to assess writing or integrate technology to support literacy instruction. Preservice teachers also still needed significant assistance considering the diversity of the students under their care.

At the urban, northeastern university, the preservice teachers improved their understanding of process writing, reading and writing instruction, and how to use the results of reading and writing assessment to better inform their instruction. However, results also showed that these preservice teachers were still uncertain about the steps involved in using the LEA approach and of their ability to integrate technology to support literacy instruction. They enjoyed creating digital stories with their students and observed first hand the many advantages of using them with youngsters.

In sum, preservice teachers successfully learned to teach reading and writing to elementary students using the digital language experience approach either in a shared writing environment or working one-on-one with children. These preservice teachers were involved in creating digital stories as an end product of the writing process, and as such were wholly immersed in teaching using the writing process approach. Coupling the use of digital stories with the LEA approach for emergent learners may provide one more avenue to allow young students to explore their language and learn new skills in a manner that is engaging and exciting to the students. In addition, coupling LEA with digital storytelling techniques can provide preservice teachers the opportunity to learn and adapt the time honored approach of the LEA with more technology advanced applications available to teachers and students today.

References

Applegate, M.D, Quinn, K.B., & Applegate, A.J. (2007). *The Critical Reading Inventory with Passages & DVD*, 2nd edition, Upper Saddle River, NJ: Pearson Education Inc.

Bedenbaugh, L. (2007). *Educational uses of digital storytelling.* Retrieved on October 27, 2007, from http://flare.ucf.edu/FLaRE_Presentations.htm.

Delpit, L. (1995). *Other People's Children: Cultural Conflict in the Classroom.* New York: The New Press.

Downing, J. (2005) *Teaching Literacy to Students with Significant Disabilities Thousand Oaks*, CA: Corwin Press, 2005, ISBN: 9780761988793

Fox, B. (2008). *Word Identification Strategies: Building Phonics into a Classroom Reading Program*, 4th Edition Upper Saddle River, NJ Prentice Hall.

Groth, L., Dunlap, K. L., & Kidd, J. K. (2007). Becoming technologically literate through technology integration in PK-12 preservice literacy courses: Three case studies. *Reading Research and Instruction*, 46, 363-386.

Hall, M. A. (1999). Focus on Language Experience Learning and Teaching. In Practical Classroom Applications of Language Experience. Boston: Allyn and Bacon.

Hayes, L. & Robnolt, V. (2007). Data-driven the professional development plan for a Reading Excellence Act school. *Reading Research and Instruction Journal*, 46, 95-120.

International Reading Association. (2004). *2003 Standards for reading professionals.* Newark, DE: Task force of the Professional Standards and Ethics Committee.

Labbo, L.D., Eakle, A.J., & Montero, M.K. (2002, May). Digital Language Experience Approach: Using digital photographs and software as a Language Experience Approach innovation. Reading Online, 5. Available: http://www.readingonline.org/electronic/elec_index.asp?HREF=labbo2/index.html.

Linek, W. M., & Nelson, O. G. (1999). Practical Classroom Applications of Language Experience—Looking Back, Looking Forward. Boston: Allyn and Bacon.

Microsoft Photostory 3. Microsoft, Inc. http://www.microsoft.com/windowsxp/using/digital-photography/photostory/default.mspx

Morrison, T.G., Wilcox, B., & Wilcox, R.T. (2008, November). *Trends and Issues in 50 Years of Literacy Research.* Presentation at the annual meeting of the College Reading Association, Sarasota, FL

Moss, B. & Bordelon, S. (2007). Preparing Students for College-Level Reading and Writing: Implementing a Rhetoric and Writing Class in the Senior Year. *Reading Research and Instruction*, 46, 197-221.

National Council of Teachers of English. (1996). *Standards for the English language arts.* Urbana, IL: A Project of International Reading Association & National Council of Teachers of English.

Pardo, L.S. (Sept/Oct 2006). The role of context in learning to teach writing: what teacher educators need to know to support beginning urban teachers. *Journal of Teacher Education*, 57, 378-394.

Pearson, P.D. (Fall 2002). Thinking about the reading/writing connection. *National Writing Project*. Retrieved on October 15, 2008 from http://www.nwp.org/cs/public/print/resource/329

Primary Resources (2008). How to create a talking book in PowerPoint 2003, retrieved on the Internet on October 8, 2008 at http://www.primaryresources.co.uk/ict/pdfs/talking_book.pdf.

Robin, B. (2005) Educational uses of digital storytelling. http://fp.coe.uh.edu/brobin/homepage/Educaional-Uses-DS.pdf

Shanahan, T. (1988). The reading-writing relationship: Seven instructional principles. *The Reading Teacher*, 41, 636-647.

Stauffer, R.G. (1969). *Teaching reading as a thinking process*. New York: Harper & Row.

Tompkins, Gail E. (2006). *Literacy for the 21st century: A balanced approach*. 4th Edition. Upper Saddle River, NJ: Pearson/Merrill/Prentice Hall.

UC Berkeley Center for Digital Storytelling http://www.storycenter.org/

Wallace, R., Pearman, C., Hail, C., & Hurst, Beth (Sept/Oct 2007). Writing for comprehension. *Reading Horizons: A Journal of Literacy and Language Arts* 48(1), 41-56.

Appendix A: Foundations of Reading

Pre-Assessment Survey
Shared Writing & the Language Experience Approach

This survey is designed to determine the extent to which the professional development provided in *Foundations of Reading and Content Reading* courses brought about change of knowledge, skills, and dispositions of elementary teacher education candidates. In particular this survey focuses on candidate knowledge of shared writing. Please answer the questions as honestly and completely as you can. The answers you provide will help the course instructor and division of education give the best possible instruction.

This survey will take approximately 5 minutes to complete. Be assured that your answers will be anonymous. Thank you for your input.

Please check the response that best represents your knowledge

1. I feel comfortable talking about and teaching writing as a content area and skill to elementary or middle level students

    _____ seldom _____ sometimes _____ frequently _____ most of the time

10. I feel comfortable talking about and teaching writing using the writing process approach

    _____ seldom _____ sometimes _____ frequently _____ most of the time

3. I feel knowledgeable about the steps for teaching writing using the writing process

    _____ seldom _____ sometimes _____ frequently _____ most of the time

4. I feel comfortable talking about and teaching using a shared writing approach

    _____ seldom _____ sometimes _____ frequently _____ most of the time

5. I feel comfortable talking about and teaching using the Language Experience Approach (LEA) to writing instruction

    _____ seldom _____ sometimes _____ frequently _____ most of the time

6. I feel knowledgeable about the guidelines for teaching using the LEA approach to writing instruction

    ____ seldom ____ sometimes ____ frequently ____ most of the time

7. I feel comfortable talking about and teaching the acquisition of language using the LEA approach to writing instruction

    ____ seldom ____ sometimes ____ frequently ____ most of the time

8. I feel comfortable talking about and teaching the formation of basic literacy concepts using the LEA approach to writing instruction

    ____ seldom ____ sometimes ____ frequently ____ most of the time

9. I feel comfortable talking about and teaching the development of reading skills using the LEA approach to writing instruction

    ____ seldom ____ sometimes ____ frequently ____ most of the time

10, I feel comfortable talking about and teaching using computer technology applications that involve students in the creation of the final product and to support student-authored products

    ____ seldom ____ sometimes ____ frequently ____ most of the time

11. In teaching writing, I feel comfortable talking about and using assessments to inform my literacy instruction

    ____ seldom ____ sometimes ____ frequently ____ most of the time

12. I know what assessments are appropriate to use in assessing writing

    ____ seldom ____ sometimes ____ frequently ____ most of the time

* Likert Scale: seldom equals 1; sometimes equals 2; frequently equals 3; and most of the time equal 4.

* Survey modeled from tool published: Hayes, Latisha L. & Robnolt, Valerie J. (2007). Data-Driven The Professional Development Plan for a Reading Excellence Act School. *Reading Research and Instruction Journal*, 46(2), 95-120.

Appendix B: Lesson Plan Rubric

Criteria	Distinguished (4)	Proficient (3)	Basic (2)	Unsatisfactory (1)
Topic/Content	Selects powerful core concepts; selects appropriate declarative or procedural knowledge; content accurate, logical, organized, credible, and in alignment with content structure; presented in steps and in logical sequence; use of varied and specific examples; aligned with learning theory	Selects accurate core concepts; selects appropriate declarative or procedural knowledge; content accurate with occasional mistakes or superficial treatment or missed alignment with content structure; presented logically with some examples; aligned with learning theory	Selects accurate core concepts; selects appropriate declarative or procedural knowledge; content presented with many mistakes or not aligned with content structure; not wholly logical or limited examples; not wholly aligned with learning theory and student developmental level	Fails to select accurate core concepts or accurate procedural or declarative knowledge; content not accurate and not aligned with content structure; not logical or no examples given; not aligned with learning theory and student developmental level
Student Development	Uses comprehensive knowledge of student development to plan appropriate learning experiences	Uses satisfactory knowledge of student development to plan appropriate learning experiences	Uses limited knowledge of student development to plan appropriate learning experiences	Fails to use knowledge of student development to plan appropriate learning experiences
Student Diversity *(learning styles, sociocultural, socioeconomic, etc)*	Uses comprehensive knowledge of student diversity to plan appropriate learning	Uses satisfactory knowledge of student diversity to plan appropriate	Uses limited knowledge of student diversity to plan appropriate learning experiences	Fails to use knowledge of student diversity to plan appropriate learning experiences

	experiences	learning experiences		
Planning Skills	Lesson plan well organized and utilized Ozarks lesson plan format; all necessary materials indicated and are "rich" (creative, engaging, varied)	Lesson plan organized and utilized Ozarks lesson plan format; all necessary materials indicated and are engaging	Lesson plan problematic and included some gaps or mistaken formatting; limited materials; long term planning not evident	Lesson plan substandard; materials or resources listed incomplete or missing or inappropriate
Objectives	Objectives clearly stated and written in measurable language; aligned with standards	Objectives clearly stated and written in measurable language; mostly aligned with standards	Objectives stated and written in measurable language but not aligned with standards	Objectives not written in measurable language
Procedures • **Before Reading (Set)** • **During Reading (Presentation)** • **After Reading (Practice and Closure)**	Procedures are appropriate in scope, sequence, and time frame; focus on core concepts and skills; aligned with objectives and assessments; reflect variety of instructional strategies to meet the needs of diverse learners	Procedures are appropriate in scope, sequence, and time frame. aligned with objectives and assessments; reflect variety of instructional strategies to meet the needs of diverse learners	Procedures are appropriate but not connected to scope, sequence, and time frame; limited alignment with objectives and assessments; limited instructional strategies	Procedures not appropriate, unclear, and/or incomplete; not clearly linked to objectives and assessments
Assessment	Assessments linked to stated objectives; clear, reasonable, measurable, and relevant;	Assessments linked to stated objectives; clear, reasonable, measurable,	Assessments linked to stated objectives but problematic; extension and higher order thinking limited	Assessments not provided or not linked to objectives; not clear, reasonable, or relevant; higher

Appendix C: *Digital Language Experience Approach Descriptive Response Form*

1. What were your students' responses to the experience you built with them?
2. What were the positives and negatives of the lesson in relation to the learning goals?
3. Can you describe times when your students knew more or less than you thought they would know?
4. How do you know your students "learned"? How did you assess them?
5. Could you or did you see how the model could be adapted for different learners?
6. What are the positives and negatives about the LEA approach as a shared writing strategy?
7. Would you use shared writing in your future classroom instruction? Why/why not?
8. What about the shared writing approach are you still unsure of or about which you have questions?
9. Would you use digital stories as a student publishing tool in your future classroom instruction? Why/why not?
10. What other observations would you like to add/share?

The Origin and Development of Ownership in a School Writing Assignment: Secondary Preservice Teachers Author a "How-To" Book

Peggy Daisey

Eastern Michigan University

Abstract

In a required secondary content area literacy course, 91 preservice teachers wrote a "how-to" book (Daisey, 2000, 2003, 2008). They completed four anonymous surveys about their ownership during the writing process. Preservice teachers' ownership of their "how-to" book increased from a mean of 6.12 to 9.53 (on a 10-point scale) during the semester. When asked to explain their ownership rating in open-ended questions, twelve categories emerged and will be shared in this paper. Preservice teachers believed there was a positive relationship between the amount of ownership they had in their "how-to" book and their rating for the likelihood to ask their future students to write a "how-to" book. Course pedagogy implications were suggested by the examination of critical points in the writing process for the enhancement of ownership.

Although students usually write for others, writers agree that they write primarily for themselves (Murray, 1982). Ownership in writing has many benefits for student writers. Students are motivated to write well if they have ownership in their work (Atwell, 1987). Ownership in writing leads to commitment and success (Blasingame & Bushman, 2005). Attitude toward writing is enhanced when students have ownership and control over learning and choice of writing topics (Prain & Hand, 1999). When young people are allowed to write about what matters to them, and when they write for authentic audiences, their motivation increases (Calkins, 1994). Cskiszentmihalyi, Rathunde, Whalen, and Wong (1997) found that motivation caused teenagers to expend more time and energy on a task, which enhanced their knowledge and ability. Students are likely to discover the power of writing to affect their lives, if their school writing is authentic and meaningful (Dudley-Marling, 1995).

Ownership throughout the Writing Process

Ownership of writing may be enhanced throughout the writing process of brainstorming ideas, drafting, revising, editing, and publishing. During the pre-writing phase, if the writer is allowed to have something to say through choice of topic, approach, or genre, then the writing is more likely to matter (Brannon & Knoblauch, 1982). Sharing expertise is one way of developing ownership. During the rough draft stage, ownership may be enhanced by providing students with an opportunity to interview classmates about their writing process (Clark, 2006). For example, Clark encourages students to draw their writing process and then share their diagram with friends (see also, Daisey, 2008). The revision stage is also fertile ground for the promotion of student ownership. Clark (2006) suggests that writers read their writing aloud to a friend, and then ask, "does this sound like me?" (p. 116). Multiple-drafts provide an opportunity for dialogue about how effectively the writer's choices have enabled the communication of his or her intentions. The teacher's role is to attract a writer's attention to the relationship between intention and effect. In this way, students may be encouraged to recognize discrepancies. A teacher may suggest ways to eliminate the discrepancies, but finally leaves decisions about alternative choices to the writer. Clark (2006) suggests that students compare edited versions of the same piece of writing and share their thoughts about them with classmates. If students are allowed to be creative and do things their own way, (for example, choose their genre or publishing format), this too is an avenue to promote pride and ownership (Koch, 1997). Evaluation is the natural conclusion of the process of response and negotiation carried through successive drafts. By responding, a teacher creates incentive for a student to make meaningful changes. By negotiating those changes rather than dictating them, a teacher returns control of the writing to the student. National Writing Project educators believe that students need to think of themselves as authors and take ownership for the direction of their learning (Wood & Lieberman, 2000). A sense of authorship brings a sense of pride and ownership for students (Bintz & Wright, 2003).

Preservice Teachers Need to Experience Writing Ownership

The promise of writing to clarify thinking and empower students will not occur without teachers who enjoy writing and understand its potential (Augsburger, 1998; National Writing Project & Nagin, 2003). Lane (1993) encourages teachers to talk about their past writing experiences and share their writing with their students. If teachers are expected to foster their students' ownership of their own learning, then preservice teachers need to experience owning their learning in their teacher education programs (Dillon, Anderson, Angio, Kahan, Rumin, & Sherman, 1995). In working with the National Writing Project, Wood and Lieberman (2000) have observed that when students resist new ways of teaching, it helps if teachers are secure about the rationale supporting their practice. This is why it is important for preservice teachers to be walked through positive writing experiences themselves

(Soven, 1996). (For more information about the National Writing Project, see Lieberman and Wood, 2003).

An Avenue to Ownership of Writing

Writing becomes accessible when respect, ownership and relevancy, as well as rule-breaking are part of the lesson (Daisey & Jose-Kampfner, 2002; Romano, 2004). Diversified writing promotes ownership (Ada & Campoy, 2004; Guzzetti & Gamboa, 2004; Maxwell, 1996; Nail, 2007). Moffett (1981) believes that writers may find their voice in school writing assignments. One example of a writing-to-learn activity that promotes ownership and voice of secondary preservice teachers is writing a "how-to" book (Daisey, 2000, 2003, 2008; Huntley-Johnston, Merritt, & Huffman, 1997). A "how-to" book describes a process and explains how to do something. While writing a "how-to" book, students become experts in their topic and must consider how to teach the process they have targeted as their topic. They must share their knowledge in a unique and creative way. For example, in "How to Go Down in History as a Somebody," a social studies preservice teacher had to research and choose leaders, analyze their qualities, and synthesize the information into steps with specific historical examples. In "How to Photosynthesize," a biology preservice teacher engaged her readers by providing this scientific information through a tale between an elderly plant and a young seedling. A physical education preservice teacher integrated her own experiences while motivating her readers to become active in "How to Kayak." A history preservice teacher revealed his historical knowledge and humor by advising his readers how to do something the wrong way, in "How to Lose Everything if You are a Russian Tsar." In past studies, "how-to" book authorship reduced the writing apprehension of secondary preservice teachers, through choice of topic, creative freedom, and division of the project into do-able steps, while building ownership and enjoyment of writing (Daisey, 2008). "How-to" book writing enhanced motivation for writing, increased identity as a writer, developed a learning community, advanced knowledge construction of content area benchmarks, and promoted reflection about the inclusion of writing in future instruction (Daisey, 2000, 2003, 2008).

Purpose of Study

In the past, preservice teachers rated their ownership in their "how-to" book projects highly (Daisey, 2008); the purpose of this study was to offer 'how-to' books as an example of a writing assignment and examine the genre's ownership-enhancing qualities that could be applied to other writing assignments. The research questions that guided this study were the following:

1. What point(s) in the "how-to" book process are critical for the development of ownership?
2. What detracts from a sense of ownership in writing "how-to" books?
3. What could be done to enhance ownership in "how-to" book writing?

4. Is there a relationship between preservice teachers with more ownership of their "how-to" book and their plan to ask their future students to write a "how-to" book?

Theoretical Frameworks

Piaget (2001) believed that learners construct their own intelligence through generating and testing hypothesis to make sense of the world they encounter. If learners have made their new understanding through their own constructivist efforts, then their learning "belongs" to them. In a related concept of scaffolding (Bruner, 1975), an adult works to support a child in achieving an intended outcome. Searle (1995) explains that scaffolding is related to control and thus to ownership. Only when teachers are ready to turn over more control to students can scaffolding be an effective classroom strategy for language development.

Advocates of the process approach to writing recognize the need for students to generate topics, draft, consider feedback and revise, receive assessment, and publish. For the process approach to be effective, teachers need to create an environment that includes time, ownership, and response (Giacobbe, 1986). Students are encouraged to "own" their ideas. Time gives room and respect for the students' own pace, while response and negotiation provide an opportunity for students to close the gap between their intended meaning and their actual, initial communication attempts. Ownership develops over time through response (Five, 1995).

Through ownership, students create new concepts and make new connections in their schemata. They select and take on projects. They make them their own, thereby making their knowledge their own. It is this ownership that fosters intellectual autonomy. Rather than adopting the role of examiner of student writing (Britton, Burgess, Martin, Mcleod, & Rosen 1975), teachers need to create environments that promote interest through authentic use of language by encouraging students to own a topic, book, activity, or process (Shannon, 1995; Willinsky, 1990). Ownership, then is a useful concept for educators who seek to understand how students learn particular content and processes under particular conditions.

Methods

This study employed a quasi-experimental design with repeated measures of matched subjects. The study took place in a Midwest university with a large teacher education program.

Participants

As part of a required secondary content area literacy course, 91 preservice teachers of diverse content areas were asked to write a "how-to" book. They were enrolled in four sections of this course during the winter semester 2008. These preservice teachers included undergraduates and students engaged in post-bachelor study for certification purposes. There were no students enrolled who were in a teacher education graduate degree program. The study included 45 males and 46 females; 85 Caucasian and six African-Americans students.

Procedures

As described elsewhere (Daisey, 2000, 2003, 2008), "how-to" books contain at least 500 words written over 20 pages including graphics, and a back cover photograph of the preservice teacher with autobiographical information. Prewriting activities include looking at lists of titles, "how-to" books by former preservice teachers, and "how-to" books at bookstores, as well as practicing writing directions. Preservice teachers submit a rough draft (with a content area benchmark), revisions, their cover, biography and resource page early. The class peer reviews throughout the process. Preservice teachers are asked to talk to their classmates throughout the semester about their "how-to" book authoring progress. When the "how-to" books are due, i.e., published, preservice teachers informally chat with their classmate authors while looking at their "how-to" books. "How-to" books were assessed by evaluating the following: (1) connection between the book's title and content area benchmark, (2) quality of first paragraph of book to grab a reader's interest by providing historical information, listing startling statistics, offering fun facts, or asking the reader a question, (3) completeness of rough draft, (4) revisions that typically included examples, (5) proof reading, (6) appearance of "how-to" book including photographs, illustrations, size and shape of book, layout of materials, attractiveness of cover, and binding, (7) resource page with at least two different types of resources including books, websites, and interviews, and (8) biographical information and photograph of preservice teacher on the back cover. (See Daisey, 2003 for additional scoring information.)

Data Collection and Analysis

Preservice teachers completed four anonymous surveys about ownership during the semester: when the "how-to" book was assigned (see Appendix 1), when the rough draft was due (see Appendix 2), when revisions were due (see Appendix 3), and when the completed "how-to" book was due (see Appendix 4). One question which asked preservice teachers to rate their ownership of their "how-to" book writing process was repeated four time, once on each survey. This question and other questions about motivation, pride, topic prior knowledge, and predictions about future instructional use of "how-to" books were Likert-like using a scale of 1-10. Means were calculated for each question by adding up all preservice teachers' answers and dividing by 91, which was the number of preservice teachers in this study. Pearson correlations were used to show the strength of the relationship between variables such as ownership, motivation, pride, topic prior knowledge, and predictions of future instructional use of "how-to" books. In each of the four surveys, an open-ended question asked for an explanation of the student's ownership rating. This question was analyzed by reading through the answers several times using constant comparison analysis (Strauss & Corbin, 1990). Key words and phrases such as "choice," "grade," "pride," and "amount of work completed" that emerged became categories to analyze. During this process, categories were grouped to form themes which were then connected to form patterns. A count was made of how many preservice teachers suggested each category of reason. Quotes from preservice teachers provided further insights into their thinking about their ownership development. The results of *t*-tests for ownership ratings between different stages of the "how-to" book writing process appear in Table 1. The categories of answers for the open-ended question about ownership ratings appears in Table 2. Correlations appear in Table 3, and means for Likert-like questions are in Table 4.

Results

Preservice teachers' ownership of their "how-to" book increased during their writing process. On the day when the "how-to" book was assigned, the mean was 6.12 (on a scale from 1-10). On the day when they peer-reviewed their rough draft, the mean increased to 8.11. Later, when student revisions were due as well as their biography and photograph of themselves for the back cover, the mean score increased to 8.74. Finally, when the completed "how-to" book was presented, the mean for ownership was 9.53. The difference between the means for each stage of the writing process was statistically significant. (See Table 1). On the day the "how-to" book was assigned, there was a wide variance (8.24) in the scores. In contrast, when the "how-to" books were due the variance narrowed dramatically to 0.63, suggesting that the preservice teachers were united in their agreement about their high rating of ownership.

Table 1: *t*-Test Results of Means for Ownership from the Four Stages of the "How-to" Book Process

	Pre	Rough Draft	Revisions	Completed Book
Pre	-----	-5.78 (p < 0.0001)	-7.62 (p < 0.0001)	-10.91 (p < 0.0001)
Rough Draft		----	-3.07 (p = 0.001)	-9.07 (p < 0.0001)
Revisions			---	-5.49 (p < 0.0001)
Completed Book				----

Preservice teachers were asked to explain their ownership rating in open-ended questions, when the "how-to" books were assigned, rough drafts were peer-reviewed, revisions were submitted, and completed books were presented. Preservice teachers, in some cases, offered responses in more than one category. Twelve categories emerged. (See Table 2).

Table 2: Reasons for Ownership (N=91)

Category	Pre	Rough draft	Revisions	Completed book
Dk topic yet	35 (38.5%)	0	0	0
Useful, has purpose	26 (28.6%)	9 (9.9%)	5 (5.5%)	17 (18.7%)
Interesting, important topic, choice	19 (20.9%)	21 (23.1%)	10 (11.0%)	9 (9.9%)
No option, doing for grade	16 (17.6%)	2 (2.2%)	1 (1.1%)	0
Understand task; confident	14 (15.4%)	4 (4.4%)	18 (19.8%)	1 (1.1%)
Just decided on topic; not done yet; wish to fix a few things	12 (13.2%)	29 (31.9%)	19 (20.9%)	4 (4.4%)
Enjoyment	7 (7.7%)	11 (12.1%)	5 (5.5%)	8 (8.8%)
Having problems	4 (4.4%)	15 (16.5%)	6 (6.6%)	2 (2.2%)
Pride	1 (1.1%)	1 (1.1%)	2 (2.2%)	26 (28.6%)
My work, words, prior knowledge	0	30 (30.0%)	35 (38.5%)	55 (60.4%)
Included words/photos of others	0	11 (12.1%)	9 (9.9%)	7 (7.7%)
More work done	0	17 (18.7%)	41 (45.0%)	16 (17.6%)

What point(s) in the "how-to" book process are critical for the development of ownership?

Beginning of the semester. At the beginning of the semester, preservice teachers based their ownership rating on the fact that they had yet to decide on a topic, thought the "how-to" book could be useful, or felt that they were writing a "how-to" book for a grade. About a third of preservice teachers (38.5%) explained that they did not have much ownership because they had yet to choose a topic. For example, a preservice teacher with a "2" ownership rating wrote, *"I think I need a topic before I 'own' it or am vested in it."*

The second most cited reason (28.6%) for ownership at the beginning of the semester was perceived usefulness of, or purpose for the "how-to" book. For instance, a preservice teacher with a "10" ownership rating wrote, *"I really love doing this sort of 'practicing' because it teaches me how to be student and also teacher…and that I truly believe will help my future students."* [sic] Preservice teachers cited interest in, or perceived importance of their choice of topic (20.9%) as a reason for their ownership at the beginning of the semester. For example, a preservice teacher with a "9" ownership rating explained, *"I feel that I have a lot of ownership in the 'how-to' book. I get to choose a topic that is of interest to me and it is also related to my subject area."* [sic]

Some preservice teachers explained their ownership rating was due to their focus on the "how-to" book as a required assignment (17.6%) at the beginning of the semester. Preservice teachers with low ownership ratings of "1" to "3" noted the assignment quality of the "how-to" book. For example, one preservice teacher explained, *"I think it will be a good experience, but right now it's more of a requirement."*

Rough draft stage. During the rough draft stage, preservice teachers based their ownership rating on their belief that they thought their chosen topic was interesting or important, they had work to finish, or were experiencing problems. Once a choice was made, there was a positive correlation between preservice teachers' prior knowledge of their topic and their ownership rating (See Table 3). For example, a physical education teacher with "8" ownership rating cited his or her own previous experiences with the topic and noted, *"I know most of this material and I am training for a marathon as well."* A small percent of preservice teachers (16.5%) cited problems as the reason for their ownership rating. A preservice teacher whose ownership rating was "7" wrote, *"I found it hard to narrow down my book and at this point I'm not completely satisfied with it."* One task that I typically have to ask of preservice teachers as part of their revisions is to add examples of what they were explaining.

Revision stage. About half of the preservice teachers (45.0%) based their ownership rating on the fact that they had completed more work. For example, a preservice teacher with an ownership rating of "9" explained, *"I'm feeling more ownership the more I work on it."* Preservice teachers felt that there was a strong relationship between ownership and the amount of work they put into their "how-to" book. There was also a strong relationship between enjoyment and ownership, as well as enjoyment and the amount of work preservice teachers were willing to invest in their how-to" book project. (See Table 4). Other preservice teachers explained their ownership rating was due to their feeling of efficacy to complete the "how-to" book successfully. Problems that were realized in the rough draft stage were resolved in the revision stage. For example, a preservice teacher with an "8" ownership rating wrote, *"I've definitely taken more ownership in my how-to book this past week. I almost considered picking a new topic, but something clicked in my revision and I'm really excited about the project again."* [sic]

Some preservice teachers (20.9%) reasoned that their ownership rating was based on their feeling that they had more work to do on their "how-to" books. For instance, a preservice teacher with an ownership rating of "9" explained, "I still want to fix a bunch of stuff."

Completed book stage. At the completed book stage, no preservice teacher rated their ownership level based on the belief that they had written their "how-to" book because they had no option or wrote it solely for a grade.

Table 3: Correlations

	r	*p*
Ownership and pride (completed book)	0.59	<0.0001
Likely to ask future students to write a "how-to" book and pride (completed book)	0.35	0.0007
Prior knowledge of topic and ownership (rough draft stage)	0.34	0.0006
Prior knowledge of topic and ownership (revision stage)	0.21	0.0246
Ideas and illustrations for how to book came from other sources and ownership (completed book)	-0.19	0.0335

Table 4: Survey Responses

	Mean
Was there a connection between your topic choice and your motivation?	8.38
If you had been assigned the topic How-to Increase the Motivation of Students to Write (in a subject area)" rather than receiving freedom of topic choice within your subject area, would this constraint have affected your ownership?	8.72
Was there a relationship between the amount of work that you put into your "how-to" book and your sense of ownership?	8.88
Was there a relationship between your sense of ownership and the amount of work you put into your "how-to" book?	9.09
Do you think that your enjoyment for the "how-to" book authoring process was related to the amount of work you were willing to exert?	9.27
Did your level of enjoyment affect the amount of ownership that you felt in your "how-to" book?	9.34
Did the addition of photographs and illustrations enhance your ownership?	8.81

Do you think there is a relationship between how much ownership you feel for your "how-to" book and the likelihood that you will ask your future students to write a "how-to" book?	8.65
How much pride do you have in your "how-to" book?	9.40

What detracts from sense of ownership in writing "how-to" books?

At the beginning of the semester, preservice teachers noted that if they had been assigned a topic rather than given a choice that their ownership would have been negatively affected. (See Table 4). An explanation for the level of ownership that appeared in the rough draft stage was the acknowledgement that some ideas and illustrations came from other sources. For example, a preservice teacher with an ownership rating of "8" admitted, *"The only things I do not own are the concepts in math that I did not discover."* There was a negative correlation between this category and the ownership rating (see Table 3).

Only four (4.4%) preservice teachers decreased their ownership rating at the end of the semester compared to their first day ratings. In all four cases, the first day rating was a "10." Three of the four preservice teachers' ownership ratings decreased to a "9," and one rating was an "8." There were two reasons mentioned during the rough or revision stages for the decrease: the knowledge that the "how-to" book would receive a grade, and the idea that the information in the "how-to" book required research and was not purely from the preservice teacher's prior knowledge of the topic.

What could be done to enhance ownership in "how-to" book writing?

When preservice teachers were asked what could have been done to increase their ownership in their "how-to" book, half (49.4%) of them felt there was nothing else that could be done to promote ownership. A preservice teacher wrote, *"if someone didn't own this project then it was their fault."* About a third of the preservice teachers (35.2%) felt that including more photographs and illustrations would have enhanced their ownership. Preservice teachers felt that there was a positive relationship between the inclusion of illustrations and ownership. (See Table 4). Eight preservice teachers noted that they would have had more ownership if they had included photographs of themselves doing the process.

Several preservice teachers (12.1%) also thought that more opportunity to talk about how they could use their "how-to" book, more time to present it to the class, or opportunity to publish it would have increased their ownership. For instance, one preservice teacher wrote, *"Maybe we could have used the how-to book for one of our (field experience) assignments. It would have been cool to use the content* (in the book) *in a classroom, and talk about the experience in [the content area reading course]."* Three other preservice teachers suggested writing a lesson plan that included the "how-to" book, asking middle and high school students in the field experience course to write a "how-to" book, or inviting former secondary preservice teachers who were student teaching (and had asked their students to write "how-to" books) to come to class and discuss their experiences.

Is there a relationship between preservice teachers with more ownership of their "how-to" book and their plan to ask their future students to write a "how-to" book?

When preservice teachers considered their "how-to" book writing experience, their responses to survey questions indicated that they felt there were strong connections among topic choice, willingness to work, enjoyment, ownership, pride, and their decisions relating to their future instruction. (See Table 4). Although there was not a statistical significant correlation between ownership and the likelihood of asking future students to write a "how-to" book, there was a positive correlation between pride and ownership. A preservice teacher with a "10" ownership rating admired his or her "how-to" book and wrote, *"I was very excited to get my book back today and see the happy/wonderful comments left for me; I felt proud to be a writer."* There was also a positive correlation between pride and the likelihood of asking future students to write a "how-to" book. (See Table 3).

Conclusions

Three themes emerged from this study: the importance of choice to motivation, the value of photographs to the promotion of motivation, and the value of breaking the writing assignment into smaller tasks.

1. Choice of a satisfying and useful topic led to motivation to work and to see through problems.

The results of this study suggested that choice of topic promoted ownership. According to Blasingame and Bushman (2005), "Choice leads to ownership, which leads to success" (p. 26). Choice was related to motivation. In order to promote ownership and motivation, teachers need to make writing seem to students like it was their idea in the first place. Allen (1995) says that when her teenage students tell her that they do not have anything to write about, she remembers Carolyn Burke's words, "It isn't that students don't have anything to write about, it is that they think that what they have to write about isn't legitimate for school" (p. 15).

The results of this study revealed that choice of topic enhanced the willingness of students to put time and energy into their writing. McClanahan (2001) notes that generally readers do not see a writer struggling with an onerous manuscript which is "delivered kicking and screaming into the light" (p. 9). Ideas may be plentiful, but what preservice teachers needed was the discipline to develop them or to continue trying when they felt they were not writing well, for example, during the rough draft stage. Writers speak of the hard work and discipline needed to write. According to Mary Heaton Vorse, "the art of writing is the art of applying the seat of the pants to the seat of the chair" (Bettmann, 1987, p. 55). Choice of topic kept preservice teachers willing to keep working to solve their writing problems.

The results of this study made clear that there was a cyclical relationship between the level of ownership and the amount of work preservice teachers invested in their "how-to" book writing project. This finding is similar to the conclusion reached by Csikszentmihalyi, et. al. (1997) that motivation promoted teenagers to expend more time and energy on a task, as well as Atwell's (1987) observation that motivation enhanced effort and success in writing. In contrast, ownership was diminished when focus was on a grade, topic was undecided or preservice teachers' topic knowledge needed to be supplemented through research.

2. Freedom to add photographs and illustrations promoted motivation and ownership.

Through "how-to" book writing, preservice teachers were allowed to have something to say. They were afforded an opportunity to consider their expertise and how to go about saying it, as they were walked through the prewriting activities. Preservice teachers were given the opportunity to combine a benchmark and their creativity. They were encouraged to break the rules (Heard, 1995) and use their voice and inventiveness to give directions from an unusual point of view or explain how to do something the wrong way in order to make their point.

3. Do-able assigned steps led to confidence and success.

The results of this study demonstrated that the combination of allowing students to make use of their prior knowledge by choosing a topic and breaking the writing project into do-able steps lead to efficacy, ownership and pride. This confidence was noted also in earlier studies particularly among minority preservice teachers (Daisey 2003, 2008).

Finally, the results of this study indicated that school writing assignments can empower students and promote positive writing identities. Writing is transformative for teachers and students (Powell & Lopez, 1989). Through writing, teachers and students may come to see themselves more clearly (Daisey & Jose-Kampfner 2002). This is because writing results in redistribution of authority in classrooms, as students' writing becomes a principle text, and the teacher is no longer the only authoritative voice (O'Loughlin, 1992). McClanhan (2001) believes that "to name the world in your own terms-tell your own story, is an activity of authority and power" (p. 3). Writing is an avenue to empower students, which is a prerequisite for the willingness to construct knowledge (Hanrahan, 1999). Preservice teachers in this study were given the opportunity to experience this transformation and empowerment.

Implications for Teacher Educators

In this study, preservice teachers were walked through a positive writing experience that promoted ownership of learning as Dillon et al. (1995) and Soven (1996) encourage teacher educators to do. Through this opportunity, preservice teachers were reminded of the importance of choice and enjoyment to promote ownership and motivation to work through a writing assignment. Teacher educators are encouraged to discuss these aspects of writing with their preservice teachers (Daisey, 2009). Ownership was prompted by use of content area prior knowledge as well as combining writing with illustrations. Teacher educators need to provide preservice teachers with opportunities to try out a variety of writing genres in order to compare and contrast the learning experience with their previous content area classroom learning experiences, in order to decide for themselves their value. Throughout the semester, preservice teachers were thinking ahead to their future teaching and promoting their future students' writing ownership. Hence, teacher educators need to ask preservice teachers to create lesson plans that incorporate a variety of forms of writing.

Limitations and Future Research

The results of this study are limited because they are self-reported. Future researchers need to ask preservice teachers to write lesson plans that include a variety of writing genres. They need to ask preservice teachers in their field experiences to ask middle and high school students to choose their topics and experience the stages of the writing process. Preservice teachers need to reflect upon this experience, contrast it with their past content area instruction, and share their thoughts with their teacher educators. Researchers need to follow secondary content area preservice teachers into student teaching and beginning teaching to study the ways positive writing experiences transform student ownership, motivation, and content achievement.

References

Daisey, P. (2000). The construction of "how-to" books in a secondary content area literacy-course: The promise and barriers of writing-to-learn strategies. In P. Linder, W. Linek, E. Sturtevant, & J. Dugan (Eds.), *Literacy at a new horizon: The 22nd yearbook of the College Reading Association* (pp. 147-158). Commerce, TX: College Reading Association.

Daisey, P. (2003). The value of writing a "how-to" book to decrease the writing apprehension of secondary science and mathematics preservice teachers. *Reading Research and Instruction, 42*(3), 75-118.

Daisey, P. (2008). Using drawings by secondary preservice teachers to study their writing process and apprehension. In M. Foote, F. Falk-Ross, S. Szabo, & M.B. Sampson (Eds.), *Navigating the literacy waters: Research, praxis, & advocacy The 29th yearbook of the College Reading Association* (pp. 201-218). Commerce, TX: College Reading Association.

Daisey, P. (2009). The writing experiences and beliefs of secondary teacher candidates. *Teacher Education Quarterly, 36,* 157-172.

Daisey, P., & Jose-Kampfner, C. (2002). The power of story to expand role models for Latina middle school students. *Journal of Adolescent & Adult Literacy, 45*(1), 587-587.

Ada, A. F., & Campoy, F. I. (2004). *Authors in the classroom: A transformative education process.* Boston: Pearson Education, Inc.

Allen, J. (1995). *It's never too late: Leading adolescents to lifelong literacy.* Portsmouth, NH: Heinemann.

Atwell, N. (1987). *In the middle: Writing, reading and learning with adolescents.* Portsmouth, NH: Heinemann.

Augsburger, D. (1998). Teacher as writer: Remembering the agony, sharing the ecstasy. *Journal of Adolescent & Adult Literacy, 41*(7), 548-552.

Bettmann, O. (1987). *The delights of reading: Quotes, notes & anecdotes.* Boston, MA: David R. Godine Publishers.

Bintz, W., & Wright, P. (2003) Teacher research: Reading & writing texts for multiple voices. *The New Advocate, 16*(1), 63-68.

Blasingame, J., & Bushman, J. H. (2005). *Teaching writing in middle and secondary schools.* Upper Saddle River, NJ: Pearson.

Brannon, L., & Knoblauch, C. (1982). On students' rights to their own texts: A model of teacher response. *College Composition and Communication, 33*(2), 157-166

Britton, J., Burgess, T., Martin, N., Mcleod, A., & Rosen, H. (1975). *The development of writing abilities* (11-18). London: Macmillan.

Bruner, J. (1975). The ontogenesis of speech acts. *Journal of Child Language, 2,* 1-40.

Calkins, L. (1994). *The art of teaching writing.* Portsmouth, NH: Heinemann.

Clark, R. (2006). *Writing tools: 50 essential strategies for every writer.* New York: Little, Brown and Company.

Csikszentmihalyi, M., Rathunde, K, & Whalen, S., with Wong, M. (1997). *Talented teenagers: The roots of success and failure.* Cambridge, England: Cambridge University Press.

Dillon, D., Anderson, L., Angio, J., Kahan, N., Rumin, A., & Sherman, R. (1995). Teaching and learning together in teacher education: "Making Easter." In S. Dudley-Marling & D. Searle (Eds.), *Who owns learning: Questions of autonomy, choice, and control* (pp. 190-213), Portsmouth, NH: Heinemann.

Dudley-Marling, C. (1995). Complicating ownership. In S. Dudley-Marling & D. Searle (Eds.), *Who owns learning: Questions of autonomy, choice, and control* (pp. 1-15), Portsmouth, NH: Heinemann.

Faigley, L., George, D. Palchik, A., & Selfe, C. (2004). *Picturing texts.* New York: W. W. Norton & Co.

Five, C. (1995). Ownership for the special needs child: Individual and educational dilemmas. In S. Dudley-Marling & D. Searle (Eds.), *Who owns learning: Questions of autonomy, choice, and control* (pp. 113-127), Portsmouth, NH: Heinemann.

Giacobbe, M. (1986). Learning to write and writing to learn in the elementary school. In A. R. Petrosky & D. Bartholomae (Eds.), *The teaching of writing: 85th yearbook of the National Society for the Study of Education* (pp. 131-147). Chicago: University of Chicago Press.

Guzzetti, B., & Gamboa, M. (2004). Zines for social justice: Adolescent girls writing on their own. *Reading Research Quarterly, 39*(4), 408-436.

Hanrahan, M. (1999). Rethinking science literacy: Enhancing communication and participation in school science through affirmational dialogue journal writing. *Journal of Research in Science Teaching, 36*(6), 699-717.

Heard, G. (1995). *Writing toward home: Talks and lessons to find your way.* Portsmouth, NH: Heinemann.

Huntley-Johnston, L., Merritt, S., & Huffman, L. (1997). How to do how-to-do books: Real life writing in the classroom. *Journal of Adolescent & Adult Literacy, 41*(3), 172-179.

Koch, A. (1997). Writing power: Opening doors to self-expression. *Winds of change, 12*(1), 14 -17.

Lane, B. (1993). *After the end: Teaching and learning creative revision.* Portsmouth, NH: Heinemann.

Lieberman, A, & Wood, D. (2003). *Inside the National Writing Project: Connecting Network Learning and Classroom Teaching.* New York: Teachers College Press.

Lunsford, A. (1993). Intellectual property, concepts of selfhood, and the teaching of writing. *The Writing Instructor, 12*, 67-77.

Maxwell, R. (1996). Writing across the curriculum in middle and high schools. Boston: Allyn and Bacon.

McClanahan, R. (2001). *Write your heart out.* Cincinnati, OH: Walking Stick Press.

Moffett, J. (1981). *Active voice: A writing program across the curriculum.* Portsmouth, NH: Heinemann-Boyton-Cook.

Murray, D. (1982). *Learning by teaching.* Upper Montclair, NJ: Boyton-Cook.

Nail, M. (2007). Reaching out to families with student-centered newsletters. *Kappa Delta Pi, 44*(1), 39-41.

National Writing Project, & Nagin, C. (2003). *Because writing matters: Improving student writing in our schools.* San Francisco, CA: Jossey-Bass.

O'Loughlin, M. (1992). Rethinking science education: Beyond Piagetian constructivism toward a sociocultural model of teaching and learning. *Journal of Research in Science Teaching, 29*, 791-820.

Piaget, J. (2001). *Psychology of intelligence.* London: Routledge.

Powell, A., & Lopez, J. (1989). Writing as a vehicle to learn mathematics and science. In P. Connolly & T. Vilardi (Eds.), *Writing to learn mathematics and science* (pp. 157-177 New York: Teachers College Press.

Prain, V., & Hand, B. (1999). Student perceptions of writing for learning in secondary school science. *Science Education, 83*(2), 151-162.

Romano, T. (2004). *Crafting authentic voice.* Portsmouth, NH: Heinemann.

Searle, D. (1995). Scaffolding: Who's building whose building? In S. Dudley-Marling & D. Searle (Eds.), *Who owns learning: Questions of autonomy, choice, and control* (pp. 185-189), Portsmouth, NH: Heinemann.

Shannon, P. (1995). Dialectics of ownership: Language as property. In S. Dudley-Marling & D. Searle (Eds.), *Who owns learning: Questions of autonomy, choice, and control* (pp. 142-152), Portsmouth, NH: Heinemann.

Soven, M. (1996). *Write to learn: A guide to writing across the curriculum.* Cincinnati, OH: South-Western College Publishing.

Strauss, A., & Corbin, J. (1990). *Basics of qualitative research: Grounded theory procedures and techniques.* Newbury Park, CA: Sage.

Willinsky, J. (1990). *The new literacy.* New York: Routledge.

Wood, D., & Lieberman, A. (2000). Teachers as authors: The National Writing Project's approach to professional development. *International Journal of Leadership in Education, 3*(3), 255-273.

Appendix 1: Beginning of the Semester-Stage Survey

1. How much ownership do you have in your "how-to" book at this point?

None   1   2   3   4   5   6   7   8   9   10   A great deal

2. Please explain your answer.

Appendix 2: Rough Draft-Stage Survey

1. How much ownership do you have in your "how-to" book at this point?

None   1   2   3   4   5   6   7   8   9   10   A great deal

2. Please explain your answer.

3. How motivated are you to write your "how-to" book based on the topic you chose?

None   1   2   3   4   5   6   7   8   9   10   A great deal

Appendix 3: Revision-Stage Survey

1. How much ownership do you have in your "how-to" book at this point?

None   1   2   3   4   5   6   7   8   9   10   A great deal

2. Please explain your answer.

3. Do you think the amount of work you have put in your "how-to" book has been related to the amount of ownership you have in it?

No relationship   1   2   3   4   5   6   7   8   9   10   A close connection

Appendix 4: Publishing Stage (Day the "How-to" Book was Due) Survey

1. How much ownership do you have in your "how-to" book at this point?

None   1   2   3   4   5   6   7   8   9   10   A great deal

2. Please explain your answer.

3. How much did adding photos/illustrations to your "how-to" book affect your ownership?

None   1   2   3   4   5   6   7   8   9   10   A great deal

4. How much did requiring your photo/biography on the back cover affect your ownership?

None   1   2   3   4   5   6   7   8   9   10   A great deal

5. What else could have been done to increase your ownership in the "how-to" book?

6. Do you think there is a relationship between how much ownership you feel for your "how-to" book and the likelihood that you will ask your future students to write a "how-to" book?

Strongly disagree   1   2   3   4   5   6   7   8   9   10   Strongly agree

7. Do you think that there is a relationship between the amount of ownership that you have in your "how-to" book and the amount of work that you are willing to put in it?

No relationship   1   2   3   4   5   6   7   8   9   10   A close connection

8. Do you think that there is a relationship between the amount of enjoyment that you have in your "how-to" book and the amount of ownership that you have in it?

No relationship   1   2   3   4   5   6   7   8   9   10   A close connection

9. How much pride do you have in your "how-to" book?

None   1   2   3   4   5   6   7   8   9   10   A great deal

10. Rather than letting you choose your topic, how much would your amount of ownership differ in your "how-to" book, if I asked you to write a "how-to" book entitled, "How to Increase the Motivation of Your Students to Write in (your subject area)?

No difference   1   2   3   4   5   6   7   8   9   10   A big difference

MENTORING STUDENTS

Progress Monitoring with Whole Text: A Comparison Study of Running Records and Curriculum-based Measures

Sandra K. Goetze

Oklahoma State University

Jacquelyn A. Burkett

Oklahoma State University

Abstract

Early literacy intervention is a critical component in helping all children learn to read. Progress monitoring within Response to Intervention models is a necessary guiding tool for good instructional practice. The purpose of this study was to compare the use of Running Records to oral reading fluency curriculum-based measures. Over a period of five months, at-risk readers in two rural schools were progress-monitored. Both the measures and the results were compared to ascertain which measure was more advantageous for planning instruction. Results indicated the Running Record reading levels were highly correlated to curriculum-based oral reading fluency measures.

R ural schools in Oklahoma and in many other states struggle to make changes between traditional models of literacy intervention and new models involving Response to Intervention (RTI) for their most struggling readers. RTI is included as part of the reauthorization of Individuals with Disability Education Act (IDEA) (United States Department of Education, 2004). RTI is, in the simplest form, a method for protecting the literacy welfare of all learners. In other words, an educator at the school monitors a child's total literacy development. When we think about RTI in the context of special education, other definitions come to mind. RTI. According to Trezek and Jarver (2008) RTI, "…can best be described as an alternative operationalized definition that may supersede the discrepancy criterion as a means for conceptualizing specific learning disabilities" (p. 14). The difficulty for schools in rural Oklahoma is how best to operationalize RTI given limited resources and the unique rural location of the schools. Many districts understand the ideas and theory behind RTI but struggle with how best to operationalize RTI within their district, especially the ongoing progress monitoring conducted by classroom teachers.

Defining RTI Models

Fuchs and Fuchs (1997) developed a 3-tier model, which initiated great challenges for schools to implement. The 3-tier model of RTI suggests good core classroom instruction at the first tier for all learners and intervention support in small groups for those learners who are not meeting established benchmarks and would benefit from more focused instruction on specific areas in literacy on the second tier. The third tier is designed for students who need extensive support in much smaller groups for a longer period of time each day. Allington (2009) suggests that at the most intensive support level, readers need one-on-one instruction. Tier three in this study focused on increasingly differentiated instruction with no more than three students in a group. Often these children were identified as needing special education services.

Although this approach is widely used, it is not the only framework for implementing RTI. Other models include Reading Recovery (Pinnell, Lyons, DeFord, Bryk, & Seltzer, 1994) or Linda Dorn's model of an extended reading and writing workshop (Dorn & Schbert, 2008). Regardless of the model, the hallmark of RTI is early literacy intervention, and RTI's key tenant is to intervene early and often with struggling readers. Clearly, there are strong arguments to support early intervention; however, the emphasis should be placed on general education curriculum and the role the classroom teacher plays (Lose, 2007).

Progress monitoring within the context of the regular classroom guided this study in these two rural schools. Classroom intervention was defined as all literacy intervention—extra support beyond core instruction—regardless of tier. The intervention took place in the classroom with the classroom teacher as a key member of the instructional collaborative team supporting students with special needs in literacy.

Progress Monitoring

Furthermore, RTI is described as a more dynamic form of assessment. Schools no longer must wait to see if students fail. According to Juel (1991), we have known for a long time that students who do not learn to read by the end of first grade will almost always remain poor readers. Progress monitoring as an ongoing assessment and instructional planning tool aids classroom teachers in moving students forward if they have literacy difficulties. "Progress monitoring is a set of assessment procedures for determining the extent to which students are benefitting from classroom instruction and for monitoring the effectiveness of the classroom curriculum (Johnson, Mellard, Fuchs, & McKnight, 2006, p. 23). These authors further add that progress monitoring needs to be a valid and efficient tool to gauge the effectiveness of intervention instruction, guide modification of instruction, and provide data for potential placement in special education.

One caveat of this notion is that progress monitoring with student data in the RTI model is relatively new for teachers to implement. Considering how to best operationalize this idea suggests challenges, especially for rural schools who often have limited resources. Progress monitoring also must provide deeper diagnostic data when students fail to respond to initial interventions, and this is not often represented in curriculum-based measures. This data, however, is easily accessible in literacy formative assessments such as running records or informal reading inventories. This use of connected text as an assessment measure seems plausible for monitoring the progress of the poorest readers since it provides the teacher with a larger window to view the reading behaviors of a child who is not responding to initial intervention (Denton, Fletcher, Anthony, & Francis, 2006).

Although this study focused on progress monitoring in rural schools, the results are relevant to urban and suburban areas that have limited resources. Progress monitoring should be a focused component of school RTI models. Additionally, pedagogical stakeholders should view progress monitoring as part of the general education system. The challenge lies in supporting classroom teachers in understanding how progress monitoring fits the teacher's role smoothly with regard to intervention (Gersten & Dimino, 2006). Since teachers have varied interests and expertise in implementing progress monitoring, it is important to explore assessment alternatives within progress monitoring models, which place inquiry and diagnostic data at the center of teacher decision-making with regard to increasing differentiated literacy instruction to support their struggling readers.

Background

Cantrick and Johnson Elementary (pseudonyms) are two rural schools in Oklahoma. These two sites serve children from rural homes as far as twenty miles from the school. William is a student attending one of the schools, and as a third grade student, William struggles with reading and language. William's school is resource poor, so the teachers at the site do not have access to a reading specialist; however, these schools recently adopted a Response to Intervention (RTI) approach with university support to better teach readers like William. Rural schools in Oklahoma often share resources such as special education teachers, reading specialists, school psychologists, and speech pathologists, which means that each site receives a small amount of time with shared teachers. Unfortunately at William's school, there was not enough money to hire even a part-time reading specialist. The teachers at both sites understood the needs of learners like William and decided to partner with a university to better understand how classroom teachers could conduct their own classroom-based intervention. After two years and just as the project was gaining some momentum, the funding from the university partner was withdrawn; however, during the partnership, teachers made a valuable investment in their own understanding and inquiry of progress monitoring to better help students like William. William continued into fourth grade and still needed support for fluency and comprehension despite his increased scores on progress monitoring data from curriculum-based measures, which indicated he was reading on grade level when in reality he was not.

Theoretical Framework

The theoretical framework of this research was situated in theories of action and "double-loop" learning (Argyris & Schon, 1974). Classrooms operate as whole and complete units as well as parts of larger organizations, namely, school districts. The rationale for the use of this theory base seeks to study observable actions and the meanings embedded in those actions. These ideas suggest that people have "maps" of how they think; this is their espoused theory. They also have ideas of action, which are observable. Argyris (1992) suggests, "There are important differences between the meanings created when people espouse their views and when they act them out" (p. 7). It is the observable ideas that guide thinking rather than their espoused ideas. Rosenfeld and Rosenfeld (2008) focused on teacher beliefs about intervention students and how these beliefs were incorporated into their instruction, which points to Argyris' theory. This indicates a need to examine the actionable and observable indicators of RTI literacy practice.

Theories of action are considered with single-loop and double-loop learning. In single-loop learning, one achieves the purpose as defined by outside influences (state requirements), and learning has a low freedom of choice. In double-loop learning, cultural factors influence outcomes; there is a sharing of control, a surfacing of conflicting views, observable data, participation in design, internal commitment, and the use of valid information. Single-loop learning creates organizations of self-fulfilling prophecies filled with error and defensiveness; whereas, double-loop learning creates organizations of inquiry.

> Individual members are continually engaged in attempting to know the organization [classroom] and to know themselves in the context of the organization [classroom]. At the same time, their continuing efforts to know and to test their knowledge represent the object of their inquiry. (Argyris & Schon, 1978)

Exploring teacher-suggested ideas for progress monitoring of effective RTI practice was critical in developing teacher tools that supported the progress monitoring research in these schools. Teacher ideas about progress monitoring and tools supported their planning of intervention instruction and theoretically grew from the notion of "double-loop" learning. The two are linked, for if the practice (action) is disconnected from teacher beliefs (espoused beliefs), the student outcomes will be problematic. The need to use the actionable beliefs as indicators ultimately led to an understanding of classroom RTI culture that enhanced overall RTI achievement for students. Teachers used one type of progress monitoring for a year and found that little diagnostic data was available from the curriculum-based measures (CBM). Their beliefs expressed during informal planning meetings over the first year indicated they felt a need to explore a more diagnostic form of progress monitoring along with the CMB measures already in place.

Purpose

The purpose of the study was to correlate two different types of progress monitoring and determine if these two tools (oral reading fluency measures and running records) accessed similar types of data to inform teacher practice and support student achievement. Oral reading fluency as an indicator during progress monitoring was studied with curriculum-based measures (CBM) along with Running Records (Clay, 1993b). Curriculum-based measures of reading fluency rely on leveled passages of text read orally by the student for one minute. The words per minute read correctly (WPRC) yield a score. Running Records record a child's oral reading behaviors, which include the types of miscues the reader makes along with accuracy and self-correction rate data along with WPRC. The latter construct of WPRC is not typically part of taking a running record, but for the purpose of this research, it was utilized as a variable.

Teachers often use a few comprehension questions at the end of a story to assess comprehension along with an oral retelling during a running record. Retelling is also a component of oral reading fluency in most CBM measures, but CBM measures do not include any comprehension questions. The broad conceptual research question asked: What can Response to Intervention planning teams learn from progress monitoring when Running Records and CBM oral reading fluency data are utilized in tandem over a period of five months? Specifically, (1) do descriptive data from CBM oral reading fluency measures and Running Records provide teachers with easily interpretable data for planning further progress monitoring instruction? (2) Is there a relationship and/or correlation between Running Records with whole text and oral reading fluency CBM measures? (3) Do Running Records provide teachers with a diagnostic picture of a reader's fluency profile including reading growth data? The reader fluency profile includes WPRC, accuracy rate, and the level of the text.

Running Records were selected as the second tool to measure oral reading fluency because according to Clay (2000), "If Running Records are taken in a systematic way, they provide evidence of how well children are directing their knowledge of letters, sounds, and words to understanding the messages in the text" (p. 3).

Research Rationale

In Oklahoma, schools are required to use one of the state-selected reading assessments. Many rural schools in the state have selected the Dynamic Indicator of Basic Early Literacy Skills (Good & Kaminski, 2002) as their assessment tool to benchmark and progress monitor students. After the first year of this project, teachers expressed an interest in exploring other types of progress monitoring tools. Teachers felt that the Dynamic Indicators of Basic Early Literacy Skills (DIBELS) provided some data but not the kinds of diagnostic data they needed to plan instruction for their struggling readers, namely, miscues and accuracy rate data. The two rural school sites, grades one through three, wanted to pilot the use of

Running Records along with the DIBELS Oral Reading Fluency (ORF) measure to determine if the use of longer connected text impacted the student assessment data in terms of obtaining more diagnostic information about the reader beyond reading rate. Teachers also wanted to understand if this new diagnostic data impacted their instruction and ultimately student achievement. Although teachers continued to progress monitor with the ORF subtest of DIBELS, they also included the reading of whole text with Running Records as they taught with a diagnostic focus (Clay, 1993b).

Evidence Base

An alarming number of children in Oklahoma are at-risk for reading failure (Dutcher, 1999). Without early detection and intervention, a struggling first grader has a 88 percent likelihood of remaining a poor reader in fourth grade, and a struggling third grader has a 74 percent chance of continuing to struggle in reading (Juel, 1988). Fortunately, three research syntheses indicate these children can be identified and provided with vital preventative reading instruction: Preventing Reading Difficulties in Young Children, National Reading Panel Report, and National Early Literacy Panel Report. Both the *No Child Left Behind Act* and Oklahoma's Reading Sufficiency Act (RSA) require schools to administer literacy screening assessments to identify and assist at-risk readers. In this state, elementary schools are administering these assessments successfully and identifying struggling readers, but they are less successful in using data to progress monitor. From the first year of the project, we know that teachers can and will use data to improve outcomes for children, but they need a cogent process for data analysis and , progress monitoring specifically.

According to many studies, the key to improving literacy outcomes for children is identifying the most at-risk learners early and then providing intensive, empirically-proven instruction to produce results (Good, Simmons, & Ka'amenui, 2001; National Institute of Child Health and Human Development, 2000; Snow, Burns, & Griffin, 1998; Torgesen, J. K., Wagner, R. K., Rashotte, C. A., Rose, E., Lindamood, P., Conway, T. et al. (1999). The most important tools in this effort are universal screening and diagnostic assessments. Universal screening tools, administered at the beginning, middle, and end of the school year, reliably identify children who are likely to have difficulties learning to read, so they can receive additional instruction (Invernizzi, Justice, Landrum, & Booker, 2005). As an outcome of this research, participants transitioned from an assessment paradigm that treated assessments as static products with little relevance to classroom work to a paradigm that treated assessment as inquiry-based, dynamic, responsive, and integral to good teaching.

The Role of Diagnostic Assessment

Providing students with a good beginning in reading is crucial to future success, and early intervention has a significant impact (Pikulski, 1994). The value of early intervention to prevent reading failure in young children is well established (Snow et al., 1998). In a study of systematic classroom assessment, Ross (2004) found a high correlation between teachers' repeated use of Running Records and student reading achievement. Regular use of progress monitoring as a systematic classroom assessment contributed to student achievement in reading (Pressley, M., Wharton-McDonald, R., Allington, R., Block, C. C., Morrow, L., Tracey, D. et al. (2001); Ross, 2004; Taylor, Pearson, Clark, & Walpole, 2000; Taylor, Pearson, Peterson, & Rodriguez, 2005).

Running Records, initially designed by Clay (1993b) for emergent readers in the Reading Recovery program, are a record of reading behaviors and strategies used as a progress monitoring tool to indicate instruction necessary for improving student reading. In addition, Running Records are an analysis of students' reading accuracy and the behaviors and strategies used during reading of leveled text (Fountas & Pinnell, 1996). The use of Running Records is supported by research, which suggests that because struggling readers have difficulty decoding, they rely on context clues found in connected text (Fawson, Reutzel, Smith, Ludlow, & Sudweeks, 2006). The researchers speculate the use of connected text during Running Records offers teachers an informative glimpse into how their at-risk readers process written language.

Regular progress monitoring with miscue analysis fits within the Response to Intervention model (Mesmer & Mesmer, 2009). In recent research on the processes of RTI, these researchers point out that as students receive intervention in an RTI model, progress monitoring data is collected on a consistent basis. They add that "the assessments should be sufficiently sensitive to small changes in the student's reading performance…. If students are showing growth on the more sensitive, micro-level progress monitoring measures, they will also be showing growth in the more comprehensive measures" (Mesmer & Mesmer, 2009, p. 283). Running Records, which focus on student growth, provide teachers with sensitive and accurate progress monitoring, which informs practice.

When analyzing miscues from Running Records, teachers gain information about readers and the reading process that informs instruction (Goodman, Bird, & Goodman, 1992). Miscues occur naturally when one reads. A concern is that by placing too much importance on how many errors a reader makes on informal reading inventories or curriculum-based measures, teacher and student may choose text that is either above or below his/her instructional level. Instead, teachers should focus on the impact miscues have on meaning. Miscue analysis gives the teacher specific information about a readers' abilities, which can be used to plan an individual reading program (Goodman, 1997).

Miscue analysis requires that the whole text be read rather than just a passage out of context. During a Running Record, the reader reads unassisted by the teacher. This allows the teacher to acquire understanding into what types of strategies the reader uses when he relies solely on his own means (Goodman, 1997). The teacher also marks the miscues the reader makes as he or she reads, noting self-corrections also.

The Role of Curriculum-Based Measures

Curriculum-based measures (CBM) are general outcome measures, which have been around since the mid-1970s. Through his extensive development and research, Deno (1985) suggested that CBMs are a measure of a student's academic performance in either basic skills or content knowledge. CMBs contain established reliability and validity, have alternative forms so that assessments can be given multiple times during a school year for progress monitoring, and are usually brief and easy to administer.

Monitoring student progress by reading CBM data has been explored extensively through oral reading fluency measures (Fuchs & Fuchs, 1999). The use of one-minute measures has emerged as a primary vehicle in schools to study progress monitoring of oral reading fluency and other reading components such as rapid letter naming, nonsense word fluency, phonemic segmentation, and comprehension (Hosp, Hosp, & Howell, 2007; Shinn, 2002). Initially, CBMs were used only for progress monitoring, but later, the use of CBMs expanded to included screening, decision making, and benchmarking.

Method

Participants

Sixty-five at-risk readers in grades one, two, and three participated in a five-month study of progress monitoring measured with the DIBELS ORF subtest and the use of connected whole text with Running Records. Both types of progress monitoring were administered to students who were identified as struggling readers. Struggling readers were defined as those students who were below the established screening benchmark according to their fall and winter ORF scores.

Approximately half of the students were from Cantrick Elementary School, and the remainder attended Johnson Elementary School. Cantrick Elementary is located in a rural community near a historically black college, and approximately thirty percent of the 205 students at the school are African American. Johnson Elementary has 140 students, and it is also a rural school; however, the minority population (about 17 percent) is composed of Native Americans. Both school communities have stable yearly enrollment, and most students complete their kindergarten through eighth grade education at the school site. Both school sites were considered at-risk for both reading and math in 2007. Since this research was conducted, both sites have been removed from the at-risk list because of increased test scores.

Data Sources and Instruments

Students were given progress monitoring assessments with the DIBELS ORF every other week by the classroom teacher. The DIBELS ORF subtest is a graded passage read for one minute by the student. Benchmarks, as established by DIBELS for oral reading fluency, were first grade benchmark for January, 20 WPMRC and May, 40 WPMRC; second grade benchmark for January, 68 WPMRC and May, 90 WPRRC; and the third grade benchmark for January, 92 WPMRC and May,

110 WPMRC. These cut scores were utilized as a baseline for serving students with intervention in the classroom for fluency. The DIBELS ORF subtest measured only WPMRC. Students were asked to retell; however, the data was not scored since benchmarking has not been established for DIBELS.

Students were also progress monitored with whole connected leveled texts and Running Records on the off weeks by two reading interventionists at the sites. The benchmarks were also applied to WPMRC with the connected whole text; however, students read longer than one minute. The Running Records were administered at the child's instructional level (94 percent accuracy rate or above), which was determined from initial classroom screening by the teachers. The running records measured words-per-minute read correctly, oral reading accuracy rate, self-correction rates, book level increases, miscue analysis, and comprehension levels. Note that although comprehension levels from four questions per reading were asked, they were not part of this correlational experiment since the other instrument did not contain comprehension questions.

Sixty-five children in grades one through three participated in the study. Data were collected on palm pilots as the children read orally for both assessments (DIBELS and the Running Records). Children were asked to retell the story after each reading session. Retellings were not scored. The data obtained from both types of assessments included words-per-minute read, oral reading accuracy rate, self-correction rates, and text level. Those data from each assessment were compared to better understand how tandem measures (CBM and Running Records) might provide more diagnostic data, which include the use of whole connected text to plan further instruction and assess progress. Additionally, this comparison was drawn to explore whether possible relationships between the two measures exist.

Running Records was selected as a generalized assessment for progress monitoring because many teachers already have knowledge of how to administer and interpret Running Records. To eliminate the variance in administering the Running Records, only two interventionists completed this part of the data collection, adding further trustworthiness to the findings. Each interventionist assessed the same child once during each of the twelve sessions to establish inter-rater reliability at 95 percent. Twelve sessions were utilized to create greater reliability of the data (Fawson et al., 2006). To lower the variance with text selection levels (guided reading levels), re-leveling of all the books took place prior to data collection (Fountas & Pinnell, 1996).

Research Design

A pretest/post-test study design was used to assess what Response to Intervention planning teams learn from progress monitoring when CBM oral reading fluency data and Running Records are utilized in tandem over a period of five months. The instruments used were the winter and spring benchmark, DIBELS oral reading fluency subtests, and twelve weekly Running Records. Leveled text from multiple publishers was re-leveled from A-Z levels (Fountas & Pinnell, 1996) to constitute the second assessment (see appendix A for book list).

The dependent variables included in the study were the measurement of words-per-minute read correctly (WPMRC) from the DIBLELS subtests, the text level of the Running Record book, Running Record WPMRC, and the Running Record accuracy rate. Descriptive data of the means and standard deviations were initially analyzed for patterns that teachers might find helpful to their progress monitoring planning. The means and standard deviations also were studied to look for changes from the winter to the spring benchmark administrations. The benchmark assessments during the winter and the spring were used to measure the effectiveness of the progress monitoring tools. This method also was used to assess treatment effect or statistical difference between the groups.

Data were recorded by the two intervention specialists using Palm Pilots and software designed for DIBELS assessment and Running Records (Wireless Generation, 2007). Those administering either the benchmarking assessments or progress monitoring selected the correct assessment by tapping on the screen. The student and the assessment then were selected from the next screen. Images of screen shots from the software are included below.

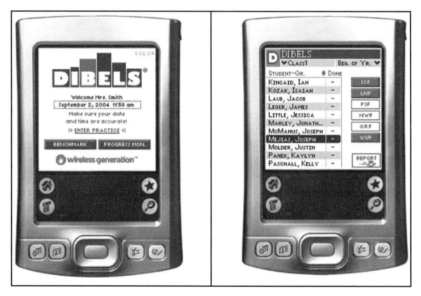

Running Record data were also captured using software developed by Wireless Generation for the Palm Pilot. Individual titles of leveled text located in the Wireless Generation electronic library were selected as part of the school's subscription to the electronic bookshelf to be downloaded onto the Palm Pilots. Screen shot images of the Running Records appear below. The first screen lists the assessment, the student's name, and the book title with level. The second screen shot is an example of how teachers may mark the Running Record, which includes a timer for recording WPMRC.

The research group (N=65) consisted of first, second, and third grade students, who were identified as at-risk of reading failure as defined by DIBELS WPMRC benchmarks for January. January benchmark levels for Running Records were established at the 94 percent accuracy rate level of text.

Data Analysis

A pretest/posttest analysis was used. Pearson's R correlations compared winter ORF measures and Running Record WPMRC and May ORF measures and the last Running Record taken for all three grades. Relationships were examined with t-test measures after the descriptive data was analyzed for patterns. The benchmark assessments during the winter and spring were used to measure the effectiveness of the progress monitoring tools. This method also was used to assess treatment effect or statistical difference between the groups.

Data from the two progress monitoring instruments (ORF and Running Records) were compared, and correlations were computed. Specifically, this comparison focused on words-per-minute read correctly from the winter benchmark and the first Running Record to the spring ORF benchmark and the last Running Record in May. The Pearson's R was calculated to determine a relationship between the two methods of progress monitoring. Student miscues were qualitatively analyzed to look for patterns in the students' miscues for further instructional planning.

The research question asked was: What can Response to Intervention planning teams learn from progress monitoring when Running Records and CBM oral reading fluency data are utilized in tandem over a period of five months? (1) Do descriptive data from CBM oral reading fluency measures and Running Records provide teachers with easily interpretable data for planning further progress monitoring instruction (descriptive data from means and standard deviations)? (2) Is there a relationship and/

or correlation between Running Records with whole text and oral reading fluency CBM measures (Pearson's R measure and correlations)? (3) Do Running Records provide teachers with a diagnostic picture of a reader's fluency profile including reading growth data (analysis of Running Record miscues)?

Running Record miscues were analyzed qualitatively for patterns of the child's progress. Since each child had twelve records, miscues were tracked and recorded on Palm Pilots, and printouts of this data were used for progress monitoring planning.

Findings

The descriptive findings from the study revealed that although students appeared to make significant progress according to the DIBELS ORF measures from the descriptive, most did not have the same level of increased improvement when whole text was used to measure oral reading fluency. The DIBELS measures tended to suggest a higher level of achievement as part of overall progress monitoring. Below are the first, second, and third grade descriptive data indicating the means for WPRMC on the DIBESL ORF and also the WPMRC with the Running Records.

Table I: First Grade, N=22

Dependent Variables	Pre		Post	
	Mean	SD	Mean	SD
ORF WPMRC	13.82	3.319	42.36	15.076
Level	2.14	.774	3.95	1.618
RR WPMRC	35.05	12.144	34.45	12.607
ACC Rate	95.77	5.665	92.59	6.434

For grade one, mean scores for both WPMRC measures went up from winter to spring; however, mean Running Record scores went down from first Running Record to the last. Mean book levels went up, and level standard deviations were the lowest of all the dependent variables. On average, readers began at level B and finished at about level D.

Table II: Second Grade, N=17

Dependent Variables	Pre		Post	
	Mean	SD	Mean	SD
ORF WPMRC	48.62	14.315	77.25	23.887
Level	4.38	1.088	8.12	3.16
RR WPMRC	50.62	20.829	57	19.47
ACC Rate	95	7.465	94.12	3.361

Second grade data (table II) reveal that WPMRC on ORF scores increased, but the standard deviation is also high. Unlike first grade data, Running Record WPMRC increased slightly from 50.62 to 57, while reading book level increased about four levels with a low standard deviation. These readers began at an average level of D books and finished, on average, at level H.

Table III: Third Grade, N=26

Dependent Variables	Pre		Post	
	Mean	SD	Mean	SD
ORF WPMRC	63.96	24.939	83	27.925
Level	5.1	1.432	11.32	4.126
RR WPMRC	62.08	20.05	57.84	13.468
ACC Rate	97.32	3.761	95	2.646

Third grade ORF data (table III) suggest that mean scores improved, but Running Record mean scores decreased. Book levels increased significantly with an average increase in reading level from 5.1 to 11.32. This is an overall mean increase of six levels, from level E to level K.

Additional descriptive data describing the book level increase from January to May is listed below. All the books read by the children during their progress monitoring period were considered a "cold" read, meaning that the child had not seen or read the text. The teacher did not give a book introduction, but rather simply asked the child to read the text. The book leveling system utilized for the study was guided reading levels A-Z (Fountas & Pinnell, 1996). Although levels were alphabetic, a change from level C to level D was denoted as one level change; this was distributed evenly across all levels. As the child read the book, the interventionist recorded the miscues. Descriptive data describing the miscues is listed after this portion.

Table IV: Book Level Increase Mean

	Beginning Level-1st Running Records with at least 94% accuracy	Last Running Records with at least 94% accuracy	Number of levels of growth from January to May
First Grade	Level B or 2	Level D or 4	2
Second Grade	Level D or 4	Level I or 8	4.4
Third Grade	Level E or 5	Level K or 11	6.34

Correlational Data of DIBLES and Running Records

Statistically significant differences (Table V) were found for students in grades first through third in terms of the ORF scores (r= .332, p< .005) and book level increases (r= .499, p< .001). There was not statistical significance when comparing the Running Record to the ORF subtest (r= .322 for winter and r= .474 for spring).

Table V: Significant Differences Grade 1

Dependent Variables	Pre		Post				r
	Mean	SD	Mean	SD	t-Ratio	Prob > t	
ORF	13.82	3.319	42.36	15.076	9.35	.001	.332
Level	2.14	.774	3.95	1.618	6.08	.001	.499
RR WPM	35.05	12.144	34.45	12.607	-0.16	.87	.006
ACC Rate	95.77	5.665	92.59	6.434	-1.46	.16	-.43

Grade two data (Table VI) also suggests statistical significance between the ORF subtest (r= .332, p< .001) and the book levels (r= .499, p< .001), while there is no correlation between the Running Record or accuracy rate and the ORF subtest (r = .552 for winter and r= -.051 for spring).

Table VI: Significant Differences Grade 2

Dependent Variables	Pre-		Post				r
	Mean	SD	Mean	SD	t-Ratio	Prob > t	
ORF	48.62	14.315	77.25	23.887	7.89	.001	.826
Level	4.38	1.088	8.12	3.16	5.04	.001	.335
RR WPM	50.62	20.829	57	19.47	.83	.423	-.178
ACC Rate	95	7.465	94.12	3.361	-.378	.710	-.312

Grade three data (Table VII) further suggests a statistical significance between the ORF subtest (r= .873, p< .001) and book levels (r= .321, p< 001). Again, there were not correlations between the ORF subtest and the Running Records (winter r= .725 and spring r = .695). It is interesting to note that r-values/correlations have a tendency to increase as grade levels increase in all cases.

Table VII: Significant Differences Grade 3

Dependent Variables	Pre-		Post				r
	Mean	SD	Mean	SD	t-Ratio	Prob > t	
ORF	63.96	24.939	83	27.925	6.98	.001	.873
Level	5.1	1.432	11.32	4.126	4.1	.001	.321
RR WPM	62.08	20.05	57.84	13.468	-1.25	.223	.549
ACC Rate	97.32	3.761	95	2.646	-3.59	.001	.54

Student Miscue Descriptive Data

Student miscues data were analyzed for reoccurring patterns in the types of miscues students made. Each Running Record was coded for standard miscues of repetitions, substitutions, omissions, self-corrections, and errors. When analyzing the error pattern of the students to plan further instruction, new types of miscues were discovered, noted, and tracked. For example, if a student was simply guessing and the word was wrong, it was recorded as a "guessing miscue" or GM. Guessing miscues often do not fit with the overall comprehension of the text. An example of a decoding miscue, or DM would have been "fielding" for the correct work "filling". Although the miscue does not make sense in the text, the student is attempting to employ some decoding strategy rather than simply guessing. Smart decoding miscues were utilized more as students began to connect with text strategically. They were categorized and marked as sDM. This type of miscue is still the wrong word, but it makes sense, and an attempt to find a similar word in structure works with the comprehension of the text. An example of the sDM might be "I'm" for "I am" or "said" for "say". The meaning is close, and it usually makes sense in the context of the sentence. Smart miscues or SM, were employed by strategic, metacognitive readers. These types of miscues often included repetitions and self-corrections. These miscues also did not disrupt meaning.

This chart was developed from the miscue data to aid in the coding process.

Figure 1: Types of Miscues

Smart Miscues (student predicting text & includes repetitions)	sm
Decoding Miscues (student attempts to decode)	dm
Smart Decoding Miscue (decoding that results in the correct word)	sDM
Guessing Miscues (guessing is the only strategy)	gm

The chart was used to code 780 Running Records over five months. Teachers used the information from bimonthly conferences with interventionists to plan further instruction that moved children from GM miscues into more sDM and finally into correct words or sm. When children were indicating slower progress with ORF data or no progress, miscues were studied. All children in the study showed this type of subtle movement over the period of the research. Teachers developed a weekly intervention log to reflect on such data.

Figure 2: Teacher Artifact

Intervention Group Information

Instructional Focus of Group: Within-Word Patterns Prosody	Week of: March 3, 2008 Time Met: 11:00–11:40
Classroom Teacher: Mrs. Y	Intervention Teacher: Mrs. X
Curriculum/Materials: Repeated Readings Word Sorts for WWP	Teaching Goal for Week: Move to new level & use WWP in writing

What was planned for each day of intervention?
Repeated Readings at current level Guided Reading New Book: Monsters (level L) SORTS Guided Writing:
T
W
TH
F

ATTENDACE AND OBSERVATION RECORDS:
Student Name: Tasha Attendance: (circle) M T W TH F NOTES: Running record indicates miscues with words that disrupt meaning. Not understanding global concept of reading to make meaning.
Student Name: Attendance: (circle) M T W TH F NOTES:

Summary of Data

Sixty-five children were post-tested with the DIBELS ORF measure, and 58 of those children increased their overall fluency rate, nearly achieving the benchmark level as specified by the state; however, when words per minute read correctly was studied with whole text the rate of reading was significantly less, and it did not approach benchmark levels. The average increase in book levels with the Running Records from January to May for grades first through third was respectively 3.5, 4.8, and 6.4 levels. The average accuracy rate for these levels was 95 percent. This indicates that students were reading at their instructional reading levels: 90-95% (Rathvon, 2004). The two measures, DIBELS ORF and Running Records, were not found to be correlated using Pearson's correlations; however, DIBELS ORF subtests and book levels were highly correlated, and there was a significant relationship between the two. It is interesting to also note that as grade levels increased the correlations began to rise, which may suggest more stable results for older readers than beginning readers and more research is needed to tease this idea out. An analysis of miscues yielded improved planning for teachers and new planning tools, which were ecologically validated.

Regular progress monitoring supports improved student achievement (Hoffman, 1991). Fawson, et al (2006) further remind us that Running Records "provide teachers with data in which to make informed instructional decisions" (p.115). These findings suggest that although students scored higher on DIBELS ORF measures than on Running Records, the oral reading fluency data resulting from whole text indicated much lower oral reading fluency scores for students overall. The correlation between DIBELS ORF measures and Running Records was not established, but as grades levels rose, correlations trended upward also. This may suggest that DIBELS may not be as sensitive to slight changes in fluency progress with poor readers when compared with whole text passages for progress monitoring. Students are managing much more information in whole text, and this is a critical consideration when measuring fluency. Overestimating progress, as suggested by the DIBELS benchmark scores, may result in students being released from intervention earlier than they are ready resulting in a false sense of achievement.

Improving Progress Monitoring

The broad conceptual research question asked: What can Response to Intervention planning teams learn from progress monitoring when Running Records and CBM oral reading fluency data are utilized in tandem over a period of five months? Specifically, (1) do descriptive data from CBM oral reading fluency measures and Running Records provide teachers with easily interpretable data for planning further progress monitoring instruction? (2) Is there a relationship and/or correlation between Running Records with whole text and oral reading fluency CBM measures? (3) Do Running Records provide teachers with a diagnostic picture of a reader's fluency profile including reading growth data?

The conceptual question was at the heart of this research in that teachers and interventionists learned that one standard measure does not give a full picture of a child's literacy progress. The CBM measures provide a quick "toothpick" approach to stick into the cake to see if it is done, while the Running Records provide the in-depth, diagnostic data teachers need for further planning. According to Shepard (1994), assessments should support instruction by modeling the dimensions of learning. An assessment that provides diagnostic data, which is relevant to further instructional planning, benefits all learners. Ross (2004) found that teachers' frequent use of Running Records was highly correlated to student achievement. This research notion stems from the idea that Running Records are more diagnostic in nature and provide the teacher with more information about how a reader is processing text. Informal measures, such as Running Records, provide credible summative decisions in a timely manner (Burgin & Hughes, 2009). Fluency can be viewed more as an outcome and process rather than just a number. While standardized measures have utility for larger picture issues in informing school or district progress overall, they do little to tell teachers what their students know and can do (Kohn, 2000).

Can descriptive data help teachers with progress monitoring?

This research project sought to understand whether oral reading fluency in progress monitoring was measured more effectively with DIBELS or whole text by comparing descriptive data. Teachers at the school sites felt confident that whole text was the better measure for progress monitoring and that students' would show greater gains with progress monitoring when reading real books. The teachers' perceptions were influenced by the double-loop learning theory, which promoted their inquiry with progress monitoring to find better tools for their planning. Because the teachers were empowered with double-loop learning, cultural factors at the sites influenced outcomes for students. There was shared control between university researchers and teachers, conflicting views with regard to assessments and observable data (book levels and accuracy rates), and participation in the design of when and how progress monitoring took place at their schools (Argyris, 1992). This promoted internal commitment by teachers and the use of valid information collected from teacher intervention logs. This theory was put into action through the teachers' struggles in using only one measure for progress monitoring, about which they had serious questions and reservations.

Interestingly, in a recent study by Doyle, Gibson, Bellenge, Kelly, and Tang (2008), DIBELS subtests were compared with Clay's (1993a) Observation Survey of Early Literacy Achievement (OS) and found that "specifically applying DIBELS criteria to the sample studied resulted in identification of a substantially reduced number of at-risk learners" (p. 157). They also suggested "serious flaws in judgments of at-riskness based on DIBELS procedures" (Doyle et al., 2008, p. 157). Although the comparison measure was different, the at-riskness level was also called into question. Students scored higher on DIBELS measures, when in the reality of reading authentic text; they processed text at slower rates and were still in need of further intervention. If only one measure was utilized, progress monitoring decisions may have been different. Teachers' insistence and intuition on adding more progress monitoring measures grew from what they knew about the culture of their rural students. Tensions created by conflicting views also supported the teachers' needs to know and tested their knowledge as it related to the culture of school.

Did scientific data yield the results teachers expected?

The findings from this study suggested that although ORF measures were not correlated moderately to Running Records, an important component of them was book level increases. Just as reading is parcel and part connecting to a whole (text meaning), literacy assessments have parts, which can meaningfully inform planning further instruction. The book levels used in Running Records is an important measure to consider and according to Allington (2009), is needed to gain fuller access to text as a critical consideration for fluency assessment when teaching struggling readers. It was also interesting to note from the data that as grade levels increased, the correlations also increased between the CBM and Running Records. This calls into question the nature of the measures used to calibrate student growth and achievement. If text level is highly correlated with ORF passages, using real text to calibrate growth makes more sense since students typically read full text rather than portions like those found on a CBM. It seems logical that as reading book level increased, reading WPMRC decreased. As learners adjust to more demanding text, fluency will decrease initially, but as a reader becomes more comfortable at that level, fluency rates will improve again. Paris and Hoffman (2004) found that informal measures can provide "multiple indicators of children's oral reading, including rate, prosody, retelling, and comprehension" (p. 207). Paris and Hoffman (2004) further states that the real benefit teachers gain is the knowledge while assessing individual children because the assessment framework provides insights about needed instruction.

Seeing the Literacy Diagnostic Picture

Teachers wanted to use whole text for progress monitoring with their students because they knew their students would engage with real reading at deeper levels. The teachers also understood that what is assessed is taught, a common assertion whose meaning is often underestimated according to Johnston and Costello (2005). It is not just about what is assessed, but rather how it is assessed that has implications for learning. Opposition from CBM research experts of fluency tools suggests that only curriculum-based measures are useful and appropriate (Deno, Fuchs, Marstin, & Shin, 2001; Denton, Ciancio, & Fletcher, 2006). While still others suggest that cultural considerations with RTI are critical in creating successful models (Klingner & Edwards, 2006). Opponents of Running Records and miscue analysis for progress monitoring often do not consider the research that has emerged supporting the validity and reliability of this form of progress monitoring (Fawson et al., 2006). Furthermore, progress monitoring with more than three, similarly leveled books, in running records provides teachers with a tool which robust. Fawson et al. (2006) point out further that with at least three records teachers will see an accurate picture of a true score.

Miscue analysis provides a wealth of information that guides instructional planning for both the process of reading and the reader (Goodman, 1997). According to Goodman (1997), it "opens up for the teacher, the reading specialist, the researcher in reading the path to how children learn to read, what they do when they read, and what strengths as well as weaknesses a reader shows when reading takes place" (p. 538).

Literacy and teacher researchers are at the beginning in understanding the role of progress monitoring in RTI, especially as it relates to the classroom teacher's perceptions of how best to plan intervention instruction. One caveat of the study is that although data were systematically collected, much more intensive studies are needed that bring teachers into the fold as researchers. Their theories of literacy teaching greatly influence progress monitoring, and often, they have a good understanding of how their students are progressing given the right tools.

Conclusion

The debate continues regarding the use of formative assessments, such as Running Records, to guide RTI progress monitoring. From this research, we are relatively certain that leveled text and a student's increasing level of text provide a good diagnostic indicator of student success. The aim of progress monitoring is to help students improve their reading abilities and data from it should support teacher planning in this direction. Standardized assessments play a role in progress monitoring, but they often do not provide a big enough picture when a student is struggling for long periods of time. Running Records fill this need, in supporting diagnostic planning.

The ability to predict when students will improve and at what rate at which this should happen is still relatively unknown. Inquiry processes like the use of Running Records to build a better diagnostic picture can help. Models to predict when a struggling reader should intersect the normal curve are yet to be discovered, especially when working with English Language Learners, but using book levels to predict progress may provide a start on this path.

References

Allington, R. (2009). What really matters in response to intervention: Research-based designs. New York: Allyn & Bacon.

Argyris, C. (1992). *On organizational learning*. Cambridge, MA: Blackwell Publishing.

Argyris, C., & Schon, D. (1974). *Theory in practice: Increasing professional effectiveness*. San Francisco: Jossey Bass.

Argyris, C., & Schon, D. (1978). *Organizational learning: A theory of action perspective*. Reading, MA: Addison Wesley.

Burgin, J. S., & Hughes, G. D. (2009). Credibly assessing reading and writing abilities for both student and program assessment. *Assessing Writing: An International Journal, 14*, 25-47.

Clay, M. M. (1993a). *An observation survey of early literacy achievement*. Portsmouth, NH: Heinemann.

Clay, M. (1993b). *Reading recovery: A guidebook for teachers in training*. Portsmouth, NH: Heinemann.

Clay, M. (2000). *Running records: For classroom teachers*. Portsmouth, NH: Heinemann.

Deno, S. L. (1985). Curriculum-based measurement: The emerging alternative. *Exceptional Children, 52*(3), 219-232.

Deno, S. L., Fuchs, L. S., Martson, D., & Shin, J. (2001). Using curriculum-based measurement to establish growth standards for students with learning disabilities. *School Psychology Review, 30*, 506-524.

Denton, C. A., Ciancio, D. J., & Fletcher, J. M. (2006). Validity, reliability, and utility of the observation survey of early literacy achievement. *Reading Research Quarterly, 41*, 8-34.

Denton, C. A., Fletch, J. M., Antony, J. L., & Francis, D. J. (2006). An evaluation of intensive intervention for students with persistent reading difficulties. *Journal of Learning Disabilities, 39*, 447-466.

Dorn, L., & Schbert, B. (2008). A comprehensive intervention model for preventing reading failure: A response to intervention approach. *Wisconsin State Reading Association Journal, 47*(3), 51-63.

Doyle, M. A., Gibson, S. A., Gomez-Bellenge, F., Kelly, P. R., and Tang, M. (2008). Assessment and identification of first-grade students at risk: Correlating the Dynamic indicators of basic early literacy skills and an observation survey of early literacy achievement. In 57th *Yearbook of the National Reading Conference* (pp. 144-159). Oak Creek, WI: National Reading Conference.

Dutcher, L. (1999). Government's "official" story masks students' reading woes: Beware of politicians bearing test scores. *Oklahoma Council of Public Affairs.*

Fawson, P. C., Reutzel, R. D., Smith, J. A., Ludlow, B. C., & Sudweeks, R. (2006). Examining the reliability of running records: Attaining generalizable results. *The Journal of Educational Research, 100*(2), 113-126.

Fountas, I. C., & Pinnell, G. S. (1996). *Guided reading: Good first teaching for all children.* Portsmouth, NH: Heinemann.

Fuchs, L. S., & Fuchs, D. (1997). Use of curriculum-based measurement in identifying students with disabilities. *Exceptional Children, 30*, 1-14.

Fuchs, L. S., & Fuchs, D. (1999). Monitoring student progress toward the development of reading competence: A review of three forms of classroom-based assessment. *School Psychology Review, 28*(4), 659-671.

Gersten, R., & Dimino, J. A. (2006). RTI (Response to Intervention): Rethinking special education for students with reading difficulties (yet again). *Reading Research Quarterly, 41*, 99-108.

Good, R. H., & Kaminski, R. A. (2002). *Dynamic indicators of basic early literacy skills* (6th ed.). Eugene, OR: Institute for the Development of Educational Achievement.

Good, R. H., Simmons, D., & Ka'amenui, E. (2001). The importance and decision-making utility of a continuum of fluency-based indicators of foundational reading. *Scientific Studies of Reading, 5*(1), 257-288.

Goodman, K. (1997). Reading diagnosis: Qualitative or quantitative? *The Reading Teacher, 50*(7), 534-538.

Goodman, K., Bird, L., & Goodman, Y. (1992). *The assessment supplement to the whole language catalog.* Santa Rosa, CA: American School Publishers.

Hoffman, J.V. (1991). Teacher and school effects in learning to read. In R. Barr, M. L. Kamil, P. B. Mosenthal, & P. D. Pearson (Eds.). *Handbook of reading research* (Vol.2, pp. 911-950). New York: Longman.

Hosp, M., Hosp, J., & Howell, K. (2007). *The ABCs of CBM: A practical guide to curriculum-based measurement.* New York: Guilford Press.

Invernizzi, M., Justice, L., Landrum, T., & Booker, K. (2005). Early literacy screening in kindergarten: Widespread implementation in Virginia. *Journal of Literacy Research, 36*, 479-500.

Johnson, E., Mellard, D. F., Fuchs, D., & McKnight, M. A. (2006). *Responsiveness to intervention (RTI): How to do it.* Lawrence, KS: National Research Center on Learning Disabilities.

Johnston, P., & Costello J, (2005). Theory and research into practice principles for literacy assessment. *Reading Research Quarterly, 40*, 256-267.

Juel, C. (1988). Learning to read and write: A longitudinal study of 54 children from first to fourth grades. *Journal of Educational Psychology, 80*(4), 437-447.

Juel, C. (1991). Beginning reading. In R. Barr, M. Kamil, P. Mosenthal, & P. D. Pearson (Eds.), *Handbook of reading research* (Vol. II, pp. 759-788). New York: Longman Press.

Klingner, J. K., & Edwards, P. A. (2006). Cultural considerations with response to intervention models. *Reading Research Quarterly, 41*, 108-117.

Kohn, A. (2009). *The schools our children deserve.* Boston: Houghton Mifflin.

Lose, M. K. (2007). A child's response to intervention requires a responsive teacher of reading. *Reading Teacher, 61*, 276-279.

Mesmer, E. M., & Mesmer, H. A. E. (2009). Response to intervention (RTI): What teachers of reading need to know. *The Reading Teacher, 64*(4), 280-290.

National Institute of Child Health and Human Development. (2000). *Teaching children to read: An evidence-based assessment of the scientific research literature on reading and its implications for reading instruction.* Washington, DC: Author.

Paris, S. G., & Hoffman, J. V. (2004). Reading assessment in kindergarten through third grade: Findings from the center for the improvement of early reading achievement. *The Elementary School Journal, 105*(2), 199-217.

Pikulski, J. (1994). Preventing reading failure: A review of five effective programs. *The Reading Teacher, 48*(1), 30-39.

Pinnell, G. S., Lyons, C. A., DeFord, D. E., Bryk, A. S., & Seltzer, M. (1994). Comparing instructional models for the literacy education of high-risk first graders. *Reading Research Quarterly, 29*, 9–38.

Pressley, M., Wharton-McDonald, R., Allington, R., Block, C. C., Morrow, L., Tracey, D. et al. (2001). A study of effective first-grade literacy instruction. *Scientific Studies of Reading, 5*(1), 35-58.

Rathvon, M. R. (2004). *Early reading assessment: A practitioner's handbook.* New York: Guilford.

Rosenfeld, M., & Rosenfeld, S. (2008). Developing effective teacher beliefs about learners: The role of sensitizing teachers to individual learning differences. *Educational Psychology, 28*, 245-272.

Ross, J. A. (2004). Effects of running records assessment on early literacy achievement. *Journal of Educational Research, 97*, 186-194.

Shepard, L. A. (1994). The challenges of assessing young children appropriately. *Phi Delta Kappen, 76*, 181-190.

Shin, M. R. (2002). Best practices in using curriculum-based measurement in a problem-solving model. In A. Thomas & J. Grimes (Eds.), *Best practices in school psychology IV* (pp. 671-693). Bethesda, MD: National Association of School Psychologists.

Snow, C. E., Burns, M. S., & Griffin, P. (Eds.). (1998). *Preventing reading difficulties in young children.* Washington, DC: National Academy Press.

Taylor, B. M., Pearson, P. D., Clark, K., & Walpole S. (2000). Effective schools and accomplished teachers: Lessons about primary-grade reading instruction in low-income schools. *Elementary School Journal, 101*, 121-166.

Taylor, B. M., Pearson, P. D., Peterson D. S., & Rodriguez, M. C. (2005). The Ciera school change framework: An evidence-based approach to professional development and school reading improvement. *Reading Research Quarterly, 40*(1), 40-69.

Torgesen, J. K., Wagner, R. K., Rashotte, C. A., Rose, E., Lindamood, P., Conway, T. et al. (1999). Preventing reading failure in young children with phonological processing disabilities: Group and individual responses to instruction. *Journal of Educational Psychology, 91*, 579-593.

Trezek, B. J., & Tarver, S. G. (2008). Prevention and identification of specific learning disabilities within the response to intervention model. *Balanced Reading Instruction, 2*, 13-24.

United States Department of Education, 2004. *Building the legacy*: IDEA 2004. Retrieved: February 2, 2007 from http:// idea.ed.gov

Wireless Generation, 2006. *Mclass Reading.* Retrieved: June 2, 2006 from http://www.wirelessgeneration.com/

Improving Reading Achievement of Low SES Minority Students With Science-Related Informational Texts and Structured Responses

Kathy E. Stephens

LeTourneau University

Abstract

The purpose of this study was to examine the impact of a 12-week science-based instructional protocol on reading achievement of low SES minority fourth-grade students. A mixed methods research design included quantitative results from reading comprehension assessments and qualitative results from student reflective journal entries. The results revealed three major findings: improved reading comprehension achievement, a narrowing of gender and ethnicity achievement gaps, and increased teacher-directed reading instructional time.

It is important to prepare intermediate-level students for a rapidly changing, highly technical world which demands that teachers equip students to achieve in all areas using strategies for comprehending a wide variety of passages (Palmer & Stewart, 2003; Snow, Burns, & Griffin, 1998; Yopp & Yopp, 2000). Similarly, finding new ways to improve reading comprehension achievement in the content areas is another vital issue facing all schools (Liang & Dole, 2006; National Institute of Child Health and Human Development, 2000; Snow et al.). With a national emphasis on testing and achievement, experts have agreed that educators must find innovative methods to help students read and comprehend all texts successfully (Bennett-Armistead & Duke, 2004; Dreher, 1998; Moss, 2004).

The National Reading Panel Report (National Institute of Child Health and Human Development, 2000) defined reading comprehension as "an active process that requires an intentional and thoughtful interaction between the reader and the text" (p. 13). Pressley (2001) emphasized the importance of connecting reading and writing with content area learning and teaching a variety of comprehension strategies to improve students' success. Furthermore, Pressley noted that effective teachers regularly include an assortment of literature experiences. Other researchers have agreed that students should interact with many types of texts, including informational books (Duke, 2004; Duke & Bennett-Armistead, 2003; Moss, 2005; Saul & Dieckman, 2005).

Informational text experiences prepare students for technological advances and information overload common with internet resources (Duke, 2006; Moss, 2004, 2005). Other research has suggested that increased use of informational text positively affects reading achievement (Stewart, 2004), and with the level of difficulty increasing in content textbooks, informational texts may provide powerful resources for enhancing the content areas (Cheak & Wessel, 2005). Other experts agree that when high-interest informational texts are included, improved motivation to read may positively affect reading achievement (Duke, 2006; Edmunds & Bauserman, 2006). These researchers have recommended that educators use informational texts to connect to real-life experiences, especially for students with limited reading experiences. Additionally, when students first experience vocabulary-rich content area textbooks in intermediate grades, reading achievement may wane (Chall, 1996). The purposeful integration of informational texts may offer teachers valuable resources for enriching textbook reading.

Correspondingly, it is during and beyond the intermediate grades that students from low-income families and minority ethnic groups often face greater challenges in both motivation and achievement (Chall & Jacobs, 2003; Chall, Jacobs & Baldwin, 1990). Reading for information is a critical skill during the intermediate grades. Reading researcher, Moss (2005) recommended that content-area instruction may be improved by including specific instructional strategies, such as the use of learning logs, along with informational texts. Moreover, reading comprehension may be improved for at-risk intermediate-level students by including high-interest informational texts within an instructional protocol (Cheak &Wessel, 2005; Smolkin & Donovan, 2001).

Purpose of the Study

Research shows that informational texts are important tools in reading comprehension instruction and achievement (Duke, 2004; Saul & Dieckman, 2005; Stewart, 2004). Therefore, this study began with a 12-week instructional protocol that integrated science-related informational texts with reading and writing activities in fourth-grade classes. This instructional protocol included teacher read-alouds, written reflections, oral discussions, and independent reading using science-based informational texts. The study sought to determine the impact of the instructional protocol on reading comprehension achievement. The research questions in this study examined the impact of including a science-based integrated instructional protocol on reading comprehension achievement of fourth-grade students, with comparisons by gender and ethnicity.

Methods

Design of the Study

A mixed methods research design was selected to examine the impact of the integrated instructional protocol, in which informational science-based texts were emphasized in the reading curriculum of intermediate classrooms. The design included a quasi-experimental component of quantitative data sources used to determine if the implementation of the protocol resulted in differences in reading comprehension achievement between intervention and nonintervention groups. The second component, a descriptive comparison, included qualitative data sources to describe further the impact of the intervention.

Participants

This study was conducted in two public school settings with comparable demographics. The intervention was conducted in a mid-sized public elementary school in Northeast Texas, located in a low socioeconomic inner-city neighborhood. The school served 464 students from prekindergarten through fifth grade, with 432 (93%) of the total population designated as economically disadvantaged according to guidelines for the National School Lunch Program, (USDA Food and Nutrition Service, 2006). The intervention fourth grade was comprised of 40 students enrolled in two self-contained classes with two primary ethnic groups, African American and Hispanic. While all 40 students participated in the instructional activities of the study, only 28 students with complete data sets were reported.

The setting for the nonintervention fourth grade group was in a school district located approximately 30 miles from the intervention campus. The nonintervention class was located on an elementary campus in a low socioeconomic inner-city neighborhood, which served 327 students, of which 281 (86%) were identified as economically disadvantaged (USDA Food and Nutrition Service, 2006). The nonintervention class, represented by three primary ethnic groups (African American, Hispanic, and White) had a population of 15 students; 14 students with complete data sets were reported in the study.

Procedures

The Literacy-based Intervention Protocol

A focal point of the 12-week intervention was teacher read-alouds using high-interest, science-based texts. The teachers read for approximately 15 to 20 minutes, 2 to 3 days each week, and guided their students in short discussions with brief written responses after the read-aloud sessions. Written responses included the book title, and (a) a summary of the big ideas, (b) a brief expository retelling, (c) a simple graphic organizer, or (d) other short written responses, recorded in reflective journals. Additionally, students read similar texts independently (or with a partner), as well as science-based student periodicals (*Weekly Reader*) for approximately 15 minutes, 3 days each week. Students then compiled written responses in their reflective journals similar to those modeled during teacher read-alouds. Since the reading intervention was implemented as part of the normal instructional environment, all students in the intervention group participated in the study's instructional activities. Students in the nonintervention group followed a regular instructional routine that did not include any emphasis on the intervention elements.

The Intervention Timeline

The principal investigator met with the participating intervention teachers three times prior to the intervention period and communicated with them through email correspondence and brief weekly school visits. The meetings were designed to (a) overview the components and goals of the study, (b) preview study materials, (c) discuss student assessment procedures, (d) provide training related to the instructional procedures, and (e) review the timeline for the study. The training also included discussions concerning (a) procedures for teacher read-alouds, (b) group discussions following the read-alouds, (c) group and individual responses using graphic organizers, (d) student paired and independent reading materials, and (e) student reflective journals.

Materials

A collection of high-interest, science-based informational children's literature was provided to each of the intervention classes as part of the instructional protocol. These grade-level appropriate books were chosen using broad categories of life science, physical science, and earth and space science included in the fourth-grade Texas science curriculum, known as the Texas Essential Knowledge and Skills (TEKS, Texas Education Agency, 2005b). A subscription to the *Weekly Reader* student magazine was also provided to the intervention students, who were given time to read and discuss the magazines each week.

Data Sources and Analysis

Quantitative Data Sources

The GMRT Comprehension Subtest. The comprehension subtest of the Gates-MacGinitie Reading Test ([GMRT], MacGinitie, MacGinitie, Maria, & Dreyer, 2000) Level 4, Form S, was used to collect normative data. The GMRT assesses the reading ability of students, ages prereading through adult. The fourth edition reported a .93 KR–20 reliability coefficient for both levels. The comprehension subtest, consisting of 11 passages and 48 questions, measures a student's ability to read and understand different types of prose (MacGinitie et al.). Prior to the first week and during the final week of the study, the GMRT comprehension subtest was administered to all students in the intervention and nonintervention groups. Normal curve equivalent (NCE) scores were analyzed using a univariate analysis of variance (ANOVA) for students in the intervention (treatment) and the nonintervention (control) groups in order to determine the impact of including an integrated instructional protocol on the reading comprehension achievement.

The Texas Assessment of Knowledge and Skills (TAKS) Test. The TAKS has been the primary measure of reading success in Texas since 1999, with successful completion of the fifth-grade TAKS objectives being a requirement for advancement to the next grade levels (TEA, 2005a). The TAKS, a standards referenced assessment, is designed to measure students' knowledge of the statewide curriculum, known as the TEKS (TEA, 2004). The Kuder-Richardson Formula 20 (KR 20) was used to determine the TAKS test reliability. While most internal consistency reliabilities range from the high .80s to the low .90s, the TAKS assessments range from 0.81 to 0.93 (TEA, 2004).

The Reading TAKS was completed after the conclusion of the intervention, and the scale scores were included as quantitative data sources for both the intervention and nonintervention groups. An ANOVA helped determine the impact of the intervention on reading comprehension achievement, and comparisons were made between the results from the intervention and nonintervention groups. TAKS scale scores were also compared by gender and ethnicity.

Qualitative Data Sources

Preservice student researchers and observational data. A group of eight senior-level preservice students assisted in gathering descriptive qualitative data during the intervention. The student researchers were enrolled in their final reading course where the principal investigator served as the course professor. Prior to the study, the principal investigator met three times with the student researchers to (a) obtain their consent to participate, (b) overview project objectives, (c) provide training for classroom observations, and (d) discuss the interview procedures. To provide consistency in data recording, the principal investigator completed one classroom observation with each student researcher, then met afterwards to compare and discuss the observational notes. After training, the student researchers traveled in pairs to the intervention classrooms and recorded global and specific field notes approximately three times (at the beginning, middle, and near the end of the intervention period). Observational field notes were recorded on the classroom observation documentation form (see Appendix A). Recorded classroom observations included topics related to teacher read-alouds, modeled written responses, student participation in whole class, paired, and independent reading activities. Observations were also completed in the nonintervention classroom by the principal investigator. In addition, communication via email between the principal investigator and the nonintervention teacher ensured that intervention procedures were not occurring.

The intervention classroom observational notes were analyzed using a constant comparative analysis method (Creswell, 1998). Specifically, an open coding method was used to determine instructional and behavioral themes and subcategories (Berg, 2004). The intervention observations were collected and read in order to discover emerging themes. This process was repeated until no new emerging themes could be found. These themes were divided into instructional and behavioral themes and subcategories, and the data was analyzed to obtain frequency counts for each of the instructional and behavioral themes and subcategories.

Reflective fourth-grade student journals. At the end of the intervention period, the reflective student journals were collected from all intervention participants. Direct quotes and visual reproductions from the entries were used as descriptive data sources. The principal investigator reviewed the journals to count and identify entries according to three categories: (a) teacher-modeled journal entries, (b) student adaptations from teacher-modeled entries, and (c) independent student entries. To address interrater reliability issues, an additional data analysis was conducted on 10% of the journal data by an outside researcher. The principal investigator and outside researcher discussed the journal responses until 100% consensus was reached.

Results

Fidelity to Implementation of Intervention

Classroom observational notes and email correspondence from the intervention teachers indicated that they closely followed the instructional protocol. The intervention teachers regularly presented the science-based texts as part of instructional mini-lessons, which connected reading and science content. Evidence from the reflective student journals also indicated a high level of participation and included multiple examples of teacher-modeled written reflections.

Quantitative Data Analysis

Impact on Reading Comprehension Achievement: Using the GMRT Data

Results by whole group. Both the intervention and nonintervention groups completed the comprehension subtest of the GMRT (MacGinitie et al., 2000) as a pretest and posttest. For analysis, the GMRT difference scores were created by computing a difference between the NCE prescores and postscores. Several statistical analyses were completed on the GMRT difference scores to determine the impact that the instructional protocol had on reading comprehension. First, the mean of the GMRT difference scores of the intervention and nonintervention were examined. The mean score results indicated that the intervention students experienced the greatest growth with 19.21 points (SD = 19.39) as compared to the nonintervention students with -10.50 points (SD = 13.83). Next, as there was a difference in the descriptive statistics, an ANOVA was conducted using the GMRT difference scores. The results showed there was a significant difference on reading comprehension between the intervention protocol group and the nonintervention students, $F(1, 40) = 26.09$, $p = .00$, $\eta^2 = .40$, with a strong effect size that indicated 40% of the variance could be explained by the intervention.

Results by gender. The differences between the intervention protocol group and the nonintervention group by gender were examined. The results showed there was a significant difference between males and females, $F(1, 38) = 6.26$, $p = .02$, with a medium effect size of η^2 = .14. Next, the GMRT differences scores of just the intervention group by gender were examined. It was found that the mean scores of the females (M = 14.37, SD = 23.13) were higher than the males (M = 5.13, SD = 21.70). However, no significant interaction was found between the effects of the intervention protocol on gender F(1, 38) = 0.11, p = .74

Results by ethnicity. The differences between the intervention protocol group and the nonintervention group by ethnicity were examined. A two-way ANOVA was conducted to determine the impact of the protocol intervention and examine ethnicity differences using the GMRT difference scores as the dependent variable, intervention status as independent variable, and ethnicity as moderator variable. Results showed a significant difference between the intervention and nonintervention students F(1, 34) = 9.05, p = .01, η^2 = .21; the medium effect size indicated that 21% of the variance could be explained by the intervention. It was found that the mean scores were higher for the Hispanic students (M = 15.29, SD = 19.50) than for the African American students (M = 9.42, SD = 24.16). However, no significant difference was observed between the African American and Hispanic students who received the intervention, F(1, 34) = 0.37, p = .56

Impact on Reading Comprehension Achievement: Using the TAKS Test Data

Results by whole group. The Reading TAKS test results were collected and analyzed using the scale scores. The TAKS scale scores were developed to ensure that performance standards could be maintained across administrations; the scale system ranges from approximately 1000 to 3200, with a passing score of 2100 for the Reading TAKS (TEA, 2004). An ANOVA was conducted with the scale scores as the dependent variable and the intervention status as the independent variable. Results indicated the mean scale score for the intervention group was 2183.50 (SD = 165.58), slightly higher than the mean scale score of 2159.43 (SD = 150.47) for the nonintervention group, but there was no significant difference F(1, 40) = 0.21, p = .65 on the TAKS measure of reading comprehension.

Results by gender. The differences between the intervention protocol group and the nonintervention group on the Reading TAKS test were analyzed by gender using a two-way ANOVA to compare the mean scale scores as the dependent variable, intervention status as the independent variable, and gender as moderator variable. The results showed there was no gender differences between the two groups, F(1, 38) = 2.32, p = .14. Next, the scores of the intervention protocol group were examined. The results showed that the female students' mean Reading TAKS scale scores (M = 2215.63, SD = 107.25) were higher than the scores of the male students (M = 2142.30, SD = 187.93); however, the differences were not significant enough to make a difference, F(1, 38) = 0.00, p = .93.

Results by ethnicity. The TAKS scale scores of both the intervention and nonintervention group were examined by ethnicity. The results showed there was no significant difference observed between the intervention and nonintervention students $F(1, 34) = 0.26$, $p = .62$. Next, just the scores of the intervention protocol group were examined. The descriptive statistics showed the mean score of Hispanic students (M=2256.33) to be higher than the African American students mean scores (M=2128.88). This mean difference was significant between the African American and Hispanic students $F(1, 34) = 5.78$, $p = .02$, with an effect size of ⊠2 = .15. The medium effect size indicated that 15% of the variance could be explained by ethnicity.

Qualitative Data Analysis
Presentation of Classroom Observational Data

Observational visits were conducted in both the intervention and nonintervention classrooms. The researcher observed every classroom, while the preservice teachers only observed the intervention classrooms. During all observations, observational notes were taken using the predetermined form (See Appendix A). Next, all observational notes were coded; categorical themes and subcategories helped with identification and analysis. A tallied frequency count was used to determine the most common themes. Subsequently from the data collected, 6 primary themes and 20 subcategories were established. Of the six primary themes observed, three major teacher behaviors were consistently noted; while student behaviors recorded were grouped into three main categories. Table 1 displays the list of the six primary themes and the frequency of occurrence noted while analyzing teacher and student behaviors as a part of the classroom observational data.

Table 1: Primary Themes From Classroom Observational Data

Teacher Instructional Behaviors
  A. Teacher read-aloud routine
    • Asked general questions or responded to students' questions-15
    • Read books aloud-11
    • Emphasized title, author, and illustrator-11
    • Displayed illustrations-10
    • Connected book information to real life examples-7
  B. Teacher-modeled written reflections
    • Displayed journal format and topic-6
    • Discussed written reflections with individual students-6
    • Led students in a collaborative writing experience-5
    • Stated expectations for written reflections-5
  C. Teacher-directed classroom procedures
    • Teacher provided instructions-16
    • Monitored students' understanding and provided positive feedback-9
    • Maintained and redirected student attention-7

Student Behaviors
  A. Student read-aloud routine
  • Responded to questions-14
  • Participated silently, although actively-13
  • Asked questions-12
  • Responded in writing to the read-aloud driven mini-lessons-11
  B. Student response to classroom procedures
  • Followed established classroom routines-8
  • Followed teacher instruction-5
  C. Student written reflections (in pairs or small groups)
  • Responded to read-alouds-11
  • Shared their writing aloud-4

Only the principal investigator conducted classroom observations of the nonintervention group. More traditional classroom behaviors were observed since the nonintervention teacher was not directed to provide specific lessons. Students in the nonintervention classroom were seated facing a lecture podium, with a white board at the front. Typically, the instruction observed focused on test preparation worksheets related to the Reading TAKS. Topical discussions or mini-lessons were not observed.

Presentation of Reflective Student Journal Results

At the end of the intervention period, the reflective fourth-grade student journals were collected from all students and analyzed for evidence of understanding of texts read. Data were gathered from the journal selections that demonstrated students' reading comprehension growth and specific influence from the instructional protocol. Table 2 includes direct sample quotes that best represent selections collected and analyzed from the students' reflective journals.

Table 2: Quotes from Students' Reflective Journals

Student A	"It is important that we don't plupot soil like throwing out paint and greese because it will weakin plants and trees." (2-22-2007)
Student B	"Nitrogen helps plants and trees grow strong roots…Potassium helps protect plants and trees from diseases." (2-26-2007)
Student C	"There are many different types of plants like clay, sand and loams. Worms help your plants grow in the soil. Don't scrap of the top soil or plants or grass will grow." (2-26-2007)
Student D	"Tropical hurricanes are the largest of all windstorms." (2-6-2007)
Student E	"When cows sit down on the ground that means that there is chance of rain. So the cows are trying to save a dry spot for themselves." (2-6-2007)

Finally, after analyses were completed, sample representative journal entries were chosen. Sample entries chosen represented the students' written responses to informational text read during the intervention period as a part of the instructional protocol. Documents included in Appendix B illustrate the most frequent types of journal entries chosen, including teacher-modeled journal entries, student adaptations from teacher-modeled entries, and independent student entries. Evidence of graphic organizers was also included.

Limitations

A number of decisions were made in planning for this study, based on the principal investigator's teaching schedule and access to public school classrooms, and these limitations may have affected the results. Because this study took place in public school classrooms, numerous factors and variables could not be controlled. Methods of instruction and teaching styles (i.e. teacher discussions, student feedback) as well as students' prior knowledge may have affected the outcomes. Results may have been influenced by factors, such as a strong emphasis on test preparation prior to the Reading TAKS. The GMRT pretest results varied widely as the participating students had differing prior knowledge as related to the test content. The study results may have been impacted by student mobility and attrition.

The number of weeks that could be devoted to the research intervention was limited by the public school calendar. A 12-week study was thus implemented and completed prior to the administration of the Reading TAKS. Only the scores of the African American and Hispanic students were included because of the small number of White students, indicating future studies should be conducted with students from other ethnic groups.

Discussion

The purpose of this study was to determine the impact of the use of high-interest, science-based informational texts within the context of an integrated instructional protocol. Results from this study revealed three major findings concerning reading comprehension instruction. First, according to the results from the GMRT and classroom observations, the intervention protocol did help to improve students' reading comprehension achievement. However, this gain was not observed in the results from the comprehension passages of the TAKS test.

Second, there was no significant difference seen in comparisons by gender in the intervention group on either the GMRT or the TAKS scores. In contrast, when the GMRT scores were compared between the intervention group and nonintervention group, there was significance found in the gender scores.

Third, the GRMT results showed there was a significant difference observed by ethnicity scores within the intervention group, as well as when comparing both the intervention group and nonintervention group. Thus, it appears that the intervention students gained in comprehension skills, gender and ethnicity gaps between

African American and Hispanic were minimized, and based on qualitative observations students successfully participated in teacher-directed reading activities.

Impact of the Instructional Protocol on Reading Comprehension Achievement

The results of this study suggested that students' reading comprehension achievement may be improved by including a literacy-based protocol, as the intervention group posted a gain of 19 points higher than the nonintervention group on the GMRT. First, according to classroom observational data, the intervention teachers appeared to follow a consistent procedure for read-alouds and discussion of texts. In addition, the intervention teachers also adhered to a consistent written reflective routine that included teacher demonstration. Observational intervention data from the protocol in this present study indicated that reading instruction included the strategies noted by Kamil (2004), thereby strengthening the findings. Kamil, while researching reading comprehension and vocabulary, observed improved student achievement when teachers regularly demonstrated new vocabulary using direct and explicit instructional strategies. As the largest GMRT comprehension subtest gain was posted by the intervention group, results also indicated that students may experience improvement in reading comprehension after participation in the strategies included in the instructional protocol.

Gender Gaps in Reading Comprehension Achievement

Findings in this study also inferred that gender-related reading achievement gaps could be minimized with increased teacher-directed reading instructional time. Results from this study reflected a current national trend with regards to reading achievement; the intervention female students demonstrated a 28-point growth in reading achievement on the GMRT, while the male students improved by only 13 points. These findings seem to suggest the importance of understanding gender differences in the classroom. In addition, the National Assessment of Educational Progress ([NAEP] Lee, Grigg, & Donahue, 2007) has provided annual comprehension achievement results showing, on average, that females outscored males on the fourth-grade exam.

Ethnicity Gaps in Reading Comprehension Achievement

Trends also noted in the fourth-grade NAEP results (Lee et al., 2007) have shown wide ethnicity gaps. Results from this study suggested that reading achievement gaps as related to ethnicity could be minimized. In the present study, a significant growth in reading comprehension achievement occurred with the intervention Hispanic students as compared to the African American students on the Reading TAKS (TEA, 2005a). Additionally, the mean Reading TAKS scale scores for both African American (M = 2128.88) and Hispanic (M = 2256.33) students were well above the state mastery standard (M = 2100). While no statistical significance was shown between intervention African American and Hispanic students on the GMRT, both demonstrated reading comprehension growth. These findings suggest that with the use of the intervention protocol, inter-minority gaps could be decreased.

According to the National Center for Children in Poverty (2006), 50% or more of American children living in poverty were minority ethnicities including African American and Hispanic. Similarly, NAEP (Lee et al., 2007) reading scores for students in the National School Lunch Program (USDA Food and Nutrition Service, 2006) were an average of 27 points lower than their peers who were not eligible for the lunch program. While a large number of the intervention students (96%) in this study also qualified for the National School Lunch Program, reading comprehension gains were reported on the GMRT. These results seem to indicate students from low-income families may benefit from the components of this integrated instructional protocol.

Teacher-Directed Reading Instructional Time

Finally, the findings in this study suggested that students may benefit from increased teacher-directed reading instructional time. Durkin (1978), a leading researcher in reading comprehension, conducted an important fourth-grade observational study, and noted that very little direct reading comprehension instruction was evident. Additionally, Ruddell and Unrau (1994), in their Sociocognitive-Processing Model, underscored the importance of the teacher's role in guiding students while interacting with the text. In this study, the instructional protocol gave emphasis to the teacher's role in demonstrating comprehension strategies regularly. Results from the observational data in the intervention classrooms indicated more direct teaching and modeling of comprehension strategies (during the instructional protocol) was evident, as compared to the nonintervention classroom. In contrast, in the nonintervention classroom, a large amount of time was devoted to procedural activities and independent student work. Results from the GMRT indicated significant gains in the intervention classrooms, with no gains noted in the nonintervention classroom. These findings suggest reading comprehension skills may be improved by intentionally increasing the amount of direct teacher instruction as a part of an instructional protocol. Gains in reading comprehension may be realized by purposely increasing structured teacher instruction with read-alouds and written responses.

Implications and Future Research

The implications of this study could be related to the findings concerning the integration of high-interest, science-based informational texts within the context of an integrated instructional protocol. First, when intermediate-level teachers utilized an instructional protocol with informational texts linked reading instruction to content area reading assignments, students' reading comprehension achievement was improved over time. Additional studies are needed in this area to determine specifically which protocol components are most effective in improving students' comprehension. Secondly, when teacher-directed reading instructional time was increased, gender and ethnicity related reading achievement gaps were minimized. In this study, when intermediate-level teachers were given the structure of the instructional protocol and the time to implement teacher-directed instruction, reading achievement was improved. More research is needed to determine the most effective teacher-directed reading strategies and how much time is needed on a daily basis. Overall, the implications of this study have far reaching possibilities for intermediate-level reading teachers, especially those teaching in schools with large populations of at-risk and minority students.

References

Bennett-Armistead, V. S., & Duke, N. K. (2004). Nonfiction reading in the intermediate grades: It's not just textbooks anymore! *Scholastic News*, Edition 2, Retrieved July 31, 2006, from http://teacher.scholastic.com/products/classmags/files/NonFict_Intermediate.pdf

Berg, B. L. (2004). *Qualitative research methods for the social sciences* (5th ed.). Boston, MA: Pierson, Allyn, and Bacon.

Chall, J. S. (1996). *Stages of reading development* (2nd ed.). New York: Harcourt Brace College Publishers.

Chall, J. S., & Jacobs, V. A. (2003). Poor children's fourth-grade slump. *American Educator*. Retrieved July 21, 2006, from http://www.aft.org/pubs-reports/american_educator/spring2003/chall.html

Chall, J. S., Jacobs, V. A., & Baldwin, L. E. (1990). *The reading crisis: Why poor children fall behind*. Cambridge, MA: Harvard University Press.

Cheak, M., & Wessel, J. (2005). Research in reading—Notes from the center for illiteracy control (CIC): A report on current research in the field of literacy. *Illinois Reading Council Journal*, 33, 65-67.

Creswell, J. W. (1998). *Qualitative inquiry and research design: Choosing among five tradtions*. Thousand Oaks, CA: SAGE Publications.

Dreher, M. J. (1998). Motivating children to read more nonfiction. *The Reading Teacher, 52*, 414-417.

Duke, N. K. (2004). The case for information text. *Educational Leadership, 61*, 40-44.

Duke, N. K. (2006). Using nonfiction to increase reading achievement and world knowedge. *Scholastic*, Retrieved July 31, 2006, from http://teacher.scholastic.com/professional/literacypapers/duke.html

Duke, N. K., & Bennett-Armistead, V. S. (2003). *Reading and writing informational text in the primary grades: Research-based practices*. New York: Scholastic.

Durkin, D. (1978). What classroom observations reveal about reading comprehension instruction. *Reading Research Quarterly, 14*, 481-533.

Edmunds, K. M, & Bauserman, K. L. (2006). What teachers can learn about reading motivation through conversations with children. *The Reading Teacher, 59*, 414-424.

Kamil, M. (2004). Vocabulary and comprehension instruction: Summary and implications of the National Reading Panel findings. In P. McCardle & V. Chhabra (Eds.), *The voice of evidence in reading research* (pp. 213-234). Baltimore, MD: Paul H. Brookes Publishing.

Lee, J., Grigg, W., & Donahue, P. (2007). *The Nation's Report Card: Reading 2007* (NCES 2007-496). National Center for Education Statistics, Institute of Education Sciences,

U.S. Department of Education, Washington, DC. Retrieved October 28, 2007, from http://nces.ed.gov/nationsreportcard/pubs/main2007/2007496.asp

Liang, L. A., & Dole, J. A. (2006). Help with teaching reading comprehension: Comprehension instructional framework. *The Reading Teacher, 59*, 742-753.

MacGinitie, W. H., MacGinitie, R. K., Maria, K., & Dreyer, L. G. (2000). *Gates-MacGinitie Reading Tests, Levels 4 & 5, Forms S & T*. Itasca, IL: Riverside Publishing.

Moss, B. (2004). Teaching expository text structures through information. *The Reading Teacher, 57*, 710-718.

Moss, B. (2005). Making a case and a place for effective content area literacy instruction in the elementary grades. *The Reading Teacher, 59*, 46-55.

National Center for Children in Poverty. (2006). *Who are America's poor children? The official story*. New York: Columbia University, Mailman School of Public Health. Retrieved July 20, 2007, from http://www.nccp.org/publications/pub_684.html

National Institute of Child Health and Human Development. (2000). *Report of the National Reading Panel, Teaching children to read: An evidence-based assessment of the scientific research literature on reading and its implications for reading instruction* (NIH Publication No. 11-4769). Washington, DC: U.S. Government Printing Office.

Palmer, R. G., & Stewart, R. A. (2003). Nonfiction trade book use in primary grades. *The Reading Teacher, 57*, 38-48.

Pressley, M. (2001). *Effective beginning reading instruction*. Executive Summary and Paper Commissioned by the National Reading Conference. Chicago, IL: National Reading Conference.

Ruddell, R. B., & Unrau, N. J. (1994). Reading as a meaning-construction process: The reader, the text, and the teacher. In R. B. Ruddell & N. J. Unrau (Eds.), *Theoretical models and processes of reading* (4th ed., pp. 996-1056). Newark, DE: International Reading Association.

Saul, E. W., & Dieckman, D. (2005). Theory and research into practice: Choosing and using information trade books. *Reading Research Quarterly, 40*, 502-513.

Smolkin, L. B., & Donovan, C. A. (2001). The contexts of comprehension; the information book read aloud, comprehension acquisition, and comprehension instruction in a first-grade classroom. *The Elementary School Journal, 1022*, 97-122.

Snow, C. E., Burns, M. S., & Griffin, P. (1998). *Preventing reading difficulties in young children*. Washington, DC: National Academy Press.

Stewart, M. T. (2004). Early literacy instruction in the climate of No Child Left Behind. *The Reading Teacher, 57*, 732-741.

Texas Education Agency. (2004). *Student assessment division technical digest 2004-2005*. Retrieved November 17, 2007, from http://www.tea.state.tx.us/student.assessment/resources/techdig05/

Texas Education Agency. (2005a). *Student assessment division*. Retrieved September 24, 2005, from http://www.tea.state.tx.us/student.assessment/resources/release/taks/index.html

Texas Education Agency. (2005b). T*exas essential knowledge and skills*. Retrieved November 17, 2007, from http://www.tea.state.tx.us/teks/index.html

USDA Food and Nutrition Service. (2006). Food and nutrition service. National School Lunch Program. Retrieved November 20, 2006, from http://www.fns.usda.gov/cnd/lunch/AboutLunch/NSLPFactSheet.pdf

Yopp, R. H., & Yopp, H. K. (2000). Sharing informational text with young children. *The Reading Teacher, 53*, 410-423.

Appendix A: Classroom Observation Documentation Form

Teacher	Students
What I Saw	What I Saw
What I Heard	What I Heard

Other Observations

Appendix B: Visual Reproduction of Student's Reflective Journal Entry

Appendix B: (cont'd) Visual Reproduction of Student's Reflective Journal Entry

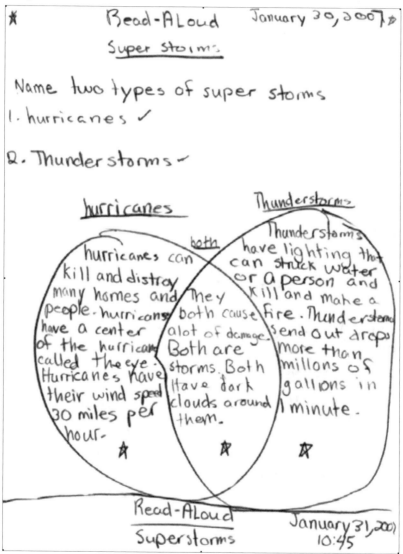

Appendix B: (cont'd) Visual Reproduction of Student's Reflective Journal Entry

1-18-07

Space
stor Death

I never Know there was a
star that Keep exploding
litle Gy litle. 150 years ago,
it was, the second bri tttest
star, now it cun't be even
seen Gy the naked eye

How many years doos a
small stor live?

How many super novas might
come in one mindium.

The Moon Seams   1-18-07
to Change

I never Know tha we
only sec one part of the
Moon never the other part

Revisiting the Affective Domain of Reading Assessment and Instruction

Brandi L. Noll
Canton Local Schools

Ruth Oswald
Evangeline Newton
The University of Akron

Abstract

Assessments in the affective domain of reading can offer insights to teachers regarding a student's interests, self-perceptions, and attitude toward reading. Thus, 27 K-5th grade classroom teachers were surveyed to identify the affective assessments they use to guide their instruction. Although 41% of survey participants reported that they used no affective assessments, 59% reported the use of one or more affective assessment methods including interest inventories, writing journals, and oral discussions. Teachers noted that time constraints and "high stakes testing" pressures constricted direct attention to the affective domain. Despite this, data analysis revealed that many teachers integrated some student-centered activities that support the affective domain into their instructional practices.

In his 2007 presidential address to The College Reading Association, Jon Shapiro observed that "even though many teachers identify the affective domain as an important area, their practice tells us it is not a priority" (p. 4). He further observed that affective aspects of students' personalities, including their interests, attitudes, and self-esteem, should be critical areas of concern for those working with readers of all ages.

The call for attention to the affective domain in education is not unique to the current era. In the fifties and early sixties Krathwohl, Bloom, & Masia (1964) developed taxonomy of educational objectives, which were divided into three domains: cognitive, affective, and psychomotor. They found that most of the objectives provided by teachers could easily be placed into one of those three major domains. These researchers raised the question whether humans ever do thinking without feeling and concluded that each person responds as a "total organism" or "whole being" when responding. Thus, while the classification (taxonomy) of affective objectives was established by these researchers, today, most educators are familiar only with the cognitive domain as articulated by Bloom's Taxonomy of Educational Objectives.

Literature Review

Although different literacy researchers include various components when writing about the affective domain, all would agree with Harris and Hodges' (1995) definition of the affective domain as "the psychological field of emotional activity" (p. 5). The affective domain includes many dimensions such as students' motivation to read, attitude toward reading, interest in reading, and beliefs about the importance of reading.

Instruments for Measuring Constructs within the Affective Domain

There are a variety of affective domain assessment instruments available which assist educators in gathering information about their students. They include instruments that educators can use to measure both the specific dimension of self-concept (Harter, 1981; Henk & Melnick, 1995) and the more general dimension of students' attitude toward reading (Tunnell, Calder, Justen, & Phaup, 1991; McKenna & Kear, 1990). Other instruments exist which give teachers more information about the interests and habits of students as readers (Moss, 2003). Some interest inventories are included in the battery of assessments used with published informal reading inventories (i.e. Flynt & Cooter, 1998). Gambrell, Palmer, Codling & Mazzoni (1996) created a questionnaire that includes many subscales of motivation including efficacy, reading challenge, reading curiosity, and aesthetic enjoyment of reading.

Attention to the Affective Domain

The National Reading Research Center (O'Flahavan, Gambrell, Guthrie, Stahl & Alvermann, 1992) found that teachers were very interested in learning more about the affective domain in reading. The survey revealed that among the top ten items that teachers wanted researched were areas that had to do with motivation to read, increasing the amount and the expanse of reading, and getting students to develop an interest in reading. However, after the National Reading Panel Report (NRP, 2000) was published the affective domain took a backseat, as the Panel emphasized the "big five" reading areas: phonemic awareness, phonics, fluency, vocabulary, and comprehension.

These five reading elements continue to be the focus of professional development for teachers as well as professional articles and books. In fact, a word search of the National Reading Panel Report found the word "phonemic" listed 752 times and the word "phonics" 178 times, while the word "motivation" was only found 19 times when not being used to describe motivation in phonics (Trelease, 2006). Furthermore, Shapiro (2007) reports that over the last 40 years, articles about the affective domain have accounted for less than 1% of the total articles published in *The Reading Teacher*.

According to the National Reading Report Card (Perie & Moran, 2005) 100% of students in kindergarten want to learn to read, but by the time they exit fourth grade only 54% reported an interest in reading daily for pleasure. By twelfth grade, the statistics are even more alarming, as the number of students reporting an interest in reading drops to 19%. This disintegration of the desire to read seems to show that as educators, we are not doing enough to capture the attention of our readers in a way that creates a passion for reading.

Research on Motivation

Motivation to read is one factor that is at the root of many problems encountered by teachers of reading, (O'Flahavan, Gambrell, Guthrie, Stahl, & Alvermann, 1992) and motivation plays a major role in student learning (Dweck & Elliott, 1983). Motivation can be achieved externally (extrinsic) or internally (intrinsic) (Wigfield, Guthrie, Tonks, & Perencevich, 2004).

Motivation is multi-dimensional and includes different psychological aspects, which operate together and influence one another. One aspect of motivation is one's self-efficacy toward reading. Schunk & Zimmerman (1997) found that a students' self-efficacy, or their judgment of their capabilities to perform a task successfully, influence their motivation to attempt tasks and work through problems to master the task.

A second aspect of motivation is self-concept, which involves the student's perception of themselves as readers (Henk & Melnick, 1995). A third aspect of motivation is engagement. Engagement has been linked to reading achievement because the experiences that children have in the classroom greatly influence their motivation to read (Campbell, Voelkl, & Donahue, 1997; Turner, 1995).

The National Reading Panel Report (2000) only looked at quantitative studies related to the affective domain that met their scientific specifications. This research does document the positive connection between motivation and achievement (Elley, 1992; Guthrie, Schafer, Wang, & Afflerbach, 1993; Purves & Beach, 1972; Walberg & Tsai, 1985; Wixson & Lipson, 1991).

Gambrell, Malloy & Mazzoni (2007) presented 10 evidence-based best practices for comprehensive literacy instruction, and motivation was number one on the list, "creating a classroom culture that fosters literacy motivation" (p. 19). These researchers concluded that, "motivation exerts a tremendous force on what is learned and how and when it will be learned…and often makes the difference between superficial and shallow learning and learning that is deep and internalized" (p. 19).

Purpose of the study

Teachers have at their fingertips a multitude of instruments already created and tested for effectiveness. These can be used to gain insight into the attitudes, self-perceptions, and interests of their students. However one question remains: Are teachers actually using them? Guided by a review of literature on effective affective domain assessment and instruction, we decided to invite practicing teachers in local school districts to share their practices in this area in order to answer the following questions.

- What, if any, assessment instruments are these practicing teachers using to plan instruction for the affective domain?
- What, if any, motivational strategies are they implementing in their classroom instruction?

Methods

Setting

Surveys were distributed to teachers in three elementary school buildings in three different school districts in northeast Ohio. District A is a large school district that includes rural, suburban, and urban areas. The school that was included in the survey has been designated by the state Department of Education as either 'Excellent' or 'Effective' over the last five years. This building, which included approximately 600 students in grades two through five, has 36 classroom and special education teachers. Sixteen of these teachers have a masters degree or higher. Forty-two percent of the students in this building qualify for the Free and Reduced Lunch Program. The student body consisted of students who were Caucasian (86.6%), African-American (7.8%), and Multiracial (4%).

District B is a large, suburban school district in northeast Ohio. It has been designated 'Excellent' for the last five years. The school, which included approximately 530 students in kindergarten through grade five, had a total of 21 teachers and special education teachers. Seventeen of these teachers hold a masters degree. Eleven percent of the students qualifies for free and reduced lunch. The student body consisted of students who were primarily Caucasian (89.5%), but also included a small population of students who were Multiracial (3.1%) or Asian/Pacific Islander (4.2%).

District C is a small, rural district in northeast Ohio. The school had approximately 400 students in Kindergarten through grade two, and was designated by the state as either 'Effective' or 'Continuous Improvement' over the last five years. Of the 17 full-time teachers and special education teachers who worked in the building, ten of them hold a masters degree or higher. Forty-four percent of the students qualify for free and reduced lunch. Eighty-three percent of the student body is Caucasian, 5.8% are African American, and 6.7% are Multiracial.

Participants

Seventy-four surveys were given to classroom teachers in three school districts. However, only 27 (36%) participants responded. Those who responded included: six Kindergarten teachers, nine first-grade teachers, six second-grade teachers, one third- grade teacher, four fourth-grade teachers, and one fifth-grade teacher. Eleven teachers from District A completed and returned the survey, seven teachers in District B, and nine teachers from District C. The majority of teachers who returned the surveys were women (93%) and were Caucasian (100%). The teachers who responded to the surveys represented a wide spectrum of teaching experience including teachers who were in their first year of teaching and teachers who had been working for close to thirty years.

Procedures

In order to determine what classroom teachers know about the affective domain, an open-ended, four-question survey (see Appendix 1) developed by the researchers was distributed to 74 classroom teachers and special education teachers. Participants were asked to complete the surveys within a one to two week period. They were also given the option of replying anonymously. Surveys were distributed during the last week of October. A contact person who worked in each building assisted the researchers. This contact person was in charge of distributing and collecting the surveys in their individual building, as well as sending reminder emails to the participants. A cover sheet explaining the research, procedures to be followed by each participant, and the timeline for participation accompanied each survey.

Limitations

Small number of participants is a limitation, as only 36% responded to the survey. A second limitation of this study is the fact that it appears that some of the participants were not clear in their understanding of what constitutes the affective domain. Some teachers contacted the survey distributor in each building stating that they were not clear in their understanding of the term 'affective domain'. Teachers who did not complete the survey may have been confused by the questions and terms used in the survey, and may have been hesitant about asking for clarification or more information. Thus, for future research, terms should be defined for the participants. Although generalizations of the findings from this study are limited, classroom teachers can reflect on these findings and evaluate their own practices regarding attention to the affective domain.

Results and Discussion

Analysis

To answer question one, what assessment instruments are practicing teachers using to plan instruction for the affective domain, a running tally was used to record the number of times each type of assessment was mentioned. In addition, how often the instruments were used, when they were used, and any other pertinent comments made by teachers were recorded.

To answer question number two, what motivational strategies are teachers implementing in their classroom instruction, teacher comments were grouped in categories. These categories were analyzed to determine if themes emerged within this group.

Assessments Used by Classroom Teachers

Eleven survey participants (41%) reported that they use no assessments for the affective domain. These teachers overwhelmingly cited time constraints and the risk of over-assessing students as the main reasons for not assessing the affective domain of their students. Many teachers felt that there was not enough time to be concerned about the affective domain as seen in the following comments:

- "We are totally focused on content and do much testing on academics, for which we are accountable. There is nothing in the content standards for affective domain."
- "We do so many reading assessments at the beginning of the year which takes a lot of teaching time, I do not want to take more time to do this kind of assessment (even though I feel it would be useful) – Time is the issue."
- "There is no time to even teach the standards, much less anything else."

The remaining 16 teachers (59%) reported the use of one or more methods of assessing areas within the affective domain including students' interests, comfort levels, and self-efficacy. The most reported method of gathering information was by a paper-pencil interest inventory used at the beginning of the school year. Eight of these participants reported using this type of inventory; however, no specific interest inventories were named. Eleven of these teachers reported using student journal writing or oral discussions as a way to gain more information about their students' interests. In their journals, students either drew pictures or wrote about their interests, or the types of literature they enjoyed. These teachers reported gathering information through discussions during circle time, or during individual student conferences and parent-teacher conferences.

Learning about the interests of their students seemed to be the area of the affective domain that these teachers utilized the most to guide instructional decisions and practices. Although teachers reported using informal methods, which included both written and oral methods to gain this information, one teacher felt that this was unnecessary, as she felt that she already knew her kindergarten students' interests. This teacher stated, "Well, to be honest, after a few years of this and as a parent, we pretty much know that girls like cats, horses, and princesses and boys enjoy the action figure of the moment, cars, trucks, and zoo animals!"

In the area of student attitude, only two teachers reported using an informal instrument, which they referred to as either a reading or literacy survey. One teacher reported using it once a year and another teacher reported using it at both the beginning and end of the year. One teacher reported using oral questioning as an informal method of gathering information regarding student enjoyment and attitude toward reading.

Interestingly, only one teacher reported the use of an instrument to measure self-efficacy in reading. This teacher reported using a 'Comfort Level Survey', but gave no details about the kinds of question this survey asked. Two teachers reported the use of an instrument that was included in the Developmental Reading Assessment they currently use. This instrument asked a handful of very broad questions related to various dimensions of motivation including interest, self-efficacy, and enjoyment of reading tasks.

The only technology-based tool used by teachers was an online learning program that included both assessments and activities for students. Both a fourth and a fifth grade teacher were using this program. Based on students' responses to online questions, the program created a profile for each individual student. This profile, which can be printed, contains several paragraphs that describe a student's interests. The program even goes a step further and matches personalized activities to the student's interests, which include Internet and downloadable resources.

Motivational Techniques Used

Results from the survey showed that these classroom teachers reported their use of a wide variety of instructional strategies that fall within the affective domain. All teachers reported using a combination of strategies that included both intrinsic and extrinsic motivators. The most widely reported strategies were under the topic of "social motivation." Strategies included explicit instruction, strategic selection of instructional texts, extrinsic rewards, and offering students a choice of texts were also frequently reported. Surprising, the use of verbal praise and instructional activities based around a common theme were both reported sparingly.

Sixty-seven percent of the responding teachers across all grade levels reported using social motivation as a technique to increase motivation to read. Students were given opportunities to share books with their classmates, to lead discussions about text, and to recommend books to others. One teacher allowed her students to bring books from home to be shared in the reading corner throughout the week. Students often read aloud to others including classmates, students from other classes, their teacher, other educators in the building, parents, and even the principal.

Carefully and strategically choosing texts for instruction and student use was reported as a technique to increase motivation to read by 13 (48%) of the survey respondents. Teachers reported using a large variety of genres, including nonfiction and fiction. A wide variety of nonfiction materials were mentioned in the survey, including the use of recipes, directions for crafts, magazines, brochures, and newspapers. Three teachers (11%) reported identifying books at appropriate difficulty levels for their students and two teachers (7 %) mentioned trying to get students interested in text based on the author (author studies). One teacher (4 %) insightfully mentioned, "standards can be taught from most any text!"

Teachers often allowed students to choose what texts they would read and use in class, where to read the texts, and how and when they would read. Eleven (41%) of the survey participants reported the use of student choice as a motivation strategy. Teachers mentioned having an extensive collection of books representing various topics, genres, and reading levels in their classroom.

Explicit instruction, including modeling, scaffolding, coaching, and stating a purpose for learning, is a strategy that many teachers reported using to support the affective domain in their classrooms. One kindergarten teacher observed that, "Just making them feel successful during shared reading experiences really motivates them." A few teachers specifically mentioned the use of pre-reading strategies that built background knowledge, got students excited, and engaged with the text. Teachers also identified making predictions based on picture walks and making personal connections to text as strategies to build confidence, interest, and motivation.

The most often mentioned extrinsic motivator from the survey was the use of rewards. Of the twelve teachers (44%) who reported using rewards, only one cited giving books as rewards. All other teachers mentioned three specific kinds of rewards: stickers, treats, and certificates. These rewards most often were tied to the achievement of reaching a reading goal, either independently or as a class.

The use of verbal praise and reinforcement were mentioned by 15% of the participants, while two other teachers mentioned that they felt a student's self-efficacy was important. A kindergarten teacher wrote, "I think how children feel about themselves and their ability is the biggest factor in liking reading." The teachers used praise as a way to make students feel better about themselves as a reader and to reward them for reading.

Eight (30%) of the responding teachers felt that by showing their own excitement about and commitment to reading, they were motivating their students. These teachers deliberately shared their love of reading. One third-grade teacher also takes advantage of silent reading time to model her own personal reading habits. "I read at the same time as my kids. I make reading important. They see how I read and want to do the same."

Six (22%) of the responding teachers felt that by actively involving their students in the processes of monitoring and reflecting about their own reading, they could increase students' motivation to read. Students used graphs and logs to monitor their independent reading and to track their progress in reaching goals. Logs were also used for personal reflections about students' reading achievements and behaviors.

Conclusions and Implications

In general, results of this survey support Shapiro's (2007) concern for the lack of attention to the affective domain in current literacy classroom practice. Of the twenty-seven teachers who responded to the survey, eleven (41%) reported that they did not use any assessments in the affective domain. The main reason given for choosing not to use these types of tools was due to the lack of time. However, one teacher's comment represents the view of many participants: "Rigorous and not developmentally appropriate standards have made teaching so challenging that it is difficult to address the needs of the whole child even though we know it's important."

It appears that in terms of assessment, teachers are regarding the state's academic content standards and motivation as two discrete categories. In fact, the teachers' responses showed that they believed that motivation does not significantly affect their students' mastery of the reading curriculum.

However, it appears that although most of these teachers placed affective factors on the backburner, some have intuitively integrated some student-centered activities that support the affective domain into their instructional practices. Many teachers identified "choice," for example, as a significant instructional practice. Some of them interviewed students to determine their interests; others built classroom libraries with a range of texts or identified themes they knew were popular with many children. Similarly, "social motivation" involved opportunities for students to share, discuss, read to, and with others. While these activities are widely accepted as effective strategies for cognitive literacy development, they also nurture the affective domain. In fact, despite the academic and time pressures they face, teachers reported using instructional strategies that promote a comprehensive view of literacy development.

Shapiro (2007) stated, "It is clear that one of the key perspectives that informs my thinking and work is that what we do in the name of improving reading ability often works against the promotion of positive attitudes toward books, toward reading, and toward oneself as a reader" (p. 5). While teachers in this survey intuitively adopted some instructional practices that support the affective domain, they had also narrowed their assessment and instructional strategies because they were superfluous to district and state mandates. Whether this attitude is a result of the National Reading Panel's emphasis on the "big five" or state and federal calls for "academic rigor" is disputable. Two decades ago, Gambrell (1996) and Guthrie (1996) were arguing for more attention to the affective domain. However, in order for students to master the "big five" and demonstrate "academic rigor," they must be motivated and engaged readers.

A very important implication of this study, then, is for educators to acknowledge openly the importance of the affective domain in literacy instruction and assessment and then to reinstate strategies and assessments in their practice that pertain to this domain. In order to become proficient readers, students must have some hope for success, must be motivated to gain new knowledge and skills, and then use these skills and knowledge so that they do not become stagnant, useless skills. As always, teachers are the most important factor to make this happen. Teachers must get to know their students through observation and conversation. Moreover, they must consider students' interests and self-concept as they plan instruction. In this time of high-stakes testing, it is critical that teachers of reading not only recognize the importance of the affective domain, but that they attend to this critical area in their daily practice.

References

Campbell, J.R., Voelkl, K.E., & Donahue, P.L. (1997). Report in brief: NAEP 1996 trends in academic progress. Washington, DC: U.S. Department of Education, National Center for Education Statistics

Dweck, C., & Elliott, E. (1983). Achievement motivation. In E.M. Heatherington (Ed.), *Handbook of child psychology:* Vol. 4. *Socialization, personality, and social development* (pp. 643-691). New York: Wiley.

Elley, W. B. (1992). *How in the world do students read? IEA study of reading literacy.* The Hague: International Association for the Evaluation of Educational Achievement.

Flynt, E. S., & Cooter, R. B. (1998). Flynt-Cooter reading inventory for the classroom. Upper Saddle River, New Jersey: Merrill.

Gambrell, L.B. (1996). Creating classroom cultures that foster reading motivation. *The Reading Teacher*, 50, 14-25.

Gambrell, L. B., Malloy, J. A., & Mazzoni, S. A. (2007). Evidence-based best practices for comprehensive literacy instruction. In L. B. Gambrell, L. Mandell Morrow, & M. Pressley (Eds.), *Best practices in literacy instruction* (3rd ed.) (pp. 11-29). New York: The Guilford Press.

Gambrell, L. B., Palmer, B. M., Codling, R. M., & Mazzoni, S. A. (1996). Assessing motivation to read. *The Reading Teacher*, 49(7), 14-25.

Guthrie, J.T. (1996). Educational contexts for engagement in literacy. *The Reading Teacher*, 49, 432-445.

Guthrie, J. T., Schafer, W., Wang, Y., & Afflerbach, P. (1993). *Influences of instruction on reading engagement: An empirical exploration of a social-cognitive framework of reading activity* (Research Report No. 3). Athens, GA: National Reading Research Center.

Harris, T.L., & Hodges, R.E. (Eds.) (1995). *The literacy dictionary: The vocabulary of reading and writing*. Newark, DE: International Reading Association.

Harter, S. (1981). A new self-report scale of intrinsic versus extrinsic orientation in the classroom: Motivational and informational components. *Developmental Psychology*, 17, 300-312.

Henk, W., & Melnick, S. A. (1995). The Reader Self-Perception Scale (RSPS): A new tool for measuring how children feel about themselves as readers. *The Reading Teacher*, 48, 470-482.

McKenna, M. C., & Kear, D. J. (1990). Measuring attitude toward reading: A new tool for teachers. *The Reading Teacher*, 43, 626-639.

Moss, B. (2003). *Exploring the literature of fact: Children's nonfiction trade books in the elementary classroom*. New York: The Guilford Press.

National Reading Panel (2000). Teaching children to read: An evidence-based asessment of the scientific literature in reading and its implications for reading instruction. Washington, DC: National Institute of Child Health & Human Development.

O'Flahavan, J., Gambrell, L. B., Guthrie, J., Stahl, S., & Alvermann, D. (1992). Poll results guide activities of research center. *Reading Today*, 10, 12.

Perie, M., and Moran, R. (2005). NAEP 2004 Trends in Academic Progress: Three Decades of Student Performance in Reading and Mathematics (NCES 2005-464). U.S. Department of Education, Institute of Education Sciences, National Center for Education Statistics. Washington, DC: Government Printing Office.

Purves, A., & Beach, R. (1972). *Literature and the reader: Research on response to literature, reading interests, and teaching literature*. Urbana, IL: National Council of Teachers of English.

Schunk, D. H., & Zimmerman, B.J. (1997). Developing self-efficacious readers and writers: The role of social and self-regulatory processes. In J.T. Guthrie & A. Wigfield (Eds.),

Reading engagement: Motivating readers through integrated instruction (pp. 34-50). Newark, DE: International Reading Association.

Shapiro, J. (2007). Another pothole in the road: Asserting our professionalism. *The Yearbook of The College Reading Association: Multiple Literacies in the 21st Century*, (28), 2-12.

Trelease, J. (2006). *The read-aloud handbook*. New York: Penguin Books.

Tunnel, M. O., Calder, J. E., Justen, J. E. & Phaup, E. S. (1991. Attitudes of young readers. *Reading Improvement*, 28, 237-243.

Turner, J. C. (1995). The influence of classroom contexts on young children's motivation for literacy. *Reading Research Quarterly*, 30, 410-441.

Walberg, H. J., & Tsai, S. (1985). Correlates of reading achievement and attitude: A national assessment study. *Journal of Educational Research*, 78, 159-167.

Wigfield, A., Guthrie, J.T., Tonks, S., & Perencevich, K.C. (2004). Children's motivation for reading: Domain specificity and instructional influences. *Journal of Educational Research*, 97(6), 299-310.

Wixson, K. K., & Lipson, M.Y. (1991). *Reading diagnosis and remediation*. Glenview, IL: Scott, Foresman.

Table 1: The Survey

Questions/Prompts
1. What grade are you currently teaching?
2. What assessments (could be formal or informal) do you currently use in the affective domain? These might be interest inventories, getting-to-know students as readers surveys, motivation scales, etc.. ___I do not use any such assessments Please explain all the reasons why you do not use one: ___I use the following Please give a short description, like what, how often, etc.
3. Please list all of the methods you can think of that you use to motivate students to read. (please include both intrinsic and extrinsic)
4. Is there any other information you wish to share about the affective domain of literacy instruction?

COGNITION, AFFECT, AND INSTRUCTION: A CYCLICAL RELATIONSHIP?

Sharon E. Green

Fairleigh Dickinson University

Elizabeth Dobler

Emporia State University

Abstract

This mixed-method study examined 22 teachers' knowledge of comprehension strategies and the ways in which this knowledge influenced their reading instruction. All were participants in an online graduate level course in reading curriculum and instruction. A key finding was the cyclical relationship between cognition, affect, and instruction. As teachers gained comprehension strategy knowledge, they began to change their classroom instruction and also reported feeling more enthusiastic and confident in teaching reading. These changes led to a further desire to increase comprehension strategy knowledge, thus creating a cyclical relationship between knowledge, affect and instruction. Preservice, inservice and teacher educators need to be aware that the development of expert strategy instruction teachers requires a multifaceted approach and a commitment to continually learning about the teaching of reading.

In the current climate of high stakes state assessments and requirements for highly qualified teachers, there is much discussion about increasing students' ability to navigate and understand text. While this is clearly important, we cannot overlook the significant role that a teacher's own knowledge of comprehension instruction plays in developing a student's reading ability. Over the past 20 years, much has been written about the use of comprehension strategies as an effective way of making meaning and about what teachers should do in order to effectively teach comprehension strategies.

The National Reading Panel Report (NICHD, 2000) and the RAND Reading Study Group (RAND, 2002) have summarized research supporting the concept of comprehension as a meaning making process. Reading research has sought to identify the specific strategies skilled readers use (Pearson, Roehler, Dole, & Duffy, 1992; Pressley, 2000) and the most effective ways to teach these strategies to students (Palincsar & Brown, 1984; Pardo, 2004; Paris, Wasik & Turner, 1991; Pressley, 2006). Research in the area of strategy instruction supports the teaching of strategies in bundles or collections (Duke & Pearson, 2002) and the importance of teacher modeling throughout strategy instruction, along with a gradual release of responsibility (Fielding & Pearson, 1994; Pearson & Gallagher, 1983; Pressley, 2006) so that students eventually use the strategies independently. Along with the research that is available in the area of reading comprehension, teacher resources for teaching comprehension strategies are abundant (e.g. Buckner, 2009; Harvey & Goudvis, 2007; Keene & Zimmerman 2007, Keene, 2008; Miller, 2002).

With all of the research and resources available in the area of reading comprehension, we still know relatively little about how much teachers understand about the comprehension process and how they pass this knowledge on to their students. Thus, the purpose of this study is to explore the ways in which a teacher's own reading practices and knowledge of strategies influences their comprehension instruction.

Related Research

The literature review for this study focuses on investigating the link between a teacher's knowledge and instructional actions. The first strand of the review began with research on the preparation of preservice and inservice teachers and how this preparation can facilitate developing knowledge of reading instruction and effective instructional practices. Second, because expertise in strategy instruction is crucial for a teacher to be able to convey the complex mental processes of comprehension to learners, the review focused on how teachers develop this expertise. Next, the review explored the varied levels of knowledge a teacher may have in regards to comprehension instruction and the depth of instruction that accompanies each level of knowledge.

Training vs. Teaching

The connection between a teacher's knowledge and practice is at the center of this study and leads to an exploration of the ways teachers are prepared to teach. While extensive research has focused on the training of teachers (e.g. Darling-Hammond, Chung, & Frelow, 2002; Griffin & Barnes, 1986), less is known about the teaching of teachers (Cochran-Smith & Lytle, 1999). Hoffman and Pearson (2000) argue that the difference between the terms training and teaching is not simply semantic. Training refers to "direct actions of a teacher designed to enhance a learner's ability" (p. 32), while teaching refers to the "intentional actions of a teacher to promote personal control over and responsibility for the learning within those who are taught" (p. 32). While a training model emphasizes skills or behavioral routines that become automatic for a teacher, a teaching model converges skills, analysis, and reflection into intentional actions designed to promote learning. In other words, teachers can be trained to become competent with regard to a specific skill, but that competency does not necessarily mean that they will use their knowledge to provide purposeful instruction. Liang and Dole (2006) suggest there must be a relationship between the teaching of comprehension strategies and a meaningful context in which to use these strategies. Teachers can facilitate the forging of this relationship by possessing a deep knowledge of the process of meaning making while at the same time being thoughtful decision makers who flexibly use this knowledge to meet the instructional needs of students.

Expertise in Strategy Instruction

In order to provide quality instruction, a teacher must have high levels of knowledge about reading and effectively convey this information to students. In other words, a teacher must be an expert. How does a teacher become an expert in comprehension instruction? El-Dinary and Schuder (1993) posit that a teacher's expertise in strategy instruction takes several years to develop and requires a multifaceted approach which includes receiving explanations and viewing models of quality strategy instruction along with coaching from master teachers. Based on the use of the transactional strategy instruction model, El-Dinary and Schuder (1993) described additional key elements that contributed to the development of teacher expertise in strategy instruction. The professional development provided to teachers must be intense at first, then gradually be reduced. In addition, the school environment must be a place where teachers feel safe to practice techniques that are new to them, especially with support of the administrator. In a related study, Duffy (1993) described teachers' journey towards becoming an expert at strategy instruction. This journey involves eight points or gates teachers pass through beginning with confusion and rejection, then moving into teacher controlling the strategy, modeling process into content, and finally being creative/inventive. Duffy called for teacher educators to play a strong role in helping teachers move along the continuum. Duffy's later work with colleagues (Anders, Hoffman, & Duffy, 2000) described ways to improve the preparation of literacy teachers to include more literacy courses, enhanced field experiences, improved qualifications of teacher educators, and collaborative efforts to improve teacher education programs. As stated previously, the development of expert teachers of strategy instruction requires a multifaceted approach involving a commitment from both the teacher and those providing preservice or inservice education.

Levels of Knowledge

An examination of the connection between cognition and classroom practice begins with an emphasis on a teacher's knowledge of comprehension strategies and moves towards application of this knowledge through instructional practices. A model of gradual release of responsibility links knowledge to practice (Pearson & Gallagher, 1983; Fielding & Pearson, 1994; Pressley, 2006) with the teacher providing an explanation, modeling, guiding practice, then independent practice. A gradual release of responsibility for comprehension instruction must begin with a teacher's deep knowledge of the process of making meaning.

Paris, Lipson, and Wixson (1994) described knowledge as a continuum a learner moves through on a journey from novice to expert which can be applied to teachers as they develop their expertise in reading comprehension instruction. This continuum begins first with declarative knowledge (knowing what), procedural knowledge (knowing how), and conditional knowledge (knowing when and why). The declarative knowledge refers to content knowledge including the components of reading. It also can refer to attitudes about teaching reading, such as "Reading is my favorite subject to teach because I love to read." or "I try to just stick with the teacher's guide when I teach reading because I am not so confident in what I am doing." Procedural knowledge refers to the how-to's in reading – how to skim, how to summarize, how to decode. Teachers at this stage are able to describe knowledge of a repertoire of basic reading strategy skills that they have often acquired through literacy courses or professional development and have refined through practice. Conditional knowledge represents the highest level of development for a teacher of reading and involves the application of reading strategies in a teacher's own reading and the sharing of these processes with students. Fitzharris, Jones, and Crawford (2008) applied this continuum to primary grade teachers and their knowledge of reading cueing systems, miscue analysis, and guided reading instruction. They found teachers to be at various stages of development in their literacy knowledge even though the teachers received the same professional development at the school. In this study, teachers' years of experience, educational background, and involvement with special education influenced their overall acquisition of new knowledge.

Research Questions

Undergraduate literacy courses lay the foundation, but teachers often find that they must combine this entry-level knowledge with experience and a more in-depth understanding of comprehension through professional development and graduate literacy courses. At the same time, teacher educators assume that what is learned at the preservice and inservice level is in fact implemented in the K-12 classroom. This study broadly seeks to examine this assumption by seeking answers to the following questions:

- What knowledge do teachers have about specific comprehension strategies?
- How does a teacher's knowledge about comprehension strategy instruction change after taking this course?
- What is the influence on a teacher's practices as a result?

The specific focus of this study is to explore the ways knowledge of comprehension strategies influences teachers' instructional decisions and classroom practices. First, we sought to identify what teachers know about comprehension strategy instruction, then to understand how this knowledge changes over the course of a graduate reading course and finally, how this knowledge influences instructional practices.

Methodology

Participants

The twenty-two participants in this study were students enrolled in an online graduate reading course as a part of a master's degree or reading specialist license. All were experienced teachers, with the level of experience varying from two years to over fifteen years. The group consisted of pre-K, elementary, middle, and high school teachers, a substitute teacher, a Title 1 teacher, and a licensed day care provider. All data collection tools were embedded within the context of the course as assignments. Upon completion of the course and submission of final grades, participants were asked if their responses could be considered as data for the study.

Questionnaire

Use of an online pre-post questionnaire containing four questions was used to determine teachers' knowledge of comprehension strategies. The first section gathered demographic data about teaching experience and current teaching responsibilities. The second section contained the four open-ended questions:

- How do you define a comprehension strategy?
- What is the easiest strategy to teach?
- What is the most difficult strategy to teach?
- Briefly, list and describe how you teach a particular strategy?

These open-ended questions were selected as a way to keep the questionnaire authentic to the course activities and served as a preview of course content for the students.

Online discussions

Discussion board contributions and virtual chat responses, which were required activities in the course, also served as data sources. Discussion topics included responses the course reading assignments and successes or failures with implementation of new information into instructional practices. Transcripts of these discussions were collected for data analysis.

Data Analysis

Qualitative Analysis

The collection and analysis of the data occurred through a mixed-method approach. Through the use of naturalistic inquiry (Lincoln & Guba, 1985), the study was designed using a natural setting (i.e. the online classroom). Answers to all of the aforementioned research questions came in part from the pre-post questionnaire and online discussion boards. Using both of these aforementioned sources, content analysis was used to identify, code, and categorize emerging themes (Patton, 1990). Themes that emerged from studying the data included new knowledge, old knowledge, self-knowledge, and instructional practices. These identified themes helped in sorting the data and in further analyzing it for patterns among and across the themes.

Quantitative Analysis

In a quasi-experimental design, the researchers developed and used a rubric that evaluated four levels of knowledge (see Table 1). Both researchers independently analyzed all pre and post questionnaire responses using the developed rubric. The rubric was a 4-point scale scoring knowledge at the Limited, Declarative, Procedural, and Conditional levels (0, 1, 2, 3, respectively). Qualitatively, the researchers reexamined any particular answers where there was a discrepancy between them in the score. Finally, a paired samples t-test was run to compare the means from the pre-posttest scores.

Table 1: Developmental Comprehension Strategy Knowledge Ruric

Levels of Knowledge	Limited Knowledge (0 points)	Declarative (1 point)	Procedural (2 points)	Conditional (3 points)
	Incomplete or incorrect information	Recognition of information, knowing what comprehension strategies are and what they are used for.	Explanations of concepts and transference of information to another similar situation, knowing how the strategy works.	Knowing when and why to use a strategy, now able to teach or apply their strategy knowledge.
	During this stage the teacher . . .	During this stage the teacher . . .	During this stage the teacher . . .	During this stage the teacher . .
Strategy Knowledge	• has incomplete or incorrect information about strategies. • confuses strategies with activities.	• provides a simple definition of what a strategy is. • describes a strategy as a general tool or plan of action. • "A plan of action."	• provides a detailed definition of a strategy and how to teach it. • describes a strategy as a tool or plan of action and how it is used. • "A tool that can be used to find an answer, remember information, or complete a task."	• recognizes that a strategy is a thoughtful choice made to achieve a • specific outcome. • "A strategy is a carefully devised plan of action used to teach students new information."

| Teaching the Strategies | • has incomplete or incorrect information about strategies.
• confuses strategies with activities.
• confuses assigning with instructing. | • knows there are strategies.
• knows that strategies should be taught.
• names a couple of strategies. | • describes individual strategies using sophisticated vocabulary (ex. context clues vs. check the picture).
• describes teaching that includes at least some aspect of the gradual release of responsibility. | • explains how to applied the strategy in own reading. gives a vivid description of how to explain the strategy to students and teach them to apply the strategy in various situations.
• Vivid description includes some or all elements of gradual release of responsibility |

Findings

Questionnaire Results

The researchers used the questionnaire responses to provide evidence with regard to comprehension strategy knowledge growth; the teachers did not simply perceive a knowledge gain, but did in fact acquire new knowledge about comprehension strategies. As demonstrated in Table 2, 27.3% of students began at the Limited stage, while 72.7% began at the Declarative stage of the rubric on the pretest. Responses to the question *How do you define a comprehension strategy?* included:

- *"a plan,"*
- *"a trick you use to figure something out"*
- *"a way of teaching that supports student learning"*
- *"a technique that will help solve a problem"*

Based on the rubric scores and the responses, most teachers appeared to have some strategy knowledge prior to taking the course.

On the posttest, teacher scores increased to 63.3% in the Declarative stage and 36.4% in the Procedural stage of the rubric. Example of responses to the query about defining a comprehension strategy included:

- *"a carefully devised plan of action used to teach students new information"*
- *"a specific procedure that helps a reader comprehend the text better"*
- *"the careful plan to achieve a particular goal"*

Overall, teacher responses displayed a higher level of knowledge about strategy instruction in general after completing the course.

Table: 2: Percentage of participants scoring at levels of knowledge rubric

Levels of Knowledge	Limited	Declarative	Procedural	Conditional
Pretest	27.3%	72.7%	0%	0%
Posttest	0%	63.3%	36.4%	0%

Quantitative Results

The questionnaire scores were also statistically analyzed. According the *t*-test results demonstrated below, teachers gained specific knowledge with regard to comprehension strategy instruction. The obtained value is higher than the critical value leading us to conclude that the difference in scores did not occur by chance but instead by treatment. Results below show that for a 1-tailed test of significance:

$$t_{(21)} = -4.693, p < .01$$
where:
$$t_{crit} = 2.518 \ (.01)$$

Online Discussions

Qualitative analysis of responses on the discussion boards and virtual chats led to the themes of previous knowledge of comprehension strategy instruction, new knowledge gained from this course, knowledge of their own comprehension strategy use (self-knowledge), and influences of the three types of knowledge on their instructional practices.

Previous Knowledge

An answer to the first research question regarding the knowledge teachers have about comprehension instruction, was revealed through the teachers' descriptions of specific instructional strategies or lack of strategies used in their teaching. One teacher wrote, *"I didn't realize there was so much to teaching comprehension, because that is not how I was taught."* For many, the knowledge gained in this course was not brand new, but their previous knowledge was refined. Several teachers expressed surprise at how much is involved with comprehension instruction, reflecting possible gaps in their old knowledge. One teacher revealed such a gap in her knowledge when she wrote, *"I thought that good readers just picked up on how to be a good reader."* Contrary to what they had previously been taught, reading a paragraph and answering questions is not comprehension instruction. A teacher commented, *"I knew about comprehension before, but in a confused, unfocused way. Now I understand everything that goes into teaching it."*

New Knowledge

In response to the second research question regarding the ways a teacher's knowledge changes, these teachers clearly perceived an increase in their own knowledge as evidenced by their responses on the pre-post questionnaire and online discussions. One new concept reiterated by several teachers of young children is the idea that the teaching of comprehension strategies can and should begin at an early age, which was not in line with their previous thinking. These teachers had believed that comprehension instruction must wait until students are adept at decoding, but now realized that strategies can be taught during read alouds. The teachers also repeatedly mentioned a newfound respect for the importance of modeling when teaching comprehension. They described previously having a vague idea that modeling is necessary, but were not sure exactly how to model the in-the-head processes involved in reading comprehension. An unexpected, yet positive result of the new knowledge seemed to be a greater sense of confidence in their teaching, as reported by the teachers. One teacher said, *"I now know how to teach the strategies instead of just telling the students about them. I feel more confident in my teaching of reading."*

Self-Knowledge

Teachers reported developing more efficient comprehension skills in their own reading because of the awareness fostered by the course activities. For example, when asked what they learned, one teacher reported, *"Improved comprehension…myself and the students have made positive gains."* Another shared, *"I've been very impressed with the amount of information that I've learned, and it has helped me to become more aware of the strategies that I use when reading myself. I was not aware of the strategies that I used until I had read the text and reflected upon them in my responses."* This and other responses describe an increase in the teachers' awareness of their metacognitive skills. On a discussion board, one teacher remarked, *"Your post reminds me of how aware I have become of my own thinking when I am reading. I'll catch myself thinking—hey, I'm making an inference here."* Another commented, *"I also hadn't realized all the things I do when I read—the strategies I used."* Further and arguably most important, the teachers recognized a deeper meaning for metacognition—the ability to understand the decisions one makes, sometimes on an unconscious level, as a reader and the influence of those decisions on understanding.

Instructional Practices

A third research question focused on the ways a teacher's knowledge about comprehension strategy instruction changed and how this influenced their instructional practices. The teachers in this study were able to clearly articulate ways their instructional practices had already changed or the plans they had made to change instructional practices in the future. A key finding in this theme was the recognition of the importance of modeling in their instruction, as briefly mentioned in the new knowledge section. The teachers described how modeling had been used previously, but not to the extent they now realized was needed in order to help students fully understand and use the comprehension strategies independently. One teacher stated, *"I have learned that modeling must be done repeatedly. There is no set amount of times that I need to model a strategy. I must model it until the students are able to implement it on their own.*" Another remarked, "*The other comment that stuck out to me was about modeling. I don't do it nearly enough in my classroom!*"

The teachers also shared a depth of understanding with regard to instruction. They described an increase in their ability to teach specific strategies as a direct result of their increased knowledge of the strategies. One teacher shared, "*I think that I look at questioning differently, I never really thought of all there was to teaching about questions until I taught the lesson. I think that can be said for all of the strategies. I did not realize there are so many levels to the strategies.*" Teachers also learned how to use their knowledge across curriculum areas. As one teacher shared, "*I have changed the way I approach the reading of the math text. I incorporate stories that are at a lower level but still use a great deal of strategies to assist their reading skills.*"

The teachers expressed surprised at the amount of knowledge they gained during the course. They described a previous surface level of understanding and reflected on how they gained a deeper understanding about comprehension strategies and how to teach them. One teacher commented, "*I think that I look at questioning differently. I never really thought of all there was to teaching about questions until I taught the lesson. I think that can be said for all of the strategies. I did not realize there are so many levels to the strategies.*" They also went on to describe how their new knowledge led to a greater sense of confidence in their teaching, which was passed onto their students. For example, one teacher shared, "*I now know how to teach the strategies instead of just telling the students about them. I feel more confident in my teaching.*" Another said, "*I feel more prepared and less nervous about teaching reading now.*"

Perhaps the most interesting finding in this category was the teachers' renewed sense of enthusiasm about their teaching of reading. One remarked, "*As I taught my strategy lessons recently, I felt like the teaching and learning was more authentic. The kids really got excited about the book we were reading together. I believe that we all enjoyed reading—even the teacher.*" Another noted, "*I have new tools for teaching and am excited about teaching once again.*" Words used to describe this enthusiasm included: "anxious to try," "looking forward to," "cannot wait," "going to have so much fun." They also made and shared concrete plans to change their instruction in the present and future.

Limitations

Limitations that should be noted include a small sample size at one university. Additionally, all data were self-reported. Outside factors, such as district professional development or other coursework could have influenced the teachers' learning, although there was no report of these aforementioned activities.

Discussion

There were two main ideas revealed in the data. First, teachers reported an improvement in their own reading comprehension skills along with a stronger awareness of their own strategy use. They also described specific ways their new knowledge of comprehension strategies created a desire to effectively pass this information along to their students. There is a clear link between developing one's own comprehension skills and the ability to teach effectively these skills to their students.

Second and arguably more important, the analysis of the data led to the identification of a cyclical learning model (see Figure 1) that includes cognitive, affective, and instructional factors. Success with comprehension instruction and enthusiasm for new learning seemed to encourage these teachers to learn more, causing reciprocal growth. As these cognitive and affective factors were identified, the idea of changing instruction emerged as a related theme. As verified by the teachers' words, they learned, became more confident, and then were able to bring changes to their classroom instruction. This was a slow process for them; they did not make these changes overnight. Many teachers sought out advice from others in the course before taking the leap themselves. Change is very difficult for people, particularly when it forces one to reflect on their own practice and accept there might be a better way to do something. As one becomes a reflective practitioner, the change process becomes easier. When cognitive, affective, and instructional aspects work together, they have a profound influence on individual teachers and on all of the students they teach.

Figure 1: The cyclical model of learning.

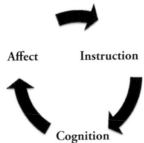

Affect   Instruction

Cognition

Conclusion

Through data analysis, it became evident that most teachers made growth with regard to their knowledge during the study (see Table 2); however, the amount of growth according to the rubric demonstrates the relatively slow process of developing expertise in teaching comprehension. Only 36% of the teachers scored in the Procedural category at the end of the course. No teachers scored in the Conditional category. Several teachers stayed flat in a given category. Upon further analysis, it should be noted that their scores did improve, but they did not improve enough to move them to a different category. For example, one teacher scored an average of 1.25 on the pretest questions and 1.5 on the posttest questions. In order to move to the next category, Procedural, she needed to score a 2.0. As described previously, the growth of a teacher with regard to instructional practices takes time. Just how much time it takes a teacher to become an expert is unknown, but some researchers estimate years (Duffy, 1993; El-Dinary & Schuder, 1993).

The teachers' words were extremely powerful. They were honest in their realizations that they lacked knowledge; however, they were also excited and rejuvenated to use their newfound knowledge both as readers themselves and with their students. Thus, we see a clear link between developing one's own comprehension skills and the ability to effectively teach these skills to students. As a result of this study, we are spending more time with the preservice and inservice teachers we work with discussing the mental processes they use as a reader and helping them to develop their own metacognitive skills. It is nearly impossible to teach someone to do something that you yourself have not done or cannot describe.

While teachers gained confidence in their own reading skills because of their increased knowledge and applied practice, they expressed a desire to share their new knowledge and experiences with other teachers. The teachers were excited about their new learning and the positive changes in their own classroom, and they wanted to give other teachers the same experience.

Implications

As teacher educators, we anticipated our students learning in the given context; however, we did not anticipate the enthusiasm that accompanied their new knowledge and how that enthusiasm influenced their instruction. We also did not foresee the immediate subsequent changes in their classroom instruction.

This study identified a need for teachers' professional development; teachers must continue to develop their content knowledge of reading. In our graduate courses, we need to dispel incorrect knowledge, clarify and solidify old knowledge and create new knowledge for our teachers. Then we must provide feedback and guidance as they implement this new knowledge into their classroom instruction. Often, this feedback and guidance is not part of a given program.

The findings from this study should not be surprising. When districts mandate scripted programs and do not allow teachers to input their own knowledge into the program and into their teaching, common sense would tell us that teachers will likely lose their desire to continue to learn. If teachers cannot use new knowledge with a scripted reading program, what would be the point of putting forth the effort to learn something new? Without this crucial knowledge, teachers are placed in a difficult position; what to do when the program does not work? Some of the teachers in this study felt frustrated, but were not sure why. Many of the teachers were previously unaware that they did not know what they needed to know with regard to reading instruction (*"I knew about comprehension, but in a confused, unfocused way"*). This unclear focus seemed to affect their dispositions about teaching which in turn influenced their classroom instruction. Figuring out what knowledge teachers really have about reading instruction is a key to good classroom instruction.

This knowledge cannot be imparted by a scripted text. Ultimately, we are reminded that teachers, not programs, teach children to read.

References

Anders, P. L. , Hoffman, J. V., & Duffy, G. G. (2000). Teaching teachers to teach reading: Paradism shifts, persistent problems, and challenges. In M.L. Kamil, P. B. Mosenthal, P. D. Pearson & R. Barr (Eds.), *Handbook of Reading Research* (*Vol. 3*. pp.) Mahwah, NJ: Erlbaum.

Buckner, A. (2009). *Notebook connections: Strategies for the reader's notebook*. Portland, ME: Stenhouse.

Cochran-Smith, M., & Lytle, S. Relationships of knowledge and practice: Teacher learning in communities. In A. Iran-Nejad and C.D. Pearson (Eds.), *Review of Research in Education* (Vol. 24, pp. 251-307). Washington, DC: American Educational Research Association.

Darling-Hammond, L., Chung, R., & Frelow, F. (2002). Variation in teacher preparation: How well do different pathways prepare teachers to teach? *Journal of Teacher Education, 53*(4), 286-302.

Duffy, G. (1993). Teacher's progress toward becoming expert strategy teachers. *The Elementary School Journal, 94* (2), 109-120.

Duke, N. K., & Pearson, P. D. (2002). Effective practices for developing reading comprehension. In A. E. Farstrup & S. J. Samuels (Eds.), *What research has to say about reading instruction* (3rd ed., pp.205-242). Newark, DE: International Reading Association.

El-Dinary, P. B., & Schuder, T. (1993). Seven teachers' acceptance of transactional strategies instruction during their first year using it. *Elementary School Journal, 94*, 207-219.

Fielding, L., & Pearson, P. D. (1994). Reading comprehension: What works. *Educational Leadership, 51*, 62-68.

Fitzharris, L., Jones, M., & Crawford, A. (2008). Teacher Knowledge Matters in Supporting Young Readers. *The Reading Teacher, 61* (5), 384-394.

Griffin, G. A., & Barnes, S. (1986). Using research findings to change school and classroom practices: Results of an experimental study. *American Educational Research Journal, 23*, 572-586.

Harvey, S., & Goudvis, A. (2007). *Strategies that work: Teaching comprehension for understanding and engagement* (2nd ed.). Portland, ME: Stenhouse.

Hoffman, J., & Pearson, P. (2000). Reading teacher education in the next millennium: What your grandmother's teacher didn't know that your granddaughter's teacher should. *Reading Research Quarterly, 35*, 28–44.

Keene, E. O. (2008). *To understand: New horizons in reading comprehension*. Portsmouth, NH: Heinemann.

Keene, E. O., & Zimmerman, S. (2007). *Mosaic of thought: The power of comprehension strategy instruction.* (2nd ed.). Portsmouth, NH: Heinemann.

Liang, L., & Dole, J .A. (2006). Help with teaching reading comprehension: comprehension instructional frameworks. *The Reading Teacher, 59*, 742–753.

Lincoln, Y. S., & Guba, E. G. (1985). *Naturalistic inquiry*. Newbury Park, CA: Sage Publications.

Miller, D. (2002). *Reading with meaning: Teaching comprehension in the primary grades*. Portland, ME: Stenhouse.

National Institute of Child Health and Human Development [NICHD] (2000). *Report of the National ReadingPanel. Teaching children to read: An evidence-based assessment of the scientific research literature on reading and its implications for reading instruction* (NIH Publication No. 00-4769). Washington, DC: U.S. Government Printing Office.

Palincsar, A. S., & Brown, A. L. (1984). Reciprocal teaching of comprehension-fostering and comprehension-monitoring activities. *Cognition and Instruction, 1*, 117-175.

Pardo, L. (2004). What every teacher needs to know about comprehension. *Reading Teacher, 58*, 272-280.

Paris, S. G., Lipson, M. Y., & Wixson, K. K. (1994). Becoming a strategic reader. In R.B. Ruddell, M.R. Ruddell, H. Singer, (Eds.), *Theoretical models and processes of reading* (pp. 788-810). Newark, DE: International Reading Association.

Paris, S. G., Wasik, B. A., & Turner, J. C. (1991). The development of strategic readers. In R. Barr, M. L. Kamil, P. Mosenthal, & P. D. Pearson (Eds.), *Handbook of reading research* (Vol. 2, pp. 609-640). New York: Longman.

Patton, M. Q. (1990). *Qualitative evaluation and research methods.* Newbury Park, CA: Sage Publications.

Pearson, P. D., & Gallagher, M. C. (1983). The instruction of reading comprehension. *Contemporary Educational Psychology 8*, 317-344.

Pearson, P. D., Roehler, L. R., Dole, J. A., & Duffy, G. G. (1992). Developing expertise in reading comprehension. In S.J. Samuels and A.E. Farstrup (Eds.), *What research has to say about reading instruction* (pp. 145-199). Newark, DE: International Reading Association.

Pressley, M. (2000). What should comprehension instruction be the instruction of? In R. Barr, M. L, Kamil, P. Mosenthal, & P. D. Pearson (Eds.), *Handbook of reading research* (Vol. 3, pp. 545-562). Mahwah, NJ: Erlbaum.

Pressley, M. (2006, April 29). *What the future of reading research could be.* Paper presented at the International Reading Association Conference, Reading Research 2006, Chicago, IL.

RAND Reading Study Group [RRSG]. (2002). *Reading for understanding: Towards an R&D program of reading comprehension.* Santa Monica, CA: RAND. October 14, 2009, from http://www.rand.org/multi/achievementforall/reading/readreport.html.

What's Old Is New Again: Is the Foundation of Comprehension Instruction Still Solid?

Stephan Sargent

Melinda Smith

Northeastern State University

Nancy Hill

Susan Morrison

Southeastern Oklahoma State University

Stephen Burgess

Southwestern Oklahoma State University

Abstract

During the past decade, a reform movement has swept across American schools designed to improve public education and rectify perceived weaknesses in our educational establishment. Perhaps no other aspect of literacy has been impacted more than reading comprehension. As a result, scripted and mandated curriculums are commonplace in many schools. This study, using a survey of 382 in-service teachers, examined whether teachers only rely on mandated resources alone or if they still incorporate other forms of research-based comprehension pedagogy to meet varied student needs. Over half of the teachers surveyed still include "best practices" in comprehension to meet the needs of individual students using research-based comprehension strategies.

"Comprehension is the reason for reading. If readers can read the words but do not understand what they are reading, they are not really reading."
(National Institute for Literacy, 2008, p.1)

During the past decade, a reform movement has swept across American schools designed to improve public education and rectify perceived weaknesses in our educational establishment. This transformation has centered on accountability—

holding practitioners, administrators, and local districts jointly responsible for student learning. The costs of this push for change in literacy instruction have been monumental. Teachers must often meet stringent requirements on many levels— national, state, district, and site. These mandates commonly include implementing required curricula and instructional programs as well as strict time allocations for reading and writing (Crawford, 2004). Perhaps no other aspect of literacy has been impacted more than reading comprehension.

Most educators agree the objective of reading is constructing meaning from the text. Comprehension is the understanding of text and often demands explanations, interpretations, applications, perspectives, empathizing, and self-monitoring. According to the National Institute for Literacy (2006), "Research over 30 years has shown that instruction in comprehension can help students understand what they read, remember what they read, and communicate with others about what they read" (p. 41). Thus, reading comprehension must remain an integral part of the literacy curriculum. Yet, is this foundation still evident amidst the superfluity of literacy mandates faced daily by reading teachers?

For decades, research-based comprehension strategies have been studied. Literacy research has shown that great improvements in comprehension have occurred when cognitive strategy instruction was used in the classroom. Techniques that foster active, self-regulated and intentional reading are especially useful (Pressley, 2000; Report of the National Reading Panel, 2000; Tierney & Cunningham, 1984, Trabasso & Bouchard, 2002). According to the National Institute for Literacy (NIFL, 2006), seven strategies are effective to bolster students' comprehension of text: monitoring comprehension, metacognition, graphic organizers, answering questions, generating questions, recognizing story structure, and summarizing (Adler, 2001). A few literacy leaders have merged theory into practice for practitioners by writing various reading programs. For example, Cunningham's "Four Blocks" approach includes "Guided Reading" (focused on comprehension instruction) that is rooted in before, during, and after reading activities to aid children's comprehension of text (Cunningham, Hall, & Sigmon 1999). Thus, teachers of reading have known and continued to learn much about comprehension.

Since the inception of the No Child Left Behind Act (NCLB) of 2001, the federal government, state governments, and local districts have played an increasingly visible and important role in reading instruction throughout the nation, aiming to help alleviate the achievement gap among minorities, disadvantaged students and students who do not fit into one of these categories (Harp & Brewer, 2005). As a result of these mandates, many schools have adopted a "scripted program" to teach children to read. This is in contrast to the International Reading Association's (IRA) Position Statement (2001) regarding reading teachers. According to IRA, excellent reading teachers "know a variety of ways to teach reading, when to use each method, and how to combine methods into an effective instructional program" (p.1). Miolosovic (2007) described an example of such mandated curriculum in an urban dictrict in the Midwest, which utilized a mandated program that relied on unauthentic text (in passages too short to develop story grammar), timed readings (using "clickers" to manage time), and scripted questions (designed similar to lower-level test questions). Milosovic contended that scripted curricula actually failed to meet the goals of increased literacy and in fact were an attack on the professionalism of the classroom teacher. As such, many reading professionals have expressed dismay at the abandonment of what research says is effective for helping students comprehend text in lieu of scripted literacy instruction (Ede, 2006).

In essence, the foundation of reading instruction seems to have crumbled. Yet, this may not be the case in many classrooms. While no one approach is best for all students, many teachers who are aware of various approaches are well suited to make an informed choice of which strategies and procedures to use in building comprehension. Ede (2006) supports this by claiming that "classroom teachers are in the best position to identify individual [students'] strengths and needs and adjust a curriculum to address them" (p. 31) as opposed to a scripted lesson.

Those who favor standardization of curriculum believe it will result in more instructional support for low-performing schools and more consistency across and within school districts with respect to what is being taught (McColskey & McNunn, 2001). Hayes (2006) noted that some research publicizing the advantages and positive benefits of mandated curriculum stresses that more attention to a uniform statewide curriculum results in clearer understandings on the part of educators as to what skills should be mastered at each grade level. Proponents also believe strict guidelines about what and how to teach result in higher scores on "high stakes" standardized tests (Ede, 2006). However, Hayes concluded that while decision makers may cling to mandates in an effort to "control" the educational system, this invariably results in a narrowing of the curriculum and a distinct reduction in the variety of instructional methods. In states with "high stakes" requirements, 80% of teachers reported that students spend more than 20% of their instructional time practicing for the standardized tests instead of teaching (Jones, Jones, Hardin, Chapman, Yarbrough, & Davis, 1999, p. 201). When the stakes for testing are high, teachers feel pressure to raise scores in any way they can (Jones et al., 1999; Hayes, 2006). Jones and her colleagues conducted a survey of teachers in a southeastern state to find the impact of testing and mandates in the schools. The teachers were asked to describe their instruction and how it had changed since an accountability program was implemented. As a direct result of the testing requirements, 67% of teachers indicated that they changed their teaching methods. Nearly 50% of these same teachers reported that "high stakes" testing, and the preparations for it, had a negative impact on students' love of learning. In light of these statistics, understanding what teachers are actually using in teaching comprehension is crucial. Although much has been learned about teaching comprehension, perhaps this knowledge is not transferring to classrooms where mandated instruction is required. Thus, this "old" knowledge may be new again to some teachers and schools.

Purpose

The purpose of this study was to discover what comprehension strategies inservice teachers actually use in their classroom amidst the mandates found in reading instruction. Specifically, the study explored the actual reading practices of teachers, especially how or if they combine effective teaching practices with mandated programs. Literacy researchers Reutzel and Cooter (2004) maintained that "not all teachers (or researchers) agree as to the best ways of teaching reading" (p. 17). As a result of this reality coupled with literacy mandates, teachers may vary dramatically in the teaching of reading and how they implement programs in the classroom.

Possible benefits of the study are abundant and include the improvement of teacher practices within the classroom, as well as, the teacher education process. Knowing whether or not teachers use effective comprehension strategies or simply abandon their use in the face of mandates will help teacher educators, school administrators, and practitioners understand how students are being taught to construct their own knowledge, which will in turn assist these teachers. Although there has been a movement to increase the use of research-based reading practices in the classroom, there is little evidence that these practices are being used. Thus, the following research question guided the study:

Question: Since the inception of the No Child Left Behind Act of 2001, the United States Federal Government, states, and local districts have played an increasingly important role in reading instruction. Scripted and mandated curriculums are commonplace in many schools. Do teachers only rely on these resources alone, or do they still incorporate other forms of research-based comprehension pedagogy to meet varied student needs?

Theoretical Framework

This study is rooted in Shulman's (1986) theoretical framework. Shulman's work contends that for teachers to be effective in the classroom, they must possess both knowledge of the content and the process of teaching the subject. If teachers are successful, they must merge knowledge of the content with effective and practical teaching principles amidst national, state, and local mandates. Thus, effective teachers of reading/literacy should possess a thorough knowledge of reading comprehension strategies (in terms of this study) to implement in literacy instruction. In addition to knowing these strategies, reading/literacy teachers must actually be able and willing to apply what helps children learn best, even in the face of scripted, mandated programs.

According to the National Institute for Literacy (2006), "Successful comprehension teachers must be strategic themselves, coordinating individual strategies and altering, adjusting, modifying, testing, and shifting tactics appropriately until readers' comprehension problems are resolved. For readers to become good reading strategists requires teachers who have appreciation for reading strategies" (p.3). Thus to be successful teachers, practitioners must have knowledge of the comprehension strategies and also know how to help students implement them. This aligns with Shulman's theory (1986).

Although college students and inservice teachers are taught research-based comprehension strategies in courses and professional development, recent trends may inhibit their implementation in the classroom. Crawford (2004) posits that mandated curriculum may "stand at odds with the principles of developmentally appropriate practice and may ultimately result in the deskilling and deprofessionalization of teachers" (p. 206). This seemingly contradicts the process/application portion of Schulman's theory (1986).Teachers should continue to use effective comprehension strategies even when faced with mandates that oppose what they have learned. Thus, exploring whether or not teachers use effective comprehension strategies or abandon these in the face of mandates is crucial.

Methods

This study is designed to explore the reading practices and habits of teachers currently in the field. The No Child Left Behind Act of 2001 (NCLB) has placed certain requirements on teachers to select programs which meet specified criteria. In this study, surveys helped examine attitudes, experiences, and practices of teachers that are related to their teaching in the classroom. Surveys aid researchers as they seek to "find out what a large group of people think about a certain teaching practice or issue" (Hubbard & Power, 1999, p. 92). This technique is especially appropriate when it is not possible to interview everyone individually, as in this study. Surveys help "tap information that would otherwise be inaccessible" (Hubbard & Power, p. 92).

Participants

The participants in this study consisted of 382 inservice elementary school teachers (all of whom are impacted by literacy mandates) who completed an on-line survey (See Appendix) that examined what mandates were present (in terms of reading instruction) as well as actual teaching practices used in the classroom. Approximately 500 surveys were distributed. Of these, 382 were completed online. Participants consisted of the 382 who returned the surveys. The vast majority of those who completed the survey were graduate students who are teaching in the elementary classroom and taking courses at the university. The participants were also invited to share the survey with other school teachers in their buildings. Approximately fifty surveys were completed by such teachers who were not enrolled in a university literacy program. Surveys were also sent to approximately thirty area school administrators asking for teacher participation. While a few teachers participated from this invitation (about fifteen), relatively few chose to participate via this route. Grade levels taught by the participants ranged from 1st through 5th grades. The ages of the participants ranged from 23 though 69, while the age of the average participant was 33. Ninety-five percent of the participants were women and 5% were men. The racial composition of the participants consisted of the following groups and percentages: White (91.6%), African American (1%), Hispanic (2%), Native American (1%), Multi-Racial (0.9%), Asian (0.5%), and other (3%). Participants answered the survey questions and submitted them electronically. The survey took approximately thirty minutes to complete.

Instruments

The survey instrument consisted of two parts. The five authors began development of the survey by discussing what information should be gleaned concerning comprehension in light of mandated instruction. First, two open-ended questions probed the participants' basic understanding of reading comprehension. These questions included:

- How do you define reading/literacy comprehension?
- Do you believe reading comprehension is important in the literacy classroom? Why or why not?

The subsequent portion of the survey explored common comprehension strategies (used over a span of grade levels) that are supported by current research and collectively incorporate the comprehension elements outlined by the National Institute for Literacy (Adler, 2001). The researchers first explored comprehension strategies supported by scientific-based research. Next, the researchers explored various reading methods textbooks used at the collegiate level to find common names (in some cases multiple names) of the comprehension strategies supported by research. The ensuing portion of the survey asked participants to indicate the comprehension technique(s) used regularly in their classrooms. For example, participants chose from KWL charts, retelling, graphic organizers, story maps, and other comprehension strategies. Also included in this section was a choice named "other" where teachers indicated other comprehension strategies used that were not part of the forced response checklist. Participants indicated if and how often they used each technique in their classrooms. Beside each comprehension strategy that teachers indicated using, they marked how often that strategy was used (once per month, once every two weeks, weekly, or daily).

Data Analysis

Once all volunteers participated in the survey, the results were analyzed. The data were analyzed using percentages. This datum consisted of a series of questions asking the participants what comprehension strategies they used. For each research-based startegy queried, percentages were calculated (see Table 1). Not only were percentages calculated for whether or not teachers used the strategy, but the researchers also noted if the participants used the strategy daily, weekly, or less than weekly.

Open-ended questions were analyzed by identifying categories that emerged from the raw data, a process known as "open-coding" (Strauss & Corbin, 1990).

Once the surveys were complete, all researchers at separate university sites individually reviewed the results of the surveys to identify broad categories. Verbatim data was stored in an electronic format, available to the researchers at the participating universities for analysis. Next, two of the researchers at a single university took a lead in the initial discussions of the open-ended questions and sought emerging themes. Differences in category identification (among these two readers) were resolved by discussing the data until a consensus was reached. During this analysis, the two researchers initally identified multiple categories that emerged from the two open-ended questions on comprehension. However, these categories were replaced with two broad categories for the open-ended questions (see Findings). These findings were shared with the entire research team, who agreed that they appropriately described the data set.

Findings

This study examined the extent to which classroom teachers used mandated resources alone or still incorporated other forms of research-based comprehension pedagogy to meet varied student needs. Eighty-five percent of the participants in the study indicated having some form of mandated reading/literacy curriculum at their schools. While teachers are required to incorporate such mandates in the curriculum, when asked about specific comprehension strategies, findings (see Table 1) indicate that teachers do incorporate research-based methods methods to ensure the needs of all their students are met, with the percentage varying by specific strategy.

Two themes emerged from the open-ended questions on comprehension. The first was that comprehension is the process of constructing meaning while reading. Eighty-six percent of the participants made a comment reflecting this sentiment. One participant noted that comprehension is "developing meaning from what is read". Because comprehending the text is the ultimate purpose of reading, having 86% of the participants mention this was not unanticipated. The second theme, which became apparent, was that children learn and use such comprehension skills while reading. Seventy-nine percent of the surveys had some reference to successful student use of comprehension strategies that have been taught. For example, one participant described how purpose-setting activities help her students understand what they read. Other skills mentioned included: comparing and contrasting, recognizing literary genres, and distinguishing facts from opinions. When discussing the strategies children utilize who are good readers, another teacher noted that her students tend to chunk phrases meaningfully as they read.

The forced-completion questions on the survey indicated that teachers are utilizing research-based strategies in their classrooms along with mandated curriculum and pedagogy. The survey revealed general strategies teachers utilize in their classrooms and the average amount of time spent on such pedagogy to enhance student comprehension (see Table 1). Also, the survey revealed that well over half of the teachers probed are using these research-based strategies on a regular basis in addition to mandated programs.

Table 1: Comprehension Strategies Used by Teachers

Strategy	Percent of Teachers Who Use This Strategy	Percent of Teachers Who Use This Strategy Daily	Percent of Teachers Who Use This Strategy Weekly	Percent of Teachers Who Use This Strategy Less than Weekly
Story Retelling	70%	38%	45%	17%
Think-Alouds	68%	53%	32%	15%
Question-Answer Relationships	65%	46%	41%	13%
KWL Charts	58%	4%	35%	61%
Story Maps	57%	13%	40%	43%
Graphic Organizers	56%	20%	45%	35%

Story retelling (Gambrell, Koskinen, and Kapinus, 1991) was the most common comprehension strategy used by teachers. Over 70% of the inservice teachers surveyed reported using this strategy. This is a strategy in which the student makes a mental representation of the story and retells the story either orally or in writing. Characters, plot, problem, and other elements of story grammar are included (Walker, 2008). Story retelling incorporates the technique of summarizing, which the National Institute for Literacy (NIFL) found to be effective for bolstering comprehension (Adler, 2001).

Think-alouds (Wilhelm, 2001) were implemented regularly by 68% of the teachers. A think-aloud allows the teacher to actually think aloud and model the process a good reader uses while reading. In turn, the student may think aloud, allowing the teacher to access his/her thought patterns (Walker, 2008). Think-alouds help students to monitor their comprehension and build metacognition. Monitoring comprehension while reading is a research-based technique recommended by the NIFL (Adler, 2001).

Perhaps surprisingly, Question-Answer Relationships (Raphael & Pearson, 1985) were used by 65% of the in-service teachers. Using this strategy, students identify sources of information needed to answer questions (Walker, 2008). The fact that so many teachers reported using Question-Answer Relationships is encouraging to the authors of this study. Generation of questions is a comprehension technique based in scientific research recommended the NIFL (Adler, 2001).

Fifty-eight percent of teachers reported using KWL Charts (Ogle, 1986). The KWL Chart is a technique used to help students brainstorm background knowledge, record information students want to learn, and record information learned. This strategy helps direct students' reading of content-area text (Walker, 2008). KWL charts help students answer self-constructed questions. Such answering of questions following reading is supported by NIFL to enhance reading comprehension (Adler, 2001). Fifty-seven percent of the teachers reported using story maps (Davis, 1994). Story maps provide students with a visual representation of the events in the text. Often, setting, problem, goal, events, and resolution are included on the map (Walker, 2008). Learning story structure is crucial, according to the NIFL, for constructing meaning from text (Adler, 2001). Finally, 56% of teachers reported using graphic organizers (DiCecco & Gleason, 2002). Graphic organizers also provide a visual representation of key words and ideas from the text (Walker, 2008). The NIFL recommends regular use of graphic organizers and provides research to show that its use positively impacts reading comprehension (Adler, 2001).

Discussion

This study explored how comprehension is being taught in the face of federal, state, and local mandates that radically influences educational practices in reading/ literacy. Ede (2006) describes the classroom environment created by government rules and regulations. However, even amidst these demands, over half of the teachers surveyed report using research-based strategies to bolster reading comprehension in addition to the often scripted curriculum.

Certainly, there is a need to prepare reading teachers to deal with the demands of mandates and societal change strategically. Teachers' attitudes, beliefs, pedagogical knowledge, and skills all play a key role in how they address and respond to the mandates imposed on them and in how they strive for quality teaching and learning in their classroom settings. According to Schulman's theory (1986), practitioners who are successful must be well versed in content and pedagogy. This is certainly true for teachers of reading.

While half of the teachers reported using one or more of these comprehension strategies regularly, half did not. This could indicate they are following the mandated program exactly without implementing research-based comprehension strategies in their classrooms. In this case, the possible benefits of the study are abundant. First, "what's old can be new again." The research-based comprehension techniques used by effective teachers may be entirely novel to some teachers only using "teacher-proof" literacy curriculums. The improvement of teacher practices within the classroom, as well as, the improvement of the teacher education process will benefit both inservice and teacher preparation programs. Using these data, programs of teacher preparation (undergraduate and graduate) can recognize what is and is not being used and help practitioners learn how to incorporate research-based comprehension strategies in their classrooms. For example, Commeyras (2007), a reading methods professor, included both research-based reading methods and an overview of popular scripted programs in her university classes to show future teachers how to merge mandated programs with quality literacy instruction.

Realizing many teachers attempt to incorporate varied modes of instruction, those involved in professional development will benefit. With increasing demands upon teachers in public schools, effective teacher preparation and continuing professional development are essential. New teachers and inservice teachers alike are expected to perform well in the classroom. Evidence, such as that found in this study, helps those involved in literacy education to know how teachers use mandated programs and what other methods are actually used. Knowing this helps those involved in teacher preparation better prepare and assist teachers who have "foundational knowledge of teaching reading to be ready for whatever mandates or choices await them in the schools where they will be teaching" (Commeyras, 2007, p. 407).

Limitations

While the study revealed much about what teachers currently use to enhance comprehension, several limitations are evident. First, this study was conducted in a four-state region of the nation. In order to generalize findings, replication of the study across the nation is needed. Moreover, subjectivity in the interpretation of open-ended surveys is a limitation. While the study utilized numerous readers and triangulation methods, varied interpretations may still be evident. Finally, the teachers' understanding of the name of the strategy could be a limitation. For example, in some regions of the nation one strategy may be known by one name, while in another area that strategy may have another title. While such an issue with terminology is negligible, it could impact the results of the survey.

Conclusions

Over the years, there have been many approaches to teaching reading comprehension. Certainly, no one approach is best for all students or all teachers. Therefore, many teacher educators acquaint future teachers with characteristics of various approaches so they will be able to make an informed choice of which strategies and procedures to use in teaching understanding of the text. No matter which approach is used to teach comprehension skills, teachers are continually challenged to meet the demands of federal, state, and local mandates. Where teachers turn for information to ensure comprehension success in their classrooms is something to ponder, keeping in mind that a child first learns to read and then reads to learn for the remainder of his/ her life. For many teachers in this study, the foundation of reading comprehension instruction seems strong. For example, 70% of the teachers surveyed reported using retelling. However, for other teachers, including effective comprehension strategies might benefit their current instructional practices. Research-based techniques such as retelling that are "old" to some teachers may be completely new to others. Therefore, "what's old is new again!"

References

Adler, C.R. (Ed). 2001. *Put reading first: The research building blocks for teaching children to read*, pp. 49-54. National Institute for Literacy. Retrieved Nov. 1, 2008, from http://www.nifl.gov/partnershipforreading/publications/reading_first1text.html.

Commeyras, M. (2007). Scripted reading instruction. What's a teacher educator to do? *Phi Delta Kappan, 88* (5), 404-407.

Crawford, P. A. (2004). "I follow the blue…" A primary teacher and the impact of packaged curriculum. *Early Childhood Education Journal, 32*, 205-210.

Cunningham, P. M., Hall, D.P., & Sigmon, C.M. (1999). The teacher's guide to the four blocks. Greensboro, NC: Carson-Dellosa.

Davis, Z.T. (1994). Effects of prereading story mapping on elementary readers' comprehension. *Journal of Educational Research, 87*, 353-360.

DiCecco, V.M., & Gleason, M.M. (2002). Using graphic organizers to attain relational knowledge from expository text. *Journal of Learning Disabilities, 35*, 306-320.

Ede, A. (2006). Scripted curriculum: Is it a prescription for success? *Childhood Education, 83* (1), 29-32.

Gambrell, L.B., Koskinen, P.S., & Kapinus, B.A. (1991). Retelling and the reading comprehension of proficient and less-proficient readers. *Journal of Education Research, 84*, 356-362.

Harp, B., & Brewer, J. (2005). *The informed reading teacher: Research-based practice*. Upper Saddle. River, NJ: Pearson.

Hayes, W. (2006). *The progressive education movement: Is it still a factor in today's schools?* New York: Rowman & Littlefield Education.

Hubbard, R.S., & Power, B.M. (1999). *Living the Questions: A guide for teacher-researchers*. Portland, ME: Stenhouse Publishers.

International Reading Association. (2001). *Excellent reading teachers. A position statement of the International Reading Association*. Newark, DE: IRA

Jones, M. G., Jones, B.D., Hardin, B., Chapman, L, Yarbrough, T., & Davis, M. (1999). The impact of high-stakes testing on teachers and students in North Carolina. *Phi Delta Kappan, 81*(3), 199-203.

McColskey, W., & McNunn, N. (2001). Strategies for dealing with high-stakes state tests. P*hi Delta Kappan, 82*(2), 115-121.

Milosovic, S. (2007). Building a case against scripted reading programs. *Education Digest, 73* (1), 27-30.

National Institute for Literacy—NIFL. (2006). Put reading first. Washington, DC: NIFL.

No Child Left Behind. (2001, January 31). Education Week. Retrieved November 27, 2007 from http://www.edweek.org/ew/articles/2001/01/31/20bushbox.h20. html?querystring=no%20child

Ogle, Donna M. (1986). A teaching model that develops active comprehension of expository text. *The Reading Teacher, 39*, 564-570.

Pressley, M. (2000). What should comprehension instruction be the instruction of? In M. Kamil, P. Mosenthal, P.D. Pearson, & R. Barr (Eds.), *Handbook of reading research, vol. III* (pp. 545-561). London: Lawrence Erlbaum Associates.

Raphael, T. E., & Pearson, P. (1985). Increasing students' awareness of sources of information for answering questions. *American Educational Research Journal, 22*, 217-235.

Report of the National Reading Panel (2000). *Teaching children to read. An evidence-based assessment of the scientific research literature on reading and its implications for reading instruction. Reports of the subgroups*. National Institute of Child Health and Human Development, National Institutes of Health.

Reutzel, D.R., & Cooter, R.B. (2004). *Teaching children to read: Putting the pieces together.* Columbus, OH: Pearson.

Shulman, L. (1986). Those who understand: Knowledge growth in teaching. *Educational Researcher, 15* (2), 4-14.

Strauss, A., & Corbin, J.M. (1990). Basics of qualitative research: Grounded theory and techniques. Newbury Park, CA: Sage Publications.

Tierney, R., & Cunningham, J. (1984). Research on teaching reading comprehension. In P.D. Pearson, R. Barr, M. Kamil, & P. Mosenthal (Eds.), *Handbook of reading research* (Vol. 1, pp. 609-655). New York: Longman.

Trabasso, T., & Bouchard, E. (2002). Teaching readers how to comprehend text strategically. In C. Block &   M. Pressley (Eds.), *Comprehension instruction: Research-based best practices* (pp. 176-200). New York: Guilford.

Walker, B.J. (2008). *Diagnostic teaching of reading.* Upper Saddle River, NJ: Pearson.

Wilhelm, J.D. (2001). *Improving comprehension through think-aloud strategies: Modeling what good readers do.* New York: Scholastic.

Appendix A: Survey

Your name _____

Your age _____

Please circle one: Female   Male

Please circle one: Caucasian   African-American   Hispanic
Other: Please specify_____

Major or degree area in education _____

When was your degree obtained? _____

Area of Specialization _____

Certification Areas _____

How many total years have you been teaching? _____

What grade level are you currently teaching? _____

Approximately how many students are in the school where you teach? _____

How many years have taught with reading as part of your curriculum coverage?
_____

How many courses have you had in special education topics? _____

How many different reading programs have you used? _____

Please list the ones that you can remember. _____

_____

_____

What program are you currently using? _____

Directions: Following are some questions related to reading comprehension. Please provide your honest answers.

What is reading comprehension? _____

_____

_____

_____

_____

Do you think comprehension is an important portion of reading instruction? Why or why not? _____

_____

_____

_____

Please place a checkmark by the comprehension technique(s) you use regularly in your classroom:

_____ **KWL charts** ____ Once per month, _____Once each 2 weeks, _____Weekly, ____ Daily
_____ **Retelling of stories** (oral and/or written)
            _____ Once per month, _____Once each 2 weeks, _____ Weekly, _____Daily
_____**Graphic organizers**
            _____ Once per month, _____Once each 2 weeks, _____ Weekly, _____Daily
_____**Story maps** ____Once per month, ____Once each 2 weeks, ____ Weekly, ____ Daily
_____**Question-Answer Relationships (QAR)**
            _____ Once per month, _____Once each 2 weeks, _____ Weekly, _____Dail
_____**Think-Alouds**
            _____ Once per month, _____ Once each 2 weeks,_____Weekly, _____ Daily
            Other: _____
            _____ Once per month, _____Once each 2 weeks, _____ Weekly, _____ Daily

Children as Authors and Illustrators: A Demonstration of the Writing Process

Janet Leigh Towell

Jane Brady Matanzo

Florida Atlantic University

Abstract

The Story Transformation Project was developed to show teachers how the writing process could be used to help children become authors and illustrators. Six master-level graduate students in a graduate reading course used variations of Writer's Workshop to teach their students how to write, illustrate, and publish story transformations of familiar folk and fairy tales. Flexibility in the assignment was a major factor in contributing to the success of the writing project in each classroom. This project was considered to be beneficial to schoolchildren, graduate students, and university professors as each was involved to some degree on their trek to becoming authors and illustrators.

As a university professor in reading and language arts, the first author became excited about the concept of children becoming authors and illustrators after attending a workshop by the British book illustrator and literacy expert, Paul Johnson, author of *A Book of One's Own* (1994). Johnson demonstrated how to make books for and by children in a variety of sizes and shapes including pop-up, shape, zigzag, accordion, origami, and flap books. Johnson's workshop not only motivated the first author to incorporate these ideas into a master-level beginning reading course but to also share the project ideas with the second author who previously had worked with elementary and middle school students to create and illustrate their own books. The authors met periodically to brainstorm ideas for implementing the writing process and Writer's Workshop through a careful selection of language arts strategies, activities, art, and traditional children's literature.

Framework

Before beginning the Story Transformation Project, the authors did a literature review to find research examples and theoretical support for encouraging children to become authors and illustrators. Yenawine (2005) suggested that visual literacy is "the ability to find meaning in imagery" (p. 845) and would be useful for an analysis of illustrations in traditional literature. Albers (2007) and Cornett (2007) described the importance of arts integration and how teaching literacy through the arts enhances creativity, comprehension, and critical thinking with diverse learners. Harste's research (2005) showed that helping learners discover unique ways of communication, sharing ideas, and furthering literacy through multiple sign systems such as reading and writing would help them become more confident and effective learners.

This learning theory of multiple sign systems introduces the concept of transmediation, which is "…a semiotic process in which learners retranslate their understanding of a text, idea, or concept through another medium" (Albers, 2007, p. 187). Transmediation and the integration of the language arts (Albers, 2007) validate the idea of children as authors and illustrators who can express their ideas through illustrations and words. Research on Writer's Workshop and the writing process (Graves, 1983; Calkins, 1994) explain the importance of meaningful conferencing with students and using innovative ideas for teaching the craft of writing. Gibson (2008/2009) showed that scaffolding through explicit instruction is essential and recommended. An effective framework, especially for primary grades, is guided writing instruction that contains four basic steps:

1. Engagement in a brief, shared experience;
2. Discussion of experience and strategic behavior for writing;
3. Time to write individually with immediate guidance from the teacher; and
4. Planned opportunity to share drafts and revised writing with audience.

According to literacy experts, the writing process is just as important as the product (Graves, 1983; Calkins, 1994; Johnson & Westkott, 2004; Ray & Laminack, 2001). During the writing process, students learn how to build their stories and by moving in and out of the writing stages, children learn that writing is not a sequential process but a cycle that can repeat as necessary to write successfully a story.

Methods

Participants

There were two groups of participants. The first group was comprised graduate students who were teachers taking an elective reading course (RED 6303 *Beginning Reading* K-3). The second group consisted of second grade to eighth grade students enrolled in public schools. The graduate students were Beth, Kathy, Anne, Connie, Alice, and Debbie (pseudonyms). Five of the students were elementary majors and one was a special education major. Their ages ranged from 30 to 50 years and their teaching experience ranged from less than five years to more than 20 years.

The 133 children were second graders to eighth graders and were primarily Hispanic and Haitian with roots from South America, Mexico, and Cuba, Haiti, and other Caribbean Islands. Generally, their first languages were Spanish or Creole with English as their second language.

Setting

There were three settings for this study: the university classroom, Title I public schools, and one teacher's home. Two components added to the graduate course the semester of the project were storytelling and bookmaking with an emphasis on English language learners.

Procedure

To initiate the Story Transformation Project, the graduate students were asked to share what they currently were doing with Writer's Workshop in their elementary classrooms. They mentioned a variety of writing strategies based on both narrative and expository text inspired by Calkins (1994) and the Four Blocks Model (Cunningham, Hall, & Sigmon, 2000), but nothing that promoted the concept of children as both authors and illustrators. The professors explained that one assignment would be the Story Transformation Project, which would require them to create innovative, original stories with children based on familiar folk, or fairy tales that ultimately would be published for classroom libraries. While doing the assignment, the graduate students were told:

- they could decide on the tale selection,
- the number of students who would participate,
- if group or individual books would be created,
- the length and frequency of working on the project, and
- how the story would be written using Writer's Workshop and incorporating the writing process.

We modeled eight steps for the graduate students using Little Red Riding Hood as the base tale. Three selections from contrasting cultures were chosen: *Little Red Riding Hood*, traditional version retold in sign language by Bornstein and Saulnier (1990); *Lon Po Po: A Red Riding Hood story from China* (Young, 1989); and *Flossie and the Fox, an African American variation* (McKissack, 1986). The steps are:

> **STEP 1. *Read aloud the chosen three or more tales beginning with the most traditional tale.*** For our purposes, the three above versions were read aloud in the order listed. It was noted that the origins of these tales began through oral storytelling and evolved through the many retellings and exposures to various ethnic groups and world regions. An extensive bibliography of additional Little Red Riding Hood variations and multiple versions of other folk and fairy tales were distributed. See Appendix A. Tales outside the list also were acceptable for the project.

> **STEP 2. *Compare and contrast the versions of the tale using a story grammar graphic organizer.*** The graduate students compared and contrasted the three versions by using a comparison chart analyzing basic story elements such as title, author, characters, setting, problem, sequence of events, solution, and ending. All three Little

Red Riding Hood versions were different. The more traditional version climaxes when a woodcutter saves Little Red Riding Hood and her grandmother from the wolf. In the Chinese version, three daughters outsmart the wolf while their mother is visiting their grandmother, Lon Po Po. In McKissack's book, Flossie outsmarts the fox on the way to her grandmother's house.

STEP 3. *Referencing the comparison chart, discuss the differences of the various versions.* An indepth discussion is encouraged to share and support the similarities and differences of the various versions' story elements. An effort near the end of the discussion should be made for readers/listeners to decide which version is preferred and why.

STEP 4. *Explain and show when possible the multiple ways tales might be transformed.* A list of eight suggestions adapted from *Living Literature* (Kasten, Kristo, & McClure, 2005) was distributed and modeled with published examples. Ways to use this list and the given examples during their projects was discussed. Suggestions included:

- Change the style from traditional to modern language (*Sleeping Ugly*, Yolen, 1997);
- Change the details, sequence, or main plot events (*Little Red Riding Hood*, Wegman, Kismaric, & Heiferman, 1993);
- Change the time and place setting, point of view, or characters (*The True Story of the Three Little Pigs*, Scieszka, 1989).
- Write a sequel to the original story (*Rumpelstiltskin's Daughter*, Stanley, 1997);
- Maintain the original story, but change the illustrations (*Rapunzel*, Zelinsky, 1997);
- Change the culture such of characters, setting, events, language or dialect (*Petit Rouge—A Cajun Red Riding Hood*, Artell, 2001);
- Make the story bilingual (*Snow White/Blancanieves*, Desclot & Blanch, 2008);
- Combine versions of different tales (*The Three Pigs*, Weisner, 2001);
- Write the story in a different format like a play, poem, readers' theatre, song, or rap (*Revolting Rhymes*, Dahl, 1982).

Using these possibilities and/or their own ideas, the graduate students determined how they would transform Little Red Riding Hood.

STEP 5. *Discuss skills/strategies/given state standards for the language arts to be taught during the projects.* Teachings could include such skills as storytelling, comprehension, critical literacy, vocabulary, grammar, and writing and publishing strategies.

STEP 6: Introduce and model a variety of graphic organizers for the initial stages of the story writing process. The graduate students learned about graphic organizers that encompassed story maps, Venn diagrams, comparison/contrast charts, storyboards, and Character Perspective Charting (CPC). CPC is useful when writing the same tale from different points of view (Shanahan & Shanahan, 1997), as it assists the reader to compare the settings, problems, themes, reactions, and outcomes of diverse versions. See Table 1.

Table 1: Character Perspective Chart

Character #1 Flossie	Character #2 Fox
Setting: Where and when does the story take place? Southern Tennessee in the Summertime	**Setting: Where and when does the story take place?** Southern Tennessee in the Summertime
Problem: What is this character's problem? To take a basket of eggs to her Grandma's	**Problem: What is this character's problem?** To eat the basket of eggs
Attempt: What does this character do to solve the problem or attain the goal? Flossie tricks the fox, telling him that he is not a fox and she is not afraid of him.	**Attempt: What does this character do to solve the problem or attain the goal?** He pleads with Flossie to persuade her that he is a fox and she should believe him!
Outcome: What happened because of the attempt? She tells him that a couple of hounds are after him.	**Outcome: What happened because of the attempt?** He runs away as fast as he can.
Reaction: How does the character feel about the outcome? Flossie is very pleased with herself because she outwitted the fox.	**Reaction: How does the character feel about the outcome?** The fox is unhappy because he didn't get to eat the eggs after all.
Theme: What point did the author want to make? Even though the pretentious fox used standard English and little Flossie spoke in Southern dialect, she proved that she was wiser than wiser than the fox. The last illustration depicts Flossie with her basket of eggs, grinning from ear to ear. Deceptive people should watch out for smart little girls!	**Theme: What point did the author want to make?** Characters are not always what they appear to be. The fox may be a sly and clever creature, but this fox was not as smart as he thought. He had to run for his life. Don't pretend to be something you're not!

STEP 7. Teach bookmaking techniques; share examples. The graduate students made a blank book covered with fabric, using a simple Japanese Book binding technique. Johnson's (1998) bookmaking techniques were reviewed. The graduate students were allowed to choose any of those formats or their own variation for

the publishing stage of the project. They were given directions for all of Johnson's formats.

STEP 8. Share transformation stories. The graduate students shared their versions of Little Red Riding Hood in class. The "Book Pass" technique was used to let everyone view each example before passing it to the next person.

The graduate students' tale selections for their Story Transformation Projects were:

- *Goldilocks and the Three Bears*: Beth
- *Stone Soup*: Kathy
- *The Three Little Pigs*: Anne
- *Cinderella*: Alice, Connie, and Debbie

Results

Beth, Reading Coach

Beth's group of third, fourth, and fifth graders in an after school program spent two weeks developing *Dreadlocks* and *the Three Hyenas*, an African American version of *Goldilocks and the Three Bears*. Student ownership was stressed, as these students were responsible for their own word processing, editing, publishing, and artwork which made them feel important. Jenny, a gifted third grader, was the plot mastermind and Linda was the lead illustrator. Beth used a storyboard for students to retell and illustrate three alternative versions of *Goldilocks* before writing and illustrating their own version using a storyboard format that was transferred to the computer. Here is the introduction to their transformation:

I'm sure you've heard of the original version of *Goldilocks and the Three Bears*. Well, *Dreadlocks and the Three Hyenas* will raise you blood pressure! Read on to see how the adventurous *Dreadlocks* charges into the woodlands to save kids but comes face to face with three wild hyenas.

Kathy, Fourth Grade Teacher

Kathy decided on Stone Soup for her project. She emphasized the brainstorming phase, encouraging her fourth graders to talk to each other to exchange ideas. Using an accordion style format for the published text, she added an author's biography page complete with self-portraits. After two weeks, Kathy and her students celebrated their work during Author's Chair. Their excitement led to inviting family members to enjoy their stories at the school. Kathy documented their class experiences in a class book entitled *The Paper Projec*t. The following excerpt reflects their author celebration:

The students created published stories that they were truly proud of. Because the books looked so professional, they wanted to share them with others. "We should invite our parents to see our work," said Sissy. "Yes, and our grandparents and aunts and uncles," Donny added. "We'll need invitations," said the teacher with paper already in her hand. The students shared their supplies to make invitations. More family members than expected came and they beamed with pride at the writing and illustrations their children had created.

Several titles of the fourth grader's books were *Moon Soup, Candy Soup, Shoe Soup,* and *Ice Cream Soup.*

Anne, Eighth Grade Teacher

Doing this project was the most challenging for Anne, a middle school English teacher. Although some eighth graders resisted a project based on *The Three Little Pigs,* their stories were quite creative. Since the time consuming project was integrated into her language arts curriculum, the students received three grades: 1) for brainstorming and completing the story-planning sheet; 2) for drafting; and 3) for publishing the final product. Story grammar was discussed including the differences between internal and external conflicts when building the plot. The craft of writing used by her students had seven parts:

1. Brainstorm ideas;
2. Sketch the basics of the story;
3. Fill in details such as character and conflict;
4. Plan the plot;
5. Plan scenes;
6. Write; and
7. Revise.

Upon completing their variations of *The Three Pigs,* the eighth graders shared their books with first grade reading buddies. When the middle schoolers realized how much the first graders enjoyed their stories, they believed that the writing project was not such a silly assignment. Titles of their books included *The Three Lobsters and the Big, Bad Shark, The Three Little Dwarf Hamsters, The Three Little Dogs,* and *The Three Little Frogs.* The author of *The Three Little Mermaids* chose to write her book in both English and Spanish, as she was bilingual.

Connie, Second Grade Teacher

Connie was on sabbatical so she worked with a colleague's second graders for one hour daily for four weeks. She and the students read five versions of *Cinderella* and completed a comparison chart. They then brainstormed possibilities for individual books. Favorite themes included sharks, snakes, Pilgrims, and flamingos. Given considerable scaffolding, the class worked on drafts, revisions, and final drafts throughout the month. Using a storyboard format, Connie helped them design a thumbnail sketch layout for the text and illustrations. Planning the layout involved student decision making as to how much text should be on each page and for the composition and design of the artwork. Some children wanted to draw the same illustration for every page. They did not understand that picture book illustrations should enhance the text so they gained that concept. Craft supplies inspired from the tissue paper collage of Eric Carle were provided for embellishing the cover. Zachary offered this excerpt from *Cinderella and the Shark*:

> *When the Shark Prince saw Cinderella and her stepsisters at the Ball, he almost fainted! He couldn't decide which one of the sisters to choose for his bride. He decided to have a contest to see who was the best swimmer. It was Cinderella! She won the contest! So the Shark Prince married Cinderella and they lived happily ever after and had many little shark pups.*

Alice, Third Grade Teacher

Alice also chose *Cinderell*a. She first read aloud a traditional version by Marcia Brown (1955) and divided her students into groups to read four additional versions. Unfortunately, the books were too difficult so she read them all orally but later felt three versions would have been more appropriate. They compared versions on laminated Venn Diagrams using post-it notes. The notes were moved as the students discussed the versions in more depth comparing story grammar elements. They brainstormed ideas and used planning sheets to compose original versions. Final copies were illustrated and handwritten on special paper with colored borders. Although the project took two months, Alice felt it was worthwhile and would do story transformations again. The authors and illustrators boasted such titles as *Cinderella in Jamaica, Cinderella Goes to Florida*, and *Miss Baird and the Princ*e that featured their teacher as a modern Cinderella!

Debbie, ESE Teacher Assistant

Debbie spent the least amount of time on the project by creating a group book with six second and third graders on Saturdays. This option was approved because her mentor did not think the project suitable for her special needs students at this time. She chose *Cinderella* to become an insect and that a group book would be originated. Six girls embraced the insect book idea and decided there should be three parts to their transformational tale: 1) Once upon a time; 2) Happily ever after; and 3) The End.

The group collaborated well and decided easily on the direction of their story. The characters were Cinderpilla, a caterpillar turning into a butterfly; Prince Pig-a-lot who lived in a mud castle; three wicked stepsister birds who lived in a treehouse, and a Fairy God-butterfly. Dried mud footprints made of play dough substituted for a glass slipper. Each participant volunteered to illustrate a different scene.

Debbie believed in the importance of integrating literacy with the performing arts. The accordion-style book was made of foam pages decorated with foam letters, ribbons, tissue paper, pompoms for the caterpillars, and pipe cleaners for the antennae. Clothespin puppets were made for the dramatization. The ending of their collaborative book was:

> *At 12 o'clock Cinderpilla, a beautiful butterfly, turned back into a caterpillar and raced through the mud around Prince Pig-a-lot's castle. He wanted to find*

Cinderpilla so he took the dried mud prints and tried to match them to the ladies of the kingdom: Holly Horse, Lilly Lion, Petunia Pig, and Susanne, the Snake. But none of them matched until he got to Cinderpilla's house. When her footprints matched the ones brought by the Prince, they both were very happy! They kissed and Cinderpilla turned back into a beautiful butterfly. Prince Pig-a-lotand Cinderpilla were married at the mud castle and lived happily ever after. THE END

Discussion

Many factors contributed to the effectiveness of using story transformations of familiar tales in a writer's workshop format to promote children as authors and illustrators. The most important factor appeared to be flexibility. The graduate students made individual decisions throughout the project regarding the specific tale to be used and how, when, and where the writing and illustrative process would be implemented. The projects could be approached from different perspectives, depending on the needs and interests of given students.

Modeling the Story Transformation Project and the use of comparison charts and storyboards made the bookmaking goal easier to meet. Studying and comparing both the verbage and illustrations of different versions before creating story transformations was helpful. Intermediate students needed less scaffolding and teachers already implementing Writer's Workshop found their familiarity simplified their teaching tasks. The challenges of Beth's group related directly to technology as their computer-crashed midway and caused anxiety for Beth and her students.

According to Graves (1983), Calkins (1994) and other writing experts, a significant block of time on a regular basis is necessary for Writer's Workshop. Writing must be an equal part with reading in a daily language arts routine. Collaborative learning communities were critical during the creation of a group book as demonstrated while creating *Cinderpilla*. This may be why most of the graduate students had their students work individually as that already was a challenge in an overly demanding curriculum. However, collaboration was invaluable with Kathy's fourth graders and with Debbie and Beth as they demonstrated the success of different small group collaborations.

The choice of alternative versions had an impact on outcomes. For example, Beth shared an African American version of Goldilocks (Kurtz, 2004), as most of her students were African American. Hence, they created *Dreadlocks and the Three Hyenas*.

Illustrations often are more important than the text as they can extend the text, which was a concept, gained by several groups. Although not required for this project, teaching the visual art elements of line, shape, color, space, texture, and form can enhance the students' knowledge and interpretation of text (Albers, 2007; Cornett, 2007). If the teacher is uncomfortable teaching this, the art teacher could join in the project to conduct mini-lessons on the above elements of composition and design and guide students in examining existing illustrations of a variety of tales. Incorporating technology through online publishing, computer graphics, and/or digital photography also are viable options for creating professional looking books produced for classroom libraries. Electronic books could be shared easily and especially with other teachers to use as bookmaking examples.

Conclusion and Implications

The concept of children as authors and illustrators is significant because it incorporates reading, writing, speaking, listening, viewing, and visual representation. The students listened to a tale while carefully studying the illustrations. Working in groups or as a whole, students compared and contrasted several versions of the same tale using graphic organizers. After discussing ideas for an original story with peers during prewriting, the students drafted individual or group versions. Following extensive revision and editing, they began the publishing process by planning text and illustration layouts based on storyboards. Language arts skills and mini-lessons were taught as needed for given groups or individuals. The cover design and book format depended on the teacher's project goals, student creativity, and materials and technology available. Sharing, using Author's Chair or invitations to family members, culminated several projects. Bourke (2008/2009) challenges educators to consider their classrooms as a "critical landscape" for creativity, discovery, and exploration (p. 311), so that students are secure to take risks by asking deeper and more relevant questions when examining and challenging both narrative and expository texts. In sharing their project reports, the graduate students accomplished this by giving students the opportunity to originate, write, illustrate, and publish innovative story transformations.

Results of the story transformation projects varied greatly; however, all projects were considered successful with the graduate students willing to do such a project again. The length of project time varied from two weeks to two months and the grade levels of more than 100 students ranged from second grade through eighth grade. At the last graduate class, PowerPoint presentations were given with the group sharing and discussing the challenges and successes of each project.

Although the results of the Story Transformation Project were considered beneficial to everyone involved, there is an obvious need for longitudinal research as there is a dearth of supportive research and professional literature. It seems important to ascertain more fully if knowledge of literature transformations, using the writing and illustrative processes repeatedly, and incorporating many language arts will make a difference in the product and be evident in long term independent transfer of knowledge and writing and illustrative experiences. Therefore, teachers and literacy educators are encouraged to collect data and note incremental self-growth longitudinally as students assume the roles and thrive as authors and illustrators.

References

Albers, P. (2007). *Finding the artist within: Creating and reading visual texts in the English Language Arts classroom*. Newark, DE: International Reading Association.

Artell, M. (2001). Petite Rouge—*A Cajun Red Riding Hood*. Illustrated by J. Harris. New York; Dial Books for Young Readers.

Bornstein, H., & Saulnier, K. L. (1990). *Little Red Riding Hood*; illustrated by B. O. Pomeroy. Washington, D. C.: Gallaudet University Press.

Bourke, R. T. (2008/2009). First graders and fairy tales: One teacher's action research of critical literacy. *The Reading Teacher*, 62 (4), 304-312.

Calkins, L. M. (1994). *The art of teaching writing*. Portsmouth, NH: Heinemann.

Cornett, C. E. (2007). *Creating meaning through literature and the arts*. Upper Saddle River, NJ: Pearson.

Cunningham, P. M., Hall, D. P., & Sigmon, C. M. (2000). *The teacher's guide to the 4 blocks: A multi-method, multilevel framework for grades 1-3*. Greensboro, NC; Carson-Dellosa Publishing Company.

Dahl, R. (1982). *Roald Dahl's revolting rhymes*. Illustrated by Q. Blake. New York: Alfred A. Knopf.

Desclot, M., & Blanch, I. (2008). *Snow White/Blancanieves: A bilingual book*. San Francisco, CA: Chronicle Books.

Gibson, S. A. (2008/2009). An effective framework for primary-grade guided writing instruction. *The Reading Teacher*, 62 (4), 324-334.

Graves, D. H. (1983). *Writing: Teachers and children at work*. Portsmouth, NH: Heinemann.

Harste, J. C. (2005, January 28). *How the arts embrace learning*. Keynote address delivered at the 2005 Georgia Read Write Now Conference, Atlanta, GA.

Johnson, K. L., & Westkott, P. V. (2004). *Writing like writers: Guiding elementary children through a writer's workshop*. Waco, TX: Prufrock Press.

Johnson, P. (1994). *A book of one's own*. Portsmouth, NH: Heinemann.

Kasten, W.C., Kristo, J.V., & McClure, A.A. (2005). *Living literature: Using chidren's literature to support reading and language arts*. Upper Saddle River, NJ: Pearson/ Merrill Prentice Hall.

Kurtz, J. (2004). *JATS fairytale classics: Goldilocks and the three bears*. Illustrated by J. Kurtz. Hyperion Books for Children.

McKissack, P. C. (1986). *Flossie and the fox*. Illustrated by R. Isadora. New York: Dial Books for Young Readers.

Marshall, J. (1989). *The three little pigs*. New York: Scholastic Inc.

Ray, K.W., & Laminack, L.L. (2001). *The writing workshop: Working through the hard parts (and they're all hard parts)*. Urbana, Ill: National Council of Teachers of English.

Scieszka, J. (1989). *The true story of the 3 little pigs*. Illustrated by L. Smith. New York, NY: Viking Juvenile Book Publishers.

Shanahan, T., & Shanahan, S. (1997). Character perspective charting: Helping children to develop a more complete concept of story. *The Reading Teacher*, 50, 668-677.

Stanley, D. (1997). *Rumplestiltskin's daughter*. New York: Morrow Junior Books.

Wegman, W., Kismaric, C., & Heiferman, M. (1993). *Little Red Riding Hood*. New York: Hyperion Publishers.

Weisner, D. (2001). *The three pigs*. New York: Clarion Books

Yenawine, P. (2005). Thoughts on visual literacy. In J. Flood, S.B. Heath, & D. Lapp (Eds.), *Handbook of research on teaching literacy through the communicative and visual arts* (pp. 845-846). Mahwah, NJ: Lawrence Erlbaum & Associates.

Yolen, J. (1997). *Sleeping Ugly*. New York: Putnam & Grosset Group.

Young, E. (1989). Lon Po Po: *A Red Riding Hood story from China*. New York: Philomel Publishers.

Zelinsky, P. O. (1997). *Rapunzel*. New York: Dutton Children's Books.

Appendix A: Bibliography of multi-cultural variations and fractured folk and fairy tales for eight selected titles

Cinderella

Buehner, C. (1996). *Fanny's dream*. Illustrated by M. Buehner. New York: Dial Books for Young Readers.

Climo, S. (1989). *The Egyptian Cinderella*. Illustrated by R. Heller. New York, NY: Harper-Collins Publishers.

Climo, S. (1993). *The Korean Cinderella*. Illustrated by R. Heller. New York, NY: HarperCollins Publishers.

Coburn, J. R. (2000). *Domitila: A Cinderella tale from the Mexican tradition*. Illustrated by C. McLennan. Auburn, CA: Shen's Books.

Coburn, J. R. (1996). *Jouanah: A Hmong Cinderella*. Fremont, CA: Shen's Books.

Cole, B. (1988). *Prince Cinders*. New York, NY: Putnam Juvenile Books.

Delamare, D. (1993). *Cinderella*. New York: Green Tiger Press (Simon & Schuster). *Venetian setting

Dwyer, M. (2004). *The salmon princess: An Alaska Cinderella story*. Seattle, WA: Sasquatch Books.

Edwards, P. D. (1997). *Dinorella: A prehistoric fairy tale*. New York: Putnam.

Goode, D. (1996). *Cinderella*. New York: Alfred A. Knopf.

Granowsky, A. (1993). *The awful Cinderella*. Orlando, FL: Steck-Vaughn.

Haddix, M. P. (1999). *Just Ella*. New York: Simon & Schuster.

Han, O. S., & Plunkett, S. H. (1996). *Kongi and Potgi: A Cinderella story from Korea*. New York: Dial.

Jackson, E. (1994). *Cinder Edna*. Illustrated by K. O'Malley. New York: Lothrop,Lee & Shepard Books.

Levine, G.C. (2000). *Cinderellis and the Glass Hill*. New York: Harper Collins.

Louie, A. L. (1982). *Yeh-Shen, a Cinderella story from China*. Illustrated by E. Young. New York: Philomel Books.

Lowell, S. (2000). *Cindy Ellen, a wild western Cinderella*. New York: Joanna Cotler Books.

Martin, R. (1992). *The rough-face girl* (Native American version). Illustrated by D. Shannon. New York: Scholastic.

Munsch, R. (1992). *Paper bag princess*. Illustrated by M. Martchenko. Toronto, ON: Annick Press.

Nhuan, N. T. (1995). *Tam Cam: A Vietnamese Cinderella story*. Fremont, CA: Shen's Books.

San Souci, R. D. (2002). *Cendrillon, A Caribbean Cinderella*. New York: Simon & Schuster.

Schroeder, A. (1997). *Smoky Mountain Rose: An Appalachian Cinderella*. Illustrated by B. Sneed. New York, NY: Dial Books for Young Readers.

Yorinks, A. (1990). *Ugh*. Illustrated by R. Egielski. New York: Michael di Capua Books.
    *Prehistoric Cinderella with a male protagonist

Goldilocks and the Three Bears

Brett, J. (1992). *Goldilocks and the three bears*. New York, NY: Putnam Juvenile Books.

Buehner, C. (2007). *Goldilocks and the three bears*. Illustrated by Mark Buehner. New York, NY: Dial Books for Young Readers.

De Luise, D. (1992). *Goldilocks*. Illustrated by C. Santoro. New York: Simon & Schuster Books for Young Readers.

Ernst, L. C. (2003). *Goldilocks returns*. New York, NY: Aladdin Books.

Flor Ada, A. (2005). *Yours truly, Goldilocks*. Illustrated by L. Tryon. New York, NY: Aladdin Books.

Turkle, B. (1976). Deep in the Forest. New York: E. P. Dutton & Co. *Wordless book

Little Red Riding Hood

Artell, M. (2001). *Petite Rouge—A Cajun Red Riding Hood*. Illustrated by J. Harris. New York: Dial Books for Young Readers.

Bornstein, H. & Saulnier, K. L. (1990). *Little Red Riding Hood*. Illustrated by B. O. Pomeroy. Washington, D.C.: Gallaudet University Press. *Told in signed English

Crawford, E. D. (1983). *Little red cap*. New York: Morrow Books.

Cross, G. (1991). *Wolf*. New York: Holiday House.

Ernst, L. C. (1995). *Little Red Riding Hood: A newfangled prairie tale*. New York: Simon & Schuster Books for Young Readers.

Forward, T. (2005). What really happened to Little Red Riding Hood. Illustrated by I. Cohen. Cambridge, MA: Candlewick Press.

Harper, W. (1967). *The Gunniwolf*. (Illus. W. Wiesner). New York: E. P. Dutton & Co.

Harper, W. (2003). *The Gunniwolf*. (Illus. B. Upton). New York: E. P. Dutton & Co.

Hyman, T. S. (1983). *Little Red Riding Hood*. New York: Holiday House.

Laird, D. M. (1985). *'Ula Li'I and the magic shark*. Illustrated by C. Jossem. Honolulu, Hawaii: Barnaby Books.

Lowell, S. (1997). *Little Red Cowboy Hat*. Illustrated by R. Cecil. New York: Henry Holt and Company.

Marshall, J. (1987). *Red Riding Hood*. New York: Puffin Books.

McKissack, P. C. (1986). *Flossie & the fox*. Illustrated by R. Isadora. New York: Dial Books for Young Readers.

Wegman, W, Kismaric, C. & Heiferman, M. (1993). *Little Red Riding Hood*. New York: Hyperion Publishers.

Young, E. (1989). *Lon Po Po: A Red-Riding Hood story from China*. New York: Philomel Publishers. *Caldecott Medal Winner

Rapunzel

Napoli, D. J. (1998). *Zel*. New York: Puffin Books.

Stanley, D. (1995). *Petrosinella: A Neapolitan Rapunzel*. New York: A Puffin Pied Piper.

Zelinsky, P. O. (1997). *Rapunzel*. New York: Dutton Children's Books. *Caldecott Medal Winner

Rumpelstiltskin

Hamilton, V. (2000). *The girl who spun gold*. New York: Blue Sky/Scholastic. *West Indian.

Moser, B. (1994). *Tucker Pfeffercorn: An old story retold*. Boston, MA: Little, Brown & Company.

Napoli, D. J. (2001). *Spinners*. New York: Puffin Books.

Ness, Evaline (1965). *Tom Tit Tot*. New York: Scribners.

Schmidt, G. D. (2001). *Straw into gold*. New York: Clarion Books.

Stanley, D. 1997). *Rumplestiltskin's daughter*. New York: Morrow Junior Books.

Vande Velde, V. (2000). *The Rumplestiltskin Problem*. Boston, MA: Houghton Mifflin.

Zelinsky, P. (1986). *Rumplestiltskin from the German of the Brothers Grimm*. New York: E.P. Dutton Publishers. *Caldecott Honor Book

Zemach, H. & Zemach, Margot (1973). *Duffy and the Devil*. New York: Farrar, Straus and Giroux. *Caldecott Medal Winner

Sleeping Beauty

Craft, M. (2002). *Sleeping Beauty*. Illustrated by K. Craft. San Francisco, CA: Chronicle Books.

Hyman, T. S. (2002). *The Sleeping Beauty*. Boston, MA: Little, Brown & Company.

Levine, G. C. (1999). *Princess Sonora and the Long Sleep*. New York: Harper Collins.

Yolen, J. (1997). *Sleeping Ugly*. Illustrated by D. Stanley. New York: Putnam & Grosset Group.

Yolen, J. (2002). *Briar Rose*: New York: Starscape Publishers.

Snow White and the Seven Dwarfs

Aiken, J. (2002). *Snow White and the seven dwarfs*. New York: Dorling Kindersley.

Desclot, M., & Blanch, I. (2008). *Snow White/Blancanieves: A bilingual book*. San Francisco, CA: Chronicle Books. *English/Spanish

French, F. (1986). *Snow White in New York*. New York: Oxford University Press.

Heins, P. (1974). *Snow White*. Boston, MA: Little, Brown & Company.

Ljungkvist, I. (2003). *Snow White and the Seven Dwarfs*. New York: Harry N. Abrams.

Philip, N. (1999). *Stockings of Buttermilk (Snow White)*. New York: Clarion Books. *Appalachian.

Poole, J. (1991). *Snow White*. Illustrated by A. Barrett. New York: Alfred A. Knopf.

The Three Little Pigs

Gantschev, I. (2001). *The three little rabbits*. A Balkan folktale. New York: North-South.

Lowell, S. (1992). *The three little javelinas*. Illustrated by J. Harris. Flagstaff, AZ: Rising Moon Publishers. *Available in Spanish

Marshall, J. (1989). *The three little pigs*. New York: Scholastic Inc.

Moser, B. (2001). *The three little pigs*. Boston, MA: Little, Brown & Company.

Rounds, G. (1992). *Three little pigs and the big bad wolf*. New York: Holiday House.

Scieszka, J. (1989). *The true story of the 3 little pigs*. Illustrated by L. Smith. New York: Viking Juvenile book publishers.

Trivizas, E. (1997). *The 3 little wolves and the big bad pig*. Illustrated by H. Oxenbury. New York: Aladdin Books.

Weisner, D. (2001). *The three pigs*. New York: Clarion Books. *Caldecott Medal Winner

Collections of Folk and Fairy Tales

Dahl, R. (1982). *Roald Dahl's revolting rhymes*. Illustrated by Q. Blake. New York: Alfred A. Knopf.

Gustafson, S. (2003). *Classic fairy tales*. Illustrated by S. Gustafson. Seymour, CT: Greenwich Workshop, Inc.

Hoberman, M. A. (2004). *You read to me, I'll read to you: Very short fairy tales to read together*. Illustrated by M. Emberley. New York: Little, Brown & Company.

Scieszka, J. (1992). *The stinky cheese man and other fairly stupid tales*. Illustrated by L. Smith. New York: Viking Juvenile Book Publishers.

Yolen, J. (2006). *Fairy tale feasts: A literary cookbook for young readers and eaters*. Illustrated by P. Be'ha; recipes by H. Stemple. Northampton, MA: Crocodile Books.

ENGAGING HIGH SCHOOL STUDENTS IN READING AND UNDERSTANDING THE CANON THROUGH THE USE OF LINKED TEXT SETS

Linda S. Wold

Loyola University Chicago

Laurie Elish-Piper

Northern Illinois University

Brigid Schultz

Loyola University Chicago

Abstract

Linked Text Sets (LTS) offer an approach to make the English curriculum meaningful to high school students by scaffolding what teens know and understand from their own lives to build a bridge to core texts from the canon. LTS include print (written-formatted texts, adolescent literature, short stories, graphic novels, poetry) and nonprint (spoken- and visually-formatted texts, music, Internet sources, DVDs, interviews) media. Print texts represent a wide range of genres, protagonists, and difficulty levels to accommodate all students. A sample LTS focused on the essential question, "What does it mean to be heroic?" is included to offer teachers and students relevant and substantive text choices for active reading that align strategically with Beowulf.

The traditional approach to teaching literature from the canon is fraught with problems. Students often find the texts too difficult to read and understand, and they complain that such texts are far-removed from their lived experiences (Bass, Dasinger, Elish-Piper, Matthews, & Risko, 2008). When a mismatch exists between the typical English curriculum and students' interests and text choices, students may become disengaged from schoolwork. In fact, 47% of students who drop out of high school cite boredom with their classes and disinterest in schoolwork as major reasons for their decision to leave school (Bridgeland, DiIulio, & Morison, 2006). With 7,000 adolescents dropping out of high school each day (Alliance for Excellent Education, n.d.), the urgency of addressing this problem is clear. While the dropout problem is daunting and beyond the full control of literacy educators, it is believed that literacy educators can make a difference by ensuring that their curriculum and instruction are relevant, meaningful, and accessible to their high school students (Alvermann, Hinchman, Moore, Phelps, & Waff, 1998). Because students' engagement increases when they are involved in reading and interpreting texts about personal life matters (Smith & Wilhelm, 2002), opportunities to experience this type of literature instruction are warranted. While such efforts at improving student engagement will not address all aspects of the dropout problem, they are a step forward in making literature study more relevant for students.

The Organization of Linked Text Sets

The use of Linked Text Sets (LTS; Wold. & Elish-Piper, 2009) is one possible way to provide access and opportunities for teen readers to engage with a wide range of texts that include both print and nonprint media. By scaffolding the exploration of various forms of texts that shed light on students' own lives, experiences, and interests, adolescents are more likely to become involved in this type of curriculum that invites thinking about multiple interpretations of texts (Moje, 2002; Greenbaum, 1994). Furthermore, LTS provide texts at varied levels to support all students, including those who read above, at, and below level. This consideration is of paramount importance because 70 percent of all ninth graders in the U.S. read below grade level, particularly students of color (Denti, 2004). As Allington (2002) argued, students "cannot learn much from texts that they cannot read" (p. 16); therefore, literacy educators must find ways to make texts accessible, engaging, and relevant for their high school students. We argue that Linked Text Sets are a promising approach to address all of these goals.

Linked Text Sets: Example of the Hero's Journey

To understand more clearly the structure and possibilities of using LTS in the high school English classroom, we offer the following example. In this LTS, *Beowulf,* a traditional canon piece, is aligned with other texts that address the hero's journey. The essential question, "What does it mean to be heroic?" guides the teachers' strategic selection of texts that meet the criteria for inclusion in the LTS. For students, the essential question provides a compelling query to guide their reading and thinking, as well as an invitation to reflect on how the question applies to their own lives and experiences. This approach empowers students to choose to read texts from both print and nonprint media that engage them in thinking— the same critical thinking that teachers hope to develop and nurture as a result of students' deep level learning.

LTS address current research (Hughes-Hassell & Rodge, 2007) that concludes that high school students yearn to read about characters they identify with, and they choose to talk about media that relates to themselves. They care about life matters and texts that honor both male and female interests; they enjoy reading magazines, and they prefer varied formats for reading such as graphic novels, Internet sources, and video options. To promote reading engagement, students' ideas must be valued when planning English instruction (Romano, 2009), particularly when selecting texts that promote indepth analysis and discussion. LTS offer a framework that is grounded in thoughtful planning that includes teen culture as a bridge to encourage students to want to read more about the world and the ever-present human conditions that are a dynamic part of daily living. Our end goal is to help students develop "a productive, tenacious attitude" (Romano, 2009, p. 31) toward learning and thinking that is meaningful across a life span. To make lessons inviting, teaching with LTS requires planning and development as described in the next section.

LTS provide differentiated reading opportunities because the selection process requires that chosen texts afford readers of all reading levels the opportunity to engage with these texts and learn from them. The texts are leveled by lexile, a standard measure that determines the reading difficulty level of the text (www.lexile.com). In this way, all levels of readers, from striving through gifted, are offered text options that are accessible to them and that they can read successfully with minimal-to-guided support by the teacher. Print and nonprint media are also differentiated by type. Print media includes basic written communication formats; nonprint media includes all other formats, such as online technology, DVDs, artwork, and radio interviews. These LTS options create opportunities for students to become successful, independent learners who gain from their active involvement in high school English course work.

To create accessibility for secondary readers, LTS offer multiple access routes. To promote text choices, teachers allow students to choose to read texts that are understandable based on standardized leveling criteria of reading difficulty (Stenner & Wright, 2002). When readers and text levels are matched for successful reading, students' comprehension increases. The text then becomes a supportive measure for scaffolding readers' understanding. Teachers also honor students' text preferences by offering a selection of texts that align with the essential question. For example, many students prefer reading literature and studying media options that are connected to their lives and experiences yet often are not included in the high school English curriculum. At times, they prefer nonprint media such as videos and internet sites rather than print media. When options invite secondary students to choose texts based on their own interests and reasons, choice will motivate them intrinsically to read (Gregory & Chapman, 2002). Nonprint media choice options may result in similar motivation for learners, particularly when text choice has not been a viable option for learning in school in the past (Wold & Elish-Piper, 2009). Once teens are intrinsically motivated to become active readers, it is more likely that they will also become engaged readers who generate questions and connect ideas beyond a single text (Moore, Bean, Birdyshaw, & Rycik (1999). Lastly, LTS address cultural responsiveness by honoring people's diversity (Koss & Teale, 2009; Short, 2007) as a way to build students' capacity to understand human experiences. In this way, high school students see the common threads that cut across gender, culture, race, and geography to bind us as humans. Geographic locations are also used to guide text selections, ensuring that the protagonists will reflect student diversity in secondary classrooms.

Developing Linked Text Sets

A single Linked Text Set can be chosen based on several criteria and involves a rigorous, three-step process for teachers. First, teachers identify one or more focal texts from the canon or their school's required reading list. The texts selected should align with the essential question under study (e.g., What does it mean to be heroic?) and provide critical thinking opportunities for students to interpret and synthesize ideas that enhance the universal themes presented in the literature.

Second, teachers determine possible text selections from sources that publish information about award-winning texts for youth. For example, the American Library Association provides booklists of award-winning titles (www.ala.org/ala/mgrps/divs/yalsa/booklistawards) from diverse formats, such as great graphic novels for teens, excellence in nonfiction for young adults, and the Stonewall Jackson awards for gay, lesbian, and transgendered titles. Notable texts are also archived on most sites to enhance access to past important resources. The National Council for the Social Studies (www.socialstudies.org/notable) offers outstanding picture book titles and also texts for struggling high school readers. To address world-mindedness (Smith, 2002), the International Board on Books for Youth (IBBY) (www.ibby.org) provides award-winning titles about protagonists from hundreds of countries around the globe. These notable resources offer potential selections for students whose reading interests vary widely. Publications also provide ongoing lists of potential text and media options, particularly the recommended texts for high school students. One such publication is the Journal of Adolescent & Adult Literacy (International Reading Association).

Third, teachers read and evaluate text selections. Each selection is reviewed and considered with the following criteria in mind so that text selections fit precisely with all indicators: 1) Aligns strategically without being forced with the essential question; 2) Provides reading access and opportunities for a specific range of readers by Lexile Level (Stenner & Wright, 2002) and readability; 3) Challenges readers by conceptual density of terms or ideas that they can learn from and understand; 4) Introduces easy-to-difficult text structure and formats; 5) Engages students in critical thinking; 6) Provides capacity for students to make textual connections; 7) Honors a world-minded focus enabling students to learn more about human experiences and events in the world at large (Short, 2007); and 8) Offers authentic print and nonprint media selections and options for both male and female adolescents that relate to their own lives.

Connecting the Theoretical Strand of the Hero's Journey in the Linked Text Sets

What does the hero's journey look like for the protagonists included in the Linked Text Sets? We build on the work of Campbell (1949) to help students understand how both the protagonists in the English canon and in adolescent literature follow distinct steps of many heroes and heroines. Rather than consider only canon texts to create a single-minded interpretation of the hero's journey, we use a synthesized view that develops from learning about each of the different heroes in the LTS and their common experiences. Students match their own protagonists' journey with Campbell's steps in which the hero hears a calling and accepts it; crosses a threshold; finds a guardian or mentor; faces a challenge; transforms a demon or difficult situation; completes the task of the calling; and returns home. At times, Campbell's guide is not a perfect match with other protagonists' journeys in the LTS, allowing some freedom in students' interpretation of the points that guide their thinking.

Sample Linked Text Set

The linked text set for the essential question, "What does it mean to be heroic?" provides strategic text selections using print and nonprint media around the hero's journey (after the canon selection, texts are listed by lexile or estimated (E) lexile level):

Print-based texts. These texts align with the essential question and provide key insights into the study of heroism. The following is a list of print-based resources:

- Anonymous. *Beowulf.* (2000). (S. Heaney, Trans.). New York: W. W. Norton & Co. (E1400 Lexile)
  Beowulf is the oldest known narrative written in English. The main sections of this epic depict Beowulf's heroic responses to cruel predators.
- Meyers, W.D. (1988). *Fallen angels.* New York: Scholastic. (650 Lexile)
  Richie Perry signs up for the Army and is sent to Vietnam right after his high school graduation. The brutality of war and the obstacles teenage soldiers encounter are presented in a straight-forward manner. Perry and his fellow soldiers struggle to survive and to do what is right when confronted with challenges that call for heroic acts.
- Johnson, A. (2005). *The first part last.* New York: Simon Pulse. (790 Lexile)
  Bobby is a typical teenager who is faced with the reality that his girlfriend, Nia, is pregnant. Through an unexpected event, Bobby finds himself functioning as a single parent to care for his infant daughter, Feather, while juggling the demands of school and the expectations of his family and friends.

The novel invites the reader to consider if Bobby is a hero or if he is just living up to his responsibilities.

- Satrapi, M. (2004). *Persepolis: The story of a childhood*. New York: Random House. (E800 Lexile)
  This autobiography in graphic novel format examines life growing up in Iran during the Islamic Revolution. Told in comic form with black and white drawings, the story begins when Persepolis is born during the Shah's regime and continues through the Revolution and war with Iraq. Persepolis embarks on her heroic journey toward adulthood in the midst of a world that has changed in   dramatic ways.
- Golenbock, P. (1992). *Teammates*. Orlando, FL: Voyager Books. (930 Lexile)
  This biography/picture book tells the story of Jackie Robinson's first year in the Baseball Major League as a player for the Brooklyn Dodgers in 1947. Robinson is a sports hero and a hero to other African-Americans for breaking the "color barrier," but Robinson's teammate, Pee Wee Reese, provides another image of a hero that requires a different type of courage.
- Budhos, M. (2006). *Remix: Conversations with immigrant teenagers*. NY: Henry Holt and Company. (E1100 Lexile)
  Budhos captures the immigrant experience of 14 high school students who negotiate their places in American society. Each reveals distinct struggles emerging from high school experiences that explain his or her heroic journey toward adulthood.

Nonprint media. The following resources reflect teens' interest in using resources that are not print-based. These nonprint media highlight a film and web site that provide strong links to the essential questions and the linked text sets.

- Lucas, G. (Producer & Writer). (1977). *Star wars* [Motion picture]. United States: Twentieth Century Fox. This futuristic epic tells the tale of Luke Skywalker as he encounters and teams up with Han Solo, Chewbacca, Ben Kenobi, C-3PO, and R2-D2 to the other two in the Star Wars trilogy chronicle Luke Skywalker's heroic journey in accordance with Joseph Campbell's stages (1949).
- My Hero Website www.myhero.com or www.miheroe.org (Spanish version). A range of visual selections from "Heroes in the News" to short films documents ordinary people demonstrating heroic deeds and highlights many adolescents who have created opportunities for others in the world.

Songs. Music that enhances the theme of the essential question of heroism and links to contemporary teen lyrics is another key aspect of nonprint media. *Hero* is a post-grunge song by the Verve Pipe which sarcastically examines the prevailing notion that famous people are heroes just by virtue of their fame. The song is available at and www.amazon.com.

Implementing the LTS

To get students interested in the unit of study and the texts they will be reading, Mrs. Gee, a 12th-grade English teacher, places poster paper around the classroom. On each piece of poster paper is one of the questions noted in Figure 1. As students enter the room, Mrs. Gee asks them to each pick up a marker and answer the questions, posting their responses "graffiti style." Each question relates in some way to the upcoming hero unit and is broad enough to engage students no matter what text or medium they choose in the unit. This Graffiti Wall Strategy (Silver, Strong, & Perini, 2001) quickly sets up an active learning environment that serves as a catalyst for engaging all students in the unit of study. With their responses posted, Mrs. Gee has students process the strategy in an active and often emotional whole-class discussion as students explain and defend their responses. Before the lesson ends, Mrs. Gee reminds students that the issues explored in the Graffiti Wall exercise are directly related to the texts that they will be reading and the questions will be revisited in the coming weeks. While students may go on to read a title different than their peers, they have begun the unit as a community of learners focused on answering the common essential question of "What does it mean to be heroic?"

Creating the active learning environment for implementing linked text sets in the classroom.

The following class period, Mrs. Gee draws students' attention to the "My Hero" website (see www.myhero.com). From this website, Mrs. Gee plays for students a four-minute clip of an interview of Ellie Wei, a high school sophomore from Los Angeles who developed a website to help those who cannot speak English learn the language. Mrs. Gee asks students to partner with another class member to determine if Ellie is a hero. She explains that heroes may be ordinary people representing physical or spiritual success. After a lively discussion, students decide that heroes are individuals who act on behalf of others solely for altruistic purposes; they are not idols who gain fame and fortune for their efforts. Mrs. Gee shares the "My Hero" website information to invite students to report on other films that link to their study of heroism. Then she presents several brief book introductions of fiction and nonfiction texts (*Fallen angels*, Myers; *The first part last*, Johnson; *Persepolis: The story of a childhood*, Satrapi; *Remix: Conversations with immigrant teenagers*, Budhos), asking students to list first and second choices for their literature circle discussion. She reminds students that the Lexile levels listed will help them know if they can read and understand the text and that they may question her for guided support in choosing texts that match reading levels. After texts are assigned, students meet in small groups to develop a plan and timeline for reading their texts. The following day, the small groups meet to discuss protagonists' dialogue and actions to determine heroic qualities. By following Campbell's steps, they interpret heroism by what the characters say and their actions to determine a match with the criteria.

Over the next week, students engage in literature discussions, revisiting self-selected questions from the initial Graffiti Wall strategy. Students assign and monitor text readings in their small groups as they add up details about heroism and use a response log to explain evidence of how each character acts heroically. During the group discussions, one student verbally monitors responses to keep the group engaged while another takes notes to contribute to the whole class discussion scheduled for the end of the week. Finally, on day five, students are given markers and allowed twenty minutes to log personal reactions to the 16-20 teacher-generated questions on the Graffiti wall (Silver, et al., 2001).

As students browse around the room studying all of the graffiti responses charted on the walls, they generate written questions and comments that prompt their thinking about themes in the journeys of the protagonists in the books they read in their literature circle groups. Their ideas contextualize the small group discussion and invite interactive talk from students who may be less willing to address the whole class. After students have had an opportunity to respond to their peers' thinking, the teacher assigns student-led discussions by naming a group of students or a spokesperson to study the responses and summarize them with the class. Then students compare peer group discussion highlights with the whole class by using their Graffiti question summaries that affirm or disconfirm their thinking. For the initial interactive discussion, the teacher selects students to create a "fish bowl" example of what this discussion looks like. Students on the outer circle of chairs surrounding the fishbowl team can challenge the students in the interior circle to provide evidence for their interpretations.

Other nonprint media are interspersed across the unit as Mrs. Gee sets the context for reading *Beowulf*. She has students read and discuss excerpts from *Remix: Conversations with immigrant teenagers* to examine how heroism can be embedded in the everyday activities of teens. She also shows excerpts from the *Star Wars* film to help students identify steps in Luke Skywalker's heroic journey. In addition, she has students consider how the term "hero" is used in popular culture by asking them to brainstorm a list of heroes, followed by listening to and analyzing the lyrics from the Verve Pipe's song, *Hero*. Finally, she asks the students to look back at their brainstormed list and determine which of the people on the list are truly heroes (according to Campbell's model) and which are merely famous.

From this type of instructional preparation that includes media that they enjoy, students are ready to delve into the canon text. Because some students will need scaffolding to read the epic text, Mrs. Gee will use guiding questions to support their inquiry about heroism and try to link it to their own personal heroic journey in high school. Mrs. Gee uses a combination of approaches to engage students in reading *Beowulf*. She provides a great deal of background information about the historical setting, the structure of an epic, and a review of Campbell's (1949) model of the heroic journey. She goes through this process to ensure that her students have the necessary background knowledge to understand *Beowulf*. Mrs. Gee reads some excerpts from the epic aloud, allowing herself some time to stop, clarify, and discuss key ideas. She has students read other sections of the epic with a partner to focus on discussing a key question designed to enhance their comprehension. Students are also assigned sections of the text to read independently as they prepare for literature discussions.

Deepening students' connections to the hero's journey. An additional post-discussion activity includes talk about students' journeys toward adulthood and what it means to make good decisions to reach their goals. The activity is anchored in Campbell's (1949) work that encourages students' personal links to learning based on their own contexts and backgrounds. As a culminating project that brings together all of their ideas and learning from the unit of study, Mrs. Gee invites her students to develop photovoice essays (Marquez-Zenkow & Harmon, 2007) in which students use articulated PowerPoint to describe oneself or another influential personal hero. Students record their perceptions about their selected heroes and explain how their journeys influenced them. The students are engaged and animated as they share their final presentations, demonstrating a clear understanding of what it means to be a hero. Throughout the unit, Mrs. Gee finds repeated evidence from students' discussions and generated questions that they appreciate the ideas and insights from *Beowulf* more now because of the explicit links made between the LTS in her teaching of literature from the canon. This specific example of an LTS shows how this approach can be used to make literature instruction accessible, relevant, and engaging for students. Other LTS may focus on essential guiding questions such as "What is my place in the world?"; "What is the American Dream?" or "What is worth fighting for?"

Final Thoughts

If our high school students choose not to read because they are not vested in reading only the classics, it is imperative that we provide innovative ways to engage learners in reading literature. It is crucial for teachers to help students become responsible adults who can read critically, synthesize ideas, and support their opinions and arguments. Linked Text Sets create opportunities for learning because they honor students' preferences and interests and provide real-world opportunities to wrestle with important questions and issues. The Graffiti Wall Strategy (Silver et al., 2001) offers further opportunities to make instruction personally relevant and meaningful for students. Such an interactive activity engages all high school students in a research-based practice that encourages student participation and provides a guiding framework for thinking about how to interpret literary elements. If high schools expect to graduate critical thinkers and decision makers, there must be increasing options for students to understand diverse human experiences from varied viewpoints that shape empathy and insights about the world in which we live. Using LTS, canon texts such as Beowulf can be meaningful tools for helping students understand human experiences and examine guiding questions that are relevant to their own lives.

References

Alliance for Excellent Education (n.d.). A framework and recommendations for federal action on secondary school reform. Washington, DC: Author. Retrieved on November 11, 2008, from http://www.all4ed.org/files/FrameworkRec_FedAction.pdf

Allington, R. L. (2002). You can't learn much from books you can't read. *Educational Leadership, 60*(3), 16-19.

Alvermann, D, Hinchmann, K. A., Moore, D. W., Phelps, S. F., & Waff, D. R. (Eds.). (1998). *Reconceptualizing the literacies of adolescents' lives.* Mahwah, NJ: Erlbaum.

Bass, J., Dasinger, S., Elish-Piper, L, Matthews, R., & Risko, V. (2008). *A declaration of readers' rights.* Boston: Allyn & Bacon.

Bridgeland, J. M., DiIulio, J. J., & Morison, K. B. (2006). *The silent epidemic: Perspectives of high school dropouts.* A report by Civic Enterprises in association with Peter D. Hart Research Associates for the Bill & Melinda Gates Foundation. Washington DC: Civic Enterprises.

Campbell, J. (1949). *The hero with a thousand faces.* Princeton, NJ: Princeton University Press.

Denti, L. (2004). Introduction: Pointing the way: Teaching reading to struggling readers at the high school level. *Reading & Writing Quarterly, 20,* 109-112.

Greenbaum, V. (1994). Expanding the canon: Shaping inclusive reading lists. *English Journal, 63*(8), 36-39.

Gregory, G., & Chapman, C. (2002). *Differentiating instructional strategies: One size doesn't fit all.* Thousand Oaks, CA: Corwin Press.

Hughes-Hassell, S., & Rodge, P. (2007). The leisure reading habits of urban adolescents. *Journal of Adolescent & Adult Literacy, 51*(1), 22-33.

Koss, M. D., & Teale, W. H. (2009). What's happening in young adult literature? Trends in books for adolescents. *Journal of Adolescent & Adult Literacy, 52,* 563-572.

Marquez-Zenkov, K., & Harmon, J. A. (2007). "Seeing" English in the city: Using photography to understand students' literacy relationships. *English Journal, 96*(6), 24-30.

Moje, E. B. (2002). Re-framing adolescent literacy research for new times: Studying youth as a resource. *Reading Research and Instruction, 41*(3), 211-229.

Moore, D. W., Bean, T. W., Birdyshaw, D., & Rycik, J. A. (1999). *Adolescent literacy: A position statement for the Commission on Adolescent Literacy of the International Reading Association.* Newark, DE: International Reading Association.

Romano, T. (2009). Defining fun and seeking flow in English Language Arts. *English Journal, 98*(6), 30-37.

Short, K. (2007). Developing intercultural understandings through international children's literature. Paper presented at the 57th annual meeting of the National Reading Conference, Austin, TX.

Silver, H., Strong, R., & Perini, M. (2001). *Tools for promoting active, in-depth learning.* Ho-Ho-Kus, NJ: Thoughtful Education Press.

Smith, D. J. (2002). If *the world were a village: A book about the world's people.* Tonawanda, NY: Kids Can Press Ltd.

Smith, M. W., & Wilhelm, J. D. (2002). "Reading don't fix no chevys": Literacy in the lives of young men. Portsmouth, NH: Heinemann.

Stenner, A. J., & Wright, B. D. (2002). Readability, reading ability, and comprehension. Paper Presented to the Association of Test Publishers, San Diego, CA.

Wold, L. S., & Elish-Piper, L. (2009). Scaffolding the English canon with linked text sets. *English Journal, 98*(6), 88-91.

Figure 1. Heroic Journey Questions for Graffiti Wall

Record questions on chart paper; intersperse around the room for students' written response:

- Think of a goal that you currently have. What could keep you from attaining that goal?
- Who is your hero?
- What kind of heroes do you admire?
- How is the "you" of today different than the "you" of five years ago?
- List one characteristic of a mentor.
- Your next-door neighbor will be starting high school next fall. What advice would you give him/her?
- Tomorrow you will be faced with a new and challenging situation that has no easy solution and may take time. What steps will you initially take?
- What are some examples of heroic acts that you, yourself, have witnessed?
- What's the best advice that you have ever been given?
- There are fewer heroes for teens to admire compared to teens of fifty years ago.
- Draw a symbol for your definition of heroism.
- Being a hero is like a trip to McDonalds because…
- Agree/Disagree. Please provide a brief comment: Who is more heroic? Vote for one. The firefighter who rescues someone from a burning building. The ordinary citizen who fights for what he believes in no matter what the consequence.